SCOTTISH COOKERY

Catherine Brown

BIRLINN

This fourth edition published in 2013 by Birlinn Ltd
West Newington House
10 Newington Road
Edinburgh
EH9 1QS

www.birlinn.co.uk

First edition published in 1985 by Richard Drew Publishing Limited
Second and third editions published in 1999 and 2006 by
Mercat Press Limited

Illustrations by Jane Glue

ISBN 978-1-78027-108-8

British Library Cataloguing in Publication Data
A catalogue record for this book is available from the British Library

Set in Adobe Caslon Pro at Birlinn

Printed and bound by Grafica Veneta
www.graficaveneta.com

Contents

Cream Sauce; Oysters on Skewers with Bacon; Mussel Brose; Mussels and Cockles in Garlic and Olive Oil; Clabbies or Mussels in a Leek and Tomato Risotto; Partan Pies; Partan Bree; Boiled Lobster to Serve Cold as a Salad; Grilled Lobster; Lobster Soup; Fruits of the Sea; Shellfish Broth; Shellfish Sauce; Orkney Squid; Sea Moss (Carrageen) Jelly; Dulse Broth with Lamb or Mutton; Hebridean Dulse Broth; Dulse Cakes; To Make a Purée (Welsh Laverbread).

Braised Red Deer with Sloe Gin; Roast Rack of Venison; Venison Pasty with Port and Mushrooms; Venison Liver; Poca Buidhe (Yellow Bag); Venison Tripe; Roast Grouse; Grouse Soup; Roast Pheasant with Fresh Herbs; Braised Pheasant with Whisky and Juniper; Bawd Bree; Elsie's Rabbit with Onions; Honeyed Rabbit; Cock-a-Leekie; Roast Chicken; Fried Chicken and Skirlie; Roast Turkey; Chestnut Stuffing; Herb and Lemon Stuffing; Cranberry and Orange Sauce; Bread Sauce.

Boiled Beef; Scotch Barley Broth; Minced Collops (Mince and Tatties); Beef Olives; Beefsteaks; Spiced Beef; Beef Cooked in Claret; Forfar Bridies; Tripe Suppers; Veal Sweetbreads and Kidneys; Sweetbread Pie; Potted Hough; Lorne Sausage; Sassermaet; A Gigot of Mutton with Caper Sauce; Roast Rack of Lamb; Grilled or Barbecued Leg of Lamb; Slow-roast Lamb Shoulder; Pickled Blackface Mutton; Scotch Pies; Stuffed Lambs' Hearts; Lamb's Fry; Haggis; Ayrshire Bacon; Baked Ayrshire-cured Ham; Ayrshire Bacon Baps; Baked Pork Chops with Chappit Tatties; Slow-roast Pork Shoulder with Fennel.

Stovies; Chappit Tatties; Oatmealed Potatoes; Dripping Potatoes; Tattie Scones; Tattie Soup; Steamed Leeks; Carrot and Bacon Soup; Glazed Carrots; Carrot Pudding; Honey and Cinnamon Carrot Cake; Rumbledethumps; Red Cabbage with Apples; Bashed Neeps;

Orkney Clapshot with Burnt Onions; Stir-Fried Kale; Green Kale Soup with Ham; Broccoli Salad; Green Pea Soup; Minted Peas with Greens; Hotchpotch; Spring Vegetable Soup; Lentil Broth.

INTRODUCTION

The Past

While Maggie puts her girdle-baked barley bannocks and oatcakes on the table with some soft cheese, Alistair goes to lift the lid of the pot on the peat fire, taking out a piece of meat and bringing it to the table. It's been in 'the salt' (a barrel of brine in the barn), he tells us. It comes, we discover, from one of his Blackies (Blackface sheep) which has roamed the rough hillsides for the best part of four years. We all get a piece of the mutton to eat with an oatcake. We marvel at its flavour. Afterwards, he chops up some kale and adds it to the pot and serves us platefuls of his broth, flavoured with barley, carrots, turnips and potatoes. Simple, sustaining and unforgettable.

I'd like to take you into the remote corner of the North West Highlands where these crofters lived. The date is 1972 and the place is a croft house on the Applecross peninsula in Wester Ross. Born at the beginning of the century, brother and sister, Maggie and Alistair, are in their seventies now and have lived here all their lives. A road has just been built round this coastline where the transport – until now – has been by boat or foot. It's a wild night outside, but there is a warm glow from a peat fire and the pot on it, slowly simmering, is filling the croft house with its fabulous aromas.

This ingenious system of self-sufficiency, making the best use of an inhospitable landscape and harsh climate, is the basis of the ancient crofting system of agriculture where scarce fertile land is divided among the population and extensive grazing land is common for all to use. These Scots, in the past, could be described as poor Northern Europeans. Without material assets, they were naturally thrifty in their ways. Their frugal, largely meatless, diet was based on broths made with vegetables, dried beans and peas, barley and lentils; brose and porridge made of oats and barley; and everything supplemented with milk, cheese and butter. Meat was a relatively rare occurrence, since animals – especially cattle – were valuable capital assets for export, not eating. Fish, on the other hand, was everyday food. Wild game, sorrel, watercress, silverweed, seaweed, garlic, nettles, hazel and beech nuts, brambles, blaeberries, cloudberries and raspberries were seasonal treats.

Before the Jacobite rebellions of the 1700s, and the exodus to the New World in the 1800s, these Highland clanspeople were expert in preservation techniques: salting, drying and smoking. Their method of cooking was ruled by their source of fuel: mostly dried-out blocks of peat turf which burned with a slow, steady glow, creating a gentle source of heat suitable for slow-simmered broths and stews. Their method of baking on an iron girdle was also ruled by the gentle peat fire. Flat unleavened breads, known as bannocks, were cut into farls (quarters) and baked on a cast-iron girdle.

The gradual deterioration of the Highland economy, after the introduction of sheep farms and the growth of shooting estates in the 1800s, led to a much less varied diet as well as a great deal of poverty. When the people were moved from the fertile glens, and rehoused at the less fertile coast, their diet suffered. The potato became a staple. The large herds of hardy native cattle were replaced by the landlord's sheep. Game, now sport for the landlord, was off the menu. Fish was their saving, a rich food supply which they exploited to the full.

South of what is called the Highland line from Stonehaven on the east coast to Dumbarton on the west, in the area described as the Lowlands, things were different. Here, there were larger areas of rich agricultural land, colonised by Benedictine and Cistercian monks in the Middle Ages. They had come with horticultural expertise and new varieties of fruits and vegetables. In other lowland areas there were also improving landlords who cleared stones, built dykes and enclosed fields. Using the Highlanders' cattle as breeding stock, some developed new breeds of cattle which have become famous worldwide for their fine-flavoured beef.

This spirit of agricultural improvement brought with it an improvement in the diet. There were better supplies of fruits and vegetables. For the more affluent, meat became a more regular item of diet, though fish remained the predominant source of protein for coastal communities and their hinterland. High food value oatmeal – the great sustainer – had overtaken barley as the staple grain in everyday brose and porridge, taken with milk, and in oatcakes eaten with cheese. The vigour and endurance of the people recorded in *Statistical Accounts*, and also noted by visiting observers, was generally attributed to the high quality of their frugal, but nutritious, diet.

The social upheaval of the Industrial Revolution, in the second half of the 1800s, altered this high quality diet. In the Lowlands it created urban slums, poverty and deterioration in diet. In the worst conditions, a kettle of boiling water for sugary tea to drink with slices of white bread and jam replaced the previous nutritious diet. In less dire conditions, the old thrifty rural diet survived in cheaply-made pots of broth using native vegetables, barley, peas and lentils along with inexpensive cuts of butcher meat. The cheap odds and ends of the carcass, tripe, liver, kidney, heart and head were highly valued. Black puddings, mealie puddings, sausages, mince and of course haggis were all useful adjuncts to the ubiquitous pot of potatoes.

Though the Lowland urban diet – at its worst – had nothing left of this previous culinary system, the rural diet survived better. It retained a more intimate link with the soil and its produce, continuing the old thrifty-cooking methods still to be found in the 1970s in Alistair and Maggie's croft house. Like others of their generation they had lived through two world wars, and during the second one had joined with the rest of the nation in the fight to keep the nation at home fed. They were well-placed to survive in the worst-case scenario – the urban population less so. But wartime rationing to save the country from starvation jolted them into a new mindset. Suburban front lawns were dug up to grow potatoes and thrifty nose-to-tail cooking became a necessity for both urban and rural. It was a relatively brief period (1940-1954) but it improved the urban diet. Everyone re-connected, more meaningfully, with their food supply; remembering how to cook good-tasting meals which made the best use of the native-grown and locally-sourced ingredients of the frugal, but nutritious, old Scots diet.

The Future

Since the end of wartime rationing the healthy benefits of the old diet have steadily been eroded. In 2006, a report from a group of health professionals, interviewing schoolchildren about their daily diet, revealed that they often started the day with one or two packets of crisps (or quite often had no breakfast at all); for lunch they might have a pastry or a roll filled with chips; sweets and coke on the way home from school; and for dinner a sausage roll, bridie or pie with chips, followed by a bought trifle or jelly and ice cream.

A technological food revolution, driven by persuasive advertising, industrialised food manufacture, factory farming and multiple food retailing, has created huge efficiencies in production and distribution. Thousands of new food products liberate, and de-skill, those who buy and prepare food. The global marketplace provides strawberries every day of the year. Yet despite the convenience and sometimes cheapness of this system, the diets of some young people have way too high levels of salt, sugar and fats. Their simultaneous loss of health is now an issue. Educators have failed to provide them with the basic nutritional knowledge to eat healthily and the skills to cook food for themselves.

Action to improve Scotland's poor health statistics was given impetus with the Scottish Diet Action Plan in 1996. It contained an ambitious set of targets which have yet to be achieved. Among the many activities it suggested, with the potential to make a difference, was setting up the government-funded Scottish Community Diet Project (now Community Food and Health). This targeted the most vulnerable in society, those most at risk from loss of health due to diet. Community food initiatives such as food co-ops and cafes, cooking and nutrition courses, and many other activities, have all focused on a health-improvement agenda. At a community-led initiative in Shotts, just outside Glasgow, they announced recently that their 'Getting Better Together' project had sold three million portions of fruit and veg.

Nothing can be more important – for future generations – than continuing the battle to achieve the targets set out in the 1996 Scottish Diet Action Plan. But the future also depends on those who shop for food and cook for themselves or their families asking some questions. Such as: Where does the food come from? How has it been produced? What's in it?

In the past this was not a problem. Butchers, bakers, greengrocers, fishmongers, once prolific on every high street, were accountable to their customers who bought from them every other day. When suspicion and doubt first surfaced with the safety of eggs in 1988, it was not so easy to get answers to troubling questions about the integrity of the new food supply. Even more troubling questions about serious health issues emerged throughout the 1990s. Consumer reason and instinct began to challenge the wisdom of technology on everything from additives to genetically modified food and a consumer-led backlash was born.

An early global voice in this subversion was the Slow Food movement. Founded in Italy in 1986, it challenged the junk-food diet of the fast-food industry. Not just for its damaging effect on people's health, but also for its damage to local food systems and traditional ingredients which are the lifeblood of local communities. Its founder, Carlo Petrini, was motivated by the arrival of the first fast food McDonalds restaurant in the centre of Rome. The movement now has followers in 150 countries.

Slow Food argues local rootedness, decentralisation and conservation of typicality. The benefits to communities of this approach are an improvement in diet; a reduction in pollution; the development of food-producing skills; and more money circulating locally – for every £1 spent in a supermarket, around 90p leaves the area, but every £1 spent in a local shop/market/farm-supplier doubles its value to the local economy.

Over quarter of a century old now, Petrini's trailblazing movement has flourished. In Scotland, Slow Food's call to subversion can be seen in new linked-up thinking, where regions with special food assets have taken up the challenge. In 1998, Argyll and the Islands Enterprise funded a local food networking project on the Isle of Arran which was published as an Arran Taste Trail. An independently written guide, it was about the producers of distinctive local foods and drinks and the shops, restaurants, cafes and hotels who were selling Arran produce. It was updated in two more editions and won a Scottish Thistle Award for best Tourism Project in 2000. It has now become the producer-led Taste of Arran brand, marketing Arran products on the island and beyond. In 2002 the first Food Network was set up in Ayrshire, growing from the Farmers' Market movement. It, and others which have followed, have also increased the availability of the region's food by setting up a membership of producers, farm-shops, delicatessens, hotels and restaurants committed to sourcing local produce.

The Soil Association took up a similar challenge with their Food Futures programme in the late 1990s. It was a three-year initiative, aimed at developing the local food economy in eleven areas of the UK, including three in Scotland: Dumfries and Galloway, Forth Valley and Skye and Lochalsh. Key individuals were brought together through workshops to investigate the potential and identify the problems. In Skye and Lochalsh there was the paradox of foreign visitors arriving in the Highlands and expecting to find the produce of Scotland's cool, unpolluted waters – langoustines, scallops, crabs, oysters, lobsters – which they could enjoy in Paris, Rome, Madrid, New York and London. Yet they were having difficulty finding them here, in their place of origin. As a result of grants from Skye and Lochalsh Enterprise, and Community Food and Health, a producer-led Food Link network was set up with its own van to collect fresh produce, dropping off orders to hotels, restaurants and shops throughout the area. Since the first year, the value of produce kept in the area has increased by around seven hundred per cent.

Similar initiatives are also up and running in other areas. Enlightened chefs and restaurant owners are now geared-up to stating on menus such local produce information as the port where the fish has been landed or the native breed of beef. The Farmers' Market movement has been an important motivator in the increased availability of local food. The first Scottish market in Perth in 1999 was a joint initiative between local food suppliers and the city council. Now seventy-one markets are established in towns and cities throughout the country.

Adding yet more power to reviving the nation's food culture has been the consumer-led Fife Diet project. This was a daring move by its founders Mike and Maureen Small, and some friends, who pledged, in 2007, to eat only Fife produce for a year. Five years on, they have an organisation of over three thousand members, funded by the Scottish Government's Climate Challenge Fund, all pledged to making their diet 80% Fife food. It has not only reduced their personal carbon footprint hugely, but also motivated producers to meet their demands. Until the project began, Fife had no local cheese. It now has the St Andrews Farmhouse Cheese Company at Falside Farm, where Jane Stewart took up the challenge, went on a cheese-making course, and now makes the excellent Anster cheese.

The momentum from all these initiatives has increased consumption of native and local ingredients. Cooking from scratch with them may not be as quick and easy as microwaving a ready-meal, but there are now liberating, time-saving gadgets and equipment which cut the time and effort. Food processors and liquidisers reduce time spent cutting, slicing and pureeing to a matter of seconds, and effort to almost zero. The microwave (especially a combination model with a convection oven and grill) reduces cooking times and is good for steaming fish and vegetables.

This book concentrates on Scottish ingredients: historic grains of oats and barley; fine seafoods; rich-tasting game; outstanding beef and lamb; slow-ripened soft fruits; hardy root vegetables; floury potatoes and distinguished cheeses. Dishes made with these ingredients bring with them an inherent quality and taste which demands that not too much is added and not too much taken away in the cooking/preparing process. And it also brings Scottish food into the twenty-first century with ingredients which continue to define the country. They have been the basis, in the past, of a diet which produced a nation of great vigour and endurance. What follows in these pages provides the means to maximise – in the future – the potential of Scottish cookery.

Catherine Brown, 2013

ACKNOWLEDGEMENTS

To each of the following I am particularly grateful for the time, information and encouragement which they gave while I was researching the first edition of the book. I hurled many awkward questions at them which they patiently answered: Dr J.J. Connell, Director, Torry Research Station, Aberdeen; Martha Crawford, Secretary of the British Deer Farmers Association, Cluanie, Beauly, Inverness-shire; Keith Dunbar of Summer Isles Foods, Achiltibuie; Sheila Harley, Scotch Quality Beef and Lamb Association; Peter Hick, Director, Reawick (Shetland) Lamb Marketing Company; Professor George Houston, Department of Political Economy, University of Glasgow; James Keay, Torry Research Station, Aberdeen; D.S. MacDonald, Oatmeal Miller and Grain Merchant, Montgarrie Mills, Alford, Aberdeenshire; Elizabeth MacIntosh, Scottish Milk Marketing Board; Professor A.D. MacIntyre, Director, Marine Laboratory, Aberdeen; Donald MacLean, Chairman of the National Vegetable Society, Dornock Farm, Crieff, Perthshire; Dr Donald McQueen, Marketing Director, Scottish Milk Marketing Board; Dr David Mann, United Biscuits, Glasgow; Rosemary Marwick of Howgate Cheeses, Penicuik, Midlothian; I.G.A. Miller, Oatmeal and Pearl Barley Miller, Kelso Mills, Roxburghshire; George Motion, Assistant Secretary, The Red Deer Commission, Knowsley, Inverness; Hamish and Livingston Neil of S.L. Neil Glasgow; Douglas Ritchie of Strathaird Sea Foods; J. Russell, Manager of the Company of Scottish Cheese Makers; Archie Sinclair, Caithness Smoking Company, Latheronwheel; Stewart Sloan of Robert Sloan, Butchers; Susanna Stone of Highland Fine Cheeses, Tain, Wester Ross; Dr Charles E. Taylor, Director, Scottish Crop Research Institute, Invergowrie, Dundee; Richard Van Oss, Director, The Game Conservancy, Fordingbridge, Hampshire; Joseph Walker of Walkers Shortbread, Aberlour; Gillan Whytock of the Advisory and Development Service, Agronomy Department, The West of Scotland Agricultural College, Auchincruive, Ayrshire.

Sincere thanks also to Iseabail MacLeod, Editorial Director of the *Scottish National Dictionary*, for editing the revised edition, also to Bruce Lenman, Professor of Scottish History at St Andrews University, and to Tom Johnstone of Birlinn for his helpful support.

For the use of their kitchens, as well as their stimulating company and help, reading and correcting recipes, my thanks to Joan Campbell and Catherine Braithwaite (my mother). And to many others who have helped in a practical way I am deeply grateful, for without their help also the book would simply not have been written.

Weights, Measures & Anglo-American Terms

Converting from Imperial to Metric

Stick to one system throughout a recipe.

Conversion from one system to another may be an exact equivalent or it may be an approximation. A few grams here or there, in many recipes, will not affect the finished result. Where it will matter is in baking recipes, such as a cake which will sink if there are not enough 'strengthening' ingredients like flour and eggs, and too many 'weakening' ingredients like butter.

Scales: Balance or Digital?

Compared with less precise balance scales, digital scales provide not just a conversion function from imperial to metric but also the ability to measure the exact equivalent, in units of 1 gram, or hundredths of an ounce. For baking, and other recipes which require precision-measuring, digital scales provide a more guaranteed chance of success.

Balance scales and measures are usually graduated in multiples of 25 g/1 oz. If the conversion of 1 oz to 25 g is made (1 oz = 28.35 g), there will be inexact conversions with 3 oz (= 85 g) and 4 oz (= 113 g). Instead of going up by 25 g I have mostly reduced 3 oz to 75 g and for 4 oz taken the jump to 125 g simply because then the metric measurements can be compared proportionately: i.e. ¼ lb = one eighth kilo; ½ lb = ¼ kilo; 1 lb = ½ kilo, etc.

For liquid measurements the same proportional system can apply, with ¼ pt = one eighth L; ½ pt = ¼ L; 1 pt = ½ L, etc. This makes measuring more convenient now all ingredients are packaged in metric.

The most important exact conversions to remember are that 500 g is actually 1 lb 2 oz and 1 litre is actually 1¾ pints.

EXACT CONVERSION FROM OUNCES TO GRAMS AND TO NEAREST 25 G FIGURE

Imperial Ounce	Exact Gram	To nearest 25 g figure
½	14.5	15
1	28	25
2	57	50
3	85	75
4	113	100 or 125
5	142	150
6	170	175
7	198	200
8	227	225
9	255	250
10	284	300
11	311	325
12	340	350
13	368	375
14	396	400
15	425	425
16	453	450

Fluid Ounce	Exact equivalent	To nearest 25 ml figure
5 fl oz (¼ pint)	142 ml	150 ml
10 fl oz (½ pint)	284 ml	300 ml
15 fl oz (¾ pint)	326 ml	450 ml
20 fl oz (1 pint)	568 ml	600 ml

Imperial/Metric Conversion to Graduated Cups

Graduated cups have the advantage of convenience, especially when scales are not available. While they are useful in such situations, and for many everyday recipes, they are less useful for recipes which need precision, like baking recipes, or for large quantities, when they become too time-consuming. Cups available in the UK (and in Australia and New Zealand) are in four sizes based on the metric system 1 cup = 250 ml; ½ cup = 125 ml; ¼ cup = 60 ml; and ⅓ cup = 80 ml.

American/Imperial Measures

The important difference in American measures is that besides retaining the imperial system, they have also retained the old British measure for 1 pint at 16 fl oz (UK now 20 fl oz), which was originally the same as the solid measure and which the British abandoned in 1825. American cups are graduated in fractions of 16 fl oz (1 cup = 8 fl oz; ½ cup = 4 fl oz; ¼ cup = 2 fl oz) which is slightly less than the metric cup at 250 ml = 9 fl oz.

American butter is packaged in 4 oz sticks, 4 to a box of 1 lb, which makes for easy and quick measuring, especially since they are usually graduated on the wrapping paper.

I have used the following table as a basis for conversion, though on occasions in the recipes I have had to adjust quantities to produce comparable results. Where the cup is described as scant then I have filled it to about ¼ in of the rim of the cup, while generous means that it was slightly heaped.

American names for commodities, where different from the British, are in brackets.

Solid ingredients	Imperial	Metric	American cups
Beans, dry	8 oz	250 g	1 c
Barley, flour	4 oz	125 g	1 c (gen)

Breadcrumbs,			
dry	4 oz	100 g	1 c
fresh	2 oz	50 g	1 c
Cocoa Powder	4 oz	100 g	1 c (gen)
Cornflour (Cornstarch)	4 oz	100 g	1 c (gen)
Currants	5 oz	150 g	1 c
Flour – Plain			
(All-purpose flour)	4 oz	125 g	1 c (gen)
Self-raising			
(Self Rising)	4 oz	125 g	1 c (gen)
Wholemeal			
(Whole Wheat)	4 oz	125 g	1 c (gen)
Glace cherries			
(Candied)	6 oz	175 g	1 c
Ground almonds	3 oz	75 g	1 c
Nuts – broken or			
coarsely chopped	4 oz	125 g	1 c
Oatmeal, fine, medium	4 oz	125 g	1 c (scant)
coarse – pinhead			
(Irish oatmeal)	4 oz	125 g	1 c (scant)
Rolled Oats (Oatmeal)	3 oz	75 g	1 c
Pearl Barley	6 oz	175 g	1 c
Rice	6 oz	175 g	1 c
Suet (shredded beef suet)	4 oz	125 g	1 c (scant)
Sugar,			
caster, granulated	7 oz	200 g	1 c
	8 oz	250 g	1¼ c
brown	5 oz	150 g	1 c (scant)
icing (confectioner's)	4 oz	125 g	1 c (gen)
Sultanas and Raisins	6 oz	175 g	1 c (gen)
Yeast, dry	2 level tsp	7 g	1 package
fresh	½ oz	15 g	1 package
			or cake

Fruit, Cheese, Vegetables, etc.

Butter and other fats	8 oz	225 g	1 c
	4 oz	113 g	1 stick
Cabbage, raw, shredded	3 oz	75 g	1 c (scant)
Carrot, 1 medium, sliced	5 oz	150 g	1 c
Cheese, Cheddar, grated	4 oz	125 g	1 c
Cream, crowdie, cottage	8 oz	250 g	1 c
Herbs, fresh	2 oz	50 g	1 c
Mayonnaise	6 oz	175 g	1 c
Meat, raw chopped or minced (Ground beef)	8 oz	250 g	1 c
Mincemeat	10 oz	275 g	1 c
Mushrooms, raw, sliced	2-3 oz	50-75 g	1 c
Onion, chopped	5 oz	125 g	1 c
Potatoes, cooked, mashed	8 oz	250 g	1 c
Treacle, black (Molasses) Golden Syrup (Light corn syrup)	12 oz	350 g	1 c

Liquid ingredients	Imperial	Metric	American cups
Water, milk, vinegar, oil, etc.	8 fl oz	250 ml	1 c (½ pt US)
	¼ pt (5 fl oz)	150 ml	¾ c (scant)
	½ pt (10 fl oz)	300 ml	1¼ c (scant)
	¾ pt (15 fl oz)	450 ml	2 c (scant) (1 pt US)
	1 pt (20 fl oz)	600 ml	2½ c
	1¼ pt (25 fl oz)	700 ml	3 c
	1½ pt (30 fl oz)	850 ml	3¾ c
	1¾ pt (35 fl oz)	1000 ml	4¼ c
	2 pt (40 fl oz)	1150 ml	5 c

Standard Measuring Spoons

These are the same as the metric measuring spoons now widely available in Britain.

All spoon measures are taken as level.

For Liquids:

1 teaspoon = 5 ml
1 tablespoon = 15 ml
American spoons
1 teaspoon = 7.5 ml
1 tablespoon = 22.5 ml

Anglo-American Cooking Vocabulary

BRITISH	AMERICAN
Cooking terms:	
Fry	Pan broil (without fat)
	Pan fry (with fat)
Grate	Shred
Grill	Broil
Gut	Clean
Knock back	Punch down
Prove	Rise
Sieve	Sift

Commodities not already mentioned in conversion table:

Anchovy essence	Anchovy paste
Bannock	Flat, round cake
Bicarbonate of soda	Baking soda
Biscuits	Cookies or Crackers
Boiling fowl	Stewing fowl
Broad beans	Windsor or fava
Cake mixture	Cake batter
Caster sugar	Granulated sugar

Cornflour	Cornstarch
Cream, single or double	Light or heavy (whipping) cream
Desiccated coconut	Flaked coconut
Dripping	Meat dripping
Essence	Extract
Flaked almonds	Slivered almonds
Haricot beans	Navy beans
Hough	Shank of beef
Icing	Frosting
Jam	Preserves
Jelly (sweet)	Jello
Rasher	Slice
Roast potatoes	Oven-browned potatoes
Scone	Shortcake, biscuit
Single cream	Light cream
Soft brown sugar	Light brown sugar
Spring onion	Green onion
Stewing steak	Braising beef
Sultanas	Seedless white, or golden, raisins
British	American

Cooking equipment:

Ashet (Scottish)	Meat dish
Baking sheet or tray	Cookie sheet
Frying pan	Skillet
Girdle	Griddle
Greaseproof paper	Waxed paper
Large pot	Dutch Oven or deep cooking utensil with a tight-fitting lid
Liquidiser	Electric blender
Roasting tin	Roasting pan with rack
Sandwich tins	Round-layer cake pans
Stew pan or pan	Kettle

Quantities produced by the recipes: servings per person

While this can only be an approximation since much depends on serving size and on the position in the meal, not to mention individual appetites, these are recommended average portion sizes per person of certain ingredients.

Soup: 250-300 ml/9-10 fl oz (larger amount if to be served as a main meal broth)

Meat and **Fish** uncooked weight: 125-175 g/4½-6 oz (without bones) 200-225 g/7-8 oz (with bones)

Rice and **Pasta:** 75 g/3 oz dry weight

Potatoes in their skins uncooked: 150-175 g/5-6 oz (less if served with several other root vegetables)

Oven Temperatures

The temperature in every oven will vary a little whether it's **gas, electric, convection, fan-assisted** or **Aga.**

In an **electric, non-fan-assisted oven**, the hottest part is at the top and the coolest at the bottom. In this oven, keep baking tins in the middle of the shelf, away from the side to prevent burning. If the heat is coming from the back it's a good idea to turn baking trays half way through the cooking.

In an **electric, convection, fan-assisted oven** the heat is circulated more evenly, making the whole oven hotter though this depends on how full the oven is and the size of the baking tins or dishes used which may impede the circulation if they are large. In theory this means that convection ovens can operate at a lower temperature than a standard conventional oven and cook food faster. The hot air circulation tends to eliminate 'hot spots' so the food should bake more evenly. The following temperatures for fan-assisted ovens may vary according to the type of oven and the volume of food being cooked. Consult the manufacturers' handbook for their recommendations.

Gas Mark	Fahrenheit	Celsius	Description
½	250	120/100 fan	Cool
1	275	140/120 fan	Very low
2	300	150/130 fan	Very low
3	325	160/140 fan	Low
4	350	180/160 fan	Moderate
5	375	190/170 fan	Moderately hot
6	400	200/180 fan	Hot
7	425	220 /200 fan	Hot
8	450	230/210 fan	Very Hot
9	475	240/220 fan	Very hot

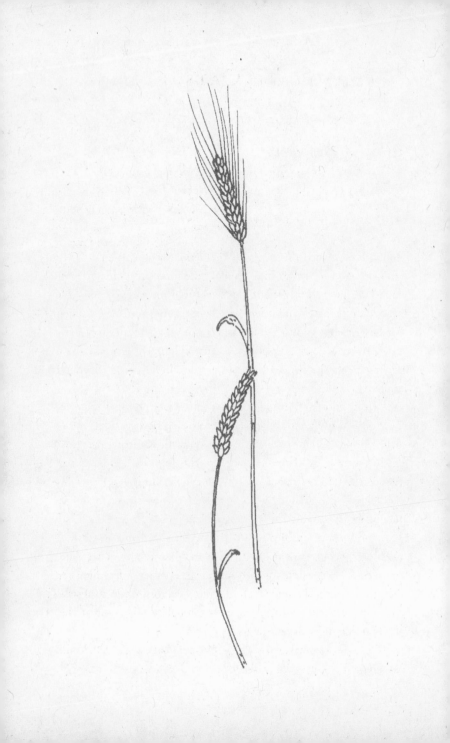

1: OATS

Oatmeal with milk, which they cook in different ways, is their constant food, three times a day, throughout the year, Sundays and holidays included . . .

J. Donaldson, *A General View of the Agriculture of the Carse of Gowrie*, 1794.

Original and frequent use of oatmeal was a mark of Scottish nationality to the extent that the English lexicographer, Dr Samuel Johnson, described the 'Scots' in his dictionary as 'oats eaters'. His knowledge of Scottish eating habits came from his travels in Scotland with his Scottish friend James Boswell in the late 1700s. He was an opinionated and often rude visitor, quite capable of making his hosts feel inferior when the fare was not to his taste. Too many bowls of Scots porridge, perhaps, prompted him to define 'Oats' as 'a grain which in England is generally given to horses, but in Scotland supports the people'.

Yet the Scots appear to have survived very well on oats and even been quite healthy, if travellers' tales are to be believed. Thomas Pennant, one of the most eminent naturalists of the eighteenth century, made a tour of Scotland not long after Dr Johnson and described the men as 'thin but strong'. Travelling people, like the drovers who herded the cattle around the country, seem to have subsisted almost totally on oatmeal carried in 'great wallets' hung round their 'broad and sturdy backs'. They mixed the oatmeal with water and baked cakes on stones heated by the fire, while soldiers carried a 'flat plate' strapped to their saddle for the same purpose. A legendary figure is the ascetic university student from a humble croft, living a subsistence existence on the bag of oatmeal brought from home at the beginning, and middle, of the term.

It is not known where or when cultivated oats originated. Wild oats are said to have been cultivated before 1000 BC by Bronze Age cave-dwellers in Switzerland. The carbonised grains of both wild and cultivated oats, along with wheat and barley, were found at digs along the Forth and Clyde Canal and at Camphill in Glasgow, and have been dated to a hundred or so years BC. Specimens are kept at the Museum of Scotland in Edinburgh.

Oats originally came from warmer countries in the east, from south-east Europe, central or western Asia or North Africa, and were certainly cultivated on the European continent before they arrived in Britain. But in the cool, moist Scottish climate, the oat kernels grow slower and therefore fill out better than in warm climates, where the growth is faster. Even oat kernels grown in the south of England are not as well filled as those in Scotland.

Oat flavour depends on many factors. The variety is important; the district where it is grown; the kind of soil; the manuring; the time of cutting the crop; and how the grain is threshed, dried and milled. Varieties of oats are continually changing and have a relatively short life compared with some of the varieties grown in the past. Around 1900, an old variety of oats known as Sandwich was favoured for its well-flavoured oatmeal. This was due to a high oil and protein content compared with the oats which are grown today – the higher the oil content the better the flavour. Oats today contain around 5-7% oil compared with only 1-2% in other cereals. Oats not only have fat in the 'germ' but also in the 'endosperm'.

From a practical storing and cooking point of view the amount of moisture is important. Most samples of newly milled meal have 6-8% moisture. At this level the meal lacks flavour and is why certain recipes say, 'Toast the oatmeal lightly in the oven before use', which will concentrate the nutty flavour. Similarly, oatcakes lightly toasted to 'harden off' will have a better flavour – the slower the process, the better the flavour. If they are dried too quickly the flavour can be harsh and fiery. This also applies to oatmeal dried in the oven before use.

Since it can become damp from exposure to the air, oatmeal should be stored well-pressed down in an airtight container. It was traditionally stored in a 'girnal' (wooden chest) – the freshly milled oatmeal tramped down, usually by children, so it would 'stay fresh' till the new harvest.

In all native oatmeal dishes such as porridge, oatcakes, brose and skirlie it's the good flavour of the meal which gives them their special character. Freshly milled meal will always produce the best flavour. If stored for too long it can develop a bitter taste or 'nip'. This is caused by 'lipase' enzymes which break down the fat into a bitter, unpleasant-tasting, fatty acid.

Traditional Milling

First the grain is dried out or 'conditioned' to a moisture content of around 15%. It's then kiln-dried: spread out on the kiln floor, which consists of perforated metal sheets with a smokeless-fuel-fired furnace some 20-30 feet below. The oats are turned by hand with large shovels until the moisture content is reduced to around 4-5%, when the meal will have taken on its mild, nutty flavour. The milling begins with shelling the husks, then the grains are ground between stone mill-wheels to the required 'cuts' or grades.

There are four water-powered, stone-ground mills and several factory mills where kiln-drying and stone-grinding is the method used.

Oatmeal 'Cuts' or Grades

> **Pinhead** – used for haggis, oatmeal loaves.
> **Rough** – used for porridge or brose, sometimes rough oatcakes.
> **Medium/Rough** – used by butchers for mealie puddings.
> **Medium/Fine** – porridge, brose, skirlie, baking.
> **Super-fine** – used in baking and in oatcakes along with a coarser grade.

To make Pinhead oatmeal the whole kernel is cut in half with any floury meal sifted out. Medium/Rough is also known as Coarse Medium. Medium and Fine grades are the most popular. There is also Oat flour which is distinct from Super-fine which still has a granule.

Other Oat Products

Rolled oats were developed in America by the Quaker Oat Company in 1877, and are made by steaming and rolling pinhead oatmeal. While they have the obvious advantage of cooking more quickly than regular meal, they have been specially heat-treated with some loss of flavour and nutrients, and this also applies to all the other 'instant' oat porridges now on the market. Jumbo Oatflakes are made by steaming and rolling the whole groat.

Dietetic Value

It has taken an American professor, James Anderson of the University of Kentucky College of Medicine, to endorse the wisdom of generations of Scots 'oats eaters'. Namely, that oats contain a gummy fibrous material (evident when porridge is made) which reduces blood cholesterol, blood sugar and fats. Researching the problems of diabetics, he discovered that oat bran is particularly rich in this 'water-soluble' fibre, much more so than wheat bran, which contains an 'unsoluble' cellulose and very little of the gum. Oats also score on value for money, since compared with other grains they contain more protein, more fat, more iron, more of the B vitamins, more calcium and also slightly more calories.

Barley

Despite the fact that today barley is mainly malted and used for distilling whisky, it was the chief crop in Scotland for all purposes from Neolithic times until the introduction of oats in the Roman period. From this time onwards the oat crop developed, but it was not until the 1700s that oatmeal became the main food crop and barley was more often used to distil whisky. Despite this, whole grains of barley continued to be used to thicken broths – as they still are today – and its milled flour was still used in bannocks. In the Highlands and Islands, and among the lower classes in the Lowlands, barley flour remained the preferred choice for making bannocks. As it still is today in parts of the Hebrides, the north of Scotland and in Orkney and Shetland.

The old Neolithic variety grown in Scotland since ancient times is known as 'bigg' or 'big' (*hordeum vulgare*) and makes a dark greyish-brown bannock. Barley from 'bigg' is called 'bere' (pronounced 'bare'). There is no sweetening in the beremeal bannock, which allows the natural flavour of the meal to predominate. It has a more distinctive flavour than oatmeal with a slightly astringent 'earthy' tang which combines well with creamy Orkney Farmhouse cheeses. Bere is ground and made into beremeal bannocks by the local bakers. Stoneground Orkney beremeal is sold in Orkney and also in many specialist shops, as well as butchers' shops and small village shops in rural areas in the rest of the country. It is mostly stoneground at water-powered mills: the Barony Mill in Birsay on Orkney and the Golspie Mill in Sutherland.

Pearl barley, which is used for thickening Scotch Broth, is widely available, while barley flour from pearl barley is less common but available in specialist shops. Like oatmeal, barley and barley flour/beremeal should both be bought in small quantities and stored in an airtight container. The flavour of barley flour is not as strong as beremeal.

Peasemeal

Roasted milled peas are used to make this very fine flour, much loved for making brose (see p.15). Yellow field peas are first roasted, which caramelises some of the sugar and darkens the colour. They are then ground through three pairs of water-powered millstones, becoming successively finer with each grinding. Peasemeal was used in a mix with other meals in bannocks and scones adding extra protein food value. It is ground at the Golspie Mill in Sutherland (see p.452).

Wheat

While the rest of the country grew mostly oats and barley, wheat flourished in the more fertile lowland areas of south-east Scotland, the Laigh of Moray, parts of Fife and Easter Ross. These areas were all developed by monastic farmers in the eleventh and twelfth centuries who grew wheat mainly as a cash crop. Not much appears to have been eaten by the common people, except at feasts and festivals. Higher up the social ladder, fine wheat bread was initially something of a prestige food which made its social descent gradually till sometime in the early 1900s, when it became a staple item of the Scottish diet.

Oatcakes

Hear, Land o' Cakes, and brither Scots . . .
Robert Burns (1759-1796)

Burns meant, of course, land of oatcakes, and not the sweet-flavoured cakes that have long been associated with the word. But why should the oatcake have come about, and why wasn't it just called oat bread or oat biscuit? It's an etymological puzzle which starts with unravelling the original meanings of loaf, bread, cake and biscuit.

Loaf, Bread, Cake and Biscuit

'Loaf' is simple – it has always meant the undivided item. 'Bread' is more complicated, since it originally meant only a 'piece' or 'bit', later referred to as 'broken bread'. The term 'a loaf of bread' really meant a loaf of 'pieces'. Eventually 'bread' became known as the undivided item. The Lowland Scots and the Northern English have retained the original meaning of 'piece' when they say 'Gie's a piece' – meaning a piece of bread.

When bread, meaning the undivided item, was baked not in a soft yeast-risen form but in an unleavened flat, round shape, it was known as a 'cake of bread'. It was usually baked hard on both sides by being turned in the process. We still talk of something being 'caked' hard. A 'cake' of soap gets its name from this too. In Wales, the North of England and Scotland (all oat-growing areas) this meaning survives in the oatcake.

'Biscuit', though it was also a round, flat, unleavened item, is derived from the meaning 'baked twice'. This was so it would keep twice as long, often to feed armies or sailors. In the mid-1500s it was described thus: 'The bread was such as was provided to serue [sic] at need, or in Wars, for it was BISCUIT, this is twice baked and without leaven or salt'. Sailors ate 'sea biscuit'.

Scots Oatcakes – shape and flavour

In their most basic and primitive form, Scots oatcakes are made with ground oatmeal, salt, a little dripping and water to mix. The Hebridean oatcake (*Bonnach Imeach*) is usually made with fairly fine oatmeal and is rolled out to between a quarter and half-an-inch thick, making it a fairly substantial cake. The Highlanders prefer a thinner, crisper variety, usually rolled out to less than a quarter-of-an-inch thick and made with medium oatmeal. Lowlanders often add some wheaten flour, which makes the texture less brittle, but they may also prefer a coarser oatmeal (pinhead) mixed with medium oatmeal, which makes an oatcake with a good bite to it. The taste in the North-East is also for a rough oatcake. The heavier Hebridean variety is the exception to the general preference throughout the country for a crisp, crunchy cake, which means it must be rolled out as thinly as possible.

Not many writers in the past mention the thickness of oatcakes, but in his diary, *Our Journal into Scotland* (1629), C. Lowther says that, 'Three travellers in the Borders had oat bread cakes, baked a fifth of an inch thick on a griddle . . .' At the other extreme there was the old festive 'mill bannock' which was made twelve inches round and one inch thick, with a hole in the middle to simulate the mill wheel.

The usual shape is a round bannock cut with a cross into four. Size depends on the size of the girdle. In pagan times, the Greeks and Romans cut crosses on their buns to represent the four seasons. Today the custom is continued with a different symbolism when crosses are put on hot cross buns.

A three-cornered piece of oatcake, scone or shortbread, the fourth part of a bannock, is known as a 'farl'. Old-fashioned, girdle-baked oatcake 'farls' are not sold commercially today since they curl up at the edges and break easily. Most commercial oatcakes are flat oven-baked and sold in packets.

The fat which is used will affect the flavour of the oatcake. Bacon fat gave a special flavour, though other fats from beef and lamb were also used. Dripping of any kind is better from the point of view of making a 'shorter' textured cake. Butter and cream will add flavour too.

Oatcakes in the diet

> For Breakfast . . . the cheese was set out as before, with plenty
> of butter and barley cakes, and fresh baked oaten cakes, which
> no doubt were made for us: they were kneaded with cream and
> were excellent.

Dorothy Wordsworth, *Recollections of a Tour Made in Scotland*, 1803.

'Oatcakes are especially good with herrings, sardines, cheese, curds, buttermilk, broth, and kail; or spread with butter and marmalade to complete the breakfast,' says F. Marian McNeill (*The Scots Kitchen*, 1929). The delicate, mealy flavour goes well with unsalted butter and some crowdie (the traditional Scottish version of cottage cheese) mixed with a little cream, the soft-cheese texture complementing the crunchy cake. All traditional soft cheeses are good with oatcakes (see p.284). The strong aromas and distinctive tang of heather honey make another good partner for an oatcake.

Records of meals show that oatcakes were commonly eaten at breakfast, dinner and supper as well as with tea at four o'clock in the afternoon. 'Oatcakes with milk' appears frequently in the diet charts of farm workers. In his *Description of Scotland*, in 1629, G. Buchanan says: 'They make a kind of bread, not unpleasant to the taste, of oats and barley, the only grain cultivated in these regions, and, from long practice, they have attained considerable skill in moulding the cakes. Of this they eat a little in the morning, and then contentedly go out a-hunting, or engage in some other occupation, frequently remaining without any other food till evening.' Highland crofters who went up into the mountains with their flocks during the summer months and stayed in primitive 'sheelins' or 'bothies', made butter and cheese with cows' and sheep's milk which they ate with oatcake, according to Thomas Pennant writing in 1772.

Burns says that they 'are a delicate relish when eaten with warm ale'. Whether this means that amongst the very poorest classes they were regarded as a luxury is not clear, but in the poorhouse diets oatcakes are never mentioned. Porridge or brose with milk, more quickly and easily made than oatcakes, were their basic fare.

GIRDLE OATCAKES
curled

Quantity for one girdle:

125 g/4½ oz medium and fine oatmeal (about half-and-half or
    all medium oatmeal)
1 tablespoon dripping, lard or butter, melted or cream
Large pinch of salt
2 tablespoons boiling water
Coarse oatmeal for rolling out

These attractive, curled triangles have a crisp, 'short' bite to them. They can be cut into 4, 6 or 8 depending on when they are to be eaten, the largest size usually served at breakfast.

Mix and roll out only enough for one girdleful at a time. Making up large quantities means that the mixture cools, making it difficult to roll.

Mixing and shaping

Mix the meals and salt. Add the fat or cream and mix through the meal. Make a well and add two tablespoons boiling water. Stir in, then knead to make it come together into a soft, firm ball. Add more water if necessary. The less water used the crisper the oatcake. Knead into a round. Dust the work surface with some coarse oatmeal and roll out to a circle about 3 mm/one-fifth inch thick. Keep bringing together round the edges to keep it from cracking. Cut with a cross into four or into six or eight. Leave to dry for about half an hour before cooking – this is not essential, but it helps to make the oatcakes curl.

Heating the girdle

(A large, heavy-based frying-pan will do instead.)

Heat the girdle slowly to get an even heat. It should be moderately hot for oatcakes, and the best way to test is by holding your hand about 2.5 cm/1 in from the surface. It should feel hot, but not fiercely so. A steady, slow heat is needed for drying out oatcakes.

Firing

Put the oatcakes on the girdle and leave till they have curled – they will curl upwards. If the cakes are too thick, they will not curl. Turn down the heat and leave for another five minutes till thoroughly dried out. This was originally done on a special toaster in front of the fire. Like toast, they should be put upright to cool since they continue to lose moisture till cold. Put in a toasting rack in a warm place to dry out thoroughly.

Note: Sometimes oatcakes were simply 'toasted very slowly at a distance from the fire, first on one side and then on the other on a toaster with open bars to let the moisture escape.' Meg Dods (1826).

Storing

Keep in an airtight tin or buried in oatmeal, which gives them a nice mealy taste. If they have been kept for more than a week it is a good idea to dry them off slightly in the oven or in front of the fire to improve the flavour.

Serving

They can be served slightly warm but not so hot that they make the butter run.

OVEN OATCAKES
very thin

350 g/12 oz medium oatmeal

50 g/2 oz coarse oatmeal

50 g/2 oz spelt or plain white flour

1 tsp honey, optional

50 g/2 oz butter

75 ml/3 fl oz boiling water to mix

Extra oatmeal for rolling out – fine, medium, coarse or pin-head

These are rich, short oatcakes which were eaten on festive occasions. They are made very thin by rolling out on a sheet of foil which is then easily lifted onto the baking tin.

To make

Preheat the oven to 350F/180C/160Cfan/Gas 4.

Use a 23 x 33 cm /9 x 13 in baking tin.

Put the meals and flour into a bowl. Mix thoroughly. Put the butter into a pan and melt with the water. When almost boiling, add to the meal with the honey and mix to a stiffish dough. It should come together easily. If it is too crumbly, add a teaspoonful of boiling water. The less water that is added, the shorter the oatcake, but too little will make an oatcake which breaks easily.

Cut a piece of foil a little bigger than the size of the baking tin and dust with coarse, medium or fine oatmeal. Dust a rolling pin with flour and roll out the mixture. For an extra crunchy texture sprinkle some pinhead oatmeal over and press in with the rolling pin. Lift, on the foil, into the baking tin. Cut into required shapes. Bake slowly without browning for 30-40 minutes till crisp.

PORRIDGE

I took my porridge i' the morning an' often got naething
again till night, because I couldna afford it.
W. Anderson, *The Poor of Edinburgh*, 1867.

Goldilocks stole her porridge in the morning, soldiers marched on their morning porridge, and the Scottish peasant for many centuries started the day with a bowl of this sustaining food.

Porridge-making is a morning ritual: the handfuls of oatmeal running through the fingers of one hand into a large, iron pot filled with boiling water, while the other hand stirs with the long, tapered stick (spurtle); then the pot left at the side of the fire giving the familiar 'plot' every few minutes just to show it is still cooking.

It's true that it was also eaten for supper, and that leftovers were poured into the 'porridge drawer' in the Scotch dresser. The cold porridge set like a jelly and slices were cut off, known as 'caulders' (Italians do this with their left-over polenta). These were taken to the fields and eaten in the middle of the day, or slices were fried and eaten at night with eggs, fish or bacon.

Type of meal

Porridge can be made with any kind of oatmeal. Finished texture and consistency is a matter of taste. Ground oatmeal will take longer to cook than rolled or jumbo oats. Pinhead and coarse oatmeal will cook faster if soaked overnight. Fine oatmeal makes a smooth, custard-textured porridge which is often given to babies.

Many ways of cooking but only one way of eating

Wooden bowls (china or earthenware plates lose heat too quickly) were filled from the central pot, often placed in the centre of the table, and the porridge was eaten with a horn spoon. The spoon was dipped into the hot porridge, leaving enough room for the milk or cream on the spoon.

A traditional hand-carved horn porridge spoon is quite large, round and deep, at least the size of a large tablespoon. To eat: the milk or cream bowl or cup is placed beside the larger one and the spoonful of hot porridge is dipped into the cold milk/cream before eating. This way the porridge remains hot which it does not when the milk/cream is added to the porridge. The essence of porridge eating is hot porridge, cold milk/cream.

Flavourings

There is nothing sacred about flavouring it only with salt. Robert Louis Stevenson made maps with **golden syrup** on top of his porridge as a child. **Honey** is another favourite. The sharp, bitter flavour of **molasses** (unsweetened treacle) is good with porridge. Farm workers in the north-east liked to eat their porridge flavoured with some of the molasses which had been bought in drums to feed the horses. Fresh **soft fruits** such as raspberries or strawberries can be stirred through, or served on top. **Nuts, seeds, raisins, prunes, dates** will all add texture and character to porridge. Some melted **chocolate** or a chocolate spread is another option. **Whisky** mixed with a spoonful of **honey** will provide a warming glow, as will a spoonful or two of **Atholl Brose**, see p.16.

TO MAKE PORRIDGE

4 servings

Put about 1.1 L/2 pt water into a pot and bring to the boil. It does reduce as it cooks, so it is very much a case of how thick you like it: use less water to oatmeal to make a thicker porridge. Sprinkle in 125 g/4½ oz oatmeal/rolled or jumbo oats with one hand, while stirring with a spurtle (long wooden stick) to prevent lumps forming. Lower the heat and leave to simmer for anything up to 30 minutes, stirring occasionally to prevent sticking. Season with a pinch of salt and serve in bowls with a smaller bowl of milk, cream, buttermilk or yogurt.

BROSE

In these barracks the food is of the plainest and coarsest description: oatmeal forms its staple, with milk, when milk can be had, which is not always; and as the men have to cook by turns, with only half an hour or so given them in which to light a fire, and prepare the meal for a dozen or twenty associates, the cooking is invariably an exceedingly rough and simple affair. I have known mason-parties engaged in the central Highlands in building bridges, not unfrequently reduced by a tract of wet weather, that soaked their only fuel the turf and rendered it incombustible, to the extremity of eating their oatmeal raw, and merely moistened by a little water, scooped by the hand from a neighbouring brook.

Hugh Miller, *My Schools and Schoolmasters*, 1854.

Brose is uncooked porridge. Sometimes, as Miller recalls, it is made with cold water, but preferably with boiling. Single men living in bothies made brose in the morning: country people working in the fields or shepherds in the hills made al fresco brose by the side of a burn. It was the quickest, cheapest way of making a meal. It was the meal which a Zurich doctor saw a shepherd making in the Swiss mountains and decided to give to his patients. 'Muesli' (from German meaning 'mashed dish') was added to the *Oxford English Dictionary* in 1933 (see **A Swiss/Scots Breakfast** p.35).

In rural areas day began at daybreak, about five o'clock, with perhaps a bowl of brose, then four or five hours later, workers would return for breakfast. Dinner was in the middle of the day, supper at night.

For brose, meal was put into a bowl – oatmeal, barley or pease meal – and boiling water, hot milk or the liquid from cooking vegetables or meat was poured over. Often a piece of butter was mixed in and perhaps some dried fruit. This was frequently a supper first course, with the meat and vegetables to follow.

OATMEAL BROSE
for breakfast

Put a handful of medium oatmeal or rolled oats into a bowl and pour over 1 cup of boiling milk to cover the oatmeal, add a small piece of butter and stir while pouring. Season to taste with salt.

PEASE BROSE
as eaten in the bothy

This is made in the same way as oatmeal brose, but instead fine peasemeal is used which gives it a richer flavour. Lots of currants and butter can be added as well as honey or sugar for sweetening.

ATHOLL BROSE
to defeat enemies

170 g/6 oz medium oatmeal
4 tablespoons heather honey
850 ml/1½ pt whisky
425 ml/¾ pt water

It was common to mix whisky with honey in the past and equally common to mix liquid with oatmeal. Bringing the two together in this potent concoction is credited to a Duke of Atholl during a Highland rebellion in 1475. He is said to have filled a well, which his enemies normally drank from, with this ambrosial mixture and they became so intoxicated that they were easily taken by his men.

Some old recipes leave in the oatmeal. But the following is reputed to have come from a Duke of Atholl and uses only the strained liquid from steeping the oatmeal in water.

To make

Put the oatmeal into a bowl and add the water. Leave for about an hour. Put into a fine sieve and press all the liquid through.

(Use the remaining oatmeal for putting into bread or making porridge – see p.13). Add honey to the sieved liquid and mix well. Pour into a large bottle and fill up with the whisky. Shake well before use.

Uses

May be drunk as a liqueur; is often served at festive celebrations such as New Year, or may be mixed with stiffly whipped cream and served with shortbread as a sweet.

BUTTERED OATS BROSE
with seeds, nuts, chocolate and dried fruits

250 g/9 oz each of:
buttered oats (see p.33)
sunflower seeds
pumpkin seeds
mixed nuts
raisins, prunes or dates
dark chocolate cut into chunks

Mix ingredients and store in an airtight container.

To make

Add water, milk, fruit juice as required. It can be soaked for a few hours. Serve with fresh fruit and yogurt or sour cream.

BANNOCKS

. . . bannocks and a shave of cheese
Will make a breakfast that a laird might please.
Allan Ramsay (1682-1758), *The Gentle Shepherd.*

In its original form, a bannock was any large, round, girdle-baked, unleavened item. The type of meal used depended on what was available, with great variations throughout the year and from district to district. Despite this, there is constant reference to barley bannocks by travellers. Thomas Pennant, in 1772, talks about the 'fresh eggs, fresh barley bannocks, and tolerable porter, together with some smoked salmon' which they enjoyed in an Inn at 'Cree in La Roche' (presumably Crianlarich, since he was travelling up Glen Falloch).

James Russell, writing in the nineteenth century, says that: 'Oatcakes and bannocks of barley meal with an admixture of pease were the ordinary table fare. Wheaten bread was scarcely known.'

Thomas Somerville, a minister in Jedburgh from 1741 to 1830, writes in his diary that, 'Though wheaten bread was partly used, yet cakes or "bannocks" of barley and peasemeal, and oatcakes formed the principal household bread in gentlemen's families; and in those of the middle class on ordinary occasions, no other bread was ever thought of.'

BEREMEAL BANNOCKS
unleavened

300 ml/½ pt milk
25 g/1 oz butter
110 g/4 oz beremeal or barley flour (may be mixed with peasemeal)
Salt to taste

Makes 1 bannock (28 cm/11 in).

Something akin to an Indian chapati since it doesn't rise, its charm lies in the barley flavour and in the contrasts of texture; the soft inside and harder, but not quite crisp, outside.

Preheat the girdle to fairly hot. Flour lightly with beremeal.

Making up the dough

Put the milk into a pan, add the butter and heat through to melt the butter; add the salt. Stir in the meal; it should come together into a softish paste. Turn out onto a floured board and knead lightly to a smooth ball, dusting well on top with barley flour. Roll out with a rolling pin to about 28 cm/11 in diameter and about 0.5 cm/¼ in) thick.

Firing

Fold bannock over the rolling pin and put on girdle. Cook on a moderate girdle till brown on one side. Turn, using a large fish slice, or cut in half and turn in two pieces. A bannock spathe, about twice the size of a fish slice, was used in the past for this. Cook on the other side for 5-10 minutes. Place on a cooling rack and eat warm with butter and cheese.

BARLEY BANNOCKS
unleavened wafer thin

Another early form was made with a much thinner mixture poured onto the girdle like large Breton pancakes (*crêpes*). Franco-Scottish connections may have had something to do with this, since there is a striking resemblance between the large Scottish girdles and the large iron plates used in Brittany for *crêpes*. In his *Travels in England and Scotland in 1799*, Faujas de St Ford talks about 'barley cakes, folded over', which probably referred to these bannocks.

115 g/4 oz beremeal or barley flour
3 eggs
25 g/1 oz melted butter
Water to mix

Makes 6-8 small, 3-4 large.

Preheat the girdle to fairly hot. Grease with oil. Mix ingredients to a pouring consistency. Pour onto the girdle and spread over girdle with a spatula till very thin. Leave to cook till lightly browned underneath. Turn and cook on other side. Cool in a tea towel on a cooling rack. Spread with butter, crowdie mixed with cream, or cream cheese, or honey or preserves and roll up to make a 'stick of rock shape' or fold in four.

ORKNEY BEREMEAL BANNOCKS
with raising agent

These are the round, light bannocks which bakers in Orkney make into rounds about the size of an outstretched hand. 15 cm/6 in approx.

125 g/4½ oz beremeal or barley flour
25 g/1 oz self-raising cake flour
1 teaspoon baking soda
Pinch of salt
30 g/1 oz vegetable fat for pastry
120 ml/8 fl oz buttermilk or fresh milk soured with the juice of
   a lemon

To make

Heat the girdle to moderately hot and flour well with beremeal.
   Sift the dry ingredients together. Rub in the vegetable fat. Make a well in the centre and add the buttermilk. Mix with a fork to make a soft elastic dough. Flour the work surface with beremeal and turn out the dough. Knead lightly for 10 seconds and roll out with a rolling pin or press out by hand. Put onto the hot girdle. Dust the top lightly with beremeal. Bake on both sides, turning once, until risen and lightly browned.

SAUTY BANNOCKS
girdle-baked

1 tablespoon syrup
275-300 ml/9-10 fl oz buttermilk or fresh milk soured with
   the juice of a lemon

125 g/4½ oz fine oatmeal

2 eggs

1 teaspoon bicarbonate of soda

2 tablespoons oil

125 g/4½ oz beremeal

This sweet, crumpet-style bannock from the North-East is called a 'Sauty Bannock'. The name is thought to come from the old superstition of adding some magic soot from the fire on special festive nights such as Halloween and Fastern's Een. It should be eaten warm from the girdle.

To make

Dissolve the syrup in the milk and add to the oatmeal. Soak overnight. When ready to cook, separate the eggs and beat the whites till stiff. Add the yolks, soda and oil and sift in beremeal. Beat with whisk till smooth. Add more milk if necessary to make a creamy consistency.

Fold in the whites of eggs. Drop in spoonfuls onto a hot girdle – they should spread to 12-15 cm/5-6 in. Fire on both sides; pile on top of one another and wrap in a cloth to keep them soft. Serve hot, with butter and jam or crowdie mixed with fresh cream.

MEALIE PUDDINGS AND SKIRLIE

It fell about the Martinmas time,
And a gay time it was then, O,
that oor guidwife had puddens to mak',
And she boiled them in a pan, O.

Anon.

In the days before the turnip was used as winter feed for animals, Martinmas, 11 November, was the time for killing the animals which could not be fed all winter. 'Mairt' was an incredibly busy time, though several families would work together. Every scrap of the animal was used – the meat mostly salted down and puddings made from the innards. Pudding is the original name for the innards of an animal. Pudding Lane in London got its name because it was where butchers washed out the innards of the animals.

Mealie puddings, black (with blood) and white (without), were made when animals were killed. This is now mostly a butcher's job, though some people still make their own. The oatmeal, onions, suet from the animal and salt and pepper were mixed in a large basin. Blood from the animal was added to make the 'bleedy' ones. The intestines were thoroughly washed, usually in a burn, and then stuffed loosely with the mixture. A writer in the *North East Review* writes nostalgically of the puddings his mother used to make – 'Come time the skins were a' filled up, and tied, and jabbit wi' a darner, and they were ready for the pot. They were biled an oor. It wis easy the langest oor I mind on. My teeth wid be watering till I slivert again, and when they lifted the lid o' the pot to see the water wisna biling in – oh! the guff that filled the kichie. The tastings, or the preens as my mother ca'ed them, were first oot and nae wirds could tell ye fit they tastit like – as the poet his't – "warm-reekin', rich," ye dinna see the like the day.'

SKIRLIE

Skirlie is made with the same ingredients as mealie puddings, but the mixture is fried in a pan. The noise of the frying or 'skirl', as in skirl of the pipes, gave it its original name of 'skirl-in-the-pan'. It can be served with roast meat and is particularly good with game, or it can also be used as a stuffing for any kind of poultry or game. It can also be made into a steamed pudding, using either a cloth or bowl.

Medium or coarse oatmeal is used. The type of fat varies, though fresh beef suet, meat or bacon dripping makes the best-flavoured skirlie. The onions also add flavour.

50 g/2 oz fat, meat or bacon dripping, butter or oil
1 medium onion, finely chopped
125 g/4½ oz medium or coarse oatmeal approx
Salt and pepper

To make

Melt the fat in a frying pan. When hot, add the onion and cook over a medium heat till reduced and lightly browned. (Some recipes add water at this point to soften the onion, but this seems to be a regional variation.) Add enough oatmeal to absorb the fat. Continue to cook over a medium heat, stirring all the time, for a few minutes. Season with salt and pepper and serve.

Variation: Skirlie Toast

This can be made with leftover meat, game, chicken or turkey. Use any of the excess dripping or gravy and mix with skirlie to make a spreading paste. Taste and season. Toast 4 slices of crusty bread or rolls. When hot, spread with skirlie and cover with thinly cut slices of leftover roast chicken, turkey, beef, lamb or game or leftover stuffing. Serve with redcurrant or rowan jelly.

OATMEAL AND BARLEY BREADS

Challenged by a Glasgow baker to make an oatmeal loaf – he thought it impossible since oatmeal has no gluten – the following breads are the results, with some help from Bernard Clayton's *The Complete Book of Breads* (1973) as well as Dan Lepard's *Short and Sweet* (2011). Lepard pioneers the theory that breadmaking does not require a kneading workout to get the best textured bread. It can be done with much less energy by a simple 10-minute resting time after the first mixing then three simple fold-push-and-stretch sessions, resting the dough in between. This way the 'strength' of the dough develops naturally.

OATMEAL BREAD or ROLLS
with molasses or treacle

175 g/6 oz rolled oats or jumbo oats
50 g/2 oz lard/butter or 4 tablespoons oil
1 teaspoon salt
85 g/3 oz molasses or treacle
450 ml/17 fl oz lukewarm water
2 x 7 g packet quick-acting yeast
625 g/1 lb 6 oz strong white bread flour
1 egg, beaten
2 tablespoons rolled oats or jumbo oats to coat tins

Makes 2 loaves

This striking loaf, richly brown on the inside, has a light, speckled crust from the rolled oats lining the tin.

Preheat the oven to 425F/220C/200Cfan/Gas 7.

Use 2 x 500 g/1 lb loaf tins.

To mix the dough

This can be done by hand or with a mixer with a dough hook. Put the oats, lard/butter or oil and salt into the bowl. Dissolve molasses in most of the lukewarm water and pour over the oats, add yeast and flour. Mix together. Using the dough hook, start the mixer on a slow speed and mix, adding more water if necessary to make a very soft, sticky dough. Beat on a higher speed for a minute until everything is thoroughly mixed. Cover the bowl with a cloth and leave for 10 minutes or longer. This allows the flour to absorb the moisture.

Knead by fold-stretch-and-rest

Oil the work surface and your hands, and turn out the dough. Scrape the bowl clean and oil it lightly. Press out the dough into a round shape. Fold in two, bringing the top edge down to the bottom edge making a half circle. Push down lightly with the 'heel' of your hand and push and stretch the dough away from you to about 5-10 cm/2-4 in. Turn the dough a quarter, clockwise, and repeat fold-push-and-stretch. After three or four times the stretchy gluten in the flour will develop and it will become more difficult to push and stretch. When this happens, stop and leave dough to relax for at least 10 minutes, or longer. Repeat push-and-stretch twice more and the dough will become smooth, silky and elastic. Put back into the bowl.

Rising the dough

Cover with a cloth and leave to rise in a warm place until it has risen by 50%.

Shaping for bread and baking

Grease tin well with lard or oil and coat the base and sides with rolled or jumbo oats. Divide the dough in half. Shape into loaves and put into tins. Cover with lightly greased cling-film and put back in a warm place till they have risen by 50% again. Brush with egg and sprinkle rolled or jumbo oats on top. Bake for 20 minutes at the high heat then reduce to 390F/200C/180Cfan/ Gas 6 and bake for another 45 minutes till the crust and base are firm and browned. Take out of tin and cool thoroughly on a rack.

Shaping for rolls

Divide into 12-14 pieces. Shape into rolls. Place on baking tray leaving space for rising. Cover with lightly oiled clingfilm and put in a warm place till they have risen again to double in size.

Baking

Brush the tops with egg and sprinkle with rolled or jumbo oats. Bake for about 25-30 minutes at the higher heat until the crust and base are firm and browned.

BUTTERMILK BREAD
with oatmeal and barley

This moist, aromatic bread is best eaten with cheese or with a thick soup-stew. It can be baked in a round bannock shape and cut in wedges, or in a loaf tin. It can also be baked in a round, ovenproof pot with a lid in the style of the cast-iron Irish bastible pot which was buried in the peat fire (see Baked in a Pot p.341).

60 g/2 oz medium oatmeal
60 g g/2 oz beremeal or barley flour
175 g/6 oz wholemeal or spelt flour
25 g/1 oz wheatgerm
1 teaspoon bicarbonate of soda
1 egg
2 tablespoons oil
Pinch of salt
250 ml/8 fl oz buttermilk or fresh milk soured with the juice of a lemon
Oil for greasing/sunflower and/or sesame seeds for coating tin/pot

Preheat the oven to 350F/180C/160Cfan/Gas 4.

Use 500g/1 lb loaf tin or 18-20 cm/7-8 in round pot with lid which can be put in the oven.

To make

Put all the meals, wheatgerm and bicarbonate of soda into a large bowl and mix well. Grease tin. Coat the greased sides with sunflower and/or sesame seeds or jumbo oats.

Make a well in the centre and add egg, oil, salt and butter-milk/soured milk. Mix together with a fork. Once they are well mixed, begin bringing in the flour from the sides. The mixing should be done as quickly as possible in a large bowl. The mixture should come together as a fairly soft dough. If it is too stiff the bread will be heavy.

Shape into a round bannock shape or put into a loaf tin or pot with a lid. Sprinkle sunflower, sesame seeds or jumbo oats on top. Put the lid on the pot. Bake for 40-50 minutes. The bannock will take 30-40 mins. To test, remove from tin or pan and knock on the base: it will make a hollow sound if ready. Remove and cool thoroughly.

Other Uses of Oatmeal and Barley

A huge pot hung over the fire which leapt in a shining black-and-steel range. A black kettle stood on one hob, a brown tea-pot on the other. Steam rose gently from the kettle and thickly from the great black pot, whence also came a continuous 'purring' noise and the wonderful smell.

Jennifer Gowan, 'Friendship is a Clootie Dumpling',
Scottish Field, July 1966.

CLOOTIE DUMPLING

If a rich, spicy and sweet Christmas pudding is for adults, this much plainer, less sweet steamed-in-a-cloth misshapen mound, with its shiny brown skin, is for children (and perhaps adults with still a wee bit of the child in them). It is traditional for birthdays, Halloween, New Year, Christmas and any other festive occasion and my childhood memories of it remain vivid.

My white-haired grandmother at the head of the table, dishing out a huge steaming dumpling to her large family, its aroma wafting across the table as we waited for our 'surprise' plateful with its silver coin wrapped in paper ... Today's generation do it differently, preferring their clootie some time after the festive meal, often in the early evening. A slice of hot clootie with a spoonful of melting brandy butter is their supper, not just on the festive day but for as long as the clootie lasts.

Its name comes from the Scots for cloth: 'clout' – pronounced cloot. It can also be cooked in a greased pudding bowl, but it will not have a skin or quite the same texture and flavour as the pudding which emerges after its long slow simmer in a pot, filling the house with its 'wonderful smell'.

A WEE CLOOTIE

This size is easier for children and first-time clootie-makers to handle. For others, double the quantity and add around an extra 7 cm/3 in to the diameter of the cloth. Adjust spices to personal taste.

2-3 tablespoons flour

125 g/4 oz beef suet, finely chopped, or Atora
   pre-prepared

100 g/3 oz self-raising flour

175 g /6 oz fine white breadcrumbs

25 g/1 oz fine oatmeal

1 teaspoon baking powder

350 g/12 oz raisins/sultanas mixed

2-3 teaspoons each of ground cinnamon, ginger and mixed
   spice

1 large tart cooking apple, peeled and grated

1 large carrot, grated

2 tablespoons black treacle

2 tablespoons golden syrup

2 tablespoons Seville orange marmalade

2 eggs

Fresh orange juice to mix

6–8 servings

Use 55 cm/22 in diameter close-textured, strong white cotton or linen cloth; length of string; large pot with lid, metal grid or small plate or saucer.

Preparing the cloth

Half-fill a very large pot with water and bring to the boil. Place a metal grid or upside-down saucer in the base to prevent the dumpling sticking. Add the cloth to the boiling water and boil for a few minutes. Clear a work surface the size of the cloth. Lift it out with some tongs, allow excess water to drip off then lay out flat on the table. While the cloth is still very hot put the flour into a sieve and dust a thick layer of flour over the whole cloth (this forms the 'skin'). Lift up cloth to shake and spread evenly. There should be a thick layer which makes the 'skin' and is the seal which prevents water from getting into the dumpling. Shake off the excess.

Mixing

Put suet, flour, breadcrumbs, oatmeal, baking powder, sultanas, raisins and spices into a large mixing bowl. Mix with a wooden spoon. Make a well in the centre. Add the apple and carrot. Put the syrup, treacle and eggs into a small bowl and mix together with a fork till the syrup and treacle are dissolved. Add to the dry ingredients. Mix by hand to get the right consistency. There should be enough moisture to make a soft but not sloppy consistency. If too soft it will crack when turned out, if too stiff it will not rise well. Add orange juice if it is very stiff.

Shaping

Put the mixture into the centre of the prepared cloth. Draw up the edges, leaving some room for the dumpling to expand, and tie tightly with string, leaving an extra length of string to tie onto the pot handles to hold the dumpling in position. Hold up the dumpling and pat it round the edges to make it a good, round shape.

Steaming

Add the dumpling to the pot. The water should come about half way up. If it comes too high, water may get in at the tied end. If possible, tie the string to the handles so that the dumpling is held up in the pot. This will help to keep its shape better. This works best if there are two handles opposite each other so the dumpling can be 'hung' from them in the centre of the pot. Bring to simmering point, cover and simmer gently for about 4 hours. Check the water-level regularly. (Alternatively use a 1.7 L/3 pt greased pudding bowl [English: pudding basin], cover the top with foil or greaseproof paper and tie securely.)

To turn out dumpling in a cloot

Fill a large basin or sink with cold water. It should be large enough to hold the dumpling. Have ready another bowl that the dumpling will just fit into. Also a large, round serving plate or ashet. Holding the dumpling by the string, dip it into cold water for about 60 seconds. This is to release the skin from the cloth. Now put it into the bowl and untie the string. Open out the cloth and hang over the sides of the bowl. Put the serving dish over the bowl, invert it and then remove the cloth carefully.

Drying off and serving

Dry off in the oven or in front of the fire until the skin forms, becoming a burnished, brown colour. (Not everyone does this and some prefer to eat it before the skin dries off.) To serve, sprinkle with soft brown sugar and eat with cream, custard and/or more soft brown sugar, also Rum or Brandy Butter. To make this: beat 250 g/9 oz unsalted butter with 250 g/9 oz soft brown sugar till creamy, then beat in 3-4 tablespoons (or to taste) rum or brandy. Pot, cover and store in the fridge. Slices of leftover dumpling can be fried with bacon and eggs, or may be wrapped in foil and re-heated in the oven or covered with clingfilm in the microwave.

Many Scots high street butchers make their 'ain clootie' (see p.442).

SWEET HAGGIS

This is really a 'white' clootie which is made in the same way but without spices. How it got its 'haggis' tag is unclear. Oatmeal and beef suet combine with dried fruit and sugar to give its distinctive character. It is eaten hot as a savoury high tea meal with leftovers cut in slices and fried or grilled with bacon and eggs. This is my grandmother's recipe from the east coast, but there are many other variations including the Hebridean 'marag gheal'. There is even a North of England version called a 'Gold Belly' described and illustrated by Dorothy Hartley in her *Food in England*, 1954.

350 g/12 oz medium oatmeal
125 g/4 oz plain flour
300 g/10 oz beef suet, finely chopped
125 g/4 oz currants
125 g/4 oz raisins
Salt and pepper
Water to mix

8–10 servings

To make

Put all the ingredients into a bowl and mix with water to a fairly stiff paste. Cook as for Clootie Dumpling.

SWEET OATEN PUDDING
with raspberries

All old Scottish cookery books have versions of this pudding. Mostly, the recipes are for a kind of rich custard thickened with oatmeal, well-spiced with nutmeg and mace, sharpened with lemon and enriched with brandy. It was often boiled in a cloth like a clootie dumpling, but it was also used to fill a pastry tart.

The following is a modern adaptation using the original flavourings and ingredients, plus raspberries for colour and flavour, but changing the method to make a light cream sweet.

450 ml/¾ pt milk
50 g/2 oz fine oatmeal
1 large egg, separated
1 small lemon, zest and juice
2 tablespoons caster sugar
5 fine-leaf sheets quick dissolving gelatine (Costa brand)
150 ml/¼ pt double cream, lightly whipped
Blade of mace
A little grated nutmeg

4 servings

Soak the oatmeal and blade of mace in milk overnight (or at least for a few hours).

To make pudding

Put the oatmeal mixture into a pan and bring to the boil, simmer for 3-4 minutes. Pour into a bowl and add the egg yolk, grated lemon rind, grated nutmeg and sugar to taste. The heat of the mixture will thicken the egg.

To dissolve gelatine

Put the gelatine into cold water for a few minutes till it softens. Remove and put into a small bowl. Cover with half the lemon juice. Put into the microwave (900W) and heat on 70% until the gelatine dissolves into the lemon juice; this should only take about a minute. Do not overheat. Leave to cool and add to the mixture.

To finish

Beat the egg white stiffly and fold into the mixture. Put some fresh raspberries into individual glasses and pour the mixture on top. When set, garnish with raspberries and cream or make a raspberry purée (p.307) and pour a layer on top when set.

BUTTERED OATS

Originally named 'Oatmeal Topping', this was an Oat Information Council recipe, circa 1984. Now a big commercial success for the breakfast cereal manufacturers, they have other names for it. The original recipe depended on the marriage of oats and butter. It's simple to make, can be made in quantity, stored in an airtight jar and used as a handy 'crumble' topping for fruit puddings.

Nuts can be added. And it can also be mixed, Cranachan-style, through cream and soft fruit. It is also good as a layer in the base of the tin when making particularly moist cakes, or as a cake topping. (See **Mincemeat Sandwich Cake,** p.368). It may also be layered with stewed apples, as they do in Denmark, using buttered oats instead of breadcrumbs.

85 g/3 oz butter
110 g/4 oz brown sugar
250 g/9 oz rolled oats
1 teaspoon ground cinnamon (optional)

Use baking tin 22 x 33 cm/9 x 13 in.

Preheat oven 350F/180C/160Cfan/Gas 4.

To make

Melt the butter in a pan and add sugar and oats. Mix well. Spread out in tin and toast in a moderate oven for about 30-40 minutes till golden brown, turning once. Leave to cool. Store in an airtight jar or tin.

DUTCH APPLE CAKE
with Buttered Oats

1 quantity Buttered Oats (see above)
4-5 medium cooking apples
1 lemon
Soft brown sugar to taste

4-6 servings

Preheat the oven to 350F/180C/160fan/Gas 4.

Use round soufflé dish or other ceramic dish approx.1.5-2 L/2½-3½ pt capacity.

To make

Make the buttered oats.

Peel, core and slice the cooking apples. Toss them in the juice of a lemon and put into a casserole with a tight-fitting lid. Bake in the oven till the apples are soft and fluffy. They should take about 30 minutes. Beat up with sugar to taste. Or stew in a pan. Cool.

Finishing the dish

Using a straight-sided soufflé dish or any other suitable sweet-dish or pie-dish, arrange a layer of oats, then apples, and so on, till all are used up. Finish with a layer of oats and leave at room temperature for about an hour for the flavours to blend. Serve with fresh cream or crème fraiche.

RHUBARB AND BANANAS
with Cinnamon Buttered Oats

Layers of buttered oats, cooked rhubarb and sliced bananas contrast both in texture and flavour in this quick-and-easy sweet.

Buttered Oats, with cinnamon (see p.33)
450 g/1 lb rhubarb
2-3 tablespoons brown sugar
2-3 tablespoons water
3 bananas
1 teaspoon ground cinnamon
Serve with crème fraiche or cream

4 servings

Preheat the oven to 350F/180C/160Cfan/Gas 4.

Use round soufflé dish or other ceramic dish approx.1.5-2 L/2½-3½ pt capacity.

To prepare

Cut up the rhubarb and place in a baking dish, sprinkle over sugar and water. Bake till just soft. Leave to cool. Put a layer of rhubarb in serving dish, cover with a layer of finely sliced bananas and a layer of oats. Repeat, ending with a layer of buttered oats and serve with crème fraiche or cream.

A SWISS/SCOTS BREAKFAST

Anton Mosimann is the Swiss chef who revolutionised the kitchens of the Dorchester Hotel in London in the early 1980s with his unstuffy approach and his passion for natural flavours (*Cuisine Naturelle*, 1985). This is the Swiss Muesli he served with his special blend of fresh fruit flavours and mellow oats piled into individual balloon brandy glasses.

125 g/4 oz rolled oats
300 g/½ pt milk
1 grated apple
50 g/2 oz chopped hazelnuts
Juice of 1 orange
Juice of 1 lemon
1 orange, segmented
1 banana, sliced
50 g/2 oz fresh pineapple, sliced
Topping:
150 ml/¼ pt double cream
50 g/2 oz brambles (blackberries)
A few strawberries and/or raspberries

4 servings

To make

Soak the oats in milk overnight. Add the grated apple, hazelnuts, orange and lemon juice, the segmented orange, banana and pineapple. Mix together. Sweeten to taste with honey. Put into serving dishes. Finish with a spoonful of whipped double cream, some brambles (blackberries) and strawberries or raspberries.

OTHER RECIPES USING OATMEAL AND BARLEY

Fresh Herring or Mackerel Fried in Oatmeal p.56. **Dulse Cakes** p.142. **Minced Collops** p.195. **Beef Olives** p.196. **Cream Crowdie (Cranachan)** p.314. **Mincemeat Cake** p.368.

2: SEAFOOD: FISH

*There is an element of exotic interest in seafood which is
perhaps not sufficiently exploited in this country.*
A.D. McIntyre (Director, Marine Laboratory, Aberdeen), *The Sea and Fresh Waters*, 1985.

'Exotic interest' in native seafood has varied during Scotland's long
relationship with this rich natural food resource. Though in the recent past it may not have been 'sufficiently exploited', a glance today
at the slabs of enterprising Scottish fishmongers shows a more adventurous choice of fish and shellfish on offer. Many seafood restaurants, bars and pierhead shellfish stalls are now also exploiting it
more actively. And there are seafood enthusiasts who have demysti-
fied the handling and cooking of native seafood specialities, some of
which have not been familiar everyday eating for many Scots. Visiting a seafood bar in Spain, while on holiday, and finding that the
shellfish on offer comes from Scottish seas, has encouraged many
Scots to take more interest in their native seafood.

The irony is that they did in the past. Scotland was once known
as the seafood-eating nation of the British Isles. Then fishing became an industry. Huge catches of fish, such as haddock, cod and
herring dominated the market and the nation's choice of seafood
narrowed. Many people lost contact with the element of exotic interest in everything to be found in seas around the Scottish coast,
resorting to this limited range, mostly sold filleted. In urban and
industrial areas, often the only fish ever eaten was a haddock fillet,
deep-fried in batter from the 'Chippie', and the sight of a fish with
a head and eye was quite disturbing to some.

Scotland's early reputation as a prolific seafood-eating nation
has its origins, first and foremost, in the rich fishing grounds around

an extensive coastline. It was a food resource fully exploited by early settlers whose 'middens' of millions of sea shells tell the story of a people dependent on seafood for survival. Large fish bones were also found in their middens. The amount and size increased after the Viking invasions, which began in the late 700s. The raiders came in boats designed to venture on the high seas, rather than potter about the shoreline. This, plus their seamanship skills, provided the basis for a seafood-eating nation with an adventurous attitude to eating a wide range of species.

The earliest recorded commercial fishing was on the East Coast, where there is an abundance of natural harbours and easy transportation. Commercial fishing in the Highlands and Islands was less successful, largely due to problems moving such a perishable food from remote areas without modern transport facilities. In these areas, especially when the crofters lost their lands in the 1800s, seafood was often their main food source. This was most evident where the Viking legacy survived on the coast, and on the islands of the West and North. In Shetland this is seen in their more adventurous attitude to eating a wider range of species, including fish heads and innards, and in pioneering fishing trips to the Faroes, Iceland and Greenland long before other fishermen.

While fishermen in those days were not concerned about saving endangered species, recent history has shown that many established species are under threat due to overfishing. To conserve stocks, those buying seafood today need to know when fish and shellfish are spawning and should not be eaten; also that it is better to vary buying habits to include less familiar species: a ling, saithe (coley) or catfish (wolf fish) rather than cod; a pollack rather than haddock; a megrim sole rather than a lemon sole. For the fact is that these less familiar species are also caught in the trawerlman's net, but if no one buys them they could become discards or made into fish meal.

The main fish being farmed in Scotland is Atlantic salmon. Scottish Government policy has encouraged this industry, despite objections from environmental and wild salmon fishing organisations who believe the industry is a threat to wild stocks. The counter-argument is that the industry has a social purpose to provide much needed work opportunities in remote areas where communities are in danger of extinction. It's a running conflict which is likely to run and run and is not limited to Scotland. Other species are farmed in smaller numbers such as sea trout, halibut, Arctic charr and rainbow trout, making up only a very small percentage of the total fish production from Scottish waters.

The Marine Conservation Society (*www.mcs.com*) provides details of the spawning periods of fish and shellfish to avoid. It also gives details of species which are under threat from overfishing as well as size details for immature fish and shellfish which should not be on sale. The Marine Stewardship Council is the organisation which certifies sustainable fisheries around the world. It provides an MSC sustainable label (blue with a white tick) for a Certified Sustainable Fishery. Up-to-date information is available at *www.msc.org/track-a-fishery*.

FISH

Atlantic Salmon
(*Salmo salar*)

Life Cycle

Hatched in the purest of Scotland's freshwater rivers, after two years or so salmon migrate to the sea and grow fat over several years, then return to their native waters, fight their way back upstream to where they were hatched and there spawn. The female lays her eggs on the river-bed and the male fertilises them. By this time, both fish are badly run down and either die or go back to sea, to return another year.

The terminology for the various stages starts with Fry, which is just after the salmon hatch and come out of the gravel, on to Parr, which is the two-year period of growth in their home river. Just before they leave, they change physically to equip them for seawater and at this point are called Smolts. Salmon which come back after one year are called Grilse, and weigh 1-4 kg depending on the richness of their sea feeding grounds. Fish which come back after two, three or four years are Adult salmon, and the best quality are caught early in the season when still fat and flavoursome from the rich sea feeding grounds. They are likely to weigh from 4 kg upwards. When, and if, they reach their place of hatching, the female spawns and the male ejects his milt on top of the spawn. After this, they either die from exhaustion and lack of food (Spent Kelts) or they make it back to sea (Mended Kelts) and return to spawn again. All Pacific salmon spawn and then die, whereas 5% of Atlantic salmon return to spawn again. They usually spend two to three winters in the sea, maximum five. The oldest recorded salmon was caught on Loch Maree in Wester Ross: it was thirteen years old and had spawned four times.

WILD SCOTTISH SALMON

The earliest commercial salmon fisheries were on the Tay, Spey, Tweed, Don and Dee, producing large catches which were eaten fresh in summer and 'kippered' (smoked), or pickled in barrels in winter. While supplies remained plentiful for the best part of the nineteenth century, there was a gradual decline in the twentieth century to the point of severe depletion. The reasons have been hotly debated. Among the main issues have been overfishing, netting at mouths of rivers, pollution from aquaculture, freshwater habitat deterioration and impediments to migration routes. In 2001 the International Atlantic Salmon Research Board (*www.nasco.int/sas/*) was set up to investigate salmon mortality.

Season-Buying

The season lasts from February to September with variations for rod-caught fish on some rivers. Most plentiful from May-July.

Stocks on some rivers may be more abundant than on others. Current scientific advice has called for reducing exploitation of as many stocks as possible to allow the species to reach conservation limits.

Avoid buying wild-caught Atlantic salmon, unless from a known and sustainable source.

FARMED SALMON

Salmon farming in open net pens began on the West Coast in 1969 and has spread to the Islands, as well as Shetland and Orkney where they market their salmon separately from the rest of Scotland. Aquaculture provides a vital source of employment in remote areas which have a declining population, and much research has been undertaken to find solutions to the problems it has created. Concerns include escaped farm fish; disease transfer between farmed and wild species; widespread use of chemicals; and the need for strict enforcement of regulatory controls.

Skilled salmon farmers can produce high-quality fish. But this depends on a number of factors, such as stocking densities and where the cages are positioned. When there are fewer fish in the cage there is less chance of disease spreading, which has been a major problem. Low stocking density, plus controlled feeding so that the fish do not get too fat too quickly, will produce the best-quality salmon. Another factor is the water current round the cages, since it has been proved that those farmed in the fast-running current between the islands in Orkney and Shetland produce a better-textured fish from swimming against the current as it rushes through the cages. Some salmon farms are registered as organic by the Soil Association, reducing the levels of disease as well as meeting organic feeding and other environmental requirements, such as ensuring that the fish in their diet is from a sustainable supply.

Farmed salmon is now Scotland's fastest growing food export, in value surpassed only by whisky.

Season-Buying

Available all year. A whole fish can be distinguished from wild salmon by its tail-fin, which is flabby, compared with the powerful tail-fin on wild salmon. A farmed fish will slip through the fingers when held clasped below the tail-fin, while a wild fish can be held without slipping.

Its fat content can also be judged by the thickness of the white fatty layers between the pink muscles. A farmed fish will most likely have a thicker fatty layer, due to its less active lifestyle and perhaps also overfeeding.

BAKED SALMON
in butter

Tibby was for cutting it in twa cuts, but I like a saumon to be served up in its integrity.
Christopher North, *Noctes Ambrosianae*, 1822-1835.

To follow Christopher North's method is difficult if you don't have a large enough fish kettle, which may have been Tibby's problem. Working in hotels has meant that I've usually had one available to cook the salmon whole. But it was in a hotel, not a mile from the finest salmon river in the area, that I first used the method below which dispenses with the kettle, with no detriment to finished flavour or texture.

The whole fish is well buttered and then wrapped in foil and baked in the oven in its own juices. Cooking food in its own juices is an old and respected method, which goes back to primitive practices when food was coated with a thick layer of clay and buried in the embers of a fire. Gypsies liked cooking hedgehogs in this way and potters used their clay to wrap up meat and fish which they cooked in the kilns. Chicken 'bricks' and cooking foil are just a modern development of this.

To bake a whole or part of a salmon or salmon trout in foil

Preheat the oven to 300F/150C/130Cfan/Gas 2.

Clean, gut and wipe salmon. Check that it will fit into the oven. If it is too large remove the head and part of the shoulders, if necessary, baking this in a separate package – it can easily be put back on again. Use double-thickness foil. Place on baking tray and brush liberally with melted butter, then place the salmon on top. Brush salmon liberally with more melted butter. Season lightly with salt and put some salt and a few lumps of butter into the body cavity. Cover with a double layer of foil and secure tightly round the edges.

Place in a cool oven and bake. Allow 12 minutes per 450 g/1lb plus 12 minutes.

If to be served hot, leave for 10 minutes before removing foil, otherwise leave in foil till cold. Skin and garnish with lemon and some greenery – the delicate, green, feathery dill or fennel, or parsley, are attractive with pink salmon. Served on an old blue-and-white ashet, the dish needs no more adorning.

GRILLED SALMON STEAK
with parsley and lemon butter

All the ghillies I've known who fish salmon rivers have an uncanny knack of cooking salmon to perfection. Though the fish was often 'poached', their preferred method of cooking was always grilled, when the fish is fresh and in its prime.

Salmon has so much natural richness, especially early in the season, that grilling preserves its flavour and texture better than frying. For such a sensitive protein as fish (it coagulates so much quicker than meat and, when over-coagulated, the muscle fibres begin to squeeze the natural juices out of the fish, destroying both its flavour and texture), grilling is a more easily regulated method and the fish can be removed from the heat and the cooking stopped when it has just set.

When eating out in a restaurant, the late Ted Reynolds, much respected senior catering lecturer at the Scottish Hotel School in the 1960s and 70s and co-author of *The Chef's Compendium* (1963), used to test a restaurant, not by the chef's saucery skills, but whether a whole fish on the bone (usually a Dover sole) was grilled to perfection.

GRILLED THICK FILLETS OF SALMON
or pollack, saithe/coley, cod, hake, ling, wolf-fish/catfish, red fish/ocean perch (either skin on or off)

4 x 175 g/6 oz fillet of (about 3 cm thick) skinned or unskinned fillet
50 g/2 oz butter, melted or 3-4 tablespoons oil
Salt
1 lemon, cut in quarters

4 servings

Use a large, shallow-sided roasting tray.

Preparing fish

Place fish in a greased roasting tray presentation side down. For skin-on fish, skin side down. For unskinned fish, flesh side down. Use butter or oil to brush top and sides of fish. Season lightly with salt. Add quartered lemons to the tray.

Grilling fish

Preheat the grill to high and grill the fish for about 4-5 minutes depending on thickness. Turn and brush other side with more oil or butter and grill until cooked through.

Check if fish is cooked by opening up gently at the thickest part, with a sharp pointed knife, when the translucent flesh should have changed to milky-opaque all the way through.

Pour over any remaining oil or melted butter and serve with the grilled lemons and the boiled new potatoes, tossed in butter and chopped chives.

POTTED SALMON

Early methods (e.g. Meg Dods' 1826 version) baked the salmon first with butter, seasoning and spices, pounded mace, cloves, black pepper and allspice. Then it was drained and the pieces packed into 'potting cans', covered with clarified butter and stored in the larder for months.

A lighter version, for immediate eating, can be made with soft cheese.

300 g/10 oz g cooked salmon, skinned and boned
(or hot smoked salmon, hot smoked mackerel, Arbroath
   smokie or white crab meat)
200 g/7 oz full fat soft cheese
1 clove garlic, crushed
1 lemon, zest and juice
Hot cayenne or ground black pepper to taste
Salt (may not be necessary if fish is salty)
Good-flavoured oil to drizzle
Warmed crusty loaf or oatcakes
Watercress or rocket salad

4-6 servings

Blending Fish

Flake fish into a food processor while making a final check for

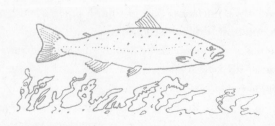

bones or shell. Add soft cheese, garlic, grated lemon zest and lemon juice. Blend to a coarse or fine texture. Taste and season according to taste.

Serving

Pile into a shallow earthware pot. Drizzle over a little good-flavoured oil. Chill in the fridge. Serve with warmed crusty loaf or oatcakes and a rocket and watercress salad.

SALMON BROTH

Stock:
Head, bones, skin and fins of the salmon
Bones from 2 white fish
2-3 tablespoons melted butter or oil
1 onion, finely chopped

Broth:
175 g/6 oz fresh salmon or 125 g/4 oz cooked
50 g/2 oz butter
1 medium onion, finely chopped
2 sticks celery, finely chopped
500 g/1 lb 2 oz small diced potatoes
2 leeks, white and green finely chopped separately
2 tablespoons double cream
Salt and pepper

8–12 servings

The delicate salmon-pink and varying shades of green make an attractive combination. It is best served as a soup/stew at lunch. It has the advantage of using up the head and trimmings of the salmon if they are available. (Fishmongers will keep them for you usually at little or no cost.)

To make stock

Wash the head and bones, removing all blood and gills. Heat the oil in a large pot and add the onions. Cook over a medium heat till they are soft. Add all the fish trimmings and continue to cook, stirring occasionally, for another few minutes. Cover with 2 L/3½ pt of cold water and bring to the boil. Skim and simmer for 20-30 minutes. Just before turning off the heat, add the fresh salmon and leave to cook in the liquor. (Do not re-cook if the salmon is already cooked.) When cooled, remove the whole pieces of salmon and break up into flakes. Strain stock.

To make broth

Melt the butter in a pot and add the onion. Cook, stirring occasionally, till soft. Add the other vegetables (the white of the leek only) and gently sweat the vegetables on a very low heat with the lid on, stirring every few minutes to prevent sticking, for about ten minutes. Add the fish stock and bring to the boil. Simmer gently till the vegetables are tender. Add the finely chopped green leek and the flaked salmon. Heat through for a few minutes, add the cream. Taste and season. Serve with crusty bread and butter.

Smoked Scottish Salmon

Preservation began with a method known as 'kippering', which can be traced back to the fifteenth century and was used to keep the fish during winter. It was a domestic operation as F. Marian McNeill describes in 1929: 'To Kipper Salmon: A Modern Method'. This involved preserving with salt, demerara sugar, olive oil, rum or whisky, and she suggests that the best smoky flavour would be achieved if the fish was smoked in an outside shed without windows used as a 'kiln', over a mixture of peat, oak chips and juniper wood. Though there are still home-made enthusiasts, using such methods in makeshift garden sheds and other contraptions, there is also a thriving industry of commercial smokers of varying sizes and types.

The basic method begins with **SALTING**, either dry or wet salting, to stabilise the salt content to around 3.5%. The most common method is to lay the fish on trays of salt and sprinkle salt over them by hand to varying degrees, depending on the taste required. Time left in the salt may be short or long depending on size and degree of saltiness required and the thickness of the fish. Smokehouses often have their own secret ingredients – sugar, juniper berries, herbs, molasses, rum or whisky – which they add at the salting stage. Small smokehouses using traditional methods will take longer to salt and dry out the fish compared with large-scale, mass-production smokers, where a fast-injection brining may be used which speeds up the process.

SMOKING: fillets are washed and left overnight to dry; laid out on wire mesh trays and wheeled on trolleys into controlled smoking kilns, to be cold-smoked at 20-30C, usually over smouldering oak chips, though some smokers continue to use some traditional peat for its distinctive flavour. During the process, the temperature and moisture content are monitored and controlled. Some curers 'rest' or 'mature' the fish for 3-4 days after smoking in a chilled temperature, which will improve the flavour by reducing the water content. In large, automated systems there is less personal control of the fish compared with smaller operations, where the gut-feeling and nose of an experienced smoker controls more carefully the finished cure. It may be sliced by hand or machine. Hand-sliced will be more expensive but will be a finer cut.

*All smoked salmon is not created equal. Most aficionados give
the nod to smoked Scotch salmon as the best . . . It is as a rule
the least oily, the most subtly flavoured, has the firmest and
most pleasing texture and the least amount of salt. It is also
the most expensive.*

New York Times, 1984.

Buying

Sweet, salty, woodsy, peaty . . . what is the best cure? Provided the
texture is as satin, the colour natural, and the balance of oil to flesh
perfect, deciding on the flavour-mix could depend on nationality.
Americans are most likely to prefer a cure dominated by woodsy flavours, with sweetness having the edge over saltiness. Italians, on the
other hand, are more likely to go for a salty cure, while in between
are the Japanese, with their liking for perfect balance. For them, the
sweet must cancel out the salt and they are not fond of woodsy or
peaty flavours.

As mass-produced smoked salmon has become much more
widely available, the trend has been to reduce this cure to its lowest
common denominator: wet, flabby smoked salmon made using fast-
curing methods have been the main problem. Smoking is a craft-
skill with a hands-on element which is not easily automated on a
large scale. There have also been cures with a bogus Scottish tag.
Hijacked for its prestige, the fish has not been Scottish but only
smoked in Scotland. Producers of such produce have been convicted
under the Trade Descriptions Act.

The best bet is to buy direct from small artisan Scottish smokers
who are within easy reach of the best supplies and select fish with
care. They often supply by mail order (see p.447).

'Top-quality wild fish, smoked in Scotland by experienced local smokers with distinctive cures, is to the mass-produced product
as "Chateau Bottled" is to "Vin Ordinaire",' says Keith Dunbar, a
salmon curer from the Summer Isles Smokehouse, 'and it ought to
be labelled as such.'

Atlantic or Pacific

Atlantic smoked salmon is longer, narrower, smaller and thinner than a side of Pacific salmon. Pacific salmon widens towards the middle and is thick and meaty. It is difficult to tell purely by colour, but the Pacific fish is closer to deep coral in colour than the Atlantic fish. In flavour and texture the Atlantic has a much more delicate flavour and a finer, more satiny, texture, which allows it – when smoked – to be sliced to translucent thinness. Pacific fish have a coarser, wider grain and a less subtle flavour.

Fresh/Frozen/Vacuum-Packed

'Fresh' smoked fish will always slice better and taste better, but provided frozen and vacuum-packed are carefully handled, there should not be too much loss of flavour or texture. To defrost, take it out of its sealed pack and place uncovered in the refrigerator. This allows it to thaw slowly and excess moisture to evaporate instead of going back into the fish. Frozen fish will never slice as thinly as non-frozen. Vacuum-packs will keep in good condition in the refrigerator for about two weeks. Once opened they should be used within the week.

Colour/Appearance

The flesh should be a natural-looking pink – beware of bright pink or orange: it may have been dyed. It should look firm and smooth, not torn or mottled, and should have a natural sheen without looking oily. Smoked salmon does go 'off', when it will have a fairly obvious rancid odour.

Preparing

Ready-sliced – the supplier should cut the slices wafer-thin, almost transparent. For the full benefit of the flavour they should be served at room temperature or very slightly cooler, so remove from the fridge at least 20-30 minutes before serving. Keep closely covered with clingfilm, since they dry out very quickly.

Whole side – place on a wooden board and prepare by trimming round the edges, if necessary. With tweezers, remove the 'pin' bones which run down the centre of the fillet if they have not already been removed. To slice, use a sharp knife with a thin flexible blade. Special knives for slicing smoked salmon may be bought from specialist suppliers. They are about 25 cm (10 in) long and have a slightly undulating edge. Keep the knife flat while cutting and make long, even strokes, working towards the tail, making paper-thin slices without tearing the flesh, which should be dense and resilient. The slices should be as large as possible, preferably one slice covering the entire plate. Do not slice more than 2 or 3 hours before use.

To serve

Go for the best quality you can afford. Cut it paper-thin for the best appreciation of the subtle flavour. Serve simply with brown bread and butter and perhaps a little pepper. 50-75 g/2-3 oz should satisfy most palates, though I have known some who could consume 125 g/4 oz at a sitting.

What to drink is a matter of taste. Scandinavians drink chilled vodka or schnapps with Gravlax, which works well but tends to anaesthetise the palate for the more subtle flavours of smoked salmon. Champagne has its followers while others prefer a White Burgundy.

Sea Trout, Salmon Trout, Brown Trout
(*Salmo trutta*)

This is a confusing species, which embraces the brown trout of rivers: the bull or lake trout of larger inland waters: and the sea trout, which is a migratory fish with a natural range from North Africa to Norway and Iceland.

Alan Davidson, *North Atlantic Seafood*, 1979.

The sea/salmon trout has a similar life cycle to salmon; it also eats the same kind of food (among other things, pink crustaceans) and therefore has the same pink flesh. It is different in size, though, smaller than salmon and with a more delicate flavour which is preferred by many. Freshwater brown trout are smaller, and their flavour is entirely dependent on the richness of their feeding grounds, which also applies to the farmed variety.

BAKED BROWN TROUT
with herbs and lemon

4 x 225 g/½ lb trout
2 tablespoons olive oil or melted butter
Sea salt
Freshly ground black pepper
4 sprigs fresh herbs (either dill, fennel, chives or parsley)
1 lemon or lime

4 servings

This is the same method as Baked Salmon – encasing the fish in foil and allowing it to cook in its own juices without drying out.

Preheat the oven to 450F/230C/210Cfan/Gas 8.

Scale and clean the trout; cut off the fins and wipe with kitchen paper. Season the inside with salt and pepper and put in herbs. Cut 4 pieces of foil into oval shapes long enough to hold the fish plus 7 cm/3 in. Brush the foil with oil or butter and lay the trout up the centre. Brush the fish with oil or butter, season with salt and pepper and place a slice of lemon on the fish. Bring up the sides of the foil to make a boat and pleat over the foil at the top to enclose the fish, pinching together with thumb and forefinger to make a scalloped edge like a Cornish pasty.

Put on a baking sheet and bake in a hot oven for 8-10 minutes.

Cooking time will depend on the thickness of the fish, so check one by opening up. Gently and carefully ease open the flesh at the thickest part along the lateral line right down to the bone. This should all be opaque. Serve in foil, first making a small slit in the foil for easier opening.

Herring
(*Chupea harengus*)

Of all the fish that swim in the sea
The herring is the fish for me.
Scottish Folk Song

It's not just songs which have been sung about this remarkable little fish. Battles have been fought over them and towns built from their profits.

The word 'herring' comes from the Germanic word, 'heer', meaning an army, which is an apt description of the shoals of herring, numbering many thousands, which swim together for protection.

Until 1963 catches had been relatively stable, then in 1969 they reached a peak when over a million tons were caught. From then on there was a steady decline, till 1976 when only two hundred thousand tons were caught in Scotland. In 1977 the Scottish herring fishing was closed.

The introduction of the purse seine net, which could catch a whole shoal of herring, meant that they were being caught more effectively than ever before. Even if the whole shoal was not caught, small numbers of remaining fish could not survive from predators without the large shoal's protection. Serious conservation methods of protecting the species were put in operation, with scientists monitoring stocks closely, setting quotas and closing down the fishing in certain areas when the fish are under pressure.

Seasons and Buying

I agree with Meg Dods (1826) when she says that herring should be eaten 'almost alive'. They are like shellfish and deteriorate quickly when dead. For some time I lived in a cottage beside the pier in Ullapool on the West Coast and could pick up a 'fry' of herring from the fish which had spilled onto the pier as the boats unloaded.

Fresh herring, or mackerel, straight off the boats is a luxury. From the fishmonger, look for firm-looking, bright fish, as they have a flabby look when past their best. Always trust the fishmonger who sells some whole from the fish-boxes when fussy buyers can be seen picking out fish, such as whole herring and mackerel, and holding them up by their tails to see how much they bend over, thus judging their freshness.

Herring are available all year round from different sources, but the heavier, fatter, late spring and summer fish will have more flavour than leaner winter fish. The amount of fat in the flesh varies throughout the annual reproductive cycle. There is a long period of starvation after spawning followed by a time of intensive feeding while the milts and roes are developing. The fat content can vary from as little as 2% to as high as 20%, so it is important to look for the plump fish which have been feeding. They have the highest fat content and therefore best flavour. The availability from certain areas around the Scottish coasts is, and always has been, unpredictable, but each ground has its season and the fishery at any one place is rarely exploited outside these periods. The **Marine Stewardship Council** (MSC) provides up-to-date information on stocks. Visit *www.msc. org/track-a-fishery* for up to date information. Herring stocks in the southern part of the Firth of Clyde are currently depleted and fish from this stock should be avoided.

Atlantic Mackerel
(*Scomber scombrus*)

A muscular fish with a streamlined body which is similar to herring in many respects. It also swims in very large shoals which makes it more liable to overfishing. It also spoils rapidly, and like herring has a rich, oily flesh, which also fluctuates according to season. It differs in flavour and in the texture of the flesh which is firmer and freer of the fine bones found in herring.

Traditional recipes serve mackerel with acid fruit sauces, gooseberry being the most common, though it is good with other sharp fruits like rhubarb, cranberries or raspberries.

Season – Buying

They spawn throughout the spring, early and late summer and stop feeding during the winter, so are at their best from April through to November.

Currently this is Scotland's most abundant species. Much of the commercial mackerel fisheries in the Northeast Atlantic have been certified as sustainable by the Marine Stewardship Council. Look for the MSC sustainable label (blue label with a white tick). Visit *www.msc.org/track-a-fishery* for up to date information

Hot smoked mackerel

Because mackerel have a high oil content, similar to herring, this cure became popular in the 1970s when the herring fishery was closed and mackerel were more widely eaten as a result. It is made with summer and autumn fish which are particularly high in oil. The fish are filleted to remove the head and bone. Single fillets with the skin on are cured in salt brine, placed on stainless-steel trays and cold smoked for an hour then hot smoked for two hours. Flavourings of pepper, herbs and spices are sprinkled over before they are smoked.

FRESH HERRING or MACKEREL
fried in oatmeal

A classic Scottish combination of oily fish and crunchy oatmeal coating.

All fish cooked with the bone left in will have more flavour. A common breakfast dish when we visited my grandmother was a large ashet piled with whole fried herring. She lived beside an East Coast fishing village and from an early age children had to master the art of removing the bones from cooked fish – or starve. She believed, as did the fisher-wives who supplied her fish fresh from the boats, that removing bones before cooking removed half the flavour.

4 fresh herring or mackerel, whole or filleted
2 heaped tablespoons medium or coarse oatmeal, lightly
  toasted
Salt and pepper
Butter and/or a neutral oil for frying

4 servings

To prepare whole herring or mackerel

Slit up the belly and remove the gut, scraping up the backbone with your thumbnail to loosen the spinal vein starting from the tail up. Cut off the head if you wish, though this is not necessary. Cut off all fins with scissors and wash. Make sure all blood is removed from the belly cavity. Salt inside. Make a few slashes into the flesh at the thickest part near the head to let the heat penetrate faster.

To fillet herring (very easy)

Place the fish, which has been prepared as above, on a board, skin-side up with the belly flaps spread out, and press with the base of your palm gently but firmly from tail to head along the backbone. The fish will flatten out as you press, and when it is fairly flat, without being squashed, turn onto the flesh side and the bone will lift out; cut at the tail to release.

To fry herring or mackerel

Heat the fat in a large frying-pan. Mix the seasonings into the oatmeal and press the wet fish into it, coating both sides – it is not necessary to moisten the fish with anything. Shake off excess oatmeal and fry. Filleted fish should be placed flesh side down first. Whole fish will take longer to cook. Test by opening carefully with a sharp pointed knife at the thickest part right down to the bone: if the flesh is still not opaque, leave for another few minutes. They should take from 5-10 minutes each side depending on the thickness of the fish.

To bone cooked fish

Following the lateral line which runs from the middle of the gill flap to the middle of the tail, cut with a sharp knife through the skin and right down to the bone in a straight line the length of the fish. Now gently ease away the fillets on either side. If the fish is cooked through they should come away cleanly, exposing the bone. To remove the bone, lift the tail and release it from the lower fillets, taking off the head if it's still attached.

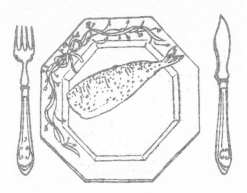

FRESH HERRINGS (or MACKEREL) AS DRESSED
AT INVERARAY
(and the Highland Sea-Lochs)

The best herrings are obtained in these localities almost alive.
Cut off the head, fins, and tails; scale, gut, and wash them.
Split and bone them or not, dust the inside with pepper and
fine salt. Place two herrings flat together, the backs outmost,
and dip in toasted oatmeal and fry them for seven minutes.
Serve hot. They are delicious; and, in the summer, add much to
the breakfasts on the steamers on the Clyde, and round all the
northeast and west coasts of Scotland.

Meg Dods, *The Cook and Housewife's Manual*, 1826.

This is a useful method for small herring: the two flesh sides
fuse together, making a moist juicy centre which contrasts with
a crisp outside.

OPEN ARMS HERRING
with Drambuie butter

4 herrings, fried in oatmeal (see p.56)
Drambuie Butter:
125 g/4 oz unsalted butter
2 teaspoons lemon juice
1 tablespoon chopped parsley
3 tablespoons Drambuie

4 servings

With fresh East Coast herring, this dish combines traditional
Herrings in Oatmeal with a Drambuie-flavoured hard butter and
lifts them out of a common, everyday dish with this simple touch.

To make the Drambuie butter

Soften the butter slightly without melting. Beat in the other ingredients. Roll into a sausage shape 2.5 cm/1 in diameter. Wrap in foil or greaseproof paper and leave to harden slightly. Cut in slices and serve two on each fish just before serving. Garnish fish with lemon wedges and watercress. To store leftover butter for future use, cut all the butter into slices. Place on tray and freeze, then put in small freezer bags and keep frozen till required. Do not keep for more than a few weeks, since the Drambuie flavour will begin to deteriorate in time.

From Chef Douglas, the Open Arms Hotel in Dirleton, East Lothian, 1984.

GRILLED HERRING or MACKEREL
with mustard

4 whole or filleted herring or mackerel
2-3 tablespoons medium oatmeal, lightly toasted
Salt and pepper
50 g/2 oz butter, melted
Mustard

4 servings

Use shallow roasting tin lined with foil.

Of the many commercial varieties of mustard the best for herring are those made with the less piquant whole mustard seeds. There is also creamy Store Mustard (p.392) which Scandinavians serve with Gravlax.

For whole herring or mackerel

Slash the skin diagonally about three times at the thickest head-end on either side: this opens up the flesh and makes it cook more evenly. Salt the inside of the fish. Mix the seasonings through the oatmeal. Now press both sides into the oatmeal and place in a roasting tin. Drizzle over melted butter and place under a hot grill. Cook on both sides for about

5-10 minutes, testing by opening up with a sharp knife when it should be opaque in the centre.

For filleted herring or mackerel

Press the wet fish into the seasoned oatmeal, shake off excess. Place skin side up in roasting tin and drizzle over butter. Grill under a hot grill, turning after about five minutes onto the other side. Test as above for doneness.

Serving

Serve with mustard and boiled, floury potatoes, skinned and sprinkled with chopped chives.

Mackerel can be served with a gooseberry or other tart fruit puree.

SOUSED OR POTTED HERRING or MACKEREL
Whole

6 fat herring or mackerel
Salt and ground black pepper
6 cloves
2 blades of mace
1 bay leaf
12 peppercorns
1 cayenne pod
300 ml/½ pt cider vinegar
150 ml/¼ pt water

6 servings

Preheat oven to 425F/220C/200Cfan/Gas 7.

If potted whole, and cooked slowly for four to five hours, the vinegar dissolves all the small bones and the cooking liquor becomes quite thick and full of flavour. A little of it should be served with the fish. Only large fatty fish should be used for this method. Poor-quality, or small, fish will not stand up to the long, slow cooking or the strong spicy flavours. Made with the season's first Loch Fyne herring, gleaming silver fish, plump and full of flavour, they are – once tasted – never forgotten.

To cook

Clean the fish and remove the heads (optional) and fins. Season the belly cavity with salt and pepper. Lay the fish, heads to tails, in a large casserole with the spices and seasonings in between. Pour over the vinegar and water. It should almost cover them. Cover very tightly and place in a hot oven for 30 minutes till the liquid begins to bubble, then reduce the heat to the lowest possible (250F/130C/110Cfan/Gas ½) and leave for 4-5 hours. Leave to cool in the liquid.

SOUSED OR POTTED HERRING or MACKEREL
Filleted

6 herring or mackerel fillets
Salt and ground black pepper
2 bay leaves
10 peppercorns
2 blades of mace
¼ teaspooon grated nutmeg
150 ml/¼ pt pickle vinegar (see p.393) or wine or cider vinegar
150 ml/¼ pt dry cider
150 ml/¼ pt water
125 g/4 oz clarified butter

6 servings

Preheat the oven to 350F/180C/160Cfan/Gas 4.

Clean and fillet the fish. Season flesh surface with salt and pepper.

For herring, roll up from head end to tail and place in shallow casserole in one layer closely packed together with the tails sticking up. Lay mackerel flat in layers. Sprinkle spices on top and cover with vinegar, cider and water. Cover and bake for 30-40 minutes or until cooked. Leave to cool in the liquor. Drain and serve.

To Pot

Drain the fish well, then pack into an earthenware pot and cover with clarified butter. They will keep in a cool place for at least four weeks.

SOUSED HERRING
Shetland-style

He had taken 13 herring, cleaned them, boned them, laid them out open and flat on their backs and applied a little salt and white pepper. He then rolled them up from head to tail and laid them in a shallow casserole large enough to take them all in one layer. He added a cup each of water and ordinary white vinegar and cooked the herrings in a moderately hot oven (400F/200C/Gas 6) for 25 minutes with the lid on and a final five minutes with the lid off "to brown the tops". The result was extremely good.'

Alan Davidson in *North Atlantic Seafood* (1979) describing Jimmy Fraser's method in his Shetland fish shop.

SWEET SPICED HERRING

250 ml/9 fl oz pickle vinegar (see p.393) or wine or cider
　　vinegar
1 medium onion, thinly sliced
175 g/6 oz granulated sugar
1 tablespoon allspice berries
1 tablespoon black peppercorns
3 small bay leaves
900 g/2 lb fresh whole herring

4 servings

Use rich fatty herring for this spicy, sweet/sour cure – lean winter herring will be overpowered by the spice.

Put all the ingredients except the herring in a pan and simmer gently for a few minutes to infuse, then leave to cool.

To prepare the fish

Clean, gut and fillet the fish. Remove skin by loosening the very thin papery skin at the tail end to get a grip of it and then pull off carefully. Cut the fillets into three or four pieces. Put into an earthenware casserole. Pour over cooled spice vinegar and leave at least overnight but preferably for 2-3 days before use. Keeps well for at least a month in a cool place.

To serve

Serve chilled, cut into small bite-sized pieces with grated beetroot in a balsamic dressing, grated raw mushrooms, chopped spring onions and sour cream (for quantities and dressing recipe see p.257).

Kipper

Some years ago, when staying at a fishing port on Lochfyneside, I used to watch the herring-boats sail in at dawn and unload their cargo, which was run straight up to the kippering sheds. Here the fish were plunged into a brine bath and thereafter hung up to smoke over smouldering oak chips, while their colour changed slowly from silver to burnished copper.

F. Marian McNeill, *The Scots Kitchen*, 1929.

Although kippers are not a Scottish invention they make up about a quarter of all the processed fish eaten in Scotland. In the 1840s, when the kipper was first developed in Newcastle, it was a saltier,

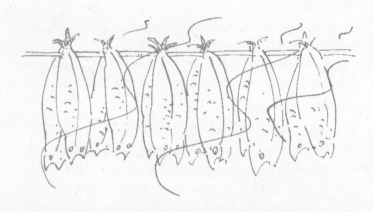

drier and darker cure. It was coloured naturally from the smoke to a dark-brown colour. During the last years of the First World War, however, a chemical dye, known as brown FK (For Kippers) was used by UK smokers, which allowed the smoking times to be reduced without loss of colour or weight. By the 1930s all the large kipper manufacturers turned to dyed kippers. Only a small number of independent smokers stuck to the traditional method. In recent years, however, the larger curers have been prompted by customer demand to make undyed kippers as concern about unnecessary additives to food has gathered momentum.

The undyed kipper, besides tasting better, can be easily distinguished from the richer brown of the dyed variety by its much paler colour. Kippers with the bone removed have a consequent loss of flavour and especially if they are frozen.

Traditional Method

They are usually brined for 30 minutes to provide a 'shine' rather than a strong, salty taste, then they are cold-smoked for between 18-24 hours over oak chips (sometimes from whisky barrels). Individual curers have their own brining recipes which give variations in flavour.

Buying

For the best flavour and keeping qualities, look for plump kippers which have a glossy shine to them, which is partly the result of the brining process but also indicates a good fat content, essential for a well-flavoured kipper.

POTTED KIPPER

2 medium to large cooked kippers, giving approximately 225 g/8 oz kipper meat
125 g/4 oz butter
1-2 anchovy fillets
2-3 teaspoons lemon juice
Cayenne pepper

4-6 servings

It is essential to use a well-flavoured, fatty kipper.

Put all the ingredients into a liquidiser or food processor and reduce to a fine paste. This will break up all the fine bones in the kipper flesh.

Adjust lemon and cayenne flavourings to taste. Serve with oatcakes which have been slightly warmed in the oven or with hot toast.

TO COOK KIPPERS

All kipper addicts have their favourite way of cooking; preferably a method which does not leave the kitchen reeking of kipper.

Grilled Kipper

This is a good method since it concentrates the flavour well, though the grill should be well lined with foil. It is not necessary to baste with butter – there should be enough natural fat in the kipper to keep it from drying out. The head, tail and fins should be cut off before grilling. Place under a medium-hot grill, flesh-side up, and cook for 5 – 10 minutes, (depending on size) on the flesh side only. Test by opening up with a sharp knife when it should be opaque in the centre.

Frying

Not a popular method with cooks, since they can't protect the frying pan with foil. It also coats an already fatty fish with another layer of fat. If frying, use a non-stick pan and place the kipper in flesh-side down. Cook for four or five minutes on either side and serve.

Jugging

This is a popular method since it doesn't involve any cooking as such, and the utensil used is easily cleaned. Place the kipper in a heated jug which is deep enough to hold it, and fill the jug with boiling water. Alternatively use a large pot, but make sure it is well heated. Cover well, and leave for at least 10 minutes. Remove the kipper and serve immediately. Some of the flavour and fat is obviously lost in the liquid, but the fish retains its plumpness and the texture of the flesh is soft and juicy.

Baking

Another method favoured by both cooks and eaters. The whole fish is wrapped in a foil parcel and placed in a moderate oven (350F/180C/160C fan/Gas 4) for 15-20 minutes. Wrap the fish individually and serve in the parcel to preserve the full aroma till it is opened.

Uncooked

In the early 1960s, TV chef Philip Harben was an early advocate of this method. He suggested the fish should be boned, sliced thinly and covered in a marinade of oil and lemon juice for several hours before eating. Later Jane Grigson suggested that the thinly sliced, raw fillets should be 'arranged in strips round the edge of some well-buttered rye bread, with an egg yolk in the middle as sauce' (*Good Things*, 1971). A deeply chilled glass of vodka or schnapps goes well with this.

Salt-Pickled Herring

This is the cure that made Scotland famous in the late 1800s as the world's largest producer of the best quality salt-pickled herring. Much of the Scottish export was to Eastern Europe, Russia, Scandinavia and Germany, where eating traditions were many and varied.

About ninety per cent of the cured fish was exported, so it's not surprising that the tradition of eating this cure only remains strong in areas where it was produced. In Scotland the most popular dish is Tatties and Herring.

TO SALT HERRING

Coarse salt
Fat, fresh herring

Use a small wooden barrel or large plastic bucket.

Begin by removing the gills and long gut from the fish, leaving on the heads. Sprinkle a thick layer of salt in the base, then set the fish in the layer with their backs uppermost, but slightly on their sides. Put in the next layer of salt, then the fish lying in the opposite direction. Continue in layers till the barrel is full. Put a plate on top to keep weighted down while the brine forms. Cover well and store in a cool place. May be used after 1-2 months. Will keep for about a year.

TATTIES 'N' HERRIN

A popular dish in the Highlands and Islands, where fishmongers will often make their own supply of salt herring to satisfy demand. The skill in eating is to add just enough piquant salt herring to every mouthful of bland, floury potato, making the perfect contrast of flavours and textures. Cold milk was the traditional drink taken with all salt fish or meat. A little butter, melting into the potato, is not traditional but worth including in this unique taste of the past.

The fish and potatoes were traditionally dished up into a 46 cm/18 in, shallow, square dish, used specially for the purpose, called a *clar* in Gaelic. Without plates or knives and forks, the potato was held in one hand and a pinch of herring was taken with the other – the herring pressed into the floury potato for a mouthful of tattie 'n' herring.

Quantities per person:
1 salt herring depending on size
250 g/9 oz floury potato (see p.248)
Butter for the potato
1 glass cold milk

To cook

Wash fish and soak overnight in cold water. Change the water twice. Wash potatoes and leave unpeeled. Put potatoes and fish into a large pot and cover with water. Bring to the boil and lower heat to a gentle simmer. Check regularly after 15 minutes and remove from the heat immediately the potatoes are cooked through. Floury potatoes can burst and break up very quickly if they are overcooked. Remove small ones when they are cooked. Drain into a colander. Cover with a teatowel to keep warm. Serve with butter and a glass of cold milk.

MARINATED SALT HERRING

Eastern European and Scandinavian countries have the richest tradition of salt herring recipes. Because the fish deteriorates so quickly they prefer to eat it preserved by a method, such as salting, which intensifies its character.

Finns, as well as other Scandinavians, have a highly developed tradition of salt herring dishes. This is one which they describe as Everyday Herring. According to F. Marian McNeill, *The Scots Kitchen* (1929), this was called a 'Pickled Herring' when the salted herring were simply marinated in vinegar, brown sugar and onions.

Pickle:
3 tablespoons sugar
1 teaspoon mustard seed
1 tablespoon whole allspice
1 tablespoon black peppercorns
3 bay leaves
3 cloves
1 lemon, thinly sliced
1 red onion, sliced
1 cup white wine vinegar

8 salt herring

4-6 servings

To make

Put all the ingredients for the pickle into a pot and bring to the boil. Simmer for 5 minutes and leave to cool.

Bone and skin the herring (see p.57). Slice into bite-sized pieces. Put into a glass jar in layers with the onions and lemon, pouring over some of the pickling liquid between each layer. Leave for a day in a cool place before using. Will keep for several weeks.

To serve

Serve chilled, garnished with chopped fresh dill. Eat with thickly buttered rye bread and ice-cold schnapps or chilled lager.

SALT HERRING SALAD
with Beetroot and Mushrooms

Balsamic and Mustard Dressing (see p.257)
4 salt herring
250 g/9 oz cooked beetroot, grated
100 g/4 oz mushrooms, grated
4 spring onions, chopped
4 tablespoons soured cream

4 servings

Dark red beetroot, shining strips of silvery, piquant herring, creamy white mushrooms and green spring onions make a stunning visual impact on the plate while the taste and texture contrasts are equally impressive.

To make

Bone and skin the herring (see p.57) and slice into small pieces. Put into a small bowl, cover and chill. Make balsamic and mustard dressing.

To assemble

Arrange a spoonful of beetroot, soured cream and mushrooms on each plate. Sprinkle over spring onions. The dressing can be mixed through the beetroot or served separately. Serve with the bowl of chilled herring, thickly buttered Oatmeal Bread (see p.24) or Barley Bannocks (see p.19) and chilled lager or vodka or schnapps.

Haddock (*Melanogrammus aeglefinus*), Cod (*Gadus morhua*) and Whiting (*Merlangius merlangus*)

More haddock is caught and eaten than any other white fish in Scotland. Cod comes next, and then whiting. These, and other demersel fish, have different habits from the herring – swimming around in much smaller shoals at the bottom of the sea, and therefore in less danger of being wiped out with one net. Even so, overfishing has caused quotas to be put on the landings of these fish too. The chemical composition of the haddock flesh is similar to that of cod and other members of the cod family, and therefore it is quite practical in recipes to interchange fish of this type.

Seasons and Buying

The prime season is from September through to February. After February they spawn, and from April to June the fish are soft and poor quality, but from about July onwards they begin to recover, and after September the flesh firms up rapidly. To help reduce the impact of fishing on fish stocks which are depleted, or being heavily fished, choose line-caught fish when available. Avoid buying haddock from West of Scotland stocks which are overfished. Marine scientists recommend a closure of this fishery.

Marine Stewardship Council Certified Sustainable Fishery

The Scottish component of the North Sea fishery, and part of the Norwegian fishery for haddock in the Northeast Arctic, are certified as sustainable by the MSC and offer the best option for haddock.

Stocks in North East Arctic (Barents and Norwegian Sea) and in the combined areas of North Sea, Kattegat and Skagerrak are at healthy, or at sustainable levels, and being fished sustainably. Haddock, however, occur in mixed fisheries with other fish such as cod, which are depleted in some areas such as the North and Irish Sea and waters west of Scotland.

Look for the MSC sustainable label (blue with a white tick). Visit *www.msc.org/track-a-fishery* for up to date information on haddock and other fish.

Other White Fish

BRILL – Spawning Habits: May to August

Buying Advice: Brill is mainly taken as by-catch in beam trawl fisheries in the North Sea. A considerable proportion of the catch is immature and the stock is over-exploited. The state of the stock in the Baltic Sea is unknown. Avoid eating immature fish (less than 40 cm) as these will not have had chance to spawn.

COD – Spawning Habits: They spawn in winter and spring from February to April.

Buying Advice: Prime season August to November. Avoid during spawning, February to April. Available all year. Cod stocks have increased in recent years. MCS advice is that stocks in the Northeast Atlantic are either overfished, or at an unknown level, except for stocks in the Northeast Arctic, Baltic, Iceland and the Faroes Plateau, and the most depleted stocks are in the Irish Sea, North Sea, and West of Scotland.

Icelandic fisheries are being overfished as quotas are being set above scientific recommendations, but the Northeast Arctic stock is healthy and is fished at a sustainable level.

Choose line-caught cod, where available, to help reduce the impact of trawler fishing on fish stocks. Longlines, however, can result in seabird by-catch. Buy fish caught using seabird-friendly methods.

Marine Stewardship Council Certified Sustainable Fishery: Part of the Norwegian long line fishery for cod, in the Northeast

Arctic, has been certified as sustainable by the MSC and is available in the UK.

FLOUNDER – (also known as Flukie) **Spawning Habits:** In the southern North Sea from February to May

Buying Advice: There are no targeted fisheries for flounder; they are taken as by-catch in trawl nets. Avoid immature fish (less than 25 cm) and fresh fish caught during the spawning season in the North Sea.

HALIBUT – **Spawning Habits:** During winter and early spring.

Buying Advice: Atlantic halibut is heavily overfished, which means it is caught in such high numbers that a sustainable fishery cannot be maintained by the current population size. Assessed as 'Endangered'. Avoid unless from a known sustainable source.

Marine Stewardship Council Certified Sustainable Fishery: Pacific halibut is less vulnerable to overfishing and fisheries are generally much better managed. Longline fisheries for Pacific halibut in US waters off Alaska, Washington and Oregon are certified as environmentally responsible fisheries by the Marine Stewardship Council (MSC). The longline fisheries for Pacific halibut in Pacific waters of British Columbia, Canada are currently undergoing assessment by the MSC.

HAKE – **Spawning Habits:** A late maturing fish, spawning from February to July in northern waters.

Buying Advice: The northern stock is classified as healthy and harvested sustainably, having recovered from unsustainable levels. The southern stock is depleted, however, and should be avoided. Avoid immature fish below about 50 cm and during their breeding season, February to July.

Marine Stewardship Council Certified Sustainable Fishery: The only hake fishery with an MSC certification is **South African, Cape hake** *Merluccius capensis*, and the deep water Cape hake (*Merluccius*

paradoxus) which is similar but slightly smaller. They breed throughout the year with peaks of reproductive activity in August and September, and can reach a size of 140 cm.

LEMON SOLE – **Spawning Habits:** Spring and summer with a peak in March-May.

Buying Advice: Prime season July-August. Not at their best from March to May during peak spawning. Does not have a designated fishery but is a trawl by-catch. Avoid immature fish under 25 cm.

LING – **Spawning Habits:** Between March and August.

Buying Advice: Deepwater stocks appear to be overfished and current management measures are not deemed sufficient to restore abundance. Scientific advice recommends that catches be limited or reduced in all commercial fisheries to allow stocks to recover. Avoid eating fish from deepwater stocks. Line caught from inshore fisheries is a more sustainable option.

MEGRIM, ABERDEEN SOLE – **Spawning Habits:** Between January and April along the edge of the continental shelf to the southwest and west of the British Isles. Also spring spawning in Iceland waters.

Buying Advice: Prime season May-June. Not at its best during peak spawning Feb-March. The state of stocks is generally unknown, but indications are that they are stable. It is a more sustainable option to plaice and sole which are overfished. Avoid eating immature fish less than 20-25 cm.

PLAICE – **Spawning Habits:** January to March.

Buying Advice: Prime season June-July. Not at their best when spawning February to March. Variable availability from January to April. Stocks have been subject to intense fishing pressure in many areas where they are now scarce. Avoid sizes below 30 cm.

POLLACK – **Spawning Habits:** Between January and April.

Buying Advice: It is taken as by-catch in trawl fisheries for cod and saithe, and it is also line-caught. The best choice to make, in terms of selectivity and sustainability, is line-caught pollack. Avoid eating immature fish (below 50 cm) and during its breeding season (January to April).

SAITHE, also known as Coalfish, Sillock, Coley and Green Cod – **Spawning Habits:** Spawns from January to March at about 200 m depth along the Northern Shelf edge and the western edge of the Norwegian deeps. Usually enters coastal waters in spring and returns to deeper water in winter.

Buying Advice: Available all year but avoid during its spawning period from January to March, and especially immature saithe below about 50-60 cm. The Northeast Arctic (Barents and Norwegian Sea) saithe stock and the combined saithe stock in the North Sea, Skagerrak, West of Scotland and Rockall, is currently healthy and above the minimum level scientifically recommended and is harvested sustainably.

To help reduce the impact of trawler fishing where fishing effort is too high (Iceland and Faroes) on fish stocks and the marine environment, choose line-caught fish where available. When buying longline-caught saithe look for fish caught using 'seabird-friendly' methods.

Marine Stewardship Council Certified Sustainable Fishery: Two Norwegian fisheries for saithe, and the German North Sea fishery, are assessed as environmentally sustainable fisheries by the MSC.

TURBOT – **Spawning Habits:** In most parts of its range, spawns in April to August.

Buying Advice: Not at their best June-August. There is no specific management of the turbot fishery except for a minimum landing size of 30 cm in Cornwall. Stock levels are unknown and the limited information available suggests that they are overfished. Avoid unless from a known sustainable source.

WITCH, also known as Witch Sole or Long Flounder – **Spawning Habits:** From March to September.

Buying Advice: Avoid eating immature fish (less than 28 cm) and fresh fish caught during the breeding season (March-September). Witch sole fisheries in EU waters outside the 6-mile limit are unregulated, i.e. there is no Minimum Landing Size (MLS) or other measures specified and so they are generally taken as by-catch in trawls targeting whitefish. In some coastal areas of England and Wales MLSs are enforced, e.g. Cornwall Sea Fisheries District & North Western and North Wales SFC prohibits the landing of witch below 28 cm.

WHITING – **Spawning Habits:** Between January and July, but mostly in spring between April and June in northern waters.

Buying Advice: Prime season August to January. Avoid fresh fish during peak spawning April-June. North East Atlantic whiting stocks are overfished and scientific advice is to reduce catches to lowest possible level. Avoid eating immature fish less than 30 cm.

Treatment and recipes for haddock may be applied to other White Fish, and even small cuts of larger fish such as brill or turbot.

WHOLE FISH – BAKED

8 sheets greaseproof paper
4 x 325 g/11 oz whole or cuts of large fish on the bone
Fresh herbs to taste (tarragon, lemon balm and dill are some
   options)
50 g/2 oz butter
1 lemon, juice of
Salt and pepper

4 servings

This is most suitable for sole, plaice, trout, sea bass, salmon, mackerel, John Dory and brill. It is a conservation method which keeps all the flavour of the fish intact in a parcel.

To cook

Preheat the oven to 450F/230C/210Cfan/Gas 8.

Wet the paper thoroughly, spread out two thicknesses. Gut the fish and lay on top. Put herbs around the fish and inside its belly cavity. Dot butter on top. Fold and wrap up as a parcel. Put on a baking tray and bake for 10-15 minutes for thin flat fish and 15-20 for thicker, round fish. Check if fish is cooked by opening up gently at the thickest part with a sharp pointed knife, when the translucent flesh should have changed to milky-opaque all the way through. Serve the parcels. The skin usually comes off with the paper.

FISH AND CHIPS

4-6 servings

'Chippies' (Fish and Chip shops) have a mystique of their own – the frying aromas and vinegar mingling in the warm shop while customers are standing in a queue waiting. It's comforting and sustaining takeaway food for cold Scottish winters, and despite competition from other fast-food outlets on the high street, the chippie shows no signs of a decline.

CHIPS to serve 2

A floury potato will make a dry chip, waxy varieties a soggy chip.

600 g/1lb 5 oz floury or medium floury potatoes (see p.248)
2 L/3½ pt groundnut or sunflower oil
Salt

FISH to serve 2

300-350 g/10-12 oz fish fillets, skinned (squid or cuttlefish cut in rings)

Salt

Egg white batter

100 g/3½ oz fine plain flour (with very low gluten content
such as Italian '00')

Pinch of salt

2 tablespoons groundnut or olive oil

100-125 ml/3-4 fl oz water

2 egg whites

To prepare potatoes

Wash and peel potatoes. Cut into chips, thin or thick. Dry thoroughly in a tea towel.

To prepare deep-fat fryer

Either use a large pan with a chip-basket or a free-standing deep-fat fryer. If using a pan with a chip basket, have the oil only a third of the way up the pan, since it rises as it cooks. Also have a fire-blanket or fire-extinguisher in the kitchen. Put oil into pan or fryer and heat to 130C/250F.

Potatoes: first slow frying to just cook through

Fill the chip-basket half-full and lower into the fat. Fry slowly till the chips are just cooked through but not browned. Time will depend on size of chips. Remove and drain on kitchen paper. They can be stored in the fridge uncovered for a day like this or they can be finished as soon as the fryer heats up again.

To fry fish: make egg white batter

Sift the flour and salt into a bowl. Make a well in the centre and add the oil and half the water. Beat together with a wooden spoon, or whisk, till smooth. Thin out with the rest of the water. It should coat the back of a wooden spoon, but not too thickly. Add more water if necessary. Leave to rest for at least half an hour or longer. When ready to use, beat the egg whites until they just hold their shape. Fold in carefully, aiming to retain as much of the air as possible.

To prepare deep-fat fryer

Either use a large pan with a fish-basket or a free-standing deep-fat fryer. If using a pan with a fish-basket, have the oil only a third of the way up the pan, since it rises as it cooks. Also have a fire-blanket or fire-extinguisher in the kitchen. Put oils into pan or fryer and heat to 190C/375F. This is usually the top heat in a fish-fryer.

To fry fish

Put onto a fork or skewer and dip into the batter, coating all sides. Lift out and hold it over the batter to let the excess batter drip off. Lower into the deep-fat fryer. At 190C, thin fillets of sole will cook in about 2 minutes. If too many pieces of food are added at once the temperature will be reduced and the crust will become soggy and the fish will take longer to cook. When cooked, remove from the fryer. Shake basket over oil to drain. Turn onto kitchen paper to drain thoroughly. Reheat oil and fry remainder of fish in the same way. Season with salt and keep warm while finishing chips.

Chips: second fast frying

Heat up oil to 190C. Lower in the chips and fry till a light golden brown. This should only take a few minutes. Drain again on kitchen paper. Serve immediately with the fish, salt and vinegar.

FRESH HADDOCK
in a light, creamy mustard sauce

This was a popular Victorian breakfast dish. Mustard with fish is an old combination.

700 g/1½ lb fresh haddock or other similar white fish fillets

2 tablespoons seasoned flour
85 g/3 oz butter and/or oil
1 teaspoon Mustard Store Sauce (p.392) or other made mustard
250 ml/8 fl oz single or double cream

4 servings

To cook

Heat about half of the butter in a frying pan. Coat the haddock in butter/oil and then in flour. Put into the pan and seal quickly on both sides without browning. Add cream and simmer gently till the fish is cooked. Remove some of the cooking liquor and mix with the mustard. Return to the pan and mix through, but do not cook any longer since mustard loses its flavour very quickly when cooked. Serve the fish and pour over sauce. Serve with stir-fried kale.

GRILLED FRESH HADDOCK
with Lemon and Parsley Butter

700 g/1½ lb fresh haddock or other similar white fish fillets
125 g/4 oz butter
125 g/4 oz breadcrumbs
Salt and pepper
Lemon and Parsley Butter:
125 g/4 oz butter
2-3 teaspoons lemon juice
Pinch of cayenne pepper
Salt
2 tablespoons finely chopped parsley

4 servings

To grill fish

Mix the seasoning through the breadcrumbs. Melt the butter. Pass the haddock through the butter, drain off any excess and then press into the breadcrumbs. Place on a buttered tray which will fit under the grill and sprinkle the fish with remaining butter. Grill gently till golden brown. Test by opening up with a sharp knife when it should be opaque in the centre

Serve with Lemon and Parsley Butter

Soften the butter slightly without melting and beat in the other ingredients. Roll into a sausage-shape and slice ¼ in thick. These can be deep frozen on a small tray and then stored in small freezer bags.

Air-dried Salted Fish: Sillocks, Cuiths, Ling, Cod and Saithe

These were an important part of the fish preservation process for excess catches before rail transport and refrigeration. Aberdeen now has the largest commercial production, and supplies areas where the cure is still popular. They also continue to be produced in some remote areas in the Highlands and Islands, and on Orkney and Shetland, by domestic curers.

Though boiling with potatoes, using the highly flavoured fish as a seasoning, is the most popular dish, the salty, flaked fish can also be mixed with mashed potatoes to make 'hairy' tatties.

Traditional method

The fish are gutted and headed, usually split if large and left whole if small. If large, the top part of the backbone is removed, then they are layered in coarse salt and completely covered. They may be left for a few days or up to a fortnight, when they are removed from the salt. They may then be washed and pressed, usually between stones, to remove as much moisture as possible, or they may simply be hung up by the tails in pairs in a cool place with a good draught until they are very hard.

RIZZARED HADDOCK
or Blawn Whiting

The small whiting, hung up with its skin on, and broiled without being rubbed in flour, is excellent. A wooden frame, called a 'hake', is used for drying fish. In Orkney, cuiths (which in Shetland they call piltocks and in the Hebrides cuddies) are prepared in this way, care being taken that the fish are perfectly fresh, newly gutted, and thoroughly cleaned, and that the salt is rubbed well in along the bones from which the guts have been removed. They may be either boiled or brandered – if boiled, they are eaten with butter, melted. They are particularly good with buttered bere bannocks or wheaten-meal scones and tea.

F. Marian McNeill, *The Scots Kitchen*, 1929.

4 whole fresh haddock or whiting (medium size, about 225 g/½ lb each)
225 g/8 oz sea salt
2 tablespoons seasoned flour
50 g/2 oz melted butter/oil

To prepare

Gut and clean the fish, remove eyes. Place fish in an ashet and sprinkle over salt. Put plenty in the body cavity and rub well into the skin all over. Leave in a cool place. The fish will absorb the salt quickly and it will be quite salty in 30 minutes. The shorter the time the less salty the fish. Remove and wipe dry. Hang up in a cool place where there is a good draught, threading a wire through the eyes or tie in pairs tied by the tail for at least 12 hours.

To cook

Make about three slashes into the skin across the thickest part of the flesh about an inch apart. Brush with butter and roll in seasoned flour. Grill till lightly browned on both sides. Serve with boiled potatoes.

Finnan Haddock – cold smoked

A good breakfast as usual in Scotland, with Findon Had-docks, eggs, sweetmeats (preserved black-currants formed one) and honey.

Robert Southey, *Journal of a Tour in Scotland in 1819.*

This notable Scottish cure is a descendant of 'speldings' which Robert Fergusson refers to in his poem, *The Leith Races*, 1773 – 'Guid speldins, fa will buy?' – and in the same year James Boswell in his diaries describes them as: 'salted and dried in a particular manner, being dipped in the sea and dried in the sun, and eaten by the Scots by way of a relish.' He also says that you could buy them in London.

Speldings were a hard, salted, unsmoked haddock, distinguished from the modern Finnans which are only lightly salted and smoked. The name 'Finnan' comes from the Aberdeenshire village of Findon where local fishwives were famed for the high quality of their cure. The advent of the railways in the late nineteenth century was responsible for changing a hard, heavily smoked fish into a much more perishable product with obvious improvements to the eating quality. A fish curer in 1882 complained that the old cures 'fell into disuse as transit improved'.

Alternative modern cures which have developed using artificial dyes are known variously as 'golden fillet' or 'yellow fillet'. They should not be confused with the traditional Finnan and should not be used as a substitute. A more genuine substitute is the Aberdeen fillet, or Smoked fillet. This is a single fillet which has been traditionally cured with no dyes, but with the bone removed before smoking and the skin left on. There are also some local variations of the basic cure such as the Pales, whose brining and smoking times are shorter than for the Finnan. They are made mainly from smaller haddock and include the Eyemouth cure and the Glasgow Pale. Some Pales are so lightly smoked that they have only the slightest smoky flavour and almost no yellow colour.

Traditional method

Gutted, headed, split fish, with the bone left in, were dry salted overnight, then smoked over soft 'grey' peat for 8-9 hours, then cooled and washed in warm, salted water.

EAST COAST FISHWIFE'S BROTH
(Cullen Skink)

This was referred to in F. Marian McNeill's *The Scots Kitchen* (1929) as Cullen Skink, though it was a common dish throughout the area. 'Skink' is an old Scots word for 'soupstew'. This recipe was given to my mother from the fishwife we were staying with while on holiday in Cullen's seatown. She made it for our 'high tea' at night and we ate it with bread and butter.

650 g/1 lb 7 oz floury potatoes
1 onion finely chopped
1 L/1¾ pts water
1 large Finnan or 250 g/9 oz Aberdeen smoked fillet
25 g/1 oz butter
100 ml/3½ fl oz milk
salt and pepper

4-6 servings

To cook

Wash the potatoes and put into a pot with the onion and water. Bring to a simmer and cook until the potatoes are almost ready. Place the Finnan on top and cook for about 5 minutes until it is cooked through. Remove from the heat and leave to cool.

To finish the broth, remove the fish. Take off the skin and remove the bones. Reserve the flakes of cooked fish. Remove the potatoes. Skin and cut roughly into bite-sized chunks. Return to the broth with the flaked fish. Reheat and add butter. Adjust the consistency with milk. Season and serve with bread and butter.

FINNAN HADDOCK
with Cheese Sauce

225 g/8 oz cooked finnan (smoked) haddock
1 teaspoonful of cornflour
6 tablespoons milk
225 g/8 oz grated extra-mature Scottish Cheddar
2 large eggs
salt, pepper and/or cayenne
4 slices of hot buttered toast

4-6 servings

The cheese and eggs combine to make a richly flavoured fondu-type sauce which is very quick and easy to make.

To make

Remove bones and skin from cooked finnan. Add a little milk to the cornflour and blend till smooth. Add remaining milk and put into a pan with the cheese. Melt the cheese over a low heat, stirring constantly. Beat the eggs together in a bowl and add a few spoonfuls of the hot cheese. Beat into the eggs with a whisk. Pour back into the pan and continue cooking over a low heat till the mixture begins to thicken. Remove from the heat. Taste and season. Add the cooked haddock and mix through. Season with salt, pepper and/or cayenne. Serve on hot toast, Welsh Rarebit-style.

BAKED SMOKED HADDOCK
and Poached Egg

Classic comfort food which can be served at any meal with oat-cakes, bread and butter or boiled floury potatoes.

750 g/1lb 10 oz smoked haddock*
250 ml/8 fl oz double cream/single cream or milk
Freshly ground pepper
Small piece of butter for greasing
4 poached eggs

*Either smoked fillets, Aberdeen fillet with the skin still on or Finnan haddock on the bone may be used – allow an extra few ounces/grams if the bone is still in.

4 servings

Preheat oven to 350F/180C/160Cfan/Gas 4.

To cook

Grease a shallow gratin dish with butter and place the fish skin-side down. Pour over cream/milk and grind some pepper on top (salt should not be necessary). Bake for 20-30 minutes giving it a shake in the middle of the cooking to re-coat the fish. Serve with the cream/milk, which will have reduced slightly and thickened, and a poached egg on top.

SMOKED HADDOCK WITH BACON
(Ham and Haddie)

750 g/1lb 10 oz Aberdeen fillet of smoked haddock
4-8 rashers of Ayrshire bacon

4 servings

Preheat the oven to 300F/150C/130Cfan/Gas 2.

Rub an earthenware dish which will hold the fillets with butter. Place fillets in a single layer and place bacon on top. Cover with foil and bake for 30 minutes. Remove the foil for the last 10 minutes to crisp the bacon. Serve with mashed potatoes.

Hot-Smoked Arbroath Smokie

Before the smoking process moved to Arbroath, to be nearer fish supplies, this cure originated at the cliff-top village of Auchmithie. Smoking barrels were dotted along the cliff and woodsmoke and cooking haddock aromas wafted upwards into the tiny village street. This early cure was longer-keeping with a darker colour and stronger flavour. The smokies were eaten heated through (often hot from the barrel) with butter and boiled potatoes.

Traditional method

The fish are gutted, headed and dry-salted for about 2 hours, depending on the size of the fish. This is to draw moisture from the fish and impart a slight saltiness. They are then tied in pairs and hung over wooden rods and left to dry for about 5 hours to harden the skin. Then the fish are placed in the smoke-pit and hot-smoked over a hardwood fire of oak or beech, covered with layers of hessian (the number of layers depends on the weather outside and may be adjusted throughout the smoking to prevent the fish smoking too quickly or too slowly). Smoking time is approximately 45 minutes.

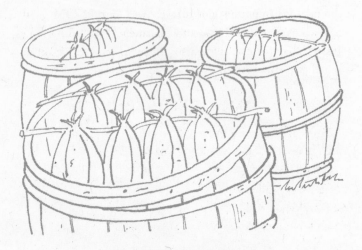

BUTTERED SMOKIE
with hot toast

4 servings

At the But 'n' Ben restaurant in Auchmithie (original home of the smokie) the chef/owner, Margaret Horn, has pioneered classic Scottish dishes such as this simple presentation of a smokie – allowing it to speak for itself without complications. For high tea, it is de-boned and opened up, spread with butter, then heated through. This 'special' on her menu comes with a pot of tea, bread and butter and traditional home baking.

4 smokies
75 g/3 oz unsalted butter, softened

To cook

Preheat the oven to 325F/160C/140Cfan/Gas 3.

Split the smokies open and remove the bone. Trim the sides of other bones and fins and place on serving plate. Spread the flesh with butter. Cover with foil and heat through in the oven for 10-15 minutes until the butter melts and they are heated through. It's important not to over-cook since the fish is already cooked and will dry out and harden if heated too long. It's essential to use unsalted butter since the smokies are already salted. Serve with bread and butter for high tea.

SMOKIE KEDGEREE

175 g/6 oz long grain rice
2 large smokies (approx 300 g/11 oz flaked fish)
2-3 hard boiled eggs
50 g/2 oz unsalted butter
2-3 tablespoons chopped parsley
Salt, ground black pepper or cayenne

4 servings

Put rice in a bowl and cover with water to about 2.5 cm/1 in above the rice. Cover with clingfilm, puncture in a few places to let out the steam and microwave (900W) for 15-20 minutes on high till soft. Or simmer in a pan till soft. Keep hot. Split the smokies open and remove the bone. Remove the cooked flesh. Peel eggs and chop whites. Melt the butter in a large pan and add the smokie flesh. Add whites and parsley. Mix together. Stir in rice. Heat through. Taste and season. Serve with yolk of egg sieved on top.

3: Shellfish & Seaweed

Very early in the spring, long before the cold east winds of March have gone, the women take up their positions. Each one has an improvised table, consisting frequently of an orange box, on which are placed saucers containing shellfish, together with the necessary condiments.

J. H. Jamieson, 'The Edinburgh Street Traders and Their Cries' in the *Book of the Old Edinburgh Club*, 1909.

Huge shellfish beds in Lowland waters provided these Edinburgh fishwives with their supplies of shellfish to sell in the streets. Taverns were also supplied with vast amounts of shellfish. A single Edinburgh tavern in the 1800s could serve ten thousand oysters a week. Though the oyster beds in the Forth became depleted through overfishing, in other parts of the country the shellfish trade survived, such as the mussels, whelks and clabbies (horse mussels), which became a street-food feature at the weekend Glasgow 'Barras'. While street-eating shellfish in towns was popular, in some parts of the Highlands and Islands shellfish had a different purpose. Used for baiting lines, it was seldom eaten. So long as there were plentiful supplies of herring and white fish, shellfish was thought of as 'last resort' food and a sign of poverty.

Enthusiasm in more recent times for shellfish eating has been encouraged by enlightened fish traders who have recognised the potential of selling seafood at its point of landing. Pioneers, such as Loch Fyne Oysters and the Macallum brothers of Troon, both began with the concept of fish shops and restaurants at the coast selling fish and shellfish straight from the boats, or from the seabed at the head of Loch Fyne.

Many restaurants are now making shellfish a feature on the menu. Some, at the coast where there are good supplies of shellfish, have set up as dedicated seafood bars. There are also thriving shell-fish bars on piers, such as the one at Oban. And as Scots rediscover the 'buried treasure' which lies beneath the unpolluted waters around their very large coastline, shellfish are out in front as top earners for Scottish fishermen. The world wants Scottish shellfish in unlimited quantities, and is willing to pay a premium price for it. This valuable Scottish asset has had a distinguished past in its native land and it deserves a future here too.

Molluscs
Scallop, King or Great
(*Pecten maximus*)

Their beautifully decorative shell gives them a charm which is only matched by the subtle and delicate flavour of the contrasting creamy muscle and orange coral inside. They call for simple recipes which preserve their unique character and flavour.

Their importance has increased steadily since the 1960s when they were first harvested from natural scallop beds by divers. In the wild they spend most of their life on the sea bed.

Scallop farming

This began in the 1970s and is still developing. It produces a more uniform supply than wild scallops. The young 'spat' are put into 'spat collectors' where they attach themselves to the sides of nets. As their shells begin to grow, they fall off the nets and are gathered into free-floating 'lantern' nets suspended in the sea water where they feed and grow. Queen scallops are left for about one to one and a half years, King scallops for about four to five. Princess scallops are gathered after about a year. Ranching or bottom culture, where the scallops are grown naturally on the sea-bed, is a method favoured by some scallop farmers. Where this takes place, Several and Regulating Orders have been granted to scallop farmers giving their stocks legal protection. The area of production is on the West Coast from Dumfries and Galloway to the Shetlands.

Identification – King, Queen and Princess

The Great or King scallop (*Pecten Maximus*) has a flat-bottomed shell and a concave upper shell with a muscle diameter of approx 5 cm. Minimum legal carapace size is 10 cm. The Queen scallop (*Chlamys opercularia*), caught in deeper waters, is smaller and the top and bottom shells are both concave. Muscle diameter is approximately 3 cm. Both the Great and the Queen scallop have creamy shells, and a creamy muscle surrounded by an orange roe, both of which are edible, but the 'frill' round the edge of the shell, which is the eyes, should be removed. The Princess scallop is the immature Queen scallop and has a reddish-pink shell with a creamy-white muscle, but the roe has not usually developed fully because of its age.

Buying

Its meat is highly esteemed and commands high prices.

Spawning Habits: Spawns during the warmer months, from March to August. It is both male and female (a hermaphrodite) having a male reproductive gland which is cream and a female gland which is orange-red: the roe or coral.

Prime season is from September to February. Minimum recommended size is 10 cm length. Those hand-selected by divers will be larger and of higher quality than those dredged from the seabed, which causes more damage to the seabed. Diving is restricted to a depth of 30 m, which gives wild populations a 'refuge' to regenerate. Dive-selected scallops are becoming more available in the marketplace and in restaurants. Check with the supplier and expect restaurants to indicate method of catching on the menu. Buying in the shell will ensure the best flavour and quality. Shucked scallops will lose flavour and quality quickly. They may also be soaked in a solution which allows them to retain moisture, rather than lose it, with a resulting loss of natural flavour as well as a reduction in size when absorbed water is expelled during cooking.

SCALLOPS IN BUTTER
with shallots and garlic

Cooking quickly and lightly preserves their full flavour. Served in their shell with aromatic butter sauce, their natural good looks speak for themselves.

8 scallops, preferably live in their shells (16 Queens)
2 tablespoons oil
50 g/2 oz unsalted butter
Sea salt
2 large cloves of garlic, crushed
2 shallots, finely chopped
2-3 tablespoons lemon juice
1 tablespoon parsley, finely chopped

4 servings

To open scallops

Slide the blade of a knife under the flat lid of the shell and cut through the muscle, keeping the blade hard against the shell so that the muscle is removed in one piece. The shell will then open. Scoop out the scallop attached to the hollow shell. Discard the frilly membrane and any brown parts. Reserve 4 good shells, clean well and put to heat through in the oven with a small nut of butter. For shucked scallops, dry well before frying.

To cook

Heat the oil in a frying pan. Season the scallops with salt and score one surface to about 5 mm/¼ in deep in a criss-cross design to allow the heat to penetrate and the flesh to cook faster. Place scored surface in the pan first and fry for 30-60 seconds, depending on thickness. They will cook very quickly. The pan should be hot enough to brown them lightly. Turn and cook 30-60 seconds on other side. Put into heated shells. Finish by adding the butter to the pan. Once it is melted and hot, add the garlic and shallots and swirl around for a minute until they begin to brown. Just before pouring over the scallops, squeeze lemon juice into the pan and finally the chopped parsley. Serve with crusty bread or hot toast.

STEAMED SCALLOPS
in a cream sauce

With no competing flavours, and against the neutral background of milk and cream, the natural flavour of the scallop flourishes. A crunchy breadcrumb topping adds texture contrast to soft scallop and creamy sauce.

8 scallops, preferably live in their shells (16 Queens)
50 g/2 oz butter
300 ml/½ pt milk
2 tablespoons cream
1 tablespoon butter and 1 tablespoon flour, i.e. kneaded butter
Salt and pepper
50 g/2 oz lightly browned white breadcrumbs

4 servings

Preparing and cooking scallops

Prepare the scallops as in the previous recipe or use shucked scallops. Put scallops in a double boiler or steamer or in a plate on top of a pan of hot water. Dot with small pieces of butter. Pour over milk and cream. Cover the pan, place it on the heat and bring the water to the boil. Remove and leave for five minutes with the lid on. The scallops should just cook through, and no more, in the latent heat. It's important not to overcook, or too much of the scallop's natural juices will go into the milk as the protein in the flesh coagulates.

Making the sauce

Drain off the cooking liquor and put into another pan. Bring to the boil and reduce slightly. Work the flour into the butter to make a smooth paste and drop very small pieces into the boiling liquid. Whisk in until all is mixed through and simmer for a few minutes to thicken. Taste and season.

Serving

Put scallops into heated shells and pour over sauce. Cover with a light sprinkling of browned crumbs and serve.

Oyster, European or Native
(*Ostrea edulis*)
Oyster, Pacific (*Cassostrea gigas*)

Oysters have been eaten with great relish in Scotland for centuries. James Hogg (1770-1835), the Ettrick Shepherd, was an avid oyster-eater and complained that 'a month without an R has nae right being in the year'. This was the heyday of the tavern oyster ploy, when native oysters were only available from September to April to avoid the spawning season. City centre life in Edinburgh revolved around the Auld Toon and even genteel Edinburgh ladies frequented the less-genteel, subterranean Oyster Cellars for 'brods' (wooden boards) of oysters and pots of porter. The night usually ended with a communal bowl of brandy punch.

Oysters were so cheap and plentiful that cooks threw handfuls into sauces, soups and stews, often a hundred at a time. What flavours they must have concocted! These native European oysters, known as 'natives', were mentioned by Martin Martin in his *Description of the*

Western Islands of Scotland (1703) as growing on 'rocks and so big that they are cut in four pieces before they are ate'. Despite much effort to protect them, the Firth of Forth 'native' oyster beds began to decline in the late 1800s and the heyday of the tavern 'oyster ploy' was over.

Much of the credit for the revival of Scottish oysters is due to the laird of Ardkinglas, Johnny Noble, and his marine biologist partner, Andrew Lane, who pioneered a new generation of Scottish oysters, discovering how to farm them successfully in the rich and unpolluted waters of Loch Fyne. One of the laird's selling points for oysters was their nutritional benefits and the feel-good factor after eating. This may have some basis of truth in the fact that they are rich in zinc – not an aphrodisiac – but a vital nutrient which stimulates the immune system and is said to help prevent tiredness and depression.

Scottish farmed oysters are a particularly good flavour since they grow naturally in the pure sea water in areas which are free from industry and shipping and where population levels are low. They are not put through sterile water tanks in order to make them safe for consumption, but are taken straight from the sea for sale, which means all the natural flavours are retained.

Lochs chosen for oyster farming must have shelter and a rich supply of natural nutrients in the waters. The most common method of farming is to put the young seed into mesh bags which are put on metal or wooden trestles at low-water mark. Allowing the oysters to be uncovered at low tide is considered important since it causes them to close tightly and survive out of the water, which is essential when they are eventually transported for sale. They are usually harvested after two summers' feeding. They are farmed on the West Coast from Dumfries and Galloway to Shetland, with some in Lothian.

EUROPEAN OR NATIVE
Ostrea edulis

This oyster ranges from the Norwegian Sea down to the Mediterranean and Morocco. It has a round, greyish-coloured shell which is less jagged than the Pacific oyster. It will vary in flavour according to its feeding and the ratio of salt to freshwater of its habitat. The location of an oyster can be identified by its flavour, and oysters from specific locations often take their name from the location. Only a small amount are farmed compared with the Pacific (*gigas*) oyster. They can reach a shell length of up to 11 cm, and occur in variable shapes.

Spawning Habits: Initially it begins life as a male, after reaching maturity (between 2-3 years old) it spawns, and then changes into a female. In Scotland, breeding normally takes place in summer between May and August. Prime season for eating is September to April. Avoid during the spawning season. Wild oyster fisheries are generally privately owned and managed by Several and Regulating Orders which prevent other fishing in the oyster bed area. The native oyster is the subject of a Biodiversity Action Plan which aims to maintain and expand where possible the distribution and abundance of natives in UK waters. The Shellfish Association of Great Britain (*www.shellfish.org.uk*) has responsibility for implementing this plan.

PACIFIC or GIGAS
Crassostrea gigas

This oyster originates from north-eastern Asia. It has an elongated oval-shaped shell which is very jagged. The location of an oyster can often be identified by its flavour according to its feeding and the ratio of salt to freshwater of its habitat. They are more widely farmed than natives. Shellfish farming is an extensive, low-impact method requiring high-quality water standards for cultivation. Maximum size 25 cm.

Spawning Habits: As with many oyster species, they develop first as males, spawn, and then later develop into females. Spawning occurs in the summer, but only in its native warm waters of the Pacific. It does not spawn in the UK's colder waters, which makes it available to eat all year. Widely available all year. May be graded by size from 1-4. Grade 1 is the largest.

Buying, Storing

Reject an oyster which is not tightly shut; if buying in a restaurant the sign of a 'good' oyster is that it should be full of liquid and look alive. The bad one is shrivelled and dried up.

Once the oysters have left the sea they should be kept in a cool place; the salad section of the refrigerator is a good place, under a damp cloth with the flat shell uppermost. They will stay fresh for four to five days, but should be eaten sooner if possible since their juices will continue to dry up on keeping.

Opening

Hold the oyster in a cloth in your left hand with the round side in the palm so that the juice is not lost. Insert a strong knife with a short rounded blade at the hinge end which should be towards you and give a quick upward turn, cutting through the muscle at the hinge. Remove any shell fragments. Loosen round the edge.

Eating

> *A genuine oyster-eater rejects all additions, – wine, eschalott,*
> *lemon, etc., are alike obnoxious to his taste for the native juice.*
> Meg Dods, *The Cook and Housewife's Manual*, 1826.

Oysters are best eaten raw on the half shell. Serve in the deep half to reserve the juice and place on a bed of ice. Serve with brown bread and butter and a chilled dry white wine. Depending on size, allow between 6-8 as a starter. Add lemon juice, cayenne pepper, chilli sauce or Tabasco to taste.

Other Ways of eating oysters

This depends on the type of oyster, since some are large and 'meaty' and lend themselves to cooking while others are best eaten live or lightly cooked. Now that they are an expensive luxury for most, adding them to pies, savoury puddings and sauces as they were in the past is seldom an option.

OYSTERS ON SKEWERS
with bacon

24 oysters,* shelled
12 rashers of unsmoked streaky bacon, cut very thinly
Freshly ground black pepper
* also suitable for clabbies and scallops.

Once known as Angels on Horseback and served as a savoury end to a meal.

4 servings

Use 4 metal skewers.

Preheat the grill to moderate. Roll half a rasher of bacon round each oyster and impale 6 on each skewer.

Grill, turning from time to time, until the bacon is cooked. Season and serve with pepper, crusty bread and unsalted butter.

Mussel
Blue or Common
(*Mytilus edulis*)
Horse or clabbie dubh (Gaelic 'black mouth'), yoag (Shetland)
(*Modiolus modiolus)*

As part of the general foraging for seafood – to eke out a meagre diet from the land – both common mussels and the larger horse mussel were eaten by Scottish peasants living in coastal areas and on islands. Mussel brose was a common dish which, according to a recipe by F. Marian McNeill (1929), was made with cooked mussels and their liquor, plus fish stock and milk. The mussels and the liquid were poured over a handful of oatmeal in a bowl in the classic brose style.

Wild and Farmed

While some mussels may be gathered wild from rocks, farming has been a common method of cultivation since the 1800s. The first record of farmed mussels in Scotland was in the 1890s, when several experiments took place on the East Coast growing mussels on ropes. This idea was abandoned following a series of disasters, but in 1966 experiments were resumed: cultivation was again on ropes and commercial ventures started in the early 1970s using ropes attached to long lines and rafts. Various methods continue to be used, with each farmer developing a system which suits his particular site. Once harvested they are washed and graded. Horse mussels are dug up from natural beds lying at the extreme low-water mark. Most farmed mussels come from the West Coast, though some also come from the East. Mussel farming is an extensive, low impact method of cultivation which has increased the abundance of mussel seed in the wild.

Identification:
BLUE or COMMON MUSSEL

Its range is throughout the North Atlantic, Mediterranean, North and Baltic Seas. It normally lives in large colonies, attaching itself to rocks and other mussels with strong, sticky threads known as *byssus*. It can be found from the high intertidal zone to the shallow subtidal zone. Colour is usually dark blue-black, though it may vary with tinges of deep bluish purple. It has become one of the most popular UK shellfish, largely due to the extensive development of farmed mussels. It is a method of aquaculture with potential for development. A mussel, farmed or wild, will vary in flavour according to its feeding and the ratio of salt to freshwater of its habitat. Some experts can distinguish the location of a mussel by its flavour.

Size and shape vary widely. Minimum recommended shell-size is 5 cm. Can grow up to 10 cm but usually is much smaller. Mussels mature when one year old and may live 10-15 years or more.

Spawning Habits: Peaks in early spring (April) and continues to late summer (August), with larvae settling after 1-6 months.

Buying Advice: Prime season after summer feeding in September to February. Avoid March, April and May. Stocks are generally considered to be under-exploited. The main methods of harvesting wild and farmed mussels are by dredging and hand-gathering. Choose mussels which have been sustainably harvested in the wild (by hand-gathering) or farmed.

HORSE MUSSEL (CLABBIES)

A larger version of the common mussel, it has a wider range and can be found in the North Atlantic, from the White Sea to the Bay of Biscay and from Labrador to North Carolina. It is also in the North Pacific. Its shell-colouring varies from shades of blue-black to purple. This is covered with a thin glossy covering (the perisostracum) which gives adults a yellow or dark brown appearance. Inside its flesh is orange. It is found, part-buried, in soft sediment or gravel in dense reefs or beds, usually subtidally, to depths of over 100 m. Some reefs may become uncovered at exceptionally low tides, when digging up with a fork is necessary to release the firm hold they have on the sea bed. Their orange muscle is sometimes considered coarse, in comparison with the smaller blue mussel. This applies more to large, wrinkled old specimens rather than younger and smoother shelled mussels, whose flavour and texture is excellent. Maximum length is 15 cm, though they have been known to grow to 23 cm. Can live up to 20 years, possibly longer.

Spawning Habits: They spawn all year round, but spawning peaks in early spring (April) to late summer (August). Not harvested commercially in the UK. Forage on seashores at low tides with a stout garden fork.

Buying

They should be bought live, all shells tightly shut. Discard any open ones. They are at their best after summer feeding and before they spawn in the spring. They can be good until February but by March are losing condition.

Preparing

Leave overnight in fresh water, then scrub clean and remove the beard – the tuft of fibres projecting from the shell which anchors it.

MUSSEL BROSE
with hot crusty bread

Simple and quick to cook: pile mussels in their shells on plates and their steaming aroma captures all the essence of the sea. In a classic Scots brose this would have been a main meal when a handful of oatmeal was put in the bottom of each bowl to soak up the mussel 'bree' (juices).

For bread:
Crusty loaf such as a baguette or ciabatta
2-3 tablespoons flat-leaf parsley, chopped
85 g/3 oz butter, softened

3-4 cloves garlic (optional)
For mussels:
2½ kg/5 lb 8 oz mussels in their shells, well scrubbed and
   cleaned
300 ml/½ pt water
Sprig of thyme
1 bay leaf
50 g/2 oz butter
Freshly ground black pepper
4 tablespoons medium or fine oatmeal (optional)
1 handful chopped parsley

4 servings

To heat through crusty loaf

Preheat oven to 350F/180C/160Cfan/Gas 4.

Wet a large, scrunched-up sheet of greaseproof paper under the
tap and spread out. Place loaf on top and slice at 2.5 cm/1 in intervals on the diagonal about ¾ of the way through. Mix parsley
with the soft butter and add garlic if using. Mix well. Open up
slits and spread cut surfaces with butter. Wrap up loosely in the
paper leaving space above the top surface. Put into a hot oven
425F/220C/200Cfan/Gas 7 for 15-20 minutes

To cook the mussels

Clean mussels and remove beards. Put the water, onion, thyme
and bay leaf into a very large pot. Bring to the boil and add mussels. Cover tightly and cook over a high heat, shaking frequently
until the shells begin to open. This will only take a minute, even
less if the mussels are small. Remove from the heat, keep the
lid on. The remainder of the mussels should open in the latent
heat – it is important not to overcook. Remove any which do
not open. Strain cooking liquor, taste for saltiness and adjust
with boiling water if necessary and stir butter in. Season with

a few grindings of pepper. Put a spoonful of oatmeal into each bowl (optional) Pour over some cooking liquor and stir in to moisten. Add mussels and pour over remaining liquid. Sprinkle over parsley. Serve with hot crusty loaf for dipping.

Other ways with cooked mussels – Mix through a creamy scrambled egg or warm them through in a little butter and fold into a soft omelette. Add to the sauce with Roast Lamb (p.218).

MUSSELS AND COCKLES IN GARLIC AND OLIVE OIL

1.25 kg/2 lb 12 oz mussels and/or cockles
3 tablespoons olive oil
3 cloves of garlic, peeled
Lemon
White pepper

2 servings

Wash the mussels/cockles and soak in salted water for 24 hours. Remove beards from the mussels.

Heat the oil in a deep sauté pan and cut the garlic in slices. Add to the oil and cook for about 30 seconds. Add the shellfish and cook over a low heat until they open, tossing or stirring from time to time. Remove from the heat, season with pepper and serve with lemon wedges and crusty bread.

CLABBIES or LARGE MUSSELS
in a leek and tomato risotto

A robust soup-stew made with risotto rice which works best with the larger and more meaty clabbies or large mussels.

8 clabbies or 16 large mussels
850 ml/1½ pt water
1 tablespoons oil

25 g/1 oz butter
2 leeks, finely chopped
350 g/12 oz risotto rice
1 tin chopped tomatoes
2 cloves garlic, crushed
Salt and ground pepper

4 servings

Preparing

Clean mussels and remove beards. Put water into a pan, bring to the boil. Add mussels, cover and cook till they just open, shaking occasionally. Strain the cooking liquor. Take mussels out of their shells. Cut into two or three pieces depending on size. Check saltiness of cooking liquor and adjust if too salty with more water.

Cooking

Heat oil and butter in a pan and add the white of the leek, cook for a few minutes until softened and then add the rice. Continue to cook for a few minutes. Then add tomatoes, garlic and enough cooking liquor to make a sloppy mixture. Cook uncovered till it is absorbed, stirring from time to time. Add more cooking liquor, as needed, without making the mixture too wet. It should take about 20 minutes to cook the rice.

Now add the green leek, stir through till softened and finally add the chopped mussels just before serving. Taste and season. Serve.

Periwinkle – Scots Whelk or Buckie
(*Littorina littorea*)

Where supplies are plentiful, local pickers collect large sackfulls from around the coasts, usually for selling on to fish markets. In the

Scottish tradition, they were most often eaten as street food, cooked and then picked from the shell with a pin, and first sold by fishwives by the plateful with appropriate condiments. Later they were sold in bags, also as street food, in places like the weekend market at the Glasgow Barras. Now they can also be found at seafood bars and shellfish stalls such as the one on Oban pier.

In times of scant food supplies they were also used by coastal and island communities to flavour, and add a few morsels of protein sustenance, to their daily broth. Children were sent to do the collecting. According to an old Hebridean recipe they were added, once cooked, with their own cooking liquor to a fish stock, made from fish bones and heads, which was then thickened lightly with oatmeal to the consistency of thin gruel.

Identification

Its range is the coastal regions of the North Atlantic where it inhabits rocky shores in all but the most exposed coastlines. In sheltered conditions it can be found clinging to rocks in sandy bays and mudflats, particularly in estuaries. It is a blue-black colour with greyish tones. It is a small marine snail, mainly found between low and high tide but can also be found at depths of 60 m in the northern end of its range.

The maximum shell size is about 3.5 cm in length, but is more commonly about 2.5 cm. Both males and females reach maturity at 1-1.2 cm. They usually live about 3 years but can survive for 4-5 years. Minimum recommended size 2 cm.

Spawning Habits: Peaks in May and June, so avoid these months.

Buying Advice: Most are collected or gathered by hand, which is a selective method of harvesting that causes least habitat disturbance. Minimum landing sizes for winkles vary between regions, but selecting larger, mature winkles (over 2cm) allows them to have spawned. Choose winkles harvested by hand-gathering methods in areas which are well managed.

A Scots whelk is an English winkle: It's not clear why many Scots decided to name the grey-black, curly-shelled winkle a 'whelk' pronounced 'wilk', but they did. The true whelk (*Buccinum undatum*) has a whiter shell and flesh and is known to Scots as the Dog Whelk; it is not generally eaten in Scotland.

Preparation

Steep overnight in fresh water to remove sand, etc.

Cooking

Place in boiling water to cover and simmer for 2-3 minutes. Drain, save liquid for using as stock.

Eating

Serve with a large pin to pick out the meat. Discard the mica-like plate, 'the eye', at the mouth of the shell.

Razor-shell Clams – Scots Spoot (*Ensis siliqua*)

'Wanted: Spoots, Spoots and More Spoots,' said a newspaper article when I was last in Orkney, spoots being what they call razor-shells there. I went spooting at the lowest of low tides and with an expert guide, but came back with nothing but mussels.
Alan Davidson, *North Atlantic Seafood* (Penguin, 1979).

These are a highly esteemed delicacy by those who catch their own seafood. Difficult to find, they are even more difficult to catch. Traditional ways of cooking and eating are similar to other similar shellfish when they are simmered in a pot till they open, then eaten in a bowl with the strained cooking liquor.

Identification

Widely found in intertidal waters throughout the UK and in temperate waters. Its shell is a glossy brown or yellowish brown with a white interior. Its muscle is a long powerful 'foot' which burrows into the sediment around the extreme low-water mark and in shallow subtidal areas. It is a filter-feeding bivalve and is capable of rapid burrowing if disturbed. The shells get their name from the shape of the oldfashioned cut-throat razor. The muscle flesh is good eating and highly esteemed in the Far East and the Continent, where Scottish razor-clam fishermen have found a ready market.

Farmed: The commercial rearing or farming of razor clams is well established in some areas of Spain and its commercial potential is now being developed in the UK and Ireland.

Spawning Habits: In summer (June–August), hours after they are fertilised, eggs develop into mobile larvae which drift with the current for 3-4 weeks and then settle, attaching themselves to sand or shell by fine, strong threads. They are relatively long-lived and may survive to 10-15 years and an average adult can reach a size of 12.5 cm. Growth stops around age 10.

Buying Advice: Buy during prime season – April, May and then September–November. Largely unavailable during the winter months from December to March. Avoid those dredged from wild stocks. Choose those harvested in the wild by sustainable methods such as hand-gathered by divers. Avoid undersized (less than 10cm) and wild-harvested during the spawning season (June–August). To forage, they can be found in reasonable numbers at the very edge of the lowest tides (equinox tides in March and September are the lowest) and especially where there are spent shells to be seen. The traditional method of catching is to walk backwards along the beach, watching for the little 'spoot' (spout) of water ejected by them as you walk over the sand. There are many different opinions about how to catch them, one method commonly used is to pour salt down the spoot hole to encourage it to come up thinking the tide is coming in. Grabbing it quickly and pulling it out is the catching technique, which may not always be successful.

Other species of razor clams found in British intertidal waters: *E. siliqua*, *E. arcuatus*.

Cooking

They can be grilled on a hot charcoal grill, when they will be ready as soon as the shells open. Otherwise they can be steamed very briefly, as for mussels. Simply open the shells, and either eat hot or cold or use to make a shellfish broth (see Mussel Brose recipe p.102) with the cooking liquor. Remove the stomach-bag and add the meat chopped finely just before the soup is served. If overcooked they become tough.

Other Scottish Molluscs
Limpet (*Patella vulgate*)
Cockle (*Cerastoderma edule*)

LIMPET

Common on Scottish seashores though not sold commercially, they are often used as fishing bait. To forage, chip them off the rocks with a sharp knife or knock them with a sharp stone. They have an interesting flavour, but if very old will be rubbery and tough to eat. A younger limpet will be less tough and will soften a bit with cooking. They are used, previously boiled, in Limpet Stovies in the Western Isles (See **Stovies** p.250). Their cooking liquid has lots of flavour and should be used as stock for making fish sauces and soups. Those found in Scottish waters have a grey, yellowish or brown shell.

Spawning Habits: September–January. Males change into females as they mature, so if wild-foraging on the seashore it is best not to take too many large ones, or the breeding potential could be threatened.

COCKLE

Its range is from the Barents Sea and the Baltic to the Mediterranean and Senegal. It is found buried in mud and sand in estuaries
and on sandy beaches, and nearly all commercial cockle-beds are on
large intertidal flats in lower reaches of estuaries. Its two identical
oval shells are scored with radiating ridges and are either a light
brown, pale yellow or a dirty white colour. It has been found in very
high densities of ten thousand per square metre. Around £20 million worth of cockles are taken from the UK's muddy beaches each
year, of which 75 per cent is swiftly exported, mostly to Holland,
Belgium, France and Spain. Companies from these countries have
started taking over the industry. It is in urgent need of a new image
in the UK since it has suffered too much as a vinegar-doused adjunct
to greasy chips, which destroys all of its natural flavour. Its shell size
is up to 5 cm long, although average sizes tend to be around 3-4 cm.
Maturity occurs at a shell length of around 2 cm.

Spawning Habits: From May to August, although exact times
will vary from region to region.

Buying Advice: Choose cockles harvested legally using sustainable methods only. Over-exploitation by mechanical harvesting and dredging causes damage to stocks, disturbance of seabed
or estuary and depletion of prey species for birds and other marine
life.

Marine Stewardship Council Certified Sustainable Fishery:
The fishery in Burry Inlet, Wales is certified as an environmentally
responsible fishery by the MSC.

Look for MSC sustainable label (blue with a white tick). Visit
www.msc.org/track-a-fishery for up to date information.

They may be eaten raw or cooked as for mussels (see p.102).

Crustaceans
Crab, Brown, Partan (*Cancer pagurus*)
Velvet Crab (*Liocarcanus puber*)

BROWN CRAB, SCOTS PARTAN

Crabs were a common shellfish, eaten by coastal communities, often used to flavour broths. It was not until the latter half of the 1900s that their commercial worth became valued (lobsters had been exported since the 1700s) when centres of intensive crab-fishing, such as in Orkney, began processing them and establishing a market for fresh crab meat.

Identification

It ranges in European coastal waters as far north as Norway but not on the American side of the Atlantic. Its shell (carapace) is a hard, reddish-brown with 'pie-crust' edge and, like other crustaceans, it sheds its shell to allow growth. Moulting takes place at frequent intervals during its first years, but only every two years after it is fully grown, when its growth slows down. The juvenile crab settles in the intertidal zone and remains in these habitats for three years, until it reaches 6-7 cm shell width, at which time it migrates to subtidal habitats.

Size: The minimum landing size is 13-14 cm carapace width (CW) in most areas of the UK. Average weight 1-2 kg. It can grow up to about 25 cm and live for up to 100 years but average age is around 25-30 years.

Spawning Habits: Mainly in the winter months.

Buying Advice: Prime season May-September. Males contain more white meat than females which have more brown meat. Males have larger claws and their tail flap is narrower and more pointed than females. Avoid from January to March and crabs which are below the minimum 13-14 cm CW, also crab claws unless it is certain they have been removed after landing. Egg-bearing or 'berried' females should be avoided at all times to allow them to spawn. Preferably buy live: they should smell fresh with no hint of ammonia and they should be reasonably lively. Lift the crab by its back to check that it is a good weight for its size.

Preparing and Cooking Crab

Measure water into large pot which will hold the crab and add an appropriate amount of salt (see p. 113). The water should be around the same saltiness as sea water so the crab will not lose flavour into the cooking liquid.

The RSPCA (*www.rspca.org.uk*) recommends that crabs should be chilled to make them insensitive before killing. To do this, put them first into the fridge for a few hours to bring down their temperature gradually. Then they can be put in the freezer until they become insensible. Check for lack of movement every 15-20 minutes and remove. They can then be killed quickly by severing the nerve centres with a small sharp screwdriver or bradawl. Crabs have two main nerve centres.

The recommended method is to lift the abdominal flap (tail flap) in the centre of the underside and pierce into the hole over the hind

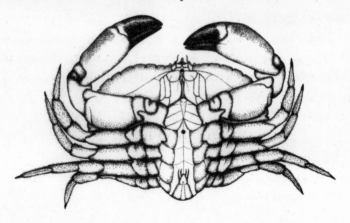

nerve centre at the so-called vent all the way through the shell, followed by a repeat of the same process on the front nerve centre, via the shallow depression at the top of the body, just above the moveable plate closed over the mouth. This should be done quickly and take no longer than ten seconds. Lay crab on the floor to give more downward pressure.

Drop the crab into the boiling salted water (use seawater or 14 g/½ oz salt per litre water). Allow 15 minutes for a 1 kg crab (add 5 minutes for every extra 500g). Remove, lay on its back and leave to cool. Repeat with second crab.

To Remove the Crab Meat

Twist off the claws and legs first. Using your thumbs together at the base of the underside of the body, push hard to release the central undercarriage from the top shell. Pull it all out and discard the small mouth with its grey stomach sac and discard the dull beige feathery 'dead man's fingers' which lie along the inside part.

To extract the meat, crack the claws and legs with crab (or nut) crackers and remove the 'white' meat. Pick the rest of the white meat from the central undercarriage with a skewer or shellfish pick. Remove the soft 'brown' meat from inside the carapace. Keep the white meat from the claws separate.

To Serve Cold as a Salad

Mix the brown meat together, taste and season. Pack into the shell on either side. Mix white meat, taste and season. Pack into the middle of the shell. Garnish with chopped parsley and serve with a lightly flavoured mayonnaise, brown bread and butter.

PARTAN PIES

4 medium sized crabs
2–3 tablespoons soft breadcrumbs
125 g/4 oz butter

½–¼ grated nutmeg
Salt and ground pepper
1 handful of chopped parsley

4 servings

The crab shell acts as a useful container for all the meat extracted. The strongly flavoured brown body meat can be flavoured with a little nutmeg and packed into the sides of the shells, leaving space in the middle for the white meat.

To cook

Preheat oven to 350F/180C/160Cfan/Gas 4

Boil the crabs and remove all meat from claws and body (see p.113). Break off edges on either side of eyes by pressing with thumbs. They should come cleanly away to open up the shell. Clean the shell.

Keep the two meats separate. Put the brown meat in a bowl and add the breadcrumbs, half the softened butter and nutmeg. Taste and season. Pack this mixture into the sides of the shell. Mix the white meat with remaining butter, season with salt and pepper and place in the centre. Cover with foil and heat through in the oven for 15-20 minutes. Serve hot.

PARTAN BREE

The crab flavour comes through strongly in this creamy soup which is thickened with rice. 'Bree' means liquid or gravy.

1 large cooked crab (see p.112)
50 g/2 oz rice
600 ml/1 pt milk
600 ml/1 pt cooking liquor from boiling the crab or water
125 ml/4 fl oz single cream
Salt and pepper
Garnish – finely chopped chives

4 servings

To cook crab (see p.112)

Remove all the meat from the crab, keeping the claw meat separate.

To make the bree

Put the rice into a pan with milk and cooking liquor or water and cook till tender. Liquidise this with the brown body meat from the crab. Put into a pot and add the white meat and cream. Reheat. Taste and season. Adjust consistency with more milk, cooking liquor or fish stock if necessary. Serve garnished with some finely chopped chives.

VELVET CRAB

To serve cold

Caught in Scottish waters, and mostly exported, this crab is similar in structure to a brown crab but with swimming legs and a more intense seafood flavour.

16 x 100 g live velvet crab
Water to cover
1 tablespoon salt

4 servings

To cook

Put crabs in a large pot, cover with boiling water, add salt, and simmer for 3-5 minutes. Drain and leave to cool.

To eat

Eat with bread and butter. Serve with shellfish crackers and lobster forks for picking out meat.

Turn crab onto its back, pull off the apron flap and push body away from shell. Remove and eat the soft brown meat from inside the shell. Remove and discard the dead men's fingers (as in brown crab, see p.113). Break body in half, leaving legs attached. Begin with swimming legs, twist off one by one and eat their attached morsels of white meat. Break large claws at a joint and crush shell to open, pick out white meat. Crush remaining body shell, and legs, for any remaining morsels of white meat.

Shell debris, and saved white and brown meat, can be used to make shellfish sauce (see p.131).

Lobster – European
(*Homarus gammarus*)

It was around the mid-1700s that creel-fishing began for crabs and lobsters. The demand for lobsters, rather than crabs, prompted English fish merchants to set up a system for shipping live lobsters to Billingsgate in a boat fitted with a supply of fresh seawater. By the early 1800s there was also a market among Scottish gourmets, when gatherings of the gastronomic Cleikum Club revealed their recipe for 'Lobster Haut Gout', involving much spicing, plus a red wine sauce. Like prime Scottish beef, the lobster was first and foremost a source of valuable income for the Scots and, except on the menus of gastronomic clubs or the tables of the rich, it was never eaten. The lobster's social divide continues and they remain an expensive luxury,

Identification

Its range is from the North Atlantic to the Mediterranean, including the North Sea, the English Channel and the west Baltic. It has a dark-blue shell (turning scarlet-red when boiled) with pale yellow markings and long red antennae. The claws are of unequal size, with one large crushing claw and a slimmer cutting claw. It inhabits rocky seabeds, living in caves and excavated burrows from the lower shore to 60 m depth. It is the most expensive shellfish from Scottish waters.

Lobster hatcheries have been set up in Orkney, Wales and Cornwall to release young lobster into the wild.

Size: Carapace length (CL: between the back of the eye socket and the furthest edge of the carapace) can grow up to 100 cm but lengths of around 50 cm are more typical. Females mature at around 7.5-8 cm (CL), at 5-7 years of age. They may live 50 years or more.

Spawning Habits: They mate in late summer when the females moult, but females can store the sperm packet over the winter, so eggs are not fertilised and laid until the following summer. Female lobsters bearing or carrying eggs are termed 'berried'.

Buying Advice: Prime season June and July, then September-November (sheds shell in August). Avoid below the legal minimum landing size, 9 cm (CL) i.e. the length between the back of the eye socket and the furthest edge of the carapace). Avoid breeding females with eggs which contribute to the breeding stock. Choose creel or pot caught lobsters. Variable availability January-March.

Marine Stewardship Council Certified Sustainable Fishery: A lobster-pot fishery off the Yorkshire coast is undergoing MSC assessment.

Look for MSC sustainable label (blue with a white tick). Visit *www.msc.org/track-a-fishery* for up to date information.

Choose a live lobster which thrashes about with some vigour when lifted. If it is sluggish in reacting, then it has probably been kept for several days out of water and without food, resulting in a loss of weight and vitality. Lift up the lobster by the back: it should feel heavy for its size.

Preparing and Cooking Lobster

Live lobster claws should be bound with heavy-duty rubber bands. The RSPCA (*www.rspca.org.uk*) recommends that lobsters should be chilled to make them insensitive before killing. To do this, put them first into the fridge for a few hours to bring down their temperature

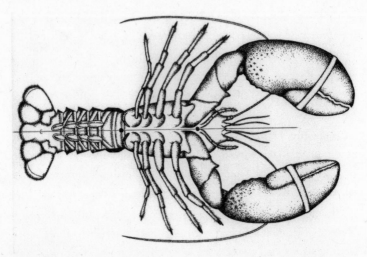

gradually. Then they can be put in the freezer until they become insensible. Check every 15-20 minutes for lack of movement and remove. They can then be killed quickly by severing the nerve centres with a heavy, sharp-pointed knife.

Lobsters have a chain of nerve centres which run along the central length of their body. These nerve centres must be destroyed by rapidly (within 10 seconds) cutting through the midline, lengthways, with a large, heavy sharp knife.

To prepare for boiling whole:

The lobster should be on a flat surface, on its back. Hold it around the top of its head with a firm pressure. Note the midline on the lobster's under-surface. Keeping the knife in line with the midline, place the knife on the head beneath the mouth parts. Cut through the head via this point to pierce and destroy the brain. Take care not to push the knife all the way through the head. Then cut through the under-surface midline to pierce and destroy the rest of the nerve chain in two stages. Starting at the midline near the junction of the tail and the thorax, the first cut is directed forwards toward the head and the second backwards down the midline towards the tail.

To prepare for cutting into two halves for grilling:

Follow the above method but instead of piercing, cut through the whole shell along the midline to give two equal halves.

To Boil

Prepare a large pot with boiling water (use seawater or 14 g/½ oz salt per litre water). Add lobsters and bring back to the boil. Cook a 750-800 g lobster for 15 minutes then add 5 minutes for every extra 500 g. Remove from pot and drain.

BOILED LOBSTER
To serve cold as a salad

When cold, cut the lobster in half. Place on a chopping board belly-side down with legs and claws splayed out. Hold the lobster body with one hand with head towards you. With a very heavy, sharp chopping knife stab the tip into the head at the central point about 2 cm behind the eyes, and with the blade facing away from your hand cut firmly all the way through. Press with your palm on the upper edge of the knife if necessary to cut through.

Remove the knife and turn the lobster round to cut through the rest of the body to the end of the tail, making two halves of lobster. Discard the black intestinal tract which runs the length of the tail. Also the small gritty sand sac behind the mouth. Besides the 'white' meat there is the soft-smooth liver meat, known as the tomalley, which is a special flavour and not to be missed.

To prepare meat for salad

1. Snap off the eight legs close to the body. Break legs at joints and pick out meat with a lobster fork.

2. Remove each claw close into the body, and bang with a wooden mallet to crack the shell. These can be left whole and served with lobster forks for picking out the meat. Or pull away

the shell and remove the meat. Remove the cartilage that runs through each claw.

3. Pull away the bony covering on the underside of the tail. Starting at the tail-end, prise out the tail meat in one piece. Discard the brown-grey feathery gills.

4. The soft grey-green liver remains in the shell. Scoop it out with a spoon and save. Lift out the inedible sand sac (stomach) and discard.

5. Lay the tail meat on a chopping board and slice into pieces about 2 cm/¾ in thick. Scrape out any remaining meat in the lobster shell.

To serve

Clean the empty tail shell and fill with the meat. Arrange the remainder attractively on a large white plate with the liver and coral (if there is any) as a garnish. Arrange claws on the plate if serving unpicked.

Serve with a lightly flavoured lemon mayonnaise, green salad, crusty bread and unsalted butter.

Chilled dry white wines or Champagne are best with cold lobster.

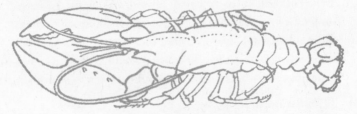

GRILLED LOBSTER

Prepare the lobster by splitting (see p.119). This method will preserve its full flavour. It is important not to overcook and dry out the flesh. The tarragon flavouring comes from fish expert Sonia Stevenson, author of *A Fresh Look at Fish*, 1996.

2 x 750-800 g/1 lb 10 oz-1 lb 12 oz live lobsters
125 g/4 oz unsalted butter
1 tablespoon tarragon leaves
Juice of a small lemon
Salt and pepper

2–4 servings

Preparing the lobster

Once the lobster is split, remove the sand sac and the coral if it is a hen lobster. This looks like a long, dark greenish-black sac running along the back under the shell. It turns a bright scarlet when cooked. Discard the white gills and the intestinal canal which runs down the middle of the tail.

Making the butter

Put the butter, coral, tarragon and lemon juice into a food processor and whizz till smooth.

Grilling

Remove claws from the body. Place claws and body shell on a baking or roasting tin, shell-side up. Put under a hot grill for 2 minutes or until they turn red. Remove. Turn over and spread cut surface with flavoured butter. Turn over the claws. Grill for 3-4 minutes, remove claws and check body. When the meat comes away easily from the shell they are cooked. Serve with the pan juices poured over. Crack the claws and arrange on the plate beside the body shell. Serve with lobster forks and finger bowls.

LOBSTER SOUP

The flavour of this depends on a slow extraction of fishy flavours from bones and heads combined with aromatic saffron.

Fish stock:
2 tablespoons oil

1 leek, sliced

1 onion, sliced

1 celery stalk, chopped

1 small head of fennel, chopped roughly

few sprigs of thyme

1-2 bay leaves

12 black peppercorns

1-2 kg/2-4 lb lobster shells and white fish bones and heads

150 ml/5 fl oz dry white wine (optional)

water to cover

For the soup:

2 large pinches of saffron

4 tablespoons boiling water

1 tablespoon oil

25 g/1 oz butter

2 large beefsteak tomatoes, skinned

2 garlic cloves, crushed

2 teaspoons flour

1.1 L/2 pt stock

150 ml/5 fl oz soured cream or crème fraiche

225 g/8 oz of lobster meat or other shellfish or fish

4-6 servings

Making the stock

Heat the oil in a large pot and when hot add the vegetables. Cook for about five minutes, stirring occasionally till they begin to soften. Clean the shellfish shells and fish bones and heads removing the gills and washing off any blood. Add to vegetables and continue to cook over a medium heat, stirring occasionally, for another 3 or 4 minutes. Cover with water and bring up slowly to a simmer. Skim and add thyme, bay leaf and peppercorns. Cook, just simmering, for about 20 minutes. Leave until slightly cooled, but not cold, and strain.

Making the soup

Pour boiling water over the saffron. Heat the oil and butter in a pan. Remove the core and seeds from the tomatoes, chop and add. Cook for a few minutes until the tomatoes are pulped. Stir in the garlic and flour.

Cook for another few minutes and then add the saffron and add the stock gradually. Bring to the boil and remove from the heat. Put into food processor and whizz till smooth. Return to the pan. Add soured cream or crème fraîche to taste. Season with salt. Add the lobster pieces, or other fish or shellfish to garnish, and just heat through. Serve.

Norway Lobster
(*Nephrops norvegicus*)

Identification

Multiply named: langoustine, Italian scampi, Dublin Bay 'prawn', or just prawn

Its range is from Iceland to Morocco and the West Central Mediterranean. There is also a colony in the Adriatic, exploited by Italy. It is caught in Scotland from the North Sea and inshore west coast waters. The carapace is pale pink, rose or orange-red; the claws are banded in red and white. It lives in burrows on the seabed and is limited to a muddy habitat, requiring sediment with a silt and clay content to excavate burrows. Its tail flesh is very highly rated.

Males grow relatively quickly to around 6 cm carapace length (CL) from tail to head, not including the claws, but seldom exceed 10 years old. Females grow more slowly and can reach 20 years old. Females mature at about 3 years. Maximum CL 24 cm.

Spawning Habits: In the autumn they lay eggs which remain attached to the tail for 9 months. Hatching occurs in the spring.

Buying Advice: Prime season October–November. Not at their best from June–August and avoid berried (egg-carrying) females, which fishermen should have released. Increase the sustainability by choosing pot or creel, caught rather than trawled. Best bought live; flavour and texture deteriorate quickly once they are dead. Buy only precooked from a reliable supplier.

There is a quality difference between live creel-caught and dead trawled. All creel-caught will be live and therefore fresher, while most of the trawled will have died during the trawling process, though there are now techniques to provide live-trawled. The better flavour and texture of a live-caught langoustine is easily recognisable and is what the European market demands.

Marine Stewardship Council Certified Sustainable Fishery: Trawl fisheries are associated with large quantities of by-catch, including overfished species such as cod and juvenile fish. The Loch Torridon creel fishery, and the Stornoway trawl fishery, have been certified as environmentally sustainable fisheries by the MSC. Look for MSC sustainable label (blue label with white tick). Visit *www. msc.org/track-a-fishery* for up to date information.

Preparing and cooking

Allow 16 large/24 small to serve 4 main course or 8 starters. Boil in seawater or water with 14 g/½ oz salt per litre) for three to four minutes, depending on size; drain. They need little preparation if being served in the shell. If they are whole, first pull off the head and claws. Then cut with a sharp knife through the bony cartilage on the underside, but do not cut through the tail meat. Open out and remove the whole tail, pick out spinal cord. Crush the claws with a wooden mallet and pick out the meat with a lobster fork. Suck out the soft head meat.

Serving

These very pretty, pink/orange-shelled creatures need no elaborate garnishing.

To serve hot in their shells

They may be tossed in butter for a few minutes till thoroughly heated through, then served in the centre of the table in the sauté pan or on a heated ashet and garnished with some colourful fresh fruits – Kiwi fruit, pineapple (use leaves to decorate), mango, strawberry. (As served by Nick Ryan at his seafood restaurant in Crinan Hotel, Argyll.) Serve with lobster forks for picking.

To serve as a cold salad

They may be left in their shells or removed and used to decorate a large, preferably white, plate. Use green salad vegetables and herbs to complement the pink/orange colour. Serve with Shellfish Sauce (see p.131) and lobster forks for picking.

To serve grilled with garlic

As recommended by David Wade of Amazon Seafoods at the wet-fish counter on Gairloch pier in Wester Ross.

'Treat the largest creel-caught as for lobster,' he says. 'Split it in half down the back. Open out and place on a baking tray. Brush with butter, sprinkle with a little dry white wine and a crushed clove of garlic. Grill until the flesh comes away from the shell and is cooked through.'

Serve with lobster forks for picking.

OTHER SCOTTISH CRUSTACEANS:
Squat Lobster (*Munida rugosa*)
Common Prawn (*Palaemon serratus*)
Northern Prawn (*Pandalus borealis*)
Squid (*Loligo forbesi*)
Sea Urchin (*Strongylocentrus droebachiensis*)

Squat Lobster

About a quarter the size of a mature Norway lobster, these tiny shellfish, packed with flavour, are much under-used but are fiddly to prepare. The best solution is to add them to a Fruits of the Sea Platter (p.129) when the eaters do the picking. Inventive Scottish chefs are now making more use of them to flavour soups and sauces. On the Isle of Arran, chef/salad-herb-and-vegetable-grower, Robin Grey, uses them as a stuffing for his courgette flowers, which he then deepfries in a light batter, Japanese tempura style.

Its range is throughout the oceans worldwide from near the surface to deep sea. There are currently 870 described species: Munida rugosa is the most commonly found squat lobster in north European waters. It is chestnut brown in colour with a greenish hint and red-tipped spines. The carapace is shiny between grooves and has scattered short hairs. It lives under stones and rocks on the lower shore and in crevices and fissures in the subtidal zone to depths of about 70 m. Though tiny compared to the European lobster, its tail flesh is an excellent flavour and highly rated.

Size: It can reach total lengths of up to 6.5 cm with a carapace length of up to 3.5 cm.

Spawning Habits: Females carry eggs during late winter and early spring.

Buying Advice: Avoid late winter and early spring.

Common Prawn

Ranges from Norway to the Mediterranean, round coastlines in inshore waters and rock pools. Alive it is almost colourless, but after cooking is an orange-red. If disturbed it shoots backwards. Eating quality of the tail flesh is highly rated.

Size: Market length from 7-8 cm. Recommended minimum length 6 cm. Maximum 10 cm.

Spawning Habits: November to June.

Buying Advice: May be caught in baited pots, fattest in September and October after summer feeding. Avoid November to June.

Northern Prawn
or Pink Shrimp, French Crevette

Its range is in the cold deep waters of the north-east Arctic, around Greenland, Norway, Iceland and the North Sea. It lives on muddy sea beds. Its live colour is red but it is usually cooked at sea when it changes to a pink colour. Tail flesh highly rated.

Size: It initially develops as a male, and then later becomes female during a 5-year life span. It takes up to three years to mature. Total adult length about 15 cm.

Spawning Habits: In summer-autumn, females move into coastal waters where eggs hatch in winter. Juveniles remain inshore for about a year before they migrate offshore as they begin to mature.

Buying Advice: The state of prawn stocks is generally unknown. Increase sustainability by only choosing prawns taken in fisheries using sorting grids to reduce by-catch of non-target species.

Marine Stewardship Council Certified Sustainable Fishery: The Northeast Arctic (Barents Sea) stock is classified as healthy and harvested sustainably and sorting grids are mandatory. The Canadian and Gulf of St Lawrence fisheries have been certified as sustainable by the Marine Stewardship Council.

Look for MSC sustainable label (blue with a white tick). Visit *www.msc.org/track-a-fishery* for up to date information.

Common or Veined Squid

Its range is in temperate and subtropical waters in the north-east Atlantic and the Mediterranean. It changes colour frequently and can instantly match the colour of the seabed it is swimming over. It has night vision, sucker-covered arms, a parrot-like beak which can slice through its prey like a razor, plus the ability to swim both backwards and forwards at high speed. Like other celphalopods it uses its ink sac to squirt a protective dark cloud to confuse predators. In early winter it comes inshore to spawn. Up to the middle of the 1900s it was more or less ignored by UK fish-eaters, but now they have cottoned on to its potential and supplies are being imported to meet demand.

Recommended size (body length from tip of nose to end of body): 15 cm.

Spawning Habits: It is fast-growing and sexually mature within its first year. The female spawns in her second year and dies soon after laying her eggs. The males live for about three years. The breeding season is between December and May.

Buying Advice: Prime season for Scottish-landed squid from the Moray Firth and west and east coasts is August, September and October though the fishing season begins in May. There are small artisanal fisheries around the UK which target squid. In Scotland there is a squid fishery in the Moray Firth where the fishermen trawl with a targeted small-mesh net. Another is the Sennan Cove squid fishery in Cornwall, where fishermen go out in small punts and fish for squid using jigs, a method of fishing similar to that of hand-lining for mackerel. Avoid eating squid taken in industrial or large scale commercial fisheries which remove large quantities of squid.

Sea Urchin

Its range in the Atlantic extends down to the English Channel and to New Jersey on the west. It is found on the lower shore among rocks, browsing on algae which it eats. It gets its name from the old name for hedgehog, an urchin, since it also has spines for protection. It is more or less spherical with the only edible part the five orange or rose-coloured ovaries inside, also known as corals. On Orkney, where they call it a 'scarriman's heid' (tramp with unruly hair), there is a tradition of eating the corals as a spread on bread instead of butter. This is a different species to the main edible sea urchin of the Mediterranean, where it is common to see basketfuls on display in markets for sale.

Size: It is a grapefruit-shaped round and can grow up to 8 cm.

Spawning Habits: in the spring.

Other Shellfish Recipes

FRUITS OF THE SEA

Shellfish traders in Scotland wish more Scots ate more shellfish in the shell. Other Europeans have no inhibitions about eating unshelled shellfish. They know how to make the most of its unique flavours, and attractive shapes and colours, by letting it speak for itself in a stunning display on a large tray of crushed ice raised up on a *fruit de mer* stand.

2-3 kg/4½-6½ lbs mixed shellfish, cooked in the shell (but
  including some raw oysters)
1 large round metal tray filled with crushed ice

1 *fruit de mer* stand (available from cookshops)
Bowl of halved lemons
Finger bowls

4–6 servings

To prepare

Pile the shellfish on top of the ice on the tray. Place stand in the centre of the table and put tray on top. Serve with shellfish crackers and lobster forks for picking. Provide plates for shellfish debris and finger bowls with wedges of lemon.

SHELLFISH BROTH

The smaller shellfish have such diverse shapes and colours, from dark-blue mussels to rusty-red squat lobsters, that a simple assembly plainly boiled in their cooking liquor is all that is necessary.

Serving can be done in two ways. Either pile all the shellfish in a very large ashet in the centre of the table and serve the broth separately in a tureen with a ladle, or arrange the shellfish in large, round, deep Scottish soup plates (or equivalent) and pour over the hot broth just before serving.

Served at the Oxford Symposium on Food and Cookery (1998) as a starter to a Scottish Feast.

2 kg/4½ lb mixed shellfish in the shell
25g/1 oz butter
1 large onion, finely chopped
Chopped parsley
Ground pepper

Serves 4

Selection of shellfish from the following:

(1) **Mussels, cockles, razor clams** – Clean well, remove beards, scrape shells if necessary.

(2) Norway lobster, squat lobster – Wash well.

To cook the shellfish

Put the mussels into a pan with about 1 cm/½ in of boiling water in the bottom. Cover and keep moving till they open, then remove from the heat. Cover and keep warm. Cook the cockles/razor clams in the same way – reserve cooking liquid, strain and keep warm.

Cook langoustine (4-5 minutes) and squat lobster (2 minutes) in boiling water, Strain and reserve liquid and keep warm.

To make the broth

Melt the butter in a large pot and when hot add the onion, cook till yellow and soft. Adjust the cooking liquid from the shellfish to make up to 1.2 L/2 pints. Some will be saltier than others, so balance the combination accordingly, adding more water if too salty. Bring up to the boil and add half the chopped parsley.

To serve

Arrange the shellfish in large deep plates or in a large tureen. Pour over hot cooking liquid. Finish by throwing a handful of freshly chopped parsley over the shellfish and serve.

SHELLFISH SAUCE
for serving with all cold shellfish

Leftover shells still hold an amazing amount of hidden flavour, which can be extracted by making this aromatic sauce to serve with any cold shellfish.

For the stock:
1.5 kg/3 lb 5 oz crustacean shells (lobster, crab, squat lobster, velvet crab, Norway lobster, Northern prawn)
2-3 tablespoons oil
2-3 tablespoons cognac

2-3 tablespoons dry white wine
250 ml/8 fl oz fish stock or water
Cream or butter to finish sauce
Salt and freshly ground black pepper

To make

Heat the oil and sauté the shells for about 5 minutes. With the blunt end of a rolling pin or other suitable instrument crush the shells quite finely. Add the cognac, flame and then add the white wine followed by the fish stock or water. Add enough water to just cover. Simmer for 20 minutes.

Strain through a strainer, pressing the shells firmly with the back of a spoon to press through all the flavour. Return stock to the pan and reduce to required consistency. It can be stored for future use or finished with some cream and or butter. Add gradually to prevent sauce separating. Serve with simply cooked shellfish.

ORKNEY SQUID

Good supplies of small, tender squid are available in Orkney. These are lightly cooked in this rich tomato sauce and colourfully finished with parsley and chives. Unless squid are very large, they cook as soon as they have heated through. Cooking for longer toughens them. Serve with a beremeal bannock for a unique taste of the islands.

4 small squid, with or without tentacles, cleaned
2 tablespoons oil
1 medium onion, finely chopped
4-5 large tomatoes, skinned and chopped
1 clove of garlic, crushed
3 tablespoons red wine
Salt and pepper

1 tablespoon chopped parsley

4 servings

To cook

Leave squid whole or cut into rings. Heat the oil in a pan and add the onion. Cook till soft then add the tomatoes and reduce slightly. Add the wine and garlic. Simmer for a few minutes to blend the flavours. Season. Add the squid and heat through. Stir in parsley. Serve with a toasted beremeal bannock (see p.18).

(From Norma Hasham, Foveran Hotel in Kirkwall, 1984.)

SEAWEEDS

In the North, and in many other places on the coast of this country, people feed upon Sloke, that is, the sea lettuce; they make Broath with it, and sometimes serve it up with butter. Some of them eat dils; ... and some eat that sort of Sea Tangle. It is a pleasant taste betwixt salt and sweet; it's eaten as a salade.

R. Sibbald, *Provision for the Poor in Time of Dearth and Scarcity,* Edinburgh, 1709.

Wet and slippery on seaside rocks, seaweeds provide a lively taste of the sea. 'Dulse and Tangel' was a favourite Leith street-cry over a hundred years ago. Around the coastal areas of the Highlands and Islands there is also evidence of widespread use of seaweed, with twenty-two recorded Gaelic names for it. Gathered from the foreshore, it was used to flavour traditional broths and add valuable nutrients such as amino acids, vitamins, minerals and iodine. Dulse was popular in broths but was also eaten raw by children. In the Hebrides the blade of sea-tangle, or redware, was cut from the fronds and stalk and roasted on both sides over embers, then eaten crumbled over a buttered barley bannock.

Orientals make the most of seaweed, doing inventive things like changing the thin, slippery fronds of sloke, which they call *nori*, into crinkly, black, paper-thin sheets which look and feel nothing like the real thing. Everyone eats it. The same nori can be found in Wales and the West Country, not in thin, dry sheets but made into a black jelly known as laverbread, sold from bowls which sit amongst the fresh fish on fishmongers' slabs in Welsh towns. 'Words cannot describe how wonderful laverbread is,' says Jackie Geer, in *The Best of Breakfasts, Recipes from Radio 4's 'On your Farm'*. 'Rolled in oatmeal and fried in bacon fat – a true gastronomic experience.'

Seaweed is nutritionally very low in fat, almost calorie-free, while at the same time containing more minerals than any other kind of food. It is high in potassium iodide. Approximately 30% of the mineral content is lost to the soaking water, so use this water as well whenever possible.

Gathering/Buying/Drying

In the yearly rhythm of the seasons, gathering wild seaweed begins after the frosts of winter have sweetened the sloke. As the days lengthen, new fronds start growing and there is the first harvest of sea moss (Irish carrageen) and kelp (Japanese kombu) to be taken. Soon after, there is a supply of the kelps to dry and store for winter use. By early summer, there is the first picking of dulse and other varieties such as sea lettuce, pepper dulse and the wracks, which all come ready in their own time throughout the summer. Then in the autumn there are second flushes of sea moss and dulse.

Some seaweed can be easily picked as the tide goes out, but many grow at the lowest tidal mark, or below it in the sub-tidal area. More of this area is uncovered when there is a low, or 'spring', tide and the sea comes up higher (springs) and goes down lower. The opposite tide is a neap tide, when the distance between low water and high water is shorter. Spring and neap tides alternate every two weeks, halfway through each phase of a new moon, or lunar month

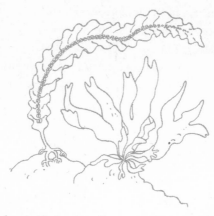

(28 days). A local tide book will give the exact tide times (see also *www.easytide.ukho.gov.uk*). The highest and lowest tides of the year are usually in February/March and September/October.

Seaweed Terms

Holdfast: the seaweed's 'root' which is attached to rock or shingle etc.

Stipe: the seaweed's 'stem' which extends from the holdfast.

Frond: the seaweed's 'leaf' which extends from the stipe.

Seaweeds have seasons of growth like other plants. They produce shoots and should be harvested before they become fertile, when they build up a bitter content which makes the flavour harsh. The season is spring to autumn. Remove the overlying seaweed and gather the tiny plants from beneath. Do not take too far down the stem, so that enough is left for the weed to regenerate. Commercial divers harvest autumn dulse, pepper dulse, daberlocks, grockle, sugar ware, finger ware and sloke (wild nori). It is air-dried in a recirculating drying oven at a low heat to preserve the flavour but remove the moisture content. It is then packed in airtight packets.

Fresh gathered seaweed should be washed in running water to remove sand, shells, etc. It is easy to dry and store. Simply lay out in a good cold current of air till thoroughly dry and store in an airtight container. It may be dried in the sun.

Dried seaweed can be bought in specialist wholefood shops. Japanese or other Oriental food shops are the best source. Since it is light and cheap to post, mail order is also a good option (see **Buying Guide** p.441).

Carrageen
Sea Moss, Carrageen Moss or Irish Moss (*Chondrus crispus*)

This is named after the village of Carrageen near Waterford in Ireland, where it is particularly plentiful. Carrageen is high in vitamin A and iodine, and it also contains B vitamins and many minerals. It is an important source of vegetable gelatines (alginates) which are used commercially for thickening soups, emulsifying ice creams and setting jellies.

Identification

It usually grows on a boulder-strewn shore near the low-water mark of spring tides, so that sometimes it can be collected only about two hours each side of the low water for a few days each fortnight. Common around British coasts, it is often hidden in rock pools under larger brown seaweeds. Sometimes it is found on the midshore.

It is small, bushy and fan-shaped with flat branched fronds widening to rounded tips. It is between 7-15cm high. Its colours range from pink through red to dark purple. When it is under water its tips can have a violet iridescence.

Sustainable harvesting

In spring and early summer. With a sharp knife cut from the top half of the plant, leaving the remainder to regenerate. Avoid dislodging the holdfast or the plant will die. When dried in the open air its colour is bleached to a pale cream. The creamier it looks the less flavour and nutrients it will have.

Best used

As vegetable gelatine setting agent for non-acid liquids, sweet or savoury. For setting milk jellies, best served with an equal quantity of whipped cream and some acid fruit or a sharp jam or jelly. Also for thickening soups and stews. Boiled with milk and honey it is good for coughs and can also help to clear chest infections. As a milk jelly, it was also given as general healing food for invalids and old people and was once sold as an invalid food.

SEA MOSS (CARRAGEEN) JELLY

This was served in the Highlands with equal quantities of thick, whipped cream and sugar. It has a mild seaweed taste which some find appealing, while others prefer to mask it with stronger flavours. The Irish serve it with fruity jams or jellies. It was also made as an invalid pick-me-up or for old people with digestive problems, for whom it was thought to have particular healing qualities.

10 g/¼ oz dried sea moss, washed
1 L/1¾ pts milk
Sugar to taste
300 ml/½ pt double or whipping cream
1 teaspoon sugar
Jar of fruity jam or jelly

Serves 4

Cooking Sea Moss

Put it into a pan with the milk and bring to the boil. Simmer gently for about 10-15 minutes until it expands and the liquid starts to thicken. Add sugar to taste. Stir to dissolve. Strain through a fine sieve into a wetted glass serving dish, pressing all the jelly through the sieve with the back of a wooden spoon.

Setting and serving

Leave to cool and set. Add sugar to fresh cream and beat till stiff. Turn out the jelly onto a plate. The Irish sprinkle some soft brown sugar over the jelly. It can be served with equal quantities of whipped cream and a pot of fruity jam or jelly.

To add an egg

Beat the egg in a bowl and sieve the cooked mixture onto it. Return to the pan and cook over a very low heat to thicken, stirring all the time. Remove, and pour into the glass serving dish. The egg can be separated and the yolk added before thickening the mixture and the white beaten till stiff and folded through once it has cooled a little. This makes a lighter-textured jelly.

Sea Moss: for thickening soups and stews

To add to soups and stews, soak in cold water for a few minutes and remove from the water, leaving behind the grit etc.; chop the carrageen finely or put some of the soup or stew liquid into a liquidiser with the carrageen and blend till smooth. While carrageen thickens a soup or stew, its delicate flavour is obscured by stronger flavours.

Dulse
(*Palmaria palmate*)

Found on both sides of the North Atlantic. Traditionally eaten in Scotland, Ireland, Greenland, Norway, France, the Faroe Islands, eastern Siberia and along the eastern coast of New England and Canada. It grows along the lower tidal area on rocks, and on other seaweeds, especially the tougher kelps.

Identification

It is a small, dark reddish-maroon coloured seaweed with leathery fronds, between 15-30cm high. When dried it is a lighter colour. It has a salty-savoury, slightly spicy flavour. It is a good source of minerals, vitamins and trace elements, and is relatively low in sodium and high in potassium. It has the highest concentration of iron in any edible food source, as well as being rich in potassium and magnesium.

Sustainable harvesting

With a sharp knife, cut off the top half of the plant so there is enough left for the plant to regenerate quickly. Its holdfast, which attaches it to rocks and other seaweeds, is not strongly attached, so care is needed to prevent dislodging it while cutting. It is one of the most commercially harvested seaweeds. Sold dried in packets as a pliable bundle of leaves. Some are more tender than others.

Uses

Dulse has a stronger flavour than carrageen and it combines well with lamb and with most root vegetables. It has an affinity with white fish like haddock, cod and whiting, rather than the stronger-flavoured oily fish, and is good with shellfish, particularly sliced very finely in accompanying salads. It is also good added to Stovies. Soak for 15 minutes then drain. Chop finely and add with the potatoes and meat (recipe p.250). It can also be used as seasoning condiment in soups, stews, mashed potatoes, stir-fries, salads, scrambled eggs, oatcakes, bannocks and soda breads. This is the seaweed Scots like to chew for its pungent flavour. It is an eating experience which may begin in childhood while beachcombing with parents who encourage seaweed-eating, when a lifelong liking is established.

Pepper Dulse
(*Osmundea pinnatifida*)

Found on many shorelines with wave-exposed rocky habitats around British coasts. It can be found from low tide to midshore.

Identification

Plants found higher up the shore are smaller and lighter in colour, while nearer low tideline they are reddish-brown and may be 8 cm long. As its name suggests it has a peppery flavour. Nutritional content: little research done.

Sustainable Harvesting

Spring and early summer. With a sharp knife, cut the top half of the plant so there is enough left for the plant to regenerate quickly. Its holdfast, which attaches it to rocks and other seaweeds, is not strongly attached, so care is needed to prevent dislodging it while cutting.

Best Used

As for dulse.

Tangle, Sugar Kelp
(*Saccharina latissima*)

Found on most shorelines with rocky habitats around British coasts. Another of the large leathery seaweeds which grow below the low tidemark in colonies known as kelp forests.

Identification

It has a long sandy-yellow to olive-brown frond, several inches wide, with slightly frilled edges, giving it a crinkly appearance. May be between 2-4 m in length. It has a short thin stipe less than 60 cm long and a small holdfast which is easily torn off rocks in stormy weather. The fronds contain a wide range of minerals, vitamins and trace elements as well as a high level of iodine, so should not be eaten in large quantities.

Sustainable harvesting

In spring from March to June, when new young shoots can be cut, as long as the holdfast is not pulled off so it can regenerate. Older plants later in the year get battered by storms and go yellow at the edges.

Best used

To make soup stock (as in Japanese Dashi) also in all bean stews to improve flavour and reduce cooking time. Also dried and crushed as a condiment. Because of its sweeter taste it can also be added to biscuits, cakes and tarts.

DULSE BROTH
with lamb or mutton

Purple autumn dulse adds its unique tang to this broth.

1.5 kg/3 lb 5 oz neck or shoulder lamb or mutton, or 500 g/1 lb 2 oz Shetland reestit mutton
3 L/5½ pts cold water
1 whole onion stuck with 3 or 4 whole cloves
Sprigs of parsley stalks, thyme, celery stalk and leek green tied in a bundle with cotton thread
Bay leaf
20 g/1 oz dried autumn dulse, cut up finely with scissors
2 onions, finely chopped
8 medium potatoes, thinly sliced
4 carrots, grated
4 celery stalks, grated or diced finely
Salt and pepper
1-2 tablespoons chopped parsley

Serves 6–8

Making the broth

Put the meat into a large pot and add the water. Bring slowly to the boil and skim. Turn down the heat and add the onion and herbs. Cook at a gentle simmer till the meat is tender and falling off the bones. Strain into a bowl. Leave the meat to cool. Remove excess surface fat.

Cooking the vegetables

Heat the fat taken off the top of the stock over a medium heat in the pot. When hot, add the onions. Cook till they are translucent and soft, stirring occasionally. Add the other vegetables stir and continue cooking for about 5 minutes, with the lid on, stirring occasionally. Add the dulse. Pour over the hot broth. Simmer till the vegetables are tender.

To finish

Cut all the edible meat from the lamb/mutton and add to the broth. Taste and season. Serve with parsley in heated bowls or deep soup plates. Eat with bannocks or oatcakes.

HEBRIDEAN DULSE BROTH

A simpler, meatless version is made in the Hebrides using cooked potatoes, peeled, drained, mashed and beaten with butter and milk. The dulse is chopped and cooked separately in water for about 10 minutes, then the dulse, and its cooking liquor, is beaten into the creamed potatoes to make a thick-soup-cum-brose consistency. Season to taste and serve in heated bowls with a knob of butter in each bowl.

DULSE CAKES

I first came across this idea in Roger Phillips' *Wild Food* (1983) but have used Scottish yellow turnips rather than the parsnips which he suggests.

250 g/9 oz carrots
250 g/9 oz yellow turnip or swede, or parsnip
75 g/3 oz rolled oats
25 g/1 oz dulse
2 tablespoons olive oil
Salt and pepper

To cook

Boil the carrots and turnip/parsnip in water till tender, drain and mash together.

Rinse the dulse and then steep in cold water for 10 minutes.

Drain (reserve the liquid for soups) and chop finely. Add to rolled oats, mix thoroughly. Put half this mixture into the vegetables, season and mix in. Shape into four round cakes. Coat with remaining oat/dulse mixture, fry on both sides in hot oil till lightly brown.

Serve as a vegetable with roast lamb or as a vegetarian dish with cheese.

Sloke (Scots, Irish), Welsh Laver, Japanese Nori *(Porphyra linearis)*

Found on many shorelines with rocky habitats around British coasts but especially on the west coast. It grows at most levels of the beach on rough-surfaced rocks and boulders, on mussels, and can almost cover concrete breakwaters. It looks like a black plastic bag which has melted. There are over a hundred species worldwide with around 6-8 species identified round British coasts, some which are very similar. They form large, thin-lobed sheets attached to the rocks by a very small disc. The species vary in colour from brown to purple to greenish. Do not use the common green variety, which is bitter. In Japan it is cultivated.

Identification

Very delicate, almost transparent frond with irregular edges. It is greenish when young, turning to brownish-purple and chocolate-black when ready to harvest. It is around 20-30 cm long and 10 cm across. It has the highest amount of protein compared with other seaweeds (37%) and has a good balance of minerals and trace elements and is especially rich in B, C and E vitamins. It is low in iodine.

Sustainable harvesting

After the first winter frosts in November or December until April. Pluck a small amount from each rock or boulder, leaving plenty to regenerate.

Best used

In Wales it is boiled to a puree (laverbread) and is sold in tubs fresh in Welsh fishmongers, markets and health-food stores. This is used rolled in, or mixed with, oatmeal, to make lavercakes.

TO MAKE A PURÉE
(Welsh Laverbread)

Rinse the seaweed well to remove all sand and dirt, then steep overnight in fresh water with a handful of salt. Drain. Put in a pan with seawater to cover and add some dripping or butter. Bring to the boil and simmer gently, beating well, and it will, like spinach, reduce to a pulp. It should simmer gently for several hours to reduce, when it will turn a very dark and glossy greenish-black. Season according to taste with pepper and more butter, some vinegar, orange or lemon juice – salt may not be needed – and serve hot or cold as a piquant flavouring for mashed potatoes and roast meats.

Welsh lavercakes: Mix 225 g/8 oz laverbread with 3-4 table-spoons oatmeal and fry in spoonfuls in bacon fat. Serve with fried bacon and cockles.

3: GAME & POULTRY

Game

Game was so plentiful, red deer, roe, hares, grouse, ptarmigan and partridge; the river provided trout and salmon, the different lochs pike and char; the garden abounded in common fruits and common vegetables; cranberries and raspberries ran over the country, and the poultry yard was ever well furnished.

Elizabeth Grant of Rothiemurchus, *Memoirs of a Highland Lady*, 1797-1827

The days of plentiful game were coming to an end by the time Elizabeth Grant was writing these memoirs. No longer a common food of the people, as it had been since the first settlers arrived in Scotland some ten thousand years ago, game was soon to achieve gourmet status for those who could afford it. Until the late 1700s, it had been an essential part of the diet of poor, as Sir Frederic Eden says in *The State of the Poor* (1797): 'There is no restraint, but 'tis every man's own that can kill it'.

There was 'restraint', though, when large areas of the Highlands became fishing and shooting retreats following the purchase of the Balmoral estate in the mid-1800s by Queen Victoria and Prince Albert. From now on the role of one of the country's most valuable food assets would be reversed, as it became illegal to shoot or catch it. Only those daring, and cunning, enough to avoid capture could now enjoy what had been part of their diet for thousands of years.

This is a legacy from the past which game-dealers and butchers have been working hard to undo and they have now succeeded in supplying a much greater variety of game to Scots consumers. It provides exciting meat for the cook. In sharp contrast to the more predictable flavours of domestic meat and poultry, it has a huge range of subtle flavours, reflecting the game animal's varied diet. In Scotland there is so much land that is free from urban pollution that the quality and range of native game is unrivalled.

Venison

. . . Dined sumptuously upon venison, a piece of Roe, dressed partly in Collops with sauce, and partly on the grid-iron.
Robert Forbes, *Diaries*, 1708-1775

Venison was the original term for the flesh of all animals and birds which were hunted, coming from Latin *venatio*, to hunt. The change in meaning seems to have been gradual over several centuries, until sometime in the 1800s, when it was exclusively applied to meat from any kind of deer.

Hunting deer on foot through rough grass, heather moors, peat bogs and rocky mountains accompanied by a local gamekeeper known as a 'stalker' – Prince Albert's favourite pursuit at Balmoral – continues on large areas of the Highlands. The deer are culled in the wild and gralloched (innards removed immediately) then transported on ponies to a collection point, where they are then transported in refrigerated vehicles to a production unit where they are skinned, inspected by a vet and hung (time depends on temperature and humidity) before being butchered into cuts.

Most Scottish wild venison was exported to Germany during the second half of the 1900s, but this has been reversed and domestic consumption is now increasing. More commercial operators in the game industry in Scotland have begun to tackle the problem of quality, which is largely to do with improving the handling and transport of deer which are not killed in the sterile environment of an abattoir. Management of deer in the wild is also important to quality, so that only animals which are in prime condition are culled for domestic consumption. More effort on this front has improved the reputation of wild venison, while there has also been more effort to market venison locally.

The Deer Commission for Scotland – now merged with Scottish Natural Heritage – is responsible for controlling the numbers of all wild deer on the hills and deciding on the annual cull. The largest herds are of Red deer; Roe deer are sold commercially in much smaller numbers, and there are a few small herds of Sika deer. There are even fewer fallow deer.

Farmed Venison

This is the modern equivalent of the early Deer Parks which controlled stocks and allowed for selective breeding. While there are a number of farms in Scotland which keep some deer, only a few are actively selling the meat commercially. The herds of deer on these farms are fairly small, so that the impact on the game market is not great. Scottish members of the British Deer Farmers Association may sell their venison to the Deer Producers Society who retail it for them, but it is also available at the farms, with some of them, like Reediehill in Auchtermuchty, developing a considerable trade for both raw meat and processed venison products.

Like farmed salmon, the meat from farmed deer should not be compared with the wild variety. The main differences are in flavour and texture. Grass-fed farmed venison is milder and the meat usually more tender, since they are all shot young. Farmed venison has the advantage of predictability for the cook but lacks the character of wild, which has the more complex flavour in the meat of animals which have foraged in a natural mountain environment.

Red Deer

The commonest variety in Scotland inhabits rough, wild, hill country. A stag weighs about 14-16 stone (cleaned): a hind 7½-11 stone.

Scottish season for stags – 1 July-20 October; **for hinds** – 21 October-15 February.

Best time for eating stags – early autumn; **for hinds** – November to mid-January.

Roe Deer

Inhabits forests, weighs about 4 stone.

Scottish season for bucks – 1 May-20 October; **for does** – 21 October-28/29 February.

Best time for eating bucks – October; **for does** – December to February.

Fallow Deer

Inhabits forests and parklands, weighs about 12 stone.

Scottish season for bucks – 1 August-30 April; **for does** – 21 October-15 February.

Best time for eating bucks – October to November; **for does** – December to February.

Sika Deer

Stag weighs 6-7 stone: hind 4½-5 stone.

Scottish season for stags – 1 August-30 April; **for hinds** – 21 October-15 February.

Hanging/Buying/Gameyness

Deer must be skinned soon after they are shot, then hung in a cool place so that the surface of the carcass is properly sealed. If this is done correctly, the meat can be hung for several weeks without going 'moochie' (mouldy from warmth and/or damp), until tender.

Age and hanging time greatly affect venison meat. Older animals will be tough, sometimes very tough, and dry. Butcher/game-dealers should be knowledgeable about the animal's history so they can advise on the likely tenderness of the meat. On well-run estates, such as the Dalhousie estate in Angus, the local butcher/game-dealer, Bruce Brymer of Brechin, is invited every year for a day's shooting, when he can see for himself the care and attention which is given to handling the carcass. He gets his estate venison when it has been hung for about a week, then he will hang it for another two to three weeks when the joints will be in prime condition. Well dried-out and 'sitting up like a good piece of beef', it will have been tenderised by enzyme action and developed a rich, gamey flavour. Gameyness is increased the longer the meat is hung and is a matter of taste. The advantage for the cook of well-hung game is its tenderness. The meat should be a dark crimson colour with pure white fat. A good covering of fat signals an animal in prime condition.

Cooking/Marinating

'Cooking large game, either wild or farmed is easy,' says Janie Hibler, in *Wild About Game* (1998), 'because there are only two basic rules to follow.

Rule 1: The tender cuts – that is the meat farthest away from the head and feet: the loin, tenderloin, steaks and chops – are cooked **hot and fast**. Without the fat layers to cook through, the heat penetrates through the muscle, cooking the meat to rare or medium rare in just minutes and minimising the loss of juices. When game meat is over-cooked, the connective tissue in the muscle contracts, squeezing out all the juices, making the meat dry and tough.

Rule 2: The tougher cuts – or those closest to the head and feet, the neck, shoulder, chuck and shank – are cooked **slow and low**.'

According to these rules, the upper part of the Haunch or Leg is a prime cut for roasting or slicing into collops (steaks). The Saddle is also a prime cut for roasting and it includes the fillets. The Saddle may be divided into loin chops for frying or grilling. The Flank may be boiled or stewed or minced for sausages. The Shoulder may be cut up and stewed or braised in a piece. The Neck may be stewed or boiled for soup. The Head may be used for broth. A good Liver is a great delicacy and can be fried or used for a venison haggis along with the Heart and Flank. Kidneys may be fried. Venison Tripe has very good flavour but must be removed from the animal and washed out thoroughly within half an hour of killing, otherwise the stomach continues to digest the contents and the flavour of the tripe is spoiled. This can be difficult if the beast has been shot on top of a mountain – farmed deer do not cause the same problem.

Marinating adds flavour to the meat while at the same time making the muscle tissues absorb more moisture. This is a slow process, so the meat needs to be in the marinade for at least a couple of hours. Acid in the marinade weakens the muscle tissue and makes it more tender.

BRAISED RED DEER
with Sloe Gin

This blend of sloes, juniper, gin and gamey wild venison is a heady mix. It's a method for mature venison and for the cuts which are less tender, requiring slow-and-low cooking such as shoulder, neck and shank. While this can also be made with a more convenient boned and rolled joint, cooking on the bone adds to the flavour.

50 g/2 oz butter, duck or goose fat
400 g/14 oz streaky bacon, chopped
3 onions, finely chopped
1 head celery, sliced
6 medium carrots, peeled and sliced
1 tablespoon crushed juniper berries
2.25 kg/5 lb shoulder, shank, neck
150 ml/¼ pt sloe gin
Salt and freshly ground black pepper
Water or stock
Rowan jelly

6–8 servings

Preheat the oven to 300F/150C/130Cfan/Gas 2.

Use a large sturdy roasting tin which can be heated on the hob or a large cast-iron pot which will go into the oven and will contain the meat snugly.

Browning the vegetables

Melt the butter or fat in the roasting tin or pot and add the bacon. Fry till it just begins to crisp. Add the onion and continue to cook till it has softened and is lightly browned. Add the celery, carrots and juniper and continue to cook for another five minutes, stirring occasionally.

Cooking the meat

Nestle the meat in among the vegetables. Add the sloe gin and enough water or stock to come halfway up the meat. Set the pan over a high heat till the liquid comes to the boil. Cover the roasting tin (or the heavy pot) with a double layer of foil. Place the lid on the pot, twisting the foil down the sides of the pot to stop moisture escaping. Put into the oven and cook for about 3-3½ hours, testing for tenderness after 2 hours. It is ready when the meat comes away easily from the bone.

Finishing the dish

Slice the meat and serve with the vegetables, pan juices, a pot of mashed potatoes and rowan jelly.

ROAST RACK OF VENISON

1 x 8-rib rack of young venison
3 tablespoons oil
1 tablespoon thyme and marjoram leaves
50 g/2 oz butter, melted
150 ml/5 fl oz robust red wine
150 ml/5 fl oz game stock or water
Salt and freshly ground pepper
Rowan jelly

4 servings

Hot-and-fast roasting on the rib bones means that the meat has its own built-in protection: preventing it drying out while also improving the flavour. For juicy, flavourful meat it must be cooked either rare or medium rare. The butcher will prepare a rack for roasting.

Preheat the oven 425F/220C/200Cfan/Gas 7.

Use a sturdy roasting tin or frying pan which is ovenproof and an instant-read internal thermometer.

Roasting

Blot the surface of the venison dry. Heat the oil in an ovenproof frying pan or roasting tin over medium-high heat until very hot. Add the rack and brown meat, turning with tongs till a deep brown – 8 to 10 minutes. Place the rack, bone side down, and pour melted butter over upper surface. Season with salt and herbs. Allow a roasting time of 12-13 minutes per 450g/1 lb for rare, 15-16 minutes medium rare. Remove from the oven about halfway through the roasting and baste the meat.

To check for doneness more accurately, use an instant-read internal thermometer. Roast until it reaches 54C for rare or 57C for medium rare. Remove, place on a warmed ashet or serving platter, cover with foil and leave the meat to rest for 10 minutes in a warm place when the meat will go on cooking, increasing its temperature by 2C.

Making the gravy

Put roasting tin or pan over a low heat and add the red wine. Scrape up all the residues from the roast and simmer to reduce and concentrate the flavours. Add the stock and continue reducing and stirring. Some juices will, by now, have dripped out of the rack and should be poured into the gravy. When it has a good consistency, season with salt and pepper.

Carving and serving

Carve down the rib bones, serve with gravy, creamy mashed potatoes and rowan jelly.

VENISON PASTY
with port and mushrooms

A modern pasty is made of what does not roast well, as the neck, the breast, the shoulder. The breast makes the best pasty.
Meg Dods, *Cook and Housewives Manual*, 1826.

Added pork fat is sometimes advised with lean venison, but Meg Dods suggests lamb or mutton fat which adds more flavour than pork. Mushrooms have a natural affinity with venison.

2 tablespoons oil
1 onion, finely chopped
750 g/1 lb 10 oz breast or shoulder of venison, diced
100 g/3½ oz firm fat from the neck or leg of lamb or mutton, finely diced
200 g/6 oz mushrooms
Salt, freshly ground pepper
½ teaspoon ground mace
½ teaspoon ground allspice
75 ml/3 fl oz venison stock or water
75 ml/3 fl oz port
1 tablespoon wine vinegar
200 g/6 oz puff pastry
For brushing – 1 egg yolk, 1 teaspoon water

4-6 servings

Preheat the oven to 400F/200C/180Cfan/Gas 6 for the first 20 minutes. Then turn down oven and cook for a further 1½–2 hours at 325F/160C/140Cfan/Gas 3.

Use a 1.2 L/2 pt pie dish and pie funnel or small cup upturned.

Cooking the meat

Heat the oil in a pan and brown the onions. Add the meat and fat. Brown lightly. Add the mushrooms and continue to cook over a low heat for another few minutes till the mushrooms soften. Mix in the seasonings, then add the stock, port and vinegar. Put the pie funnel in the centre of the pie dish and pour the mixture into the pie dish. Leave to cool.

Making the pasty

Roll out the pastry about 2.5 cm/1 in wider than the rim of the dish. Place pie dish on top of pastry and cut round. Wet the pie dish edge and place extra strip round the edge. Press well. Wet the pastry edge and place the oval piece of pastry on top. Press to seal the edge. Decorate the edge and also the top of the pastry with scraps made into leaves. Make two holes for steam to escape. Brush with egg yolk and bake at the high temperature to puff up the pastry then reduce to the lower temperature to cook the meat. Cover the pastry with foil if it is browning too much. If necessary, fill up the pasty with hot stock or water through one of the holes before serving.

VENISON LIVER

A gamekeeper all his life, Peter MacIntosh, of Braemar and Knoydart, knew how to judge a good liver. The innards are the keeper's perk and he would fry only the best (the quality of the liver is a good guide to the health of the animal and is judged by a vet before the carcass is exported). But Peter's test of quality was to put his first finger and thumb on either side of the liver and press together. If there was too much resistance then the liver would be tough to eat. But if finger and thumb came together easily then it was good for frying. His wife had died and he was no longer stalking the high hills but lived alone in a remote bothy on the Knoydart estate at the head of Loch Nevis, watching the salmon river for poachers and cooking for himself. His timing was always perfect and the liver served up just pink in the middle and well browned and crisp on the outside. He ate it with oatcakes and butter for high tea or for breakfast with crisp fried bacon.

4 rashers of bacon
4 slices venison liver about 1 cm/½ in thick
3 tablespoons milk
1 tablespoon seasoned flour

To cook

Put the bacon into a hot pan and fry till crisp. Remove and keep warm. Meanwhile soak the liver for a few minutes in milk, drain and coat in seasoned flour. Fry very quickly on both sides in hot bacon fat. Serve with the bacon and toast or oatcakes and butter.

POCA BUIDHE (Yellow Bag) VENISON TRIPE

Venison tripe
4-5 medium onions, sliced thinly
125 g/4 oz butter
125 g/4 oz flour
1 L/1¾ pt milk
salt and ground pepper

This was another of Peter's favourites which bears no resemblance to cow's tripe. It looks more like a mushroom stew, but with its own distinctive flavour. This recipe is from another nose-to-tail game cook, Mary Holmes, who taught me how to make it and encouraged me to serve it on the hotel menu as 'Pocha Buidhe', translated – for those who asked – as a 'local venison dish'.

To prepare the tripe

The tripe must be cleaned immediately after the deer has been gralloched on the hill (see p.147). It should then be soaked for 24 hours in cold salted water. Rinse out thoroughly under a running tap and then simmer for 6-8 hours in plenty of water.

To make pocha buidhe

Drain and cut tripe into 2.5 cm/1-inch squares. Fry the onions in butter till soft and yellow. Add the flour and cook for a few minutes. Gradually add the milk, then the tripe and seasoning, and simmer for about an hour, adding more milk if necessary. Serve with a pile of hot buttered toast.

Red Grouse
(*Lagopus Scoticus*)

Nothing is better for a spartan lunch by the spring on a hill-side than half a cold grouse with oat-cake, and a beaker or two of whisky and water.

A.I. Shand, *Shooting*, 1902.

Red grouse live on the high heather moors eating, besides heather, a number of other herbs and grasses which give them their special flavour. Native to Scottish moors, they are wild birds and cannot be hand-reared, though their survival can be protected by human 'management' of their native habitat. To create a mosaic of heather plants at various stages of growth as the grouse habitat, different areas of the hill are burnt each year to help the heather regenerate. This system provides a good supply of young shoots, important for their diet, plus older, well-grown heather as cover for their nests. Availability is variable depending on how well grouse moors have been managed, and the weather. Cold, wet conditions when the young chicks are vulnerable lead to fatalities. Grouse-shooting parties are usually highly organised, with groups of beaters driving the birds forward towards the guns.

Also in the grouse family are black grouse (blackcock); wood or great grouse (capercaillie); and the white grouse (ptarmigan). The blackcock's habitat can be threatened by intensive land development, draining and forest clearance, and therefore needs careful management, which can include controlled shooting. For a number of environmental reasons, the Scottish population of capercaillie of around 10,000 pairs in the 1960s declined to fewer than 1,000 birds by the end of the century. Though it was in danger of extinction, it is now making a modest recovery, but it is unlikely to become a target for shooting parties in the foreseeable future. Ptarmigan inhabit the rocky mountain tops and are elusive and rare birds which are only shot if there is an obvious surplus.

Season – 12 August to 10 December.

Judging age

One method is to look at the two outer primary feathers. If the bird is young they will be pointed, whereas old birds have more rounded, tattered and sometimes faded feathers.

Another method which is recommended by the Game Conservancy is the Bursa test. The Bursa is a blind-ended passage on the upper side of the vent. In all young game birds it becomes much reduced or may close completely when the bird reaches sexual maturity. The presence of a normal Bursa is a certain test for a young bird. Insert a matchstick which has been burnt at one end, so that it is narrow but not too sharp, or a quill.

Yet another guide is to look at the claws. Adult grouse shed their nails between July and September so that if a nail is in the process of shedding then it is an old bird. If it has already been shed there may be a transverse ridge where the old nail was attached, though this may fade after a month or two, which again indicates an old bird.

Hanging

Young birds are often shot and eaten the same day (as they are at the opening of the grouse season on the Glorious Twelfth of August). Game enthusiasts do not recommend this practice, arguing that there is no real grouse flavour when they are so fresh. Among those of this opinion was Winston Churchill, who on one occasion refused to eat grouse caught and served up for him on the twelfth of August. However, they should not be hung for more than 2-4 days, depending on temperature and humidity. Their distinctive flavour is lost if they become too gamey.

ROAST YOUNG GROUSE

4 young grouse approx 600 g/1 lb 5 oz each
Salt and freshly ground black pepper
6 tablespoons duck fat or lard
4 slices of bread
125 g/4 oz softened butter

4 servings

This is the hot-and-fast method, which only works if the grouse is young and tender. To judge the grouse's age see p.158.

Preheat the oven to 450F/230C/210Cfan/Gas 8.

Use an ovenproof frying pan or sauté pan and an instant-read thermometer.

Preparing the grouse

Heat 5 tablespoonfuls of the duck fat or lard in a large, ovenproof frying pan or sauté pan over a high heat. Meanwhile season the grouse inside and out with salt and pepper. When the fat is very hot add the grouse, first lying them on their sides to brown the legs. Turn the heat down to medium and fry gently for about 2 minutes, then turn the birds onto the other legs and repeat for another 2 minutes. Then turn onto the breasts and brown for about 1 minute. Finally turn onto the backs to finish the browning.

Roasting

Put into the oven and roast for 6 minutes. Remove from the oven and test for readiness by pressing with thumb and forefinger over the breast at the thickest part. It should feel firm with a slight 'give'. If it feels too soft, put it back in for another minute or two.

Using an instant-read thermometer, the internal temperature should reach 54C for rare or 57C for medium rare. Overcooked it will be dry and have lost its flavour. Place on their breasts on a heated serving dish, cover with foil and keep in a warm place for about 10 minutes to rest the meat. They will go on cooking in the latent heat and the internal temperature will increase by 2 degrees C.

Serving

Return the frying pan or sauté pan the birds were roasted in to a gentle heat and add the remaining duck fat or lard and the butter. Add the slices of bread and fry in the pan juices, turning once. Place each slice on the serving platter under the grouse. (Meg Dods, in 1826, served her grouse on 'buttered toast soaked

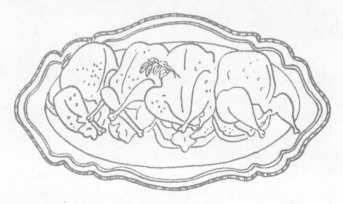

in the dripping pan' and recommends that the toast be sprinkled first with a little lemon juice.) If the livers and hearts are available they can also be fried in butter and spread on the bread.

Garnish with some watercress or rocket. Optional extras: **Bread Sauce** (see p.180), **Spiced Damsons** (see p.390), game chips (crisps).

The best way to appreciate all the complex flavours in different parts of the bird is to pick it up and chew off the bone. Serve with finger bowls.

GROUSE SOUP

But, oh! my dear North, what grouse-soup at Dalnacardoch. You smell it on the homeward hill, as if it were exhaling from the heather . . . As you enter the inn the divine afflatus penetrates your soul. When upstairs, perhaps in the garret, adorning for dinner, it rises like a cloud of rich distilled perfumes through every chink on the floor, every cranny of the wall.

Christopher North, *Noctes Ambrosianae*, 1822-35.

I make this with the debris from roast grouse or with older birds. This method can also be used for other game birds, singly or in combinations. It is certainly the best way to extract every last ounce of flavour from game bones and meat.

For the stock:
3 grouse (or the bones and legs from 4-6) or other game birds
2 L/3½ pts water or poultry stock
6 crushed juniper berries
Bundle of fresh herbs including parsley
2 sticks of celery
To finish the soup:
50 g/2 oz solidified fat from the stock or 2 tablespoons oil
25 g/1 oz butter
2 rashers of bacon, finely chopped

2 medium onions, finely chopped
4 stalks celery, finely diced
4 shallots, finely chopped
2 tablespoons long-grain polished rice, washed and drained

6–8 servings

Making the stock

Remove the breast meat from the grouse if using whole birds. Put the carcasses into a pan, cover with water/stock and add juniper berries, herbs and celery. Bring to the boil, cover and simmer gently for 1-2 hours. Strain, leave to cool and skim off any excess fat and reserve. Remove any edible meat from the carcasses and chop finely for adding to the broth at the end. Discard the remaining bones.

Finishing the soup

Melt the fat/oil and butter and cook the onions and bacon till lightly browned and crisp. Add the other vegetables and the rice. The grouse breast meat, chopped finely, may be added at this point or it may be kept for a separate dish. Cover and sweat over a very low heat for about five minutes, stirring occasionally.

Add the strained stock, bring to the boil and simmer until the vegetables are just tender and the rice cooked. If there is any other edible grouse meat from the carcasses, add at this point. Taste and season. Add parsley. Serve with boiled floury potatoes in their skins.

Pheasant

It was called the Phasian Bird when it lived beside the river Phasis near the Black Sea, but the Greeks took it to Rome and the Romans took it with them as their empire expanded, when it arrived in Britain. It does not frequent the high hills, or eat very much heather, so its flavour is milder and less distinctive than grouse.

If well hung, it has a mildly gamey flavour which becomes stronger, as it does with all game, when it is eaten cold. It is cheapest to buy during the height of the season and is more generally available than grouse since, unlike grouse, it can be hatched and reared in pens when young, then released into the wild.

Season – 1 October to 1 February.

Judging age

The Bursa test (p.158) can be applied to both the cock and hen bird. In young birds the Bursa will be approximately 2.5 cm/1 in. In old birds it may be closed completely.

Hanging

Pheasant should be hung by the head and the time will depend on the preferred taste, the age of the bird and also the weather. The longer it is hung the more its flavour develops. In cool, dry conditions it can be hung for up to two weeks. More mature birds become more tender the longer they are hung. Young birds can be hung for a shorter time, when their flavour will be less gamey.

ROAST PHEASANT
with fresh herbs

The secret of keeping this dry bird moist and succulent is to roast quickly and keep turning it in the oven so that it self-bastes. Most of the roasting time should be on its breast, so that the juices are running into it, rather than out. Ideally it should be roasted on a spit. All problems of basting and turning small game birds, which dry out so quickly in the hot oven, vanish if you are able to spit roast, while the results are the best ever.

1¼-1½ kg/2½-3 lb young pheasant
125 g/4 oz butter
4 large sprigs of parsley

4 sprigs of fresh tarragon
Sheet of fresh pork fat for barding or 2 rashers of bacon

2-3 servings

Preheat the oven to 375F/190C/170Cfan/Gas 5.

Use a small roasting tin with a rack and an instant-read internal thermometer.

Preparing the bird

Put two sprigs of parsley and two of tarragon in the cavity with about half of the butter. Spread the remaining butter over the breast. Put the remaining herbs on top and cover with pork fat or bacon rashers. Wind some strong thread round the fat or bacon to hold it in place.

Roasting

Put the pheasant on its side on a rack in a shallow roasting tin and roast for 10 minutes. Turn onto other side, baste and roast for another 10 minutes. Now turn onto its breast, baste and roast for about 20 minutes. Remove from the oven, take off the barding fat and return to the oven for another 5 minutes, placing it breast side up to brown the skin. It should take about 45 minutes in all. To test the pheasant for doneness, pierce the meat near the thigh and leg joint. If the juices which run out are pale pink the bird will be juicy but slightly underdone. If the

juices are clear then it is thoroughly done. This may take up to an hour, so be prepared to continue with the basting, since the breast meat loses its juices very quickly if overcooked.

Using an instant-read thermometer, the internal temperature should reach 54C for rare or 57C for medium rare. Overcooked it will be dry and have lost its flavour. Place on its breast on a heated serving dish, cover with foil and keep in a warm place for about 10 minutes to rest the meat. It will go on cooking in the latent heat and the internal temperature will increase by 2 degrees C.

Serve with gravy made from a reduction of the pan juices and a little stock or water and with some oyster mushrooms (ordinary ones will do if they are not available) sliced, sautéed in butter and garnished with some chopped parsley and tarragon.

BRAISED PHEASANT
with whisky and juniper

This method keeps the pheasant moist and succulent. It also adds some mellow whisky flavours from Auchentoshan, a Lowland malt. Peaty island malts are too strong for pheasant, but there are all the Speyside malts which should work well, also others such as the characterful Glenmorangie from Easter Ross.

2 tablespoons oil or butter
1 x 1¼-1½ kg/2½-3 lb pheasant
1 medium onion, finely chopped
125 ml/4 fl oz Auchentoshan whisky
150 ml/5 fl oz game stock or water
1 tablespoon juniper berries
125 ml/4 fl oz whipping cream
1 teaspoon lemon juice
Salt and pepper

2 servings

Preheat the oven to 375F/190C/170Cfan/Gas 5.

Use a cast-iron casserole with lid.

Braising the bird

Melt the fat in the pot and brown the pheasant on all sides. Remove and add onions and cook till golden brown. Return the pheasant to the pan and pour over half the whisky. Flame, and when the flames die down, add stock and juniper berries. Cover well, and bake in the oven for 45 minutes or until tender. Test after about 40 minutes, when the leg should come away easily. It could take up to an hour depending on the age of the bird. Remove the bird and cut into 4 joints (2 legs and 2 breasts).

Finishing the dish

Keep the joints warm and covered while finishing the sauce. Strain the sauce and then return to the cooking pot. Add the remaining whisky, cream and lemon juice and reduce to a good consistency. Taste and season. Return the pheasant to the sauce and serve.

Hare

Not so highly regarded as other game meat, yet Scottish hares which have exercised well on the mountains have a superb flavour. They need a 'slow-and-low' method of cooking which allows their rich flavour to develop to its full potential. Hare is available in season from game butchers or dealers.

Season – no close season, but may not be sold March to July inclusive. The best time for eating is October to January.

Judging age

A young hare will have soft thin ears which tear easily and white sharp teeth, whereas an older hare will have tougher ears and larger, yellower teeth. The coat of an older hare will be rougher.

Types

Brown Hare – weighs up to 3.5 kg/7 lb.

Mountain Hare or **Blue Hare** – weighs between 2-2.4 kg/5-6 lb. Regarded as the best-flavoured. It has the same open season as the Brown Hare but it is not suitable for roasting and should be stewed or braised or made into soup.

Hanging

Hares should be hung head downwards, ungutted, for 1-2 weeks, again depending on the weather, preferred taste and toughness of the hare. Place a bowl with a teaspoon of vinegar in it (this stops the blood congealing) underneath the head to catch the blood.

Skinning

Make a circular cut through the fur just above the back heel joints. Make a lengthwise cut along the inside of the leg on both sides and pull the skin off both legs. Tie the paws together and hang up somewhere. This is not essential but makes the skinning job easier and means that the blood is collecting at the top end and is therefore less likely to spill out all over the place when the belly is opened up.

Make a slit at the base of the tail from the top of one hind leg to the top of the other. Peel the skin back gently, turning it inside out and leaving the tail attached to the body. Now peel the skin down over the body and forelegs to the shoulders. Make a circular cut through the fur on the front legs just above the paws and then slit the skin along the inside of the leg. Peel back the skin on both legs. Peel the skin from the neck and then over the head as far as the ears, cut off the ears at the base and pull away the rest of the skin. It may be necessary to loosen round the eyes and mouth.

With a very sharp knife open up the belly. Draw out and discard all the intestines leaving the liver, heart, lungs and kidneys. Take out the kidneys; remove the liver carefully, remove the gall bladder and discard. Put the liver into a bowl with 1 teaspoon of vinegar. Position the bowl underneath the body and make a slit in the diaphragm at the base of the chest and allow the blood to run out. When you have collected the blood, pull out the heart and lungs and place in the bowl.

BAWD BREE

A mature, well-hung hare is essential for this traditional soup/ stew or 'mouthful soup' as it is aptly described in *The Household Book of Lady Grisell Baillie* (1692-1733). 'Bawd' is the old Scots word for hare and 'Bree' simply means gravy, juice or liquid in which something is cooked.

1 hare
2.75 L/5 pts cold water
Bundle of fresh herbs
50 g/2 oz butter
4 sticks celery, chopped
3 carrots, diced
1 small piece turnip, diced
1 large onion, finely chopped
2 tablespoons flour
2 tablespoons oil
3-4 tablespoons port
Salt and ground black pepper
To serve:
4 boiled mealy potatoes
Rowan Jelly

Preparing the hare

Skin and clean, reserving the blood, liver, heart, and kidneys (see Skinning p.167). Remove the fleshy pieces from the back and legs and cut into neat pieces. Place the remainder of the carcass in a pot with the cold water and leave overnight.

Making the stock

Bring the carcass and water to the boil, skim and then add the herbs. Simmer for 1 hour. Strain. Add butter to the pot and when hot add the vegetables. Cook gently, stirring occasionally, for 5-10 minutes till they begin to soften. Add the stock.

Finishing the dish

Flour the reserved hare flesh. Slice the kidneys and heart and flour. Melt oil in a pan and fry till lightly browned. Add to the bree (stock and vegetables) and simmer gently till the meat is tender.

Press the liver through a sieve and mix with the blood. Mix the blood/liver, which has had vinegar added at the cleaning-out stage, with the remaining flour and gradually add some of the hot cooking liquid. Pour back into the pan and heat through to thicken. It should not boil. Add the port. Taste and season. Serve in wide deep soup plates with a boiled mealy potato in the centre of the plate and rowan jelly on top.

Rabbit

Rabbit meat was popular in the early 1900s. Rabbit-catchers, employed by farmers, set traps and kept control of the population. Rabbits were cheap and plentiful until myxomatosis was introduced in the belief that this was an easier method of rabbit control, but it put an end to cheap and plentiful supplies. It took decades for the rabbits to become immune to the disease, and meanwhile two generations lost the rabbit-eating habit. Today, rabbits are more available and have more flavour and character than intensively reared chicken. They are best eaten fresh, though they can be hung. They should be skinned first (see instructions for Hare p.167).

Buying/Cooking

Look for soft ears and sharp teeth, which indicate a young rabbit. They should be plump with a smooth fur. There is no close season. They can weigh from ½-1½ kg/1-3 lb – 2 small or 1 large for 4 servings.

Lowland Scots have always eaten more rabbit than Highlanders. The most popular method of cooking was with onions, though other traditional methods include potted rabbit using the same method as for potted beef hough and sometimes mixing the beef and rabbit hough; roasted young rabbit; minced rabbit which was sometimes shaped into a meat roll with pork and onions; and rabbit soup and pies.

ELSIE'S RABBIT WITH ONIONS

My father's first job before breakfast, when working as a young boy on a farm in an Angus glen during the 1920s, was collecting rabbits caught in snares. On his return, he delivered the rabbits to Elsie, the farmer's daughter, who had a repertoire of a hundred ways with rabbit. But this one with onions was everyone's favourite. For the best flavour use roast dripping. Some butchers sell it in tubs as 'dripping for stovies' when it will have a bottom layer of dark brown meat juices to add even more flavour.

50g/2 oz roast dripping
2 medium onions, sliced
1 rabbit, skinned, cleaned and jointed
1 tablespoon flour, seasoned with salt and pepper
Salt and ground pepper

4 servings

To cook

Melt the dripping in a pan and brown the onions. Coat the rabbit with flour. Brown the rabbit well. Add seasoning and enough water to cover. Simmer gently until the rabbit is tender. Taste and season. Serve.

HONEYED RABBIT

Heather honey, tomatoes and a hint of garlic lift this rabbit stew out of the ordinary.

For the sauce:
3 tablespoons oil
1 medium onion, finely chopped
750 g/1 lb 10 oz tomatoes, skinned and chopped
4 tablespoons milk
4 tablespoons heather honey
1 clove of crushed garlic
To finish the dish:
4 tablespoons oil
50 g/2 oz flour
1 rabbit, cleaned and jointed
Salt and pepper
2 tablespoons parsley, chopped

3–4 servings

Making the sauce

Heat the oil in a sauté pan with a lid and add the onion, cook till soft without colouring, then add the tomatoes, milk and honey and simmer to reduce. When it is a good, thick consistency, add the crushed garlic, salt and pepper to taste.

Finishing the dish

Heat the oil in a pan and dip the rabbit joints into the tomato sauce (this helps to make more flour stick and gives a better crust) then into the flour. Brown the rabbit in the oil on all sides and then add the sauce. The liquid should almost cover the rabbit. Cover with a lid and simmer gently till tender, adding more stock or water if necessary. Taste and season. Sprinkle over chopped parsley and serve.

Other Scottish Game

Sizes and seasons. All dates inclusive.

Duck

MALLARD: 1.1-1.3 kg (2½-2¾ lb), 2-3 servings. **Season** – below high-tide mark, 1 September to 20 February. Elsewhere – 1 September to 31 January.

TEAL: 300-370 g (11-13 oz), 1 serving. **Season** – as for Mallard.

WIDGEON: 700-900 g (1½-2 lb), 2 servings. **Season** – as for Mallard.

Goose

PINK-FOOTED: 2.7-3.2 kg (6-7 lb), 6 servings. **Season** – as for Mallard.

GREYLAG: 3.7-5 kg (8-11 lb), 6 servings. **Season** – as for Mallard.

WOODPIGEON: 500-600 g (1-1¼ lb), 1 serving. No close season.

BLACK GAME: 1.4-1.8 kg (3-4 lb), 3 servings. Season – 20 August to 10 December.

PTARMIGAN: 400-600 g (1-1¼ lb), 1 serving. **Season** (Scotland only) – 12 August to 10 December.

PARTRIDGE: Cock 350-450 g (13-15 oz); Hen 400 g (12½-14½ oz), 1-2 servings. **Season** – 1 September to 1 February.

COMMON SNIPE: 100-130 g (3½-4½ oz), 1-2 per person. **Season** – 12 August to 31 January.

WOODCOCK: 230-400 g (8-14 oz), 1 serving. **Season** – 1 September to 31 January.

Poultry

While recipe books today never mention the sex of domestic poultry, this was important in early cookery books. A sinewy, elderly male cockerel required slow-and-low methods of cooking which led to the invention of *cock-a-leekie* and *coq au vin*, Meanwhile, the female hen might be fattened for hot-and-fast methods, or she might be kept for eggs and breeding till too elderly to be roasted, when a slow-and-low cock-a-leekie might be her fate. Most homes kept a few hens which ate up leftover scraps and scratched in the backyard for what they could find. When unexpected visitors arrived, someone was sent out to catch, and wring a young hen's neck and get it ready to cook.

While gastronomes of the day debated the merits of a mature cockerel versus an elderly hen for their cock-a-leekie (they preferred the former) the debate today is about its diet and the method of rearing: caged or free-range, organic or corn-fed? The choices are more complicated, but the simple flavour partnership of chicken and leeks lives on.

COCK-A-LEEKIE

Though written recipes for this broth first appear in the 1700s, its origins are thought to date back to medieval times, when adding sweet ingredients, such as prunes or raisins, to savoury recipes was common. In this case they may have been added to offset the bitter flavour in mature leeks. Perhaps this is not such a problem today, but they do add something unique to the broth's character.

How it was served varied. In peasant homes the tough old cockerel might be removed from the pot and the edible bits cut up, to be eaten by hand (knives and forks were seldom available for everyone) with oatcakes or bannocks, followed by platefuls of the leek broth (they all had a hand-carved horn spoon). Or it may have been served in the broth, as they do in peasant food cultures around the world, when an island of large chunks of vegetables and meat is surrounded by the liquid broth. No tough old cockerel, though, for Lady Grisell Baillie (1665-1746) of Mellerstain House, whose menu describes her Cock-a-Leekie as 'Chicken soup with chickens in it'.

A traditional Scottish soup plate is deep, and as wide as a meat plate, so meat could be cut with a knife and fork. This recipe makes use of the leftover carcass, legs and wings from a roast chicken (or other roast poultry/game).

1 large roast chicken (and/or other poultry or game)
carcass remains including meat from wings and legs (see
    recipe p.175)
2.75 L/5 pts cold water
Bundle of fresh herbs, thyme, bay leaf, marjoram
125 g/4 oz stoned prunes
2-3 medium onions, finely chopped
1 kg/2 lb 4oz leeks
125 g/4 oz long grain rice
Salt and pepper
2 tablespoons chopped parsley

8-10 servings

To make the stock

Pick off all the meat remaining on the carcass, and from the wings and legs. Chop roughly into even, bite-sized pieces, and reserve. Soak the prunes in boiling water. Put the remaining bones and skin in a large pot and cover with cold water. Bring to the boil, add herbs and simmer gently for an hour. Strain, leave to cool. Remove excess fat and reserve.

Finishing the broth

Heat the reserved fat (or use 2-3 tablespoons oil if not enough fat) over a medium heat in a large pot and add the onions. Cook

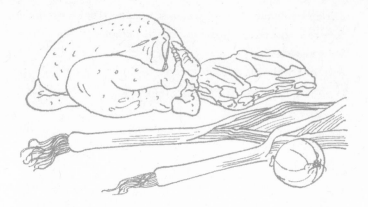

till soft and yellow. Meanwhile clean the leeks and chop finely, separating the white from the green. Add the white to the onions, stir well, cover and leave to sweat for about five minutes, stirring occasionally. The leeks should be soft now. Add the strained stock. Wash the rice and add. Simmer until the rice is cooked. Add the green leek and chicken meat. Drain and add the prunes. Taste and season. Bring back to a simmer to soften the leeks. Serve immediately. If the green leeks are overcooked at this stage they will lose both their bright green colour and fresh flavour. Sprinkle chopped parsley into each plate and pour over broth.

ROAST CHICKEN

This makes full use of the oven by roasting chicken and vegetables in separate roasting tins.

1.5-2 kg/3 lb 5 oz-4 lb whole chicken
4-5 tablespoons oil
Salt to taste
2 salted anchovies, chopped
50 g/2 oz pickled capers
5-6 heads of garlic (optional)

2-3 kg/4½ -6½ lb vegetables: choose from potatoes, parsnips, carrots, turnip, carrot, onion, squash, pumpkin
2-3 sprigs rosemary
Red wine/water or stock for gravy

Preheat the oven to 450F/230C/210Cfan/Gas 8.

Use 2 large sturdy roasting tins and an instant-read meat thermometer.

Preparing vegetables

Peel vegetables and cut root vegetables, pumpkin, squash and onions into roughly the same size. Leave the peppers whole. Put into one of the roasting tins with the rosemary sprigs. Drizzle over some oil, rub all over and sprinkle lightly with salt. Slice almost through the base of the garlic but leave a bit of the root still attached so the cut cloves are not exposed. Put the garlic, anchovies and capers in the base of the other roasting tin.

Roasting chicken

Place chicken in the roasting tin with the anchovies and capers. Drizzle over oil and rub all over. Lightly sprinkle salt all over. Lay on one side. Roast for 40 mins. Check if the garlic is soft and remove. Turn the chicken onto its other side. Reduce the heat to 220C/200Cfan/Gas 7 and roast for another 40 minutes. Remove from the oven and turn onto its back to brown the breast.

Continue to roast at this temperature until the juices run clear (no pinkness from blood) when the thickest part of the thigh is pierced with a skewer. Or use an instant-read internal meat thermometer inserted into the leg which should reach 70C. Remove from the oven and place on top of the vegetables. Cover and keep warm.

Roasting vegetables

Add the vegetables to the oven when you reduce the heat to 220C/200Cfan/Gas 7. Roast for 40 minutes. Turn vegetables. If some look dry, drizzle over more oil. Keep turning them in the oil to prevent them drying out until they are lightly browned and soft.

Making gravy and serving

Add red wine/water or stock to the pan juices in the chicken's roasting tin and stir to scrape up all the debris and juices. Squeeze the cooked garlic cloves out of their skin and mash into the liquid. Boil up to reduce. Taste and season. Serve with the chicken and vegetables.

Use chicken carcass and leftover chicken meat/excess fat to make Cock-a-Leekie (see p.173).

FRIED CHICKEN
and Skirlie

1.1 kg/2 lb 12 oz chicken thighs
Salt and ground pepper
4 tablespoons oil
450 g/1 lb onions, thinly sliced
450 g/1 lb mushrooms, sliced
100 ml/3½ fl oz crème fraiche
15 g/½ oz flour
Stock or water
Skirlie, see p.22

Serves 4-6

Use 25-30 cm/10-12 in sauté or frying-pan with lid.

To prepare and fry chicken

Dry chicken joints and sprinkle lightly with salt. Heat the oil in pan over a moderate heat and when hot add the chicken, skin-side down. Fry slowly till the skin is golden brown and crisp. If necessary turn up the heat to brown skin. Turn and fry on the other side. It should take about 30-40 minutes. Remove to a plate.

To fry onions and mushrooms

Fry the onions in the oil till crisp and golden brown. Add mushrooms and continue to fry until they are soft and lightly browned. Turn down the heat.

Finishing and serving

Put flour into a sieve and sift over the onions and mushrooms. Stir in flour till well blended. Add the crème fraiche and simmer gently to thicken the sauce. Add stock or water to adjust consistency. Taste and season. Return chicken to the pan and heat through. Serve with skirlie and creamed or baked potatoes.

Optional flavourings: black olives and preserved lemons; serve with steamed rice or couscous.

ROAST TURKEY

'Oysters! Oysters! madam: there is no other turkey stuffing worth the attention of a Christian eater,' is the opinion of Dr Jekyll, recorded in *The Cook and Housewives Manual* by Meg Dods (1826) when the question of 'Stuffing for Turkey' is debated among the gastronomes of the Cleikum Club. He speaks at a time when oysters were cheap and plentiful, and consumed in everything from stews to stuffings.

Other ideas for the turkey from the club-members included stuffing with truffles and ham: giving the bird 'three days to take the flavour'. But chestnuts are also considered, mixed with ham or pork sausage, mace, nutmeg, parsley and butter. And for a sauce, chestnuts were chopped and 'stirred into a thickened strong gravy, with a glass of Sherry or Madeira'.

Advance preparation

Chestnut and Herb Stuffings, Cranberry and Bread Sauces.

Chestnut Neck Stuffing*

500 g/1lb 2 oz unpeeled chestnuts to yield approx 280-300
   g/9-10 oz peeled
50 g/2 oz chopped bacon
50 g/2 oz butter
125 g/4 oz fresh white breadcrumbs
1 tablespoon finely chopped parsley
grated zest of a lemon
½ teaspoon each mace and nutmeg
salt and ground pepper
1 egg

To make:

Slit chestnuts all round and place on a baking tray. Put in oven
(425F/220C/200Cfan/Gas 7) and roast for 30-35 minutes or
until the skins are crisp and curling away from the chestnut.
Remove from the oven and leave to cool a little. Remove skins.
The chestnuts should be cooked. Either chop finely or blend in
processor till fine, but not too fine.

Melt the butter and fry the bacon till lightly crisp. Mix in
breadcrumbs, add all the other ingredients and bind together
with egg.

Herb and Lemon Stuffing*
for the Body Cavity

2 onions, finely chopped
125 g/4 oz butter
175 g/6 oz fresh white breadcrumbs
50 g/2 oz chopped bacon
2 tablespoons parsley, finely chopped
2 tablespoons thyme, finely chopped

*Reduce stuffing quantities for smaller birds or make the same quantity
and put the excess into the baking dish and bake separately.

grated zest of 2 lemons
1 teaspoon ground mace
Salt and pepper
1 egg

To make

Melt the butter and cook the onion over a gentle heat till transparent but not browned. Add bacon and cook till crisp. Add breadcrumbs, parsley, lemon, thyme and mace. Season. Bind with egg.

Cranberry and Orange Sauce

500 g/1 lb 2 oz fresh or frozen cranberries
250 ml/8 fl oz fresh orange juice
1 cinnamon stick
4 cloves
1-2 tablespoons sugar
2 tablespoons port

To make the sauce:

Put the cranberries in the food processor and whizz till fine. Put into a pan with the orange juice, cinnamon, cloves and sugar. Bring to the boil, cover and cook for about five minutes. Stir in the port. Put into serving dish till required.

Bread Sauce

1 onion
5-10 whole cloves, or half a nutmeg
1 bay leaf
8 black peppercorns
450 ml/16 fl oz milk
50 g/2 oz butter
85 g/3 oz 2 day old white bread, crusts removed

2 tablespoons double cream
Salt

To infuse the milk

Stud the onion with cloves (quantity depends on amount of clove flavour preferred). Add with bay leaf and peppercorns to a pan (grate in nutmeg if using instead of cloves) and pour over the milk. Bring up to boiling point and simmer for a few minutes. Remove from the heat and leave to infuse for a few hours or overnight.

To make the sauce

Strain the milk and return to the pan. Add the breadcrumbs and the butter, bring up to a slow simmer over a very low heat. Stir frequently to prevent sticking. When the sauce has thickened, remove from the heat and stir in the cream. Cover and keep warm.

TO ROAST TURKEY

1 turkey 6 kg/13 lb (allow 450 g per person plus 2-3 kg extra
   for leftovers)
250g/9 oz unsalted butter, softened
Grated zest of a lemon
2 cloves garlic, crushed (optional)
8-10 rashers of streaky bacon
2 tablespoons plain flour
1 L/1¾ pt chicken or vegetable stock
125 g/4 oz cooked chestnuts, finely chopped
Sherry or Madeira to taste
Salt and pepper

Preheat oven to 425F/220C/200Cfan/Gas 7.

Use extra wide foil and an instant-read internal thermometer.

To prepare turkey for roasting

Loosen the skin over the breast and legs by pushing your fingers carefully between skin and flesh. Cut out the wishbone (this makes it easier to carve). Spread the softened herb butter under the skin, making sure there is plenty over the breast and tops of the legs, which are most likely to dry out.

Pack the chestnut stuffing into the neck cavity, leaving room for expansion. Fold under the skin and secure with cocktail sticks. Pack the herb stuffing into the body cavity. Leave room for expansion. Truss, with the wings folded under the body and the legs tied together. Weigh the turkey and allow about 20 minutes per 500g/1lb 2oz.

Put turkey into the roasting tin on its back. Put bacon over the breast and legs. Cover with foil and make a complete seal by securing foil tightly round the edges of the roasting tin.

To roast

Place in the oven and roast for an hour at the high temperature.

Reduce the heat to 350F/180C/160Cfan/Gas 4 and continue roasting. Remove from the oven and baste with the juices halfway through. After two and a half hours check if cooked.

To check

Either put a skewer into the thickest part to check if the juices are clear (if so, it's cooked) or pinkish (it's not cooked). Or insert a meat thermometer into the breast or the leg at the thickest point without touching the bone. When the temperature reads 70C remove from the oven and place on a serving dish. Cover with foil and rest for 30-45 minutes in a warm place.

To make gravy and serve

Sift flour over the residue juices in the roasting tin and scrape everything in the tin together. Add the stock gradually, stirring all the time, and bring to the boil to thicken. Add any more juices which have come from the turkey while it has been resting. Add chestnuts, sherry or Madeira. Taste and season. Pour into a gravy boat.

Serve turkey with cranberry, bread sauce, gravy, roast potatoes and brussels sprouts.

4: MEAT

Scotland's hill and upland farms provide ideal breeding grounds for beef cattle and sheep that come to maturity on the lush pastures of the Scottish lowlands.

Scotch Quality Beef and Lamb Association 1990s

Beef

Cattle ran wild like game in the forests and hills of Britain 700 years ago, give or take a century. Six wild bulls are mentioned as part of the feast given for George Neville when he was installed as Archbishop of York in 1466. But according to C. Ann Wilson in *Food and Drink in Britain*, 'by Elizabeth I's reign (1558-1603) the wild forest cattle had retreated from lowland Britain but were still to be found in the remote parts of Wales and in Scotland.'

Once domesticated, they became an important part of the Highland economy in Scotland, with thousands sent every year to markets in the south along ancient drove roads. This trade flourished until the 1745 Rebellion changed the fortunes of the Highland Jacobite clans and their cattle droving traditions. In the 1800s, large flocks of sheep were introduced by landowners who cleared the people and their livestock from the most fertile areas.

Though large-scale cattle rearing never returned to the Highlands, in the north-east some enterprising Scottish farmers, who knew a good thing when they saw it, began the process of moulding together the most valuable characteristics of the native black hornless breed. From obscurity among the hills and glens, they succeeded in breeding Aberdeen Angus cattle which would become a prime beef breed, renowned worldwide.

Three men were principally responsible – Hugh Watson (1780-1865) of Keillor in Angus; William McCombie (1805-1880) of

Tillyfour in Aberdeenshire and Sir George Macpherson Grant (1839-1907) of Ballindalloch in Banffshire. Keeping a sharp eye on utilitarian qualities, while they built up their families of cattle, they rated hardiness very highly. They had to survive harsh winters. They also had to be able to thrive on the available low-quality pasture and rough grazing; not only thrive but also mature early, by converting these simple rations quickly and effectively into high-quality, well-marbled, good-flavoured beef.

While previously the Highland cattle drover had transported the animals on the hoof for fattening to the richer pastures of Norfolk and Suffolk, Watson was the first to fatten them himself. Now the Angus and Aberdeenshire beef-breeders began to 'fix' their own breed. In 1850 the railway line to London was complete and now they could send their most valuable carcasses on an overnight train.

The new Aberdeen Angus breed's main rival was Amos Cruickshank's Scotch Shorthorn (established in Aberdeenshire in the 1830s, though the breed originated in Yorkshire in the 1700s). It could be fattened more rapidly, but did not milk so well and was less hardy than the Aberdeen Angus. The two were eventually crossed to become the source of most prime beef produced in Scotland. The Polled (hornless) Cattle Herd Book was set up in 1862 and the Aberdeen Angus Cattle Society inaugurated in 1879.

Since this time, many changes have occurred in the Black Angus breed, as it is commonly known. For most of the first fifty years of the twentieth century the demand was for a small, thick, heavy bull with its fat-marbled meat making a high ratio of fat to meat. This was reversed with entry to the EU, when the fashion developed for a taller, leaner animal with a much lower percentage of fat. Continental breeds were introduced with a leaner, fleshier carcass, initially the Charolais, but later the Simmental and Limousin, which led to a loss in the pure-bred stock of the native breeds. When they were crossed with the native breeds, though the meat was often given the native breed name, it was often less than fifty per cent native breed.

Though this intermingling with Continental breeds became well established in the second half of the 1900s, a counter-movement was also afoot to reverse the ultra-lean approach, recognising that such meat lacks the flavour and character which the pioneer breeders of the 1800s had dedicated their lives to perfecting in native Scottish breeds.

Referring to this fashion for lean Continental beef, Jim Jack, Aberdeen Angus President in 1994, said: 'This meat does not have the succulence and flavour that the consumer requires. Thus the aim now is to have meat that has marbling of fat through it, to give a product that is succulent and tasty.'

Similar comments came in 1995 from Sir Alistair Grant, chairman of the Safeway supermarket chain. Reporting to the Agricultural Scottish Affairs Committee, he suggested that something positive could be done to reverse the situation: 'The intermingling of French breeding stock, particularly Charolais, has produced a beef type which is not particularly Scottish. Over a long period we could attend to that, so that we produced a larger Scottish breed with a bit more fat and have the best of both worlds.' He had just bought his first pure-bred Aberdeen Angus heifer.

Also in 1995 an Angus farmer, Geordie Soutar, with some of the pioneering beef-breeding instincts of the early improvers, decided to concentrate on establishing a herd of pure-bred Angus. He remembered the fine qualities of the meat from the smaller animals and set about building up bloodlines which would reverse the infiltration of Continental genes. It has taken some time to archive, but there are now enough breeding heifers to remove the pure-bred Angus from the endangered species list. Besides selling semen and embryos around the world, Soutar also sells his Angus beef to some local butchers (see p.442).

Of the pure native breeds, besides the Angus and the Beef Shorthorn, there are three other native breeds protected by breeding societies which hold the records of pedigree herds: the Galloway is of slower growth, but very hardy, and its breeding society was established in 1877; the picturesque horned Highland cattle, also renowned for their hardiness, were established in 1884; and the Luing, established on the island of Luing in 1966, and also noted for producing good beef in poor, wet conditions. All native breeds originally thrived on a grass diet, and also 'finished' (i.e. fattened up for market) on grass, of which there is an abundance in Scotland. Besides careful breeding, this was the other asset in native breeds which added to their fame, for it produced exceptionally good-flavoured beef, compared with the beef from animals finished on grain. An EU protection order has been applied for to cover UK Traditional Pasture Reared Beef, which would give it a Traditional Speciality Guaranteed status (see below).

Buying/Cuts of Beef

The late twentieth century will no doubt be remembered for the un-savoury facts which emerged about the degenerative disease in cattle, bovine spongiform encephalopathy (BSE), and its tragic effects on human health. Most breeders of prime beef in Scotland were not involved in the intensive systems which resorted to feeding sheep offal to cattle, which appears to have caused the problem. Only a small percentage of cases were reported in Scotland. Three-quarters of the beef produced in Scotland is reared in an outdoors-extensive system. These are known as beef-suckler herds, where the calves are weaned naturally from their mothers and animals graze on pasture and silage, sometimes outdoors throughout the winter if the breed is a hardy one with a thick coat, such as the Galloway or Highland.

As more interest has been created about the origins of beef supplies and methods of production, some butchers have established, at the point of sale, more information about the beef they're selling. The fashion for lean Continental breeds was largely supermarket-led. Their fresh, pink, lean beef could be produced cheaply by reducing hanging times, so the meat could be sold with a much higher percentage of water than had previously been the case. Among the pioneers calling for a return to the old quality and flavour found in fat-marbled native breeds, properly hung for 2-3 weeks, was butcher and beef farmer, Michael Gibson of Forres. In the 1980s when the craze for leanness was at its height, he drew attention to high-quality, low-quantity, fat-marbled Highland beef. It was not a story the beef marketing organisations wanted to broadcast and he was not popular. But others followed him, and many farmers now recognise that there is a market for well-hung, fat-marbled native breeds from extensive, and more environmentally friendly, systems of production.

A number of labelling schemes have been set up to provide customer confidence about beef's origins; among them is a European Union regulation set up in 1993 to provide a system for the protection of food names on a geographical or traditional recipe basis, similar to the familiar 'appellation controlee' system used for wine. The three schemes, Protected Designation of Origin (PDO); Protected Geographical Indication (PGI); and Traditional Speciality Guaranteed (TSG), highlight regional and traditional foods whose authenticity and origins can be guaranteed through an independent inspection system. Orkney Beef and Lamb and Shetland Lamb have PDO status, while Scotch Beef and Lamb have PGI status. As mentioned above, UK Traditional Pasture Reared Beef has applied for TSG status.

BOILED BEEF

This universal dish has many variations around the world, from the sophisticated Austrian *Tafelspitz*, made with sirloin and served with chive mayonnaise and apple purée mixed with grated horseradish, to the more everyday English Boiled Beef and Carrots.

Combining soup and meat courses in one pot is central to the Scottish culinary tradition. A north-east farmer's daughter, Ethel McCurrach, recalls how:

'On Sundays a 14 pint pot was used. That meant there was enough for Monday (Yavils)* and Tuesdays (Ley),* as well as half a

*Refers to the farming system of 2nd and 3rd year corn rotation.

turnip plus a few carrots as well as the beef. Now if a dumpling was needed for the dinner [12 noon] it was tied in a cloth and boiled in amongst the broth, if not a mealie pudding mixture was tied tightly in a cloth and boiled amongst the broth. All that was then needed to finish off a full three-course meal was a pot of boiled potatoes. Two pots for a three-course meal that would last three days – it would be a "pot man's" dream in a hotel kitchen today.'

In the north-east the meat was usually removed from the pot and served first while hot. It was sliced by the master of the house. Farm servants often did not have knives or forks, so they ate the meat with their fingers, taking pieces from the central platter. Then the broth was served into wooden bowls and they supped it with their hand-carved horn spoons.

For Boiling a Whole Piece of Beef

2-2¼ kg/4-5 lbs beef brisket, nineholes, silverside or hough
Cold water to cover
1 onion stuck with a few cloves
1 bay leaf
2-3 sticks celery, cut in four
1 sprig rosemary
6 carrots
1 large turnip
1 leek
12 even-sized, floury potatoes, washed but unpeeled
Salt and pepper
2-3 tablespoons parsley, chopped
Dumplings instead of potatoes:
125 g/4 oz plain flour
50 g/2 oz shredded suet
1 teaspoon baking powder
Cold water to mix
Salt and pepper

8-10 servings

Use a pot which will hold the beef and vegetables neatly. It is important not to have too large a pot with too much water, since the flavour of both vegetables and meat will end up diluted in the liquid.

Place the meat in the pot, cover with cold water and bring to the boil. Remove the scum. Add onion, bay leaf, celery and rosemary. Cover and simmer until the meat is just tender – approximately 1-2 hours depending on toughness of meat. Add carrots and turnips towards the end of the cooking time and the potatoes for the last 20 minutes until soft. Taste and season.

To serve

Arrange the meat on a large ashet and carve in fairly thick slices. Surround with vegetables and pour a little of the broth on the meat to keep it well moistened. Sprinkle over parsley. Give each person a cup of broth. Serve with Mustard (p.392), Apple chutney (p.391) or any other sharp pickles and some coarse salt.

Dumplings

These may be added to the pot instead of potatoes about 20 minutes before serving.

Mix together the flour, suet, baking powder, cold water and salt and pepper. Drop in spoonfuls on top of the meat and vegetables, cover and simmer gently till they are well risen.

For Boiling Pieces of Beef

Geordie Kelly was the Scots/Irish cook on the *Clara*, a coal-carrying puffer sailing the Hebridean coasts in the 1920s. His recipe for B'il't' Beef is described by Victor MacClure, who sat in the galley with him shelling peas and scrubbing carrots while gazing out to the islands of Colonsay and Mull, as Geordie taught him the art of boiling beef.

'"Boiled" beef,' Geordie said, 'is a misnomer. You only drop your meat into boilin' water to give it a skin that'll keep it sappy [moist]. If it was put into the pot in one piece like the Frenchies do it, you might need to give it five minutes real boilin'. But it's quite enough, when it's in bits like this, to bring it back to the boil for a jiffy. An' that's all the actual boilin' you ever give it. All it wants after that is as much heat as'll just keep the liquor saying "plup!" six to twelve times a minute. In the piece you would allow about twenty minutes for each pound-weight and twenty minutes over. You can hardly spoil the meat by simmering too long, except that in the piece it'll likely fall to bits when you try to carve it. But simmering, mind! If you boil meat – that's to say at the heat of water for makin' tea – you'll get somethin' as tough and tasteless as cahootchy [indiarubber]. An' nothin' in the world'll make it worth eatin' again.

'Of course,' Geordie went on, 'a certain amount o' the meat juice leaks out into the liquor. That's what makes the broth. An' when you come to put in the vegetables, somethin' o' their juice gets into the meat, helpin' its flavour. But the notion is to keep all the virtue you can in the beef, so you don't do anything to encourage it to give its juices out. That's why you don't salt your liquor until meat an' vegetables are nearly ready.'

Victor MacClure, *Good Appetite My Companion*, 1955.

2 kg/4 lb 8 oz brisket or other boiling cut

2 L/3 ½ boiling water

Bunch of parsley

Few peppercorns (my addition – not Geordie's)

Bay leaf

Sprig of thyme

12 medium carrots, sliced

12 white turnips, sliced

2 kg/4 lb 8 oz fresh peas in their pods (summer)

4 leeks (winter)

4 shallots, finely chopped

Salt and pepper

8–10 servings

Cut the meat up into portion-sized pieces and put into the water with parsley, peppercorns, bay leaf and thyme. Bring to the boil and then skim. Reduce the heat to a very gentle simmer. Cover and cook till almost tender. Add the carrots and turnips and simmer for half an hour.

Finally shell the peas or chop leeks finely and add with the shallots. Taste and season. Simmer for five minutes and serve with floury boiled potatoes (see p.248).

SCOTCH BARLEY BROTH

Bit it's sorroo and grief if there's no bilan' beef
An' ye canna hev broth, on 'e Sunday.
Donald Grant, *Broth on 'e Sunday*, 1961.

This traditional broth occupies the high ground between soups on the one hand and stews on the other. Meg Dods describes it, and a variety of other substantial Scottish soups, as *Soup and Stew or Mouthful Soups*.

Some Scottish men are highly skilled broth-makers, taking time and effort to achieve perfection. Such was auld Andra, an ex-Glasgow shipwright whose magnificent Scotch Broth was something of a legend, and the highlight of the week, for Madeleine Gibb when she was a teenage apprentice to Andra's dressmaker daughter during the depression in the 1920s. Monday they had 'stovies' made from the leftovers of the Sunday roast, Tuesday was 'cooheel', but on Wednesday it was Andra's Special. Cooled and reheated overnight, the flavour developed and it tasted even better on Thursday. Andra was ever ready to reel off the recipe for the broth, which was made in a huge iron pot over the kitchen range. The procedure started at nine o'clock by filling the pot with cold water.

'Intae this,' commanded the receipt, *'fling a sma' haunfie o' coorse saut. Whan it biles pit in yer beef, a guid, fat, twa-pun piece. Then hauf-a-pun o' weel-washed baurley and twa pun o' well-soakit peas.'* About ten-thirty Andra added *'wan guid swede turmut, fower carrots, eicht guid leeks and a wee tait o' sugar.'* Before departing for his *'bit dram'* he added *'twa guid haunfies o' choppit greens and eicht tautties';* and on his return – exuding the rich and heady perfume of the Special, he stirred in another *'haunfie'* – this time of parsley which, with canny forethought, he had chopped before setting forth.

Madeline Gibb, *Scotland's Magazine*, December 1960.

Earlier recipes from the more affluent nineteenth century have a much higher proportion of beef and fewer peas and barley, but the basic ingredients remain the same, as do the three basic stages.

Cooking the meat/barley/peas

For the best flavour use about 450 g/1 lb of beef to every 1.1 L/2 pts of cold water. A cheap cut like nineholes (thick flank) or hough (shin), though other cuts suitable for boiling, and larger or smaller pieces, can be used. Use for this quantity 25 g/1 oz barley and 15 g/½ oz split peas which have both been steeped in hot water overnight with a small nut of butter, which will give the broth a good lithing (thickening). All of this should be put on to boil with a little salt and a bunch of sweet herbs for at least an hour before the vegetables are added.

Note: Since it is difficult to know exactly the toughness or tenderness of the meat, boil till tender and then remove and keep warm. If the vegetables are finely chopped they will cook faster. If to be served in larger pieces with the meat then they should be added sooner.

Adding the vegetables

Those which take longest to cook should be added first and

others added so that all vegetables are just cooked through without being overcooked, at which point the broth is ready to serve.

The proportions and the combinations are a matter of taste, except that almost everyone would agree that carrots and yellow turnips (swedes), leek (king of the broth vegetables) and parsley are essential. Only Mrs Cleland, writing in 1759, varies widely from this, when instead she uses 'four or five heads of celery washed clean and cut small [this was to 12 pts of water] and a few marigolds. Let this boil an hour. Take a cock or large fowl, clean picked and washed, and put into the pot; boil it till the broth is quite good, then season with salt, and send it to table, with the fowl in the middle.'

Potatoes can be cooked in the broth, as in Andra's version, or cooked separately but served with the broth, a single potato as an island in the middle of the broth. Or they can be served with the meat as the second course. Floury potatoes will disintegrate quickly once they are cooked and will dissolve into the soup if they are cooked too long.

Use a medium-sized carrot, a quarter of a medium-sized turnip and two leeks with a long 'flag' of dark green to the 1 L/1¾ pts water. Peel and dice the carrot and turnip and add first. Chop the leek and add (leek white only) when the carrot and turnips are about half cooked. Add a teaspoonful of sugar at this point.

Finishing the broth

When all are tender, remove from the heat and add a good handful of chopped parsley and the dark green of the leek, very finely chopped. Taste and season. Serve as a main course with the meat chopped and added, or as a first course with the meat and potatoes to follow.

MINCED COLLOPS
(Mince and Tatties)

I dinna like hail tatties
Pit on my plate o mince
For when I tak my denner
I eat them baith at yince.

Sae mash and mix the tatties
Wi' mince intil the mashin,
And sic a tasty denner
Will aye be voted 'Smashin!'

J. K. Annand, *A Wale o' Rhymes*, 1989.

A popular, everyday Scottish dish, always eaten with mashed potatoes and commonly known as 'Mince and Tatties'. Collops is a term for thin slices of meat of any kind, usually taken from the leg, but with no bone. This version is based on a simple recipe given by Mrs Dalgairns in 1829, which depends for flavour on a very thorough browning of meat and onions. The Scots tradition is to use the best quality steak minced.

2 tablespoons oil/fat for browning
1-2 onions, finely chopped
700 g/1 lb 10 oz steak, minced
Salt and ground pepper
1 tablespoon medium or fine oatmeal (optional)

4-6 servings

To cook

Heat the oil/fat in a pan, and when it is quite hot add the onions. Cook slowly till a good, rich, dark golden-brown, then add the mince. Break up with a fork and keep stirring while it is browning. This should be done slowly (it takes about 10-15 minutes). After this, the meat is really cooked and simply needs moistening and seasoning before serving. Add about 300 ml/10 fl oz water or stock, bring up to a simmer and add oatmeal and simmer for about 5-10 minutes. Taste and season. Serve with mashed/creamed potatoes ('tatties') or dumplings (see p.190) also known as doughboys or doughballs. Serve with a tangy chutney or a dash of Worcestershire Sauce.

Note: For convenience, carrots and turnips are often cooked in mince, which lengthens the cooking time once the liquid has been added, but at the same time brings additional flavour. They should be very thinly sliced to reduce cooking time.

BEEF OLIVES

Rolls of thinly sliced beef or veal are stuffed to make this economical dish. Some butchers in Scotland use a cut called Beef Ham to make their own beef olives, which they stuff with sausagemeat. The one used here is breadcrumb-based and flavoured with lemon and herbs, though a favourite sausage can be used instead.

For the stuffing:
25 g/1 oz butter or 1 tablespoon oil
1 small onion, finely chopped
85 g/3 oz fresh breadcrumbs
1 tablespoon chopped parsley
1 tablespoon chopped lemon thyme
Grated rind of 1 lemon
½ beaten egg
Salt and pepper
For the olives:
500 g/1 lb 2oz stewing steak, cut thinly
2 tablespoons oil or dripping
1 onion, finely chopped
425 ml/¾ pt water or stock

1 tablespoon of Japanese miso (optional)
400 g/12 oz carrots, thickly sliced
Salt and ground pepper

4 servings

To stuff olives

Heat the butter/oil in a pan and when hot add the onion. Cook till soft. Add all the stuffing ingredients and mix well. Beat the steak with a rolling pin or meat bat till it is fairly thin. Cut into 4 strips about 10 x 20 cm/4 x 8 in each. Place a spoonful of stuffing on each piece; roll up and wind some strong thread round to hold in place. Or substitute four sausages for the stuffing, removing the casings.

To cook

Heat oil/dripping in a pan and brown the onion, then add olives and brown. Add water or stock, or dissolve miso in water and add. Add carrots and seasoning. Bring to the boil. Simmer gently till tender. Taste and season. Serve with creamed potatoes or **Skirlie Toasts** (see p.23).

BEEFSTEAKS

Lucky Laing . . . contrived to make her shop in the gloomy old Tolbooth a cosy little place, half tavern, half kitchen, whence issued pretty frequently the pleasant sounds of broiling beefsteaks, and the drawing of corks from bottles of ale and porter.
Marie W. Stuart, *Old Edinburgh Taverns*, 1952.

The taste for simple, old-fashioned meat dishes served at steak restaurants is as much a part of our eating-out scene today as it was more than two hundred years ago. Beefsteaks were then – as they are now – one of the most popular restaurant dishes.

The Rules of the Beefsteak Club, which was established in 1734, were: 'Pound well the steak till all the fibres are broken.

Don't spare the coal. Turn it frequently. Take care the fat is more done than the lean. Take care the juice is allowed now and then to fall in the dish. Butter the steak but do not season till dished.'

So, except for beating 'till all fibres are broken' the Club's rules remain – almost three centuries on – the wisest moves for the best results. Perhaps today a new one could be added: that the steak must come from a native Scottish breed, grass-fed, with fat-marbled flesh, hung till a mature flavour, and not from a grain-fed Continental breed, lean-fleshed, vacuum-packed and with a minimum of fat.

Potatoes:
4 large floury baking potatoes
Oil or butter
Sea salt
4 teaspoons crème fraiche
Chopped parsley
Salad:
1 round lettuce
100 g watercress or rocket
1 tub cress
Balsamic dressing (see p.257)
Steaks:
4 x 175-225 g/6-8 oz rib eye steaks
Oil for brushing
Sea salt and ground pepper
50 g/2 oz unsalted butter, softened
Dijon mustard or horseradish sauce

Serves 4

To bake potatoes

Preheat the oven to 425F/220C/200Cfan/Gas 7. Wash potatoes, stab with a fork a few times. Rub with butter or drizzle over some oil and lightly sprinkle with sea salt. Put into a roasting tin and bake for about an hour depending on size, turning once.

To make salad

Wash and dry lettuce leaves. Put into the serving bowl with the rocket or watercress and toss together. Cut cress and sprinkle on top. Serve with balsamic dressing (see p.257).

To grill steaks

Have steaks at room temperature. Heat a griddle pan or non-stick frying pan over a high heat till very hot. Brush steaks with oil on both sides. Place on hot pan and cook for 2 minutes on one side till sizzling and caramelised. Turn over and cook for another 2 minutes. The meat will be rare at this point. Season to taste with salt and pepper. For medium rare, turn again and cook for another 2 minutes on either side. Remove to a heated serving dish. Spread the meat with butter, pour over pan juices. Cover with foil and rest for five minutes.

To serve

Cut potatoes with a cross, press sides to open up and put a teaspoon of crème fraiche on top. Sprinkle with parsley. Serve steaks whole or carve into slices. Serve with juices poured over, mustard/horseradish/sea salt, green salad and balsamic dressing.

SPICED BEEF

Dry Spicing

This preservation method adds a rich, mellow flavour to beef. It's a lighter cure, compared with early methods when the meat was simply buried in dry salt in a stone trough in the winter months. Spices were added but the salt dominated. Now there is less need to use so much salt and subtle blends of spices add a rich and distinctive flavour to the meat. It is a popular Christmas feature on festive tables in Ireland and some butchers make their own versions.

Cuts

It is not really worth spicing anything under 2 kg/4½ lbs, since the purpose is to have a supply to last several weeks. A 3-5 kg/6½-11 lb piece is best. Prime cuts like a middle rib of roast make superb spiced beef, also silverside, rump and 'salmon' cut, but equally successful are the cheaper brisket and nineholes.

There should be a good mix of fat and lean. The fat is necessary to keep the meat moist during cooking, but also fat is a good absorber of flavour during the spicing process. The meat should have all bones removed and may be spiced rolled and tied, or unrolled. Penetration of the spices is quicker and more thorough in unrolled meat. Also, because the meat is flatter, more of it is sitting in the spicing liquor. It is important from this point of view to have a bowl or dish which fits the meat neatly. Pieces which are a fairly uniform shape like the salmon cut or silverside will not need rolling or tying before cooking but rib roast, brisket and nineholes will need some tying.

A cut of beef 2-5 kg/4½-11 lb
125 g/4 oz brown sugar
25 g/1 oz allspice
25 g/1 oz juniper berries
25 g/1 oz black peppercorns
15 g/½ oz coriander seeds
½ grated nutmeg
2-3 crushed cloves of garlic
125 g/4 oz salt

Spicing

Put the meat into a fairly closely fitting dish and rub all over with the brown sugar. Cover well and leave for 2 days in a cool place, turning each day.

Pound all the spices and garlic together in a mortar. Experiment with spice combinations – cloves will dominate so should be used sparingly. The spices can be ground coarsely in a grinder but not to a fine powder, since this will be more difficult to remove from the outside surface of the meat at the end of the spicing which will make the meat too spicy if it is to be baked.

Mix spices with the salt and rub into the meat. Cover with foil or a tight-fitting lid and turn the meat every day. Leave for about 4-5 days for thin cuts, 6-8 for thicker. Old recipes recommend a month minimum but this makes a very strongly spiced beef.

Cooking

For boiling – (best for tougher cuts like brisket and nineholes) wipe off excess spice and put in a pot of boiling water, bring back to the boil and skim well. Add **1 stick of celery; an onion stuck with a few cloves; 1 carrot; 1 small piece of turnip; bunch of parsley and thyme; a tablespoon peppercorns**. Bring back to the boil and simmer over a very low heat, allowing 30 minutes per 450g/1 lb plus 30 minutes, or till tender.

For braising – Wipe off the excess spice. Melt **2 tablespoons oil** in a pan and add **2-3 chopped carrots, 1 small turnip** and **1 medium onion, chopped,** and sauté till lightly browned. Place the meat on top. If it has no fat cover a 'skin' of fat can be used instead (available from butchers). Add enough water to cover the vegetables completely and come about halfway up the meat. Cover with a double layer of foil and then a tightly-fitting lid and bake at 300F/150C/130Cfan/Gas 2 for 30 minutes per 450 g/1 lb plus 30 minutes, or until tender.

Pressing

Remove when cooked, wrap tightly in foil while still hot and put between two boards with a weight on top, leave overnight.

Serving

It can be eaten hot, but the spice flavour is best appreciated when cold. Serve as a starter or main course or in an open or closed sandwich with pickles, chutneys, mustards, zesty salads or beetroot cooked and grated with a balsamic dressing (see p.257).

BEEF
cooked in claret

We have one great advantage, that makes amends for many inconveniences, that is, wholesome and agreeable drink, I mean French Claret . . .

Edward Burt (Chief Surveyor to General Wade during the making of roads through the Highlands), *Letters from a Gentleman in the North of Scotland* (1724-28).

With so much borrowing back and forward between Scotland and France, the use of French claret to cook Scottish beef seems an obvious combination. The cheapest, toughest cuts of beef can be used in this slow-and-wet method which will provide more flavour from harder-working muscles like the leg.

For the meat:
4 tablespoons oil
1.4 kg/3 lb stewing steak, cut into 4 cm/1½ in cubes
5 cloves garlic, crushed
40 g/1½ oz plain flour
1 bottle fruity young claret (Burgundy, Cotes-du-Rhone or Beaujolais)
1 teaspoon sugar

Bunch of fresh herbs
Salt and freshly milled black pepper
For the trimmings:
150 g/5 oz streaky bacon
6-8 small shallots
400 g/14 oz small button mushrooms

6-8 servings

Preheat the oven to 350F/180C/160Cfan/Gas 4.

Use a large cast-iron casserole and a large frying or sauté pan.

To cook

Heat the oil in a casserole over a medium heat and brown the meat. Add the garlic and sift over flour. Stir for a few minutes, then add wine, sugar, herbs and seasoning. Cover and bring up to a simmer, stirring to prevent sticking. Cover and put in the oven for 1-1½ hours. Test for tenderness after an hour.

Meanwhile, cook the trimmings. Heat a large frying or sauté pan and fry the bacon till lightly brown. Add the onions and cook for about 10 minutes, turning occasionally. Then add the mushrooms, keep turning and cook gently for another 10 minutes or until both onions and mushrooms are cooked. Keep aside till serving.

Remove meat from the oven and stir in the trimmings. Taste and season. Heat through for five minutes and serve with chopped parsley and baked potatoes or Dauphinoise potatoes (see **Gratin Dauphinoise**, p.405).

FORFAR BRIDIES

These convenient hand-held delicacies were made by itinerant sellers who mostly plied their trade at local fairs and markets. They may have taken their name from one such seller, Maggie Bridie of Glamis, though another story goes that because of their lucky horseshoe shape they were served at weddings and took their name from the bride.

Today they are a bakers' speciality, like a Cornish pasty turned on its side but filled only with beef. Forfar is an important centre of the beef trade in Angus and the first bridies I bought in Forfar were made by a local butcher, who used the very best rump steak for filling – the crisp pastry was made with beef dripping.

Shortcrust pastry:
85 g/3 oz butter
85 g/3 oz beef dripping
100 ml/3½ fl oz boiling water
350 g/12 oz plain flour
Salt
To prepare the meat
500 g/1 lb 2 oz rump or topside
85 g/3 oz beef suet, finely chopped
2 onions, finely chopped
Salt and ground black pepper to taste

Makes 4

Preheat the oven to 400F/200C/180Cfan/Gas 6.

To make the pastry

Cut the butter and beef dripping into small pieces and put into a bowl. Pour over boiling water and beat with a whisk till creamy. Add flour and salt. Stir to mix in. Bring together and knead till smooth. Wrap in clingfilm and leave in fridge for at least an hour before use. Divide into four and roll out into large ovals. Leave to rest for about an hour.

To prepare the meat

Beat out the steak with a meat-bat or rolling-pin and cut up roughly into 1 cm/½ in pieces. Put the meat into a bowl with the onions and suet, season and divide into four. Cover half of each oval with the meat, leaving about 1 cm/½ in round the edge for sealing. Wet edges, fold over and seal. Crimp edge with fingers. Make a hole in the top and bake on a greased baking sheet for about 45 minutes.

TRIPE SUPPERS

The frequenter of Douglas's, after ascending a few steps, found himself in a pretty large kitchen – a dark fiery Pandemonium, through which numerous ineffable ministers of flame were continually flying about, while beside the door sat the landlady, a large fat woman, in a towering head-dress and large flowered silk gown, who bowed to everyone passing. The House was noted for suppers of tripe, rizzard haddocks, mince collops and hashes which never cost more than sixpence a head.

Robert Chambers, *Traditions of Edinburgh*, 1868.

Even cheaper Tripe Suppers were provided for the poor at 'eating houses' in the industrial towns of the late nineteenth century. W. Anderson, writing in *The Poor of Edinburgh and Their Homes* (1867), describes how they were allowed 'as muckle as a man can eat' for a penny, and a plate of potatoes for another penny.

Tripe is a dish which arouses extreme emotions, for and against. Those who enjoy nose-to-tail eating of the kind Fergus Henderson celebrates with such enthusiasm in his St John restaurant in London will have no problem with this dish. A simple stew or hotpot of tripe, potatoes and onions, its advantage is that everything is cooked in one pot.

1 kg/2 lb 4 oz prepared tripe cut into 5 cm/2 in squares
2-3 medium onions, finely sliced
1.25 kg/2 lb 13 oz potatoes, sliced thinly
1 marrow bone/or knuckle of veal/or ham bone

Water or stock to cover
Seasoning:
3-4 bay leaves
1 tablespoon fresh thyme leaves
1 heaped tablespoon crushed garlic and salt
2-3 tablespoons chopped parsley

6-8 servings

Use a 1.4 L/8 pt oven casserole.

Preheat the oven to 275F/140C/120Cfan/Gas 1.

To cook

Place the meat bone in the base of the casserole. Arrange the tripe, onions and potato in layers with seasoning in between – finish with a layer of potato.

Press down well and pour in water to cover. Bring to the boil. Cover with a double layer of foil under a tightly-fitting lid and bake for 3-4 hours. Serve with lots of freshly chopped parsley.

VEAL SWEETBREADS AND KIDNEYS

On Monday 21 March 1737, the Murrays of Ochtertyre near Crieff had 'sweetbread and kidneys' for supper. According to the household accounts they had 'killed an oxe' that day and for several days following they ate tripe in a variety of guises. The theory that innards went to servants, the workhouse poor, or were thrown to the dogs, was not the case at Ochtertyre. According to the household accounts, servants fared very well, frequently eating beef and pig as well as 'puddings and hagas'. If sweetbreads are not available use all kidneys.

500 g/1 lb 2 oz veal (or lamb's) sweetbreads
250 g/9 oz veal (or lamb's) kidneys
Juice of half a lemon

Salt

For the sauce:

4–5 tablespoons unsalted butter

2 tablespoons Madeira

425 ml/15 fl oz double cream

1 teaspoon grated nutmeg

Salt, freshly milled black pepper

4 servings

To prepare both throat and heart sweetbreads

Wash well in running water for a few minutes and then leave them to soak for an hour with a tablespoon of salt. This removes traces of blood. Drain, rinse and put in enough cold water to cover. Add the lemon juice and a pinch of salt, bring to the boil and simmer until the sweetbreads become firm and white. This will only take a few minutes for lamb's sweetbreads; veal's will take longer depending on size. Don't overcook. Drain them, reserving the cooking liquid for stock, and refresh under cold running water. Remove the skin and membranes, tubes and hard bits, etc. For a firm texture, they may be pressed between two plates or boards with weights on top, and left overnight.

To make the sauce

Melt the butter in a pan. Slice the sweetbreads into 2.5 cm/1 in pieces. Skin and slice the kidneys in similar-sized pieces. Toss both in butter and cook quickly for about five minutes. Remove with a slotted spoon and keep hot. Add the Madeira to the pan and boil for 2–3 minutes, mixing with the pan juices. Add the cream and nutmeg, and reduce for about ten minutes. Adjust seasoning and pour very hot over the sweetbreads.

Serving

They can be served plainly on hot buttered toast or fried bread. Sometimes they are served in small pastry cases or on a bed of spinach. Lady Clark of Tillipronie served them with sorrel, a piquant foil for mellow sweetbreads.

SWEETBREAD PIE

Sweetbreads are a natural ingredient for pies and have been used for centuries in all kind of combinations highlighting their distinctive flavour and texture. The subtle blend of pork, bacon, mushrooms and garlic in this pie is based on Jane Grigson's recipe in *Good Things*, 1971.

Shortcrust pastry:
50 g/2 oz lard
50 g/2 oz butter
50 ml/2 fl oz boiling water
175 g/6½ oz plain flour
Salt

For the filling:
500 g/1 lb 2 oz veal sweetbreads
350 g/12 oz lean pork and/or veal
250 g/9 oz back pork fat
2 rashers unsmoked Ayrshire bacon
2 large eggs
1 heaped tablespoon flour
2 tablespoons oil
125 g/4 oz mushrooms, finely chopped
1 onion, finely chopped
1 clove garlic, crushed

8 servings

Preheat the oven to 350F/180C/160Cfan/Gas 4.

Shortcrust Pastry

Cut the butter and lard in small pieces into a bowl and pour on the boiling water. Whisk them together till the fat is all melted and mixed through – this can also be done in a processor. It should make a thickish creamy mixture, but this depends on how well the fat creams. It does not matter if the fat and water are still separated at the end of whisking. Now add the flour and salt and mix in, cover and place in refrigerator till hard – about an hour.

For the filling

Prepare the veal sweetbreads as described on p.207.

Put the pork or veal, pork fat and bacon into a food processor and whizz till coarsely blended. Add the eggs and the flour and mix through by hand.

Heat the oil in a pan and cook the mushrooms, onion and garlic together till soft.

Line a 1.75 L/3 pt capacity loaf tin with the pastry, keeping enough aside for the lid.

Lay in a third of the pork mixture and put half of the mushroom mixture on top. Arrange half of the sweetbreads on top of this. Continue – pork/mushrooms/sweetbreads – finishing with a layer of pork. Mound up nicely to support the pastry. Roll out lid, wet edges and cover. Decorate and brush with egg.

Bake for 1 hour (protect the lid if necessary). Serve warm or cold.

Note: May be made as a meat loaf without pastry in an earthenware meat-roll jar (but cover with double layer of foil – leave off towards the end of the cooking to brown top. Cool and press under a light weight overnight.

POTTED HOUGH
(Jellied Meat)

A traditional economy food which was made with the tough parts of the animal, plus bones for flavour and setting properties (from the gelatine). It was originally a high tea dish, eaten with hot buttered toast and is still a popular item in traditional butchers' shops. Made in varying sizes, there are subtle differences in the flavour of potted hough. Made at home, it can be used as the basis for useful stock by adding a few extra bones: then the leftover jellied stock can be used for soup. Some butchers add salt-pickled beef.

1 kg/2 lb 4 oz hough (shin of beef)
Nap bone (put in more if making extra stock)
Blade of mace
3 or 4 whole cloves
Salt and pepper

4-6 servings

To cook

Place the ingredients in a large pan, cover with water and bring to the boil. Skim off scum, add mace and cloves and simmer until the meat falls off the bones. This takes around 2-3 hours. Strain. Leave stock to get cold overnight, when it should set to a firm jelly. Remove the excess fat layer on top and use as dripping. Leave the meat to cool, then chop finely or put into a food processor with some stock and whizz till fairly fine.

To finish

Put the meat into a pan and cover with jellied stock. The proportion is a matter of taste, add more stock if you like a jellied result, less if you like it meatier. Bring to the boil and simmer for a few minutes. Leave to cool. Taste and season. Pour into wetted moulds and leave to set. Turn out to serve.

Other Traditional Beef Products – Lorne Sausage, Sassermaet, Suet and Dripping

LORNE SAUSAGE

A square, sliced sausage which was named after the Glasgow Music Hall comedian, Tommy Lorne, who liked to joke about this 'squeer' sausage. The square shape was designed to fit sandwiches, made with a 'square loaf' which fitted into the square tin lunchboxes which Glasgow working men took with them every day to their work.

The sausage is made with minced beef and fat, plus a starchy binder, seasonings and water. This is then put into a Lorne tin, the surface pressed by hand and the tin inverted onto a tray. It is left to harden in the refrigerator before slicing.

SASSERMAET

This is a Shetland version of a Lorne sausage using minced beef and spices. There is also a pork version. In its earliest form it was a winter preservation item made by the crofter. The chopped meat was heavily spiced and packed into an earthenware crock. When it was required it was mixed with breadcrumbs and chopped onions, bound together with egg or milk and fried. The spices used are black pepper, white pepper, ground cloves, allspice and cinnamon.

SUET

This is the fat from the loin and kidney region in a beef carcass. Its primary use was as an ingredient in traditional boiled/steamed puddings. Those of the savoury variety were part of the staple diet as a high calorie starchy filler in the days before potatoes. Suet is still an essential ingredient for clootie dumpling, Christmas pudding and mincemeat. It is a creamy white, hard fat and may be sold by the butcher straight from the carcass, in which case it must have the sinewy membranes removed before chopping. This will give a better flavour than the ready-prepared shredded suet, which is made from beef kidney suet. The ready-prepared shredded vegetarian suet lacks flavour.

DRIPPING

This is the fat carefully collected in the roasting tray after meat has been cooked. Butchers, who cook their own meats, pour it into clean pots and allow it to cool. Some sell it with a layer of the meat juices in the base of the pot underneath the dripping: this is sold as 'Stovie dripping'. It may be used as a spread on hot toast, or in sandwiches, especially those made with the roast meat. Also used for basting meat, roasting potatoes and making **Skirlie** (see p.22).

Lamb and Mutton

Such a display of mutton broth…and roasted jiggets of lamb.
D.M. Moir, *Mansie Wauch*, 1828.

Sheep and goats were the first wild animals gathered into herds by prehistoric man, who saw the advantage of having milk and meat 'to hand'. Indigenous in the wild to parts of the Near East, it was probably in Iraq, around 9,000 BC, that they were domesticated and nomadic herdsmen began to moved westwards with their herds.

They reached Britain about 4,000 BC, when sheep and goats became established as valuable milk, meat and wool producers. In the Middle Ages the Border hills were well trodden by sheep, which helped keep the English wool trade in business, as well as providing milk for cheese. Sheep and goats were also kept in the Highlands and Islands for meat, milk, cheese and wool, but in much smaller numbers compared with the Borders. Just a few sheep and goats were kept for domestic use and practically none were exported. The vast army of sheep which came nibbling their way up strath and glen as a result of the mid-1800s Clearances were not for local use but to supply meat for growing urban markets. In some areas, such as the Borders, they continued to supply wool for the textile industry.

Breeds

While England can name some forty native breeds, Scottish sheep husbandry is mostly based on the native Blackface and North and South Country Cheviots, with some local variants such as Shetland, Soay and North Ronaldsay. Much cross-breeding goes on to improve stock and give a good proportion of meat to bone, as well as tender, well-flavoured flesh. There have been similar developments to those in beef breeding, where leaner, larger Continental breeds were introduced to produce larger, leaner cuts. The disadvantages of this policy have been made clear in the lack of flavour and character in meat from these animals, as in beef from Continental breeds.

The **Blackface** or 'Blackies' are considered among the hardiest, surviving the worst snowstorms on open hills and still producing healthy lambs in the spring. They have a wild look which characterises their temperament as tough, courageous and determined animals, whose natural instincts keep them foraging for food in the most appalling conditions. They predominate on the vast areas of wild hill country, and most of the UK flock are in Scotland. There are several distinct types within the breed. These have evolved over the years, influenced by climate, environment and grazing quality. There are three main types: the Perth type, a large-framed sheep found mainly in north-east Scotland, south-west England and Northern Ireland: the **Lanark** type, which is dominant in much of Scotland and areas of Ireland, is of medium size, with shorter wool than the **Perth** type; and in the north of England there is also the large-framed **Northumberland Blackface** with its softer wool. Breeders on the Isle of Lewis in the Hebrides describe their Blackface as **Hebridean**.

The breed can be traced back to the twelfth century, when they were mentioned by monks who exported their wool. But it was James IV of Scotland who began improving the breed, establishing a flock in the Ettrick Forrest in the 1500s. In the early 1800s they were taken, along with Cheviots, to the Highlands and by the end of the century had become the dominant breed. Such is the pursuit of excellence in the breed that a Blackie tup was sold at Perth in 1997 for a record £85,000.

'This small hill lamb is perhaps the finest quality in the world, giving a carcase free from superfluous fat and waste. The lightweight carcass satisfies a high demand in the marketplace whether it is sold through Smithfield, a High Street butcher, the supermarkets or the continent.' *British Sheep* (The National Sheep Association 1982).

The **Cheviots**, named after the Cheviot Hills which extend across the border between Scotland and England, are also hardy hill sheep, more often found on upland farms and grass-covered 'white' hills rather than 'black' hills, which are heather-covered. They produce a lightweight carcass, low in fat with a high percentage of well-flavoured lean meat, and are one of the oldest breeds in Scotland. Their history goes back at least to the fourteenth century, when they were bred for their wool by the monks of the Border abbeys. To improve the wool quality, Merino sheep were introduced and the wool-manufacturing towns of Selkirk, Galashiels, Hawick and Langholm became famous for their woollen products.

It was in the Borders that the North Country Cheviots were first developed. Crossed with a variety of other breeds, besides the Merino sheep, they became known as 'Northies' when they were established in Caithness as a breed, displacing the people during the mid-nineteenth-century Clearances. Today the breed is still found mainly on the colder, more exposed, east side of Scotland, from Shetland to the Borders. It is a tough breed which produces a large carcass with a high proportion of lean to fat.

Shetland sheep, which graze on rough grasslands, heather and seaweed on the Shetland shores, are one of the smallest British breeds, retaining many of the characteristics of wild sheep. They are hardy and self-reliant, surviving severe gales and winter blizzards. Because it is impossible to be more than three and a half miles from the sea anywhere on the islands, the air, activated by the strong winds, carries salt over all the pastures. This, combined with the seaweed which they eat, gives the meat a unique, slightly gamey flavour which has been favourably compared with the much-praised French Agneaux de Pré-Salé, which are the lambs fed on the salty grasses of the northern coastal region of France. Like the Shetland lamb, the Pré-Salé is five to nine months old at the time of killing, but because of the poor-quality winter grazing, Shetland lamb is smaller in size. Despite this, the harsh environment has ensured that only the fittest lambs survive, making them well-conditioned, hardy and vigorous.

Shetland sheep were also kept for their very fine, soft wool which was carded and spun in the croft houses. This wool was not clipped but 'rooed' – pulled away by hand when the sheep started to lose its coat in summer, the finest wool coming from the neck. It was this neck wool which was used in the famous shawls which are so fine they can pass through a wedding ring. Shetland lamb has never become widely known on the British mainland, partly due to distance and difficulties of transport. The scarcity of numbers has also been a limiting factor. The lambs are normally born from May onwards and do not become available until October or November. The difficulties of marketing this distinctively flavoured breed has been overcome by sheep farmer Ronnie Eunson, through making contacts with specialist butchers who market his lamb on the Scottish mainland, and in London by David Lidgate, in Holland Park.

Other native breeds:

At present these are being preserved from extinction by the Rare Breeds Survival Trust, and include the **Boreray** from the island of Boreray in the St Kilda group; also the **Soay** sheep from the St

Kilda islands, and **North Ronaldsay** sheep from the Orkney island where they live entirely on a diet of seaweed on the shore. A stone dyke round the whole island fences the sheep out of the precious arable land, which is kept for other livestock. The sheep's seaweed diet produces a uniquely flavoured meat and milk with a high iodine content.

Four breeds – Soay, North Ronaldsay, Shetland and Castlemilk Moorit – are classed under the general heading of Scottish Primitive Breeds. Associated with the far north and west of Scotland, they are thought to be not too different to Neolithic sheep. In the Hebrides and Shetland they have been influenced by breeds brought by the Vikings from Scandinavia. After a long period of decline, the primitive breeds are now being recognised for both their genetic and commercial factors. Studies indicate that the fatty acid composition of primitive sheep is different to commercial breeds, making them a more healthy eating option since they have a lower proportion of the more harmful saturated fatty acids.

Other breeds: English Leicesters, Suffolks, some of the Down breeds and continental breeds including Texels (from the island of Texel off the north-west coast of Holland) are used for crossing with the native Scottish breeds, but usually there will be some Blackie in the cross to give hardiness.

Availability/Buying

Lamb: Most lambing takes place on hill sheep farms during April, though some low-ground farms may start as early as February. A few low-ground farms produce early lambs from the end of December. Born and reared indoors in intensive systems, they are available in limited quantities for Easter, but because of high production costs they are expensive and they lack flavour.

Scottish lamb is at its best, and most plentiful, from July through to December. Most of the lamb from Scottish hill farms comes on the market from October onwards. Killed before its first birthday it is still lamb, but thereafter is a hogget (a year-old sheep which becomes mutton, a mature sheep, after its second birthday). Flavour depends on breed, age, feeding and hanging.

The Blackface Sheep Breeders Association (*www.scottish-black-face.co.uk*) aims to market the slower growing lamb in November. Its selling point is its excellent flavour. Though it lacks a large carcase size, by Continental standards, Blackies have a well-rounded muscle, a small amount of bone and, given their active lifestyle, not a high percentage of surplus fat. All primitive breeds provide small joints of fine-flavoured meat.

Mutton: This was a highly valued meat from sheep for centuries. Bred first and foremost for their wool, it was only after a couple of years, once they had produced a fleece or two, that they were killed. Most were kept a lot longer.

After World War II all this changed, as the wool trade declined and faster-reared and faster-cooked lamb became the preferred choice. For most people mutton slipped into oblivion. Yet mutton enthusiasts continued to wax lyrical about its charms, while others wanted to forget the tough-as-boots old mutton they had to eat during the war. So mutton was minced and put into pies, or eaten by ethnic communities who knew how to cook it slow-and-wet, or it was exported.

Now there is a crisis among hill sheep farmers, and those on remote Scottish islands, who must get better prices for their mutton if they are to survive. They have vast areas of rough grazing which is ideal for nothing much else than rearing mature sheep. They are being supported by a growing movement in the UK, set up in 2004, which has campaigned to bring back over-two-year-old mutton to the nation's dinner tables (see www.muttonrenaissance.org.uk). They are dealing with issues of quality and supply in their effort to reverse its fortunes and save the hill and island sheep farms from extinction.

It is available from October to March. Farmers who sell through farmers markets often have supplies of mutton, while another source is Halal butchers, though their mutton may not be hung very long. For optimum flavour, all mutton requires a hanging time of at least seven days.

A GIGOT of MUTTON
with Caper Sauce

This is made with two-year plus mutton. Between four and five-year-old was rated the best. Many ideas for cooking mutton are to be found in nineteenth and early twentieth-century cookery books. Mrs Beeton is a good source, but also Meg Dods, in this recipe for four to five-year-old mountain or wether (castrated male) mutton, in *The Cook and Housewife's Manual*, 1826:

Simmer in an oval-shaped pot that will just hold it, letting the water come very slowly to the boil. Skim carefully. Boil sliced carrots and turnip with the mutton, and the younger and juicier they are the better they suit this joint. All meat ought to be well done, but a leg of mutton not overdone, to look plump and retain its juices. About two hours slow boiling will dress it.

Garnish with slices of carrot. Pour caper-sauce over the meat, and serve mashed turnip or cauliflower in a separate dish.

ROAST RACK OF LAMB

Roasting on the rib bones provides its own built-in rack, protecting the meat and preventing it drying out while retaining flavour. For juicy, flavourful meat a rack should be cooked either rare or medium rare. An instant-read thermometer to check the internal temperature of the meat is a useful tool to prevent overcooking.

A rack can be either single (quicker) or double (longer). For a 'Guard of Honour', two racks the same size, with the end of the rib bones trimmed, are interlaced, making a tunnel between them for the stuffing.

For a single rack, buy one with 8 uncut chops and ask the butcher to prepare – he should saw through the backbone but not remove, since it protects the meat while cooking and can be removed before carving. He may trim the ends of the bones, but this is not essential.

For a double rack, ask for two matching racks from the same animal if possible. The top 2-3 inches of the ribs need to be stripped to allow the two sides to interlace.

1 rack (8 chops) or 2 racks (8 chops each) of lamb
Herb and Lemon Stuffing for double rack (see p.179):
Salt and pepper
3 tablespoons oil
1 tablespoon thyme leaves
50 g/2 oz butter (½ stick)
150 ml/5 fl oz stock or water
Salt and freshly ground pepper

4 servings

Preheat the oven 450F/230C/210Cfan/Gas 8.

Use a sturdy roasting tin.

Preparing the meat

Weigh the meat. Allow a roasting time of 12-15 minutes per 450 g/1 lb for underdone pink meat. Put the meat in a dish and rub with oil and thyme over the outer meat surfaces. Grind some black pepper on top. Cover and leave for a few hours or overnight.

Roasting a single rack

4 servings

Place the rack, bone side down, in a roasting tin and baste with any excess oil. Season fat surface with salt. Roast for 10 mins at high heat, then reduce the temperature to 425F/220C/200Cfan/Gas 7. Before the estimated time, check the internal temperature on an instant-read thermometer. It should reach 54C for rare or 57C for medium rare. Remove, place on a warmed ashet or serving platter, cover with foil and leave the meat to rest for 10 minutes in a warm place, when the meat will go on cooking in the latent heat, increasing its temperature by 2C.

Making the gravy

Add stock or water and scrape up all the residues from the pan. Simmer for about five minutes to reduce and concentrate the flavours, stirring all the time. Some of the juices will, by now, have dripped out of the rack and should be poured into the gravy. When it has a good flavour, season with salt and pepper.

Carving and Serving

Carve down the rib bones. Serve with gravy, creamy mashed potatoes and an apple and mint or redcurrant jelly.

Roasting a double rack

8 servings

Preparing the meat

As for single rack (above). Make the stuffing. Marinate the meat with oil and herbs.

To stuff

In the dish they have been marinating in, lay one rack on its side, meat side down, and cover the rib cage with the stuffing. Press into the bone till it is evenly packed. Put the other rib on top, meat side up, and interlace the bones. Press all well together and tie with string. Weigh and allow a roasting time of 12-15 minutes per 450 g/1 lb for underdone pink meat.

Roasting

Put into roasting tin standing upright. Pour over any excess oil and herbs in the dish. Season with salt and freshly ground pepper. Put into the hot oven for 15 minutes. Lower the heat 350F/200C/180Cfan/Gas 6. Before the estimated time, check the internal temperature on an instant-read thermometer. It should reach 54C for rare or 57C for medium rare. Remove, place on a warmed ashet or serving platter, cover with foil and leave the meat to rest for 10 minutes in a warm place when the meat will go on cooking in the latent heat, increasing its temperature by 2C.

Make gravy/rest/and serve as for single rack above.

Carve by following the rib bones and cutting two chops together with the stuffing in the centre.

GRILLED OR BARBECUED LEG OF LAMB

This is best barbecued over charcoal with a handful of fresh rosemary thrown over the hot coals before and during the cooking. To make the piece of meat a uniform thickness so that it cooks evenly, it is boned out first. If necessary, ask a butcher to do this.

1 leg of lamb
Marinade:
450 ml/15 fl oz robust red wine
4 tablespoons olive oil
1 medium onion, finely sliced
1 carrot, thinly sliced
6 parsley stalks
2 bay leaves
A sprig of rosemary
1 clove garlic, crushed
1 teaspoon salt
Freshly ground black pepper

To make the marinade

Mix all the marinade ingredients together.

To bone out the meat

Begin by loosening the pelvic bone, following the contours of the bone. When the ball-and-socket joint that connects the pelvic bone to the thighbone is exposed, cut through the tendons joining the bones. Make a straight cut down the length of the thighbone on the inside of the leg, and again following the contours of the bone, loosen the flesh from the bone.

Marinating the lamb

Flatten out the meat with a meat-bat or rolling-pin. It should be a fairly even thickness. Place in a dish which it will fit into neatly and add marinade. Leave for 12-24 hours, or longer, and turn once or twice.

To cook the lamb

Grill or barbecue over a high heat for about 10-15 minutes, depending on the degree of pinkness required. For the best flavour and succulence it should be cooked rare to medium rare. Keep turning and baste frequently with a little of the marinade to keep it moist. Make a gravy with some of the strained marinade and the pan juices if grilled. Serve with a green salad and baked potatoes.

Note: If the grill-pan is not large enough to cope with a whole leg it can be roasted in a very hot oven – 450F/230C/210Cfan/ Gas 8 for 15 minutes per 450g/1 lb. Turn and baste once or twice during the cooking. Leave to rest for 10 minutes in a warm place before serving.

SLOW-ROAST LAMB SHOULDER

Not the traditional lamb roast joint but, unlike the leg, it can be left in the oven without worry about overcooking. It may not carve so neatly into slices as a leg, but what it lacks in shape it makes up for in flavour.

1 lamb shoulder on the bone (approx. 2.225 kg/5 lb)
1 head garlic
2-3 sprigs rosemary
3-4 tablespoons oil
Juice of 1 lemon
1.5 kg/3 lb 5 oz carrot, turnip, onion, celery, peeled weight
Sprigs of rosemary and thyme
Sea salt
450 ml/15 fl oz white wine/water or stock
Salt and ground pepper

6-8 servings

Use a large roasting tin, 23 x 28 cm/9 x 11 in, which will hold the shoulder.

Preheat the grill to high. Preheat the oven to 325F/160C/140Cfan/Gas 3.

Slow-roasting the meat and vegetables

Cut the vegetables into chunky pieces and put them with the thyme and rosemary into the roasting tin. Drizzle over oil, coating all the vegetables. Divide up the garlic head into cloves, smash each clove with the side of a large chopping knife and remove skin. With a long sharp knife make deep slits in the flesh of the lamb and push cloves into the slits. Make surface slits in the fat and push through sprigs of rosemary. Put shoulder on top of vegetables skin side up. Rub the skin with oil and sprinkle over lemon juice. Add 250 ml/8 fl oz wine or water. Cover with two layers of foil and seal round the edges.

Cook slowly for 3-4 hours till the meat is tender and coming away easily from the bone. Remove foil and roast for 20-30 minutes at a high heat (450F/230C/210Cfan/Gas 8) to crisp and brown the skin.

Finishing and serving

Remove from the oven. Strain off the juices into a pan. Adjust consistency with some wine. Bring up to a simmer and reduce a little. Taste and season. Serve with the meat and vegetables and roast or baked potatoes.

PICKLED BLACKFACE MUTTON

This salt-sugar pickle adds extra flavour and character to more mature mutton from native breeds such as the Blackface (Blackie), while adding to its shelf-life.

Pickle mix:
2 L/3 pt 10 fl oz water
600 g/1 lb 5 oz coarse sea salt
250 g/9 oz brown muscovado sugar
1 sprig bay leaves
1 sprig thyme
5 crushed juniper berries
5 crushed peppercorns
Cooking mix:
3 medium onions stuck with 3 cloves
bay leaf
8 peppercorns
3 carrots, peeled and chopped in two
Small turnip, peeled and chopped roughly in large pieces.

To make the pickle

Boil the ingredients, stirring to dissolve, and leave to simmer for about 10 minutes. Leave to cool. Put the cold pickle into a large earthenware crock, plastic bucket with a lid or other suitable container which will hold a whole leg. Immerse the meat and keep below the surface by laying a heavy plate on top. Cover and keep in a cool place. Pickle time should be shorter if the meat is thin and boneless, longer if it is thick and with bone. For a 3 kg/6lb 12 oz leg of mutton on the bone, between 12 and 24 hours will produce a well-flavoured result. The longer it is left in, the stronger the result. If kept in a cool dark place, the pickle mixture will keep for several months and can be used again.

To cook the meat

Rinse under cold water; put into a pot which it will fit into neatly. Add onion stuck with cloves, bay leaf, peppercorns, carrot and turnip. Cover with cold water and bring up to the boil, skim. Turn down heat to low and simmer gently, covered with a tight-fitting lid, till the meat is tender. Remove and serve hot with boiled floury potatoes or cold with oatcakes and butter.

Use the cooking liquor to make broth, adjust saltiness if necessary by adding more water.

This pickle can also be used for pork, duck and chicken.

SCOTCH PIES

Scottish bakers make these pies in a special pie-making machine which moulds the shape. They are made with a hot-water pastry and mostly filled with minced beef, though the original filling was mature mutton. Other more modern fillings include macaroni and cheese.

The small, hand-held pies have straight sides and are usually about 7.5-8.5 cm (3-3½ in) in diameter by 4 cm (1½ in) deep. They are noted for the space above the pie lid and the top edge of the pie which is filled with beans, mashed potatoes or gravy. Often sold as a hot takeaway by bakers and fish and chip shops, they are also standard fare at football matches with a cup of hot Bovril. They were a popular tavern food, and Grannie Black's tavern in Glasgow's Candleriggs district once had a reputation for the best mutton pies, costing two pence, which were commonly known as 'Tuppenny Struggles'.

Nose-to-Tail Cooking

Heads are available, though not on display. Sometimes difficult to get if there is a circus in town since they are favourite food for lions and tigers. I suppose the same holds true if you live near a zoo.

The blood makes black puddings, with sieved oatmeal, or groats, or rice . . . The head, trotters and breast of mutton, with some of the superfluous fat on this last cut off, make, with vegetables, the best broth, and afterwards all the meat is useful in other ways. The sheep's head, whole, is served with feet ('trotters') round as garnish, and with broth as sauce; or cut up in squares in dressed sauce as an entrée, vegetables in centre and fried brains as garnish; or can be boiled and turned out of a mould solid.

The boiled breast of mutton used to boil with Sheep's Head, can afterwards be crumbled, with mixed herbs, and broiled or baked a nice brown, to eat hot. If for upstairs, serve a sharp sauce in a boat with chopped gherkins or capers in it.

Kidneys can be sliced for breakfast, with bacon, or in an omelet, and the liver sliced and fried and served with bacon and fried potatoes.

The sheep's heart is hard if roasted; it is better stuffed and braised – but must be eaten at once – it chills so immediately. A sheep's sweetbread is not worth cooking though in the lamb it is excellent. A lamb's head can be served upon a 'fugie', a mince of heart, sweetbread, liver etc. but no kidneys. Make it savoury.

Much of the rest is used for Haggis. Any bits not otherwise wanted are very welcome additions to the scraps set aside for the keeper's dogs.

From *The Cookery Book of Lady Clark of Tillypronie* (1909).

STUFFED LAMBS' HEARTS

Stuffing:
25 g/1 oz butter or 1 tablespoon oil
1 onion finely diced
150 g/5 oz white breadcrumbs
1 tablespoon chopped parsley

1 tablespoon thyme leaves
Grated zest of 1 lemon
1 egg
Salt and ground pepper
Hearts:
2 tablespoons oil
2 carrots, ¼ turnip, 3 sticks celery and 1 onion, peeled and
  roughly chopped
6 lambs' hearts
Strong thread to wind round
15 g/½ oz flour
Salt and ground pepper
Stock or water

6–8 servings

Use a thick-based or cast-iron oven-proof pot with a tight-fitting lid.

Preheat oven to 350F/180C/160Cfan/Gas 4.

Making the stuffing

Heat the butter/oil in a pan, and when hot add the onions. Cook till soft but not coloured. Add the breadcrumbs, parsley, thyme, lemon zest, salt and pepper. Mix through, then add the egg and bind it all together.

Preparing, stuffing and cooking the hearts

Cut off any arteries and trim round the top. Slit the cavity open with scissors to make a space for the stuffing. Wash under running water to remove all traces of blood. Fill cavities with stuffing. Wind some strong thread round to hold in stuffing, or skewer top edges together. Heat the oil in an ovenproof pot over a medium heat till hot, add the onions and brown lightly. Then add the other vegetables and cook for a few minutes. Sieve flour over the vegetables and stir in. Add seasoning. Place the hearts on this base of vegetables. Add stock or water to cover the vegetables. Cover and put in the oven for 2½-3 hours till tender. Remove the lid for the last 30 minutes or so to brown the hearts and reduce the cooking liquid.

Serving

Remove hearts from the pot and unwind the thread. Taste and season the cooking liquor. Return hearts to the pan and serve with creamed potatoes.

LAMB'S FRY

Very thin strips of liver, kidney and heart are cooked very quickly to preserve flavour and texture.

4 tablespoons oil
2 lambs' hearts
200 g/7 oz lambs' liver
200 g/7 oz lambs' kidney
1-2 cloves crushed garlic
1 handful of chopped parsley
Lemon juice
Salt and ground pepper
4 slices of hot buttered toast or fried bread

4-6 servings

Use a non-stick wok or frying or sauté pan.

To prepare the meat

Split heart in half. Wash off all blood. Remove excess fat and tough tubes/gristle etc from the heart. Wash and dry. Cut meat in strips, lengthwise. Remove tough tubes etc from the liver. Wash and dry. Cut into thin strips. Cut kidney in half. Remove the tough core. Wash and dry. Cut into strips roughly the same size as the other meats.

To cook

Heat the oil till fairly hot, but not smoking, in a wok (or frying or sauté pan) and add the heart. Toss in the oil for about a minute. Add the rest of the meat. Continue tossing in the hot oil. Add the garlic. When they begin to look cooked – they will only take a few minutes – cut a piece open to test. When still lightly pink add parsley, a squeeze of lemon juice and salt and pepper. Toss and serve on hot buttered toast or fried bread.

HAGGIS

Liver, heart, kidney and lungs, still attached to the windpipe, are thoroughly washed in the sink, then put into a huge stock pot with the windpipe hanging over the side of the pot. A jar underneath catches the drips as the pluck (innards) cooks, quietly disgorging blood and other impurities into it.

This haggis recipe is in *The Glasgow Cookery Book* first published in 1910 (revised for the Centenary Edition in 2010) and is made with a sheep's pluck chopped and mixed with oatmeal, onions and spices, which is more or less the type most Scottish butchers make with their own secret variations.

Qualities of a good Haggis

Fine or coarse? Spicy or oniony? Meaty or mealy?

The texture, flavour and content of haggis provides as many choices as there are haggis-makers. Heated debates arise when a haggis has been made with pig or ox liver. It's not a proper Scotch haggis, some say. Arguments of this type are inevitable, but there are some basic rules: no tough gristly bits; a moist consistency; a firm texture; not dry or crumbly; and no cheating by adding the flavour-enhancer MSG (monosodium glutamate) – yes, it does happen.

Traditional Method

(Quantities of suet, onions and oatmeal vary according to size of pluck.)

1 sheep's stomach bag and pluck (liver, heart and lungs)

50 g/2 oz butter

4 medium onions, finely chopped

250 g/9 oz pinhead oatmeal, sometimes a mix of medium and
pinhead (toasted)

200 g/7 oz beef suet, finely chopped

1 tablespoon fresh herbs, chopped finely

Salt to taste

Freshly ground pepper

Ground allspice

Preparing the pluck and bag

Wash the stomach bag under running cold water, scrape and clean well. Leave to steep overnight in cold water. Wash the pluck and put it in a pan of boiling water. Let the windpipe hang over the side of the pot and have a small jar underneath to catch the drips. This might seem an unnecessary procedure but it removes impurities and makes it possible to use the cooking liquor (stock) to flavour and moisten the haggis. Bring up to the boil and skim. Simmer gently till all are tender – this depends on the age of animal but is usually between one and two hours. Leave to cool in its own liquor overnight.

Making the Haggis (the next day)

Heat the butter in a pan and add the onions. Cook till soft and uncoloured. Toast the oatmeal in the oven till thoroughly dried out but not browned. Cut off the windpipe, trim away all skin and black parts. Chop or mince the heart and lungs, grate the liver. Add the oatmeal, salt, pepper, herbs and allspice. Gradually add enough cooking liquor to make a soft consistency, neither too wet or too dry. Mix well. Fill the bag slightly more than half full; it needs space to expand. Press out the air, sew up open end. Wrap loosely in a large piece of foil and place in a pot of gently simmering water. Simmer for 3 hours. The bag may be cut into several pieces to make smaller haggis, in which case cook for only 1½-2 hours.

Serve hot with 'tatties' – creamed potatoes; 'neeps' – mashed yellow turnip (see p.266). May be served with spicy or fruit chutneys, wholegrain or Dijon mustard.

OTHER WAYS OF SERVING

'Haggis meat, by those who cannot admire the natural shape,' says Meg Dods, *'may be poured out of the bag, and served in a deep dish. No dish heats up better.'*

Meg's method works well for leftovers, and Burns' Suppers for large numbers, but covering tightly with foil is essential. Some pieces of butter on top will ensure moistness. Slices of haggis can be grilled, fried or wrapped in foil and baked in the oven, also with a bit of butter on top. This can be served as part of a Mixed Grill or for breakfast with bacon and egg. A fried slice goes well with **Burnt Onions** (see p.268) or in a roll with some spicy chutney (a haggisburger). It can also be mixed with mince in a Shepherd's Pie. A mild-flavoured haggis can be used as a stuffing.

In fact it is so versatile that a book on many 'ways to use haggis' (*The Macsween Haggis Bible*, 2013) has been written by Jo Macsween, daughter of the late Charles Macsween, the Edinburgh haggis butcher who created a stir when he invented a haggis without a pluck at the request of the Scottish Poetry Library in 1984. It includes vegetables, spices, oatmeal, nuts and brown rice and has become popular among both non-meat and meat-eaters.

Other variations, past and present, include: adding the juice of a lemon or a little 'good vinegar'; flavouring with cayenne pepper; adding less or more oatmeal; using a variety of 'cuts' of oatmeal (see p.3); using less or more suet; using sheeps' tongues and kidneys instead of the lights; substituting soaked bread or crisped crumbs for some of the oatmeal. There is no end to haggis permutations.

Origins of Haggis Pudding

Though the habit of cooking the chopped innards of an animal in its stomach bag goes back to the beginnings of cookery, its development in Britain has taken some curious twists. How it got its name, for a start, remains a riddle. Could it have come from the French *hachis*, meaning 'mince'? Or was it named after an early word for a magpie – *haggas*? Another possibility is that it came from the Old Norse verb *To hag*, meaning 'to hack or chop'. An even more intriguing question is why it was so loved by everyone in England, for the best part of four centuries, but was suddenly rejected in the middle of the 1700s when it became a distinctly Scotch haggis.

The evidence of haggis's popularity in England, prior to this, goes back a long way, to the first record of it in the English Harleian manuscript of 1430 for *Hagws of a schepe*. Then in 1597, in his *Good Huswifes Jewel*, Thomas Dawson gives another English recipe *To make a Haggas pudding* using a calf's innards. More evidence of its popularity is confirmed by Gervase Markham, writing in *The English Huswife* (1615) when he says that, '. . . oat-meale mixed with blood, and the Liver of either Sheepe, Calfe or Swine, maketh that pudding which is called the *Haggas* or *Haggus*, of whose goodnesse it is in vaine to boast, because there is hardly to be found a man that doth not affect [like] them'. The chef to royalty, Robert May, devotes a section to *Sheeps Haggas Puddings* in his *Accomplisht Cook* (1660), establishing that it was not just a cheap peasant dish but celebrated by the highest in the land.

A recipe for a *Scotch haggas* in 1747 by the English cookery writer, Hannah Glasse, is an early sign that there was something distinctly Scottish about it. Confirmation that the haggis had become Scotch comes from the novelist Tobias Smollett. Though a Scot himself, his English hero in the novel *Humphry Clinker* (1771) says, 'I am not yet Scotchman enough to relish their singed sheep's-head and haggice.' His female companion was also unable to partake, turning 'pale' at the sight.

Meanwhile, in Scotland, a recipe for *Good Scotch Haggies* appears in Susanna McIver's *Cookery and Pastry* (1773) which is made, like Hanna Glasse's recipe, with a calf's pluck and 'a piece of beef', plus oatmeal, suet, onions and spices. It could have been this haggis which Burns eulogised when he wrote 'The Address' some thirteen years later. What prompted him to do so is yet another puzzle.

It was during his first visit to Edinburgh in 1786 that he wrote the poem, possibly inspired one night when invited to say an impromptu grace before dinner as a steaming haggis was dished up. Moved by the sight before him, he decided to make his feelings known about how he rated the virtues of the haggis, compared with what he had observed in other places during his few months in Edinburgh. He was in much demand by the intelligentsia, who had recently moved into their elegant New Town houses, and a welcome guest at their dinner tables. Was this where he came across those 'that ower their French ragout' looked down 'wi' sneering, scornfu' view on sic (such) a dinner'?

Lodging in the Old Town, his daily fare in the taverns would certainly have included the 'singed sheep's-head and haggice' which Smollett's hero had rejected. Burns saw it differently. Here was a dish which symbolised ingenuity and thrift. It was honest peasant food which had made the 'haggis-fed' Scot strong and healthy. 'Oh how unfit,' he opines, is the fate of those who turned pale at the sight of it.

After his death in 1796, Burns's poem might have remained an interesting piece of culinary history. But this was Scotland, still recovering from the loss of both crown and parliament. There was a concern among many that the country would also lose its native culture. Among those who were keen that the Scots language should not be lost was Sir Walter Scott, who wrote himself in Scots and also encouraged many of the bright young talents of the day to write, like Burns, in Scots.

He was also involved in a Burns celebration in 1815: a dinner in Edinburgh when 'The Address' and the 'Haggis' joined forces. Burns Clubs had already been set up by this time, and would eventually grow into a national and international movement. But in the early decades of the 1800s, Scott's support of haggis as an icon of nationalism was influential. He must have relished the sentiments in the poem. Always the dramatist himself, he would have loved the ritual address, tartan, bagpipes etc. And he would have enjoyed eating the haggis dinner too. If the descriptions of his eating habits by his biographer son-in-law, John Gibson Lockhart, are anything to go by, Scott was a nose-to-tail man, nothing wasted. His cook at Abbotsford would have been well-practised in this culinary art.

Though haggis was still made in the domestic kitchen, at least until the mid-1950s, much of the production has been taken over by high street butchers. When many of them closed in the second half of the 1900s, with the rise of supermarkets, haggis production did not decline. Those surviving on the high street just made more, while others opened haggis factories to increase their output. Though peak production is mid-January for Burns Night, there is also a daily demand throughout the year. No need for a preservation order to prevent Scotch haggis falling into oblivion.

The first 'Scotch' Haggis recipe?

A Good Scotch Haggies

Make the haggis-bag perfectly clean, parboil the draught; boil the liver very well, so as it will grate; dry the meal before the fire; mince the draught and a pretty large piece of beef very small; grate about half of the liver; mince plenty of the suet and some onions small; mix all these materials very well together, with a handful or two of the dried meal; spread them on the table, and season them properly with salt and mixed spices; take any of the scraps of beef that are left from mincing, and some of the water that boiled the draught, and make about a choppin of good stock of it; then put all the haggis meat into the bag, and that broth in it; then sew up the bag: but be sure to put out all the wind before you sew it quite close. If you think the bag is thin, you may put it in a cloth. If it is a large haggis, it will take at least two hours' boiling.

From *Cookery and Pastry*, Edinburgh 1773, by Susanna McIver.

Pork and Bacon

The Scottish Pork Taboo

Was it a foolish prejudice or just a shortage of pig food? It's a question which has mystified antiquarians, anthropologists, folklorists and modern historians over the years. Though there is evidence that pork was eaten in prehistoric Scotland, and in the Middle Ages too, at some point after this its consumption declined. The American anthropologist Eric B. Ross (*The Riddle of the Scottish Pig*, 1983) has suggested that this was a result of the loss of oak and beech forests, which made it uneconomic to raise pigs. Now sheep were more suited to the treeless landscape and, as pigs decreased, so sheep multiplied.

This was certainly true, as many travellers in Scotland noted in the 1700s that there was an almost complete absence of pigs in certain parts of the country. In particular, it seems, this was the case in the Highlands, in fishing communities and generally in the lower classes throughout the country.

There is one folklorist theory that suggests this can be dated back to a religious cult in pre-Roman times. Others suggest that it was a Christian taboo, related to biblical beliefs that pork was 'unclean' and a symbol of the devil – as an old Galloway grace before meat confirms in its last line *'Bless the soo for Satan's sake, he was yince a soo himsel'* (from Dr Trotter's *Galloway Gossip*). Whatever the reason for the pig's rejection in Scotland, its effect can be seen in the lack of cooking traditions for it, compared with England's rich pork and bacon specialities.

The pig's revival in Scotland was encouraged in the 1800s by new developments in cheesemaking, particularly in the dairying areas of South West Scotland. Now the pig, once again, had a source of cheap food in whey, a cheesemaking by-product. And foolish prejudices, where they existed, began to die out.

AYRSHIRE BACON

This is a curing method which depends on high-quality pork. At Ramsay's Wellriggs factory, one of the largest Ayrshire bacon-curers in the area whose tradition goes back four generations, they buy pigs which are fatter than normal which they pay a premium for.

'Because it's better fed, and has a bit more fat,' says Andrew Ramsay, 'the pig has a better flavour. That's half the battle. No point in having a pig that's half starved and tastes like rubber.'

The curing method removes both skin and bones before wet-salting. The back or cutlet part is not separated, so that once cured the whole piece is rolled up tightly with the fat side out to make the traditional round-shaped rasher. It's usually salted for two days, then dried out for two to three weeks and is usually unsmoked. This traditional method does not use phosphates after the meat has been brined to replace the water content lost in the brining process. When phosphates are used, bacon shrinks and oozes water when it hits the frying pan.

The traditional method should also be distinguished from what is often called 'Ayrshire-style' bacon. This will look like the traditional round Ayrshire shape, but the fat will have a waxy look and will be softer than the traditional cure. This is because the pigs are 'plotted' after killing. Plotting is a mass-production method which involves putting the carcass into boiling water to soften the skin. Then it is put into a tumble-drier with friction pads which take off the hair, and finally it is blast-dried with a gas-blower. This method will not produce the same high quality as the traditional cure, which preserves the flavour and texture by chilling the carcass and removing the skin by hand when it is cold.

BAKED AYRSHIRE-CURED HAM

In late November, the cold room in Ramsay's Wellriggs factory is many hams deep with orders waiting for collection. Some have been treated with a spiced cure, which they make to order from an old family recipe.

'Look for a short shank on a whole ham on the bone,' says Ramsay. 'Avoid the long one. The broad, plump joint with a good layer of fat is the best buy.'

For end-of-the-year festivities, a whole ham is something worth celebrating in its splendid entirety. Also there are leftovers: a source of many more cooking-free meals. Either on, or off, the bone the method is the same. Large, whole hams on the bone will usually be too large to boil in a pot. They should be cooked in foil, leaving room round the joint for cooking in the steam. Alternatively, smaller joints, which will fit into a pot, can be simmered in water till almost tender, then removed and finished in the oven as for 'Glazing'. This method provides useful stock for soup.

Yield: depends on size of ham

1.8-6 kg/4-13 lb ham (on the bone for larger sizes)
3-5 tablespoons dark brown sugar
1-2 tablespoons whole cloves
Preheat the oven to 400F/200C/180Cfan/Gas 6.

Use extra-width foil for large ham on the bone and a large roasting tin.

To prepare ham for baking

Put two pieces of double-thickness foil which are large enough to cover the ham comfortably, crosswise in the roasting tin. Place the ham on top and bring up each piece of foil to meet in the middle making an enclosed 'tent' over the ham. Do not wrap tightly since the ham should cook in the steam. Twist all edges together to make a perfect seal.

To bake ham

Put into the oven and bake for 35 minutes per 500g/1lb 2oz. Slice off a piece with a sharp knife near the end of the cooking time to test if the meat is tender. When ready, remove from the oven.

Glazing

Turn up oven to 435F/220C/200Cfan/Gas 7. Fold down the foil. Remove the skin with a very sharp knife, taking care not to remove too much fat. Score the fat lightly with the sharp knife into a diamond pattern.

Push a clove into the joins of all the diamonds. cover the whole surface with sugar and return the ham to the oven for about 30-40 minutes till crisp and browned. Serve hot with creamed potatoes, minted peas (see p.274) and spicy mango chutney.

To boil ham

Put into a large pot and cover with cold water. Bring up to a gentle simmer and simmer for 35mins per 1 kg. Test for readiness with a skewer inserted into the meat or cut off a sliver with a sharp knife and taste for tenderness. If overcooked it will be difficult to carve hot. Or check internal temperature with an instant-read thermometer when it should reach 68C. Remove from the pot and follow 'Glazing' instructions above. Serve with creamed potatoes, minted peas (see p.274) and spicy mango chutney.

Use the cooking liquor to make lentil or pea and ham soup.

AYRSHIRE BACON BAPS

For regular picnic use, the best sandwich in the world, and the most filling, is made by slitting baps, buttering both inside pieces and closing them over a thick slice of spiced bacon which is a Scottish delicacy of which we are justly proud.
Donald and Catherine Carswell, *The Scots Week-end*, 1936.

BAKED PORK CHOPS
with Chappit Tatties

4 x 175-200 g/6-7 oz pork chops
1 large egg
1-2 tablespoons milk
125 g/4 oz white breadcrumbs
Salt and ground pepper
2-3 tablespoons oil

Serves 4

Preheat the oven to 350F/180C/160Cfan/Gas 4.

Use a large roasting tin, greased.

Preparing the chops

Beat the egg and milk together. Season breadcrumbs with salt and pepper. Dip the chops in the egg and milk. Drain and press all sides into the breadcrumbs. Shake off excess and place in roasting tin.

Baking

Drizzle a little oil over the chops and bake in the oven for 45-50 minutes or until crisp and brown.

Serve with **Chappit Tatties**, see p.252.

SLOW ROAST PORK SHOULDER
with fennel

A shoulder of pork is the best cut for this long slow method, since the meat is layered with fat which keeps it moist. Aromas of aniseed fennel seeds, pungent garlic and sharp lemon blend together with hot chilli during the cooking to give this pork its unique flavour.

1.8-2.25 kg/4-5 lb shoulder of pork boned* with skin on
2 heads of garlic, peeled cloves
125 g/4 oz fennel seeds
2-3 small dried red chillies
Juice of 2 lemons
3 tablespoons oil

Serves 6-8

Preheat the oven to 450F/230C/210Cfan/Gas 8.

Use a ceramic dish or roasting tin 23 x 28 cm/7-11 in.

Preparing the meat

Using a very sharp knife, score the whole surface with deep cuts about 2 cm/¾ in apart, which go through the skin and fat layer into the flesh. Crush peeled garlic cloves with the fennel seeds, pepper and chillies in a pestle and mortar. Or crush the garlic and whizz in a food-processor with the fennel and chillies to break up the fennel seeds a little. It should be a coarse consistency. Press this mixture into the deep cuts on the surface. Also make some incisions in the underside of the meat and push some of this mixture in.

Cooking

Place the meat in the roasting tin and roast at a high heat in the oven for about 30 minutes or until the skin begins to crackle, blister and brown. Turn the oven down to 250F/130C/110Cfan/

*add an extra 1-2 kg if on the bone

Gas 1. Pour over half the lemon juice and 2 tablespoons oil. Cover meat tightly with foil and cook until the meat is tender for about 3-4 hours, shorter or longer depending on the toughness of the shoulder. Give it a further basting of more lemon juice and olive oil about half-way through the cooking.

Finishing

Remove the meat from its cooking dish/tin and keep warm. Add some more lemon juice to the cooking juices, mix well and spoon over the meat. Serve each person with some of the crisp skin and pieces of meat.

Wild Boar

In mythology, wild boar is a symbol of terrifying strength. Hunted to extinction in Britain in the 1600s, it was the prized meat of the feast. And now it's back. Not roaming wild, but fenced in by wild boar farmers who recognise its value. It is a hardy animal with tough feet and a thick coat which protects it well from life in a cold northern climate. It also makes good use of scrub-woodland, rough grass and bog, all in plentiful supply in Scotland. On wooded hillsides overlooking the Beauly Firth, a herd of pure-bred wild boar forage for bugs, beasties, roots and hazel nuts. 'We do supplement their diet with local organic root vegetables, and some barley,' says farmer Lucinda Spicer. But it is their natural, primitive diet, plus an energetic lifestyle, which produces the dark-red, characterful meat more like beef than pork. If it is too light a shade of red the boar may have been crossed with a domestic pig. Wild boar makes very good sausages and outstanding bacon. Not to mention delectable black puddings, which are made by Andrew Johnston at Hilton Wild Boar – another pioneering wild boar farmer in Perthshire who sells his boar meat and products at Perth Farmers' Market. All pork recipes can be made with boar (see **Buying Guide** p.442).

5: VEGETABLES, SOUPS & OTHER DISHES

Potatoes

We were conducted…into a room where about twenty Scotch Drovers [cattle drivers] were regaling themselves with whisky and potatoes.
Robert Chambers, *Walks in Edinburgh*, 1825.

Potatoes were a newcomer to Scotland, only grown for a few decades, when these drovers were filling up on boiled tatties washed down with drams of strong whisky. They were the latest superfood. Soldiers on the march during the Napoleonic Wars, it had been discovered, could survive very well on them. They were more nourishing than any of the grains, since they contained all the necessary vitamins, minerals, proteins, calories and cellulose for a human diet. Why it took thousands of years for them to arrive in Scotland, since they were first discovered in South America by Stone Age humans, is another story.

'Papas' had become a staple crop among the icy, windswept high peaks of the Andes when the inventive Incas discovered the method of freeze-drying. Known as *chunos*, thousands were stored in warehouses in times of plenty, which gave the Incas the power to control and conquer others when food became scarce. *Chunos* are still on sale in the street markets of Peru and Bolivia. On first sight, they look like little grey pebbles, but steeped in water for a few hours, they soften and can be boiled and eaten, flavoured with mountain herbs.

The first Europeans began to write about potatoes in 1537, when Cieze de Leon joined an expedition to what is now Colombia. A little later in the century another Spaniard, Juan de Castellonos, described the potato as something like a truffle, about the size of an egg, round or elongated, and white, purple or yellow in colour – 'floury roots of good flavour, a delicacy to the Indians and a dainty dish even for the Spaniards'. The first mention of them being grown in Europe as food is believed to be in 1573, when '19lb of potatoes' appears in the account books of the Hospital de la Sangre in Seville.

The new superfood was not initially welcomed by everyone. Some thought them lacking flavour. In Scotland, there was a gradual, if reluctant, acceptance of the potato in Scotland, as their cultivation was encouraged. J. Walker describes the early difficulties of establishing the potato crop in his *Economic History of the Hebrides and Highlands* (1808) – 'Typical of the suspicion with which new methods were viewed was the attitude to the introduction of potatoes: in 1743 the Chief Clanranald brought a small quantity for the first time to South Uist, but the farmers suffered imprisonment before they would submit to planting them. When autumn came they brought the 'obnoxious roots' to the Chief's door, protesting that he might force them to plant them, but not to eat them. Hunger was, however, a more effectual argument, and within twenty years many Highlanders were subsisting on potatoes for nine months of the year.' Their original use as food reserves to the Incas was now finding its way into the Old World.

While Ireland had started growing them in the 1600s, it was the late 1700s before they were being widely grown in Scotland. They were mostly welcomed in areas where there was an impoverished smallholding peasantry, poor communications and lack of monetary resources. In addition to their superfood status, their ability to flourish in difficult conditions was an important factor in their development as a staple crop in both Scotland and Ireland. They arrived at a crucial time in the history of both countries, as a vital saviour from a widespread and increasing deterioration, cultural, social and economic, in the life of the people. While Ireland was, by this time, more or less totally dependent on potatoes, regional differences of climate and custom in Scotland meant that some parts depended on them more than others. In the Highlands and Islands, coinciding with the Clearances, they became an important staple item of diet. Their advantage, growing underground, meant they were less susceptible to the vagaries of weather than oats and barley. They also produced more food per acre (four families growing potatoes could survive on land that once supported one family growing grain) and they combined well – not just with whisky – but also with other staples such as milk, cheese and fish. Elizabeth Edmondston, writing in *Sketches and Tales of the Shetland Isles* (1856), says that, 'Fish with oat bread or potatoes . . . without any accompaniment at all, forms the three daily meals of the Shetland cottager.' Though Lowlanders grew potatoes to eat themselves, they also used them as animal feed.

But despite these variations, the Scots by this time valued potatoes so highly they often referred to them as 'meat'. Compared with the varieties preferred in England, which were a wetter, more waxy-textured potato, Scottish and Irish potatoes had a high dry-matter content, giving them a low water content and a better flavour. Throughout the 1800s, ready-cooked 'mealie [floury] tatties' still in their skins were commonly sold from farm carts in the city streets in Scotland.

When tragedy struck in Ireland in 1845–46 with the potato crop ruined by blight, breeders set about developing new varieties which would be blight-free, sourcing new potato cultivars from South America. Among them was an amateur Scottish breeder, William Paterson of Dundee, who invested a small fortune gathering stocks from abroad which were not affected with the virus, and successfully raised several distinct varieties, including Victoria (1863), which has since been used widely by breeders. In 1891 William Sim of Fyvie bred the very popular Duke of York, while Archibald Findlay of Auchtermuchty was possibly the most influential breeder with his successful British Queen, Catriona and Majestic: the varieties which are reputed to have fed Britain through two world wars. Meanwhile in 1901, on the Isle of Arran, the local shopkeeper in Lamlash, Donald McKelvie, was given some potatoes from a friend, and in a few plots he began to breed potatoes, becoming one of the best known breeders of his day and awarded an MBE in 1925 for his services to potato-breeding. McKelvie's contribution to the development of potato variety was particularly important, since his varieties have been used for future development. Arran Pilot and Arran Victory are still popular, and one of the most widely grown modern varieties, Maris Piper, was bred from McKelvie's Arran Cairn.

In *A Book of Arran Verse* (1930) he is celebrated:

> Donald o' tattie fame
> – Health to McKelvie!
> Long shall we praise his name
> Whilst Arranmen delve ye.
> 'Arran Chief', 'Arran Rose',
> 'Comrade' and 'Ally',
> Yea where the 'Consul' grows –
> Health to McKelvie!

The Development of Traditional Potato Varieties

Old traditional varieties such as Arran Pilot, Craig's Royal and Epicure have given way to Pentland Javelin, Estima, Wilja, Maris Peer and Maris Bard. Similarly, traditional maincrop varieties such as Majestic, King Edward and Redskin have been largely displaced by Desiree, Maris Piper, the Pentland varieties (particularly Pentland Crown) and Record, although King Edward has retained a place of some importance.

N.A. Young, *The European Potato Industry*, 1981.

These changes in potato varieties were largely to do with improving yields and reducing disease. But the result was often a wetter potato which had less dry matter and less flavour. For the first half of the twentieth century, the most popular dry 'floury' or 'mealy' potatoes with a good flavour were Golden Wonder, Kerr's Pink, Majestic and King Edward, which accounted for 75 per cent of the potato acreage in Scotland. By the end of the century, however, they were down to 5-10 per cent, and it looked as though they might be about to sink into oblivion.

Like the revival of beef-as-it-used-to-taste, there has been revival of old – now often called 'heritage'- potatoes. Among many old varieties which have made a comeback there are such characters as the very dry blue-skinned Arran Victory, named by MacKelvie to celebrate the end of World War I (1918); the good-flavoured British Queen (1894); the crofter's Shetland Black (1923); the red-fleshed Highland Burgundy Red (1936); the Orcadian Keppleton Kidneys; Charles Spence's Dunbar Rover (1936) with its snowy-white flesh and excellent buttery flavour; and many others.

That these old varieties were not lost is thanks to potato enthusiasts such as the late Donald MacLean, Chairman of the National Vegetable Society, who wrote in the Scots Magazine in October 1978: 'This autumn I will be harvesting small amounts of over 200 varieties and disposing of them all over the UK to appreciative gourmets and enthusiasts, thus in small measure, keeping alive my kind of dodos and dinosaurs.'

He felt that there should be a wider choice of potato at the point of sale, considering the valuable contribution Scottish potato-breeders had made in the past. He also campaigned for better labelling, so that varieties would be clearly labelled and individual quality judged more easily. There were many old varieties which he felt were worth keeping.

Among them he particularly rated **DUKE OF YORK**, a low-yielding potato which was first raised in Aberdeenshire by W. Sim in 1891. But due largely to low yields, compared with its rivals, it fought a losing battle and was for years only grown by specialist allotment holders or people like MacLean. It is a yellow-fleshed potato with an outstanding flavour, which is at its best when young.

As maturity is reached the flavour is less intense and it disintegrates easily when boiled.

KING EDWARD, which is a floury, maincrop potato, was the UK's most popular potato for the first half of the century. It was raised in 1902 by an unknown gardener in Northumberland and first named 'Fellside Hero', It has a pale-yellow flesh and aromatic flavour. It is at its best roasted or baked. It was abandoned by many growers because it is not an easy potato to grow, requiring good irrigation and a strong soil with plenty of organic matter. It does not do well on heavy, acidic or sandy soils.

GOLDEN WONDER, raised by John Brown near Arbroath in 1906, is a late maincrop potato with a good flavour and an unusually thick, brown, rough skin. It has a very high dry matter content which has made it the premium floury/mealy tattie in Scotland and Ireland. Also there is **KERR'S PINK**, which was raised by J. Henry of Banff and first named Henry's Seedling when it won a Gold Medal in 1916. Henry sold all the seed to a Mr Kerr, who renamed it and launched it on the market in 1917. For the next fifty years it remained among the top ten varieties in the UK. Easier to grow than King Edward and a bigger cropper than Golden Wonder, it continues to dominate the acreage of floury potatoes in Ireland. Though it is traditionally a maincrop potato, many Irish growers harvest the crop early and sell it as an early potato.

While McLean pursued his potato preservation activities on his Perthshire farm, others at the Scottish Plant Breeding Institute at Pentlandfield near Edinburgh were busy breeding the **PENT-LAND** varieties: Pentland Crown (1958); Pentland Dell (1960); and Pentland Squire (1970) and the still popular first early, Pentland Javelin (1968), bred at Pentlandfield by Jack Dunnet. And in the Carse of Gowrie at the Scottish Crop Research Institute (now the James Hutton Institute, JHI) new potato varieties were continually being investigated. They had a collection of Andean potato varieties which had been started when some pioneering breeders in the early

1900s had returned to the Andes in search of undeveloped varieties. This became known as the Commonwealth Potato Collection and remains at the Carse of Gowrie site where some eighty ancestor potatoes varieties are now grown annually, making a direct link to where the potato story started thousands of years ago.

Cooking qualities

Floury (mealie) varieties: Best for – jacket; also boiled in their skins, since they can disintegrate quickly if boiled too quickly; roasted unpeeled in wedges; mashed and for crisp dry chips: Arran Pilot (Sco)*; Arran Victory (Sco); British Queen (Sco); Cara; Catriona (Sco); Dunbar Rover (Sco); Dunbar Standard (Sco); Edzell Blue (Sco); Epicure; Golden Wonder; Innovator; Kerr's Pink (Sco); King Edward; Keppleton Kidney; Majestic (Sco); Mayan Gold (Sco); Red Duke of York; Red King Edward; Record; Rooster; Sante; Sharp's Express; Shetland Black (Sco); Yukon Gold.

Salad (both floury and smooth) varieties: Best – left in their skins; boiled; steamed or roasted whole in their skins: Annabelle; Anya; Bambino; Carlingford; Charlotte; Corolle; Duke of York; Exquisa; Inca Dawn; Kestrel (Sco); Maris Bard (Sco); Maris Peer (Sco); Nicola; Pentland Javelin (Sco); Pink Fir Apple; Rocket; Roseval; Salad Blue (Sco); Jersey Royal; Witchill.

Smooth (waxy) varieties: Best for – boiled and in sauces since they hold their shape; for very smooth mash; for soggy chips: Arran Comet (Sco); Arran Pilot (Sco) Apache; Bonnie Dundee (Sco); Chopin; Desiree; Estima; Harmony; Home Guard; Lady Balfour; Marabel; Maris Piper (Sco); Marfona; Melody; Mozart; Nadine; Osprey; Romano; Saxon; Vales Sovereign; Vivaldi; Wilja.

To peel or not to peel?

Cooking in their skins retains the maximum food value, since all

*(Sco) Scottish bred.

potatoes have valuable vitamins and minerals just under the skin which are removed if peeled. In some potatoes removing the skin may also remove some of their flavour.

Buying and storing

> *In a parking space at the side of the A77 a few miles north of Girvan there is a white van with a sign: AYRSHIRE EPI-CURES. A row of cars are parked beside it and the queue at the van is for a bag of the season's first earlies lifted that day.*
> *The Herald Magazine*, June 1997.

While there are other varieties of early potato (Rocket and Maris Peer) grown along this fertile coastal strip, it's Epicure which locals rate the best. Simply boiled and eaten with melted butter and chopped chives, they are regarded as 'your dinner', and sales of meat are said to drop for the first few weeks of the earlies. They lose their fresh, new flavour very quickly and should be eaten within 24 hours of lifting. The sooner the better.

The **First Earlies** season on the warmer, wetter West Coast begins a few weeks earlier than the East, but they are mostly available from the end of May through June, while **Second Earlies** start in July and go through into the end of August.

The **Maincrop** lifting starts at the end of September. Scottish children get a couple of weeks' holiday in October – once known as their 'tattie holidays' – when they went to the fields to help lift tatties. Now it is done mechanically, but the school holiday remains.

All sacks of potatoes sold to the market must bear the variety name which the retailer must display.

To store, keep in a cool, dark place: warmth makes them sprout, damp encourages storage diseases, and light turns them an unhealthy green. Polythene bags cause problems if potatoes are kept too long in them, since they can't breathe properly and condensation accumulates in the bag and causes rotting.

STOVIES

This dish may have been influenced by early and close ties with France; certainly it makes the same use of the thinly sliced potatoes, cooked slowly, as the French do in their *Gratin Dauphinois* (see p.405).

The origin of the word 'stovie' is not clear. Some, including F. Marian McNeill (*The Scots Kitchen*, 1929) suggest it comes from the French verb '*étuvé*' (meaning stewed) which would confirm the French tie-in. But there is also the old English verb 'to stove', meaning to cook on the stove (cooker). It was originally applied to the idea of 'sweating'. Gervase Markham, in *The English Huswife* in 1615, talks about letting a bird 'stove and sweate [*sic*] till evening', while later recipes show that it becomes more associated with stewing, but remains a cross between sweating and stewing – as in stovies.

STOVIES
one recipe but many versions

This economy, leftover dish based on potatoes and onions lends itself to individual likes and dislikes. There is no classic recipe, but the opportunity to experiment with the remains of other dishes while adding new flavours and textures. Some like a floury potato which will break up and make soft-textured stovies, while others like their stovies with a waxy variety to stay intact. Some like their onions well-browned, while others don't. Though it originated as a weekday meal made from the leftovers of the Sunday joint, there is no reason, today, why it can't be made from scratch – grilled bacon used instead of leftover roast, and a spoonful or two of Japanese miso if there is no leftover gravy or stock.

In some parts of the country it is a popular through-the-night pot on the stove at Hogmanay, often served with a jar of piquant pickled beetroot or some other favourite pickle or chutney.

100 ml/3½ fl oz fat, dripping from meat or bacon or oil
600-800 g/1 lb 5 oz-1 lb 12 oz onions

1.5 kg/3 lb 5 oz potatoes
125 ml/4 fl oz stock, leftover gravy or water
Or 1-2 tablespoons Japanese miso
Leftover meat or grilled bacon
Salt
Ground black pepper, grated nutmeg or ground allspice
2-3 tablespoons chopped parsley, chives or spring onions

4-6 servings

Use a 30-35 cm/12-14 in sauté or frying pan with lid.*

To make

Slice the onions thinly or put into a food processor with the slicing disc and whizz. Melt fat/oil in a large sauté or frying pan with a tight-fitting lid. When hot, add onions. Reduce the heat and fry until they are soft and greatly reduced. Continue to reduce and brown if preferred. Slice potatoes to preferred thickness. If using floury potatoes they can also be unevenly sliced, so that the thin ones reduce to a mush while the thick ones stay whole when cooked. Waxy potatoes which will not break up are best sliced the same size so they are all soft at the same time. They can be sliced thinly in a food processor using the slicing disc. Add to the onions and stir well.

Place lid on the pan and leave to cook for about 5 minutes, stirring when necessary to prevent sticking. The heat must be at its lowest possible. Add water, stock or gravy from a roast to moisten and prevent sticking, or mix some miso to a paste with water and add for extra flavour if necessary. The less water added the drier the stovies. Cover and cook till potatoes are soft, stirring occasionally to prevent sticking.

Finishing

Add cooked meat and mix through the stovies. Taste and season.

*Half-quantity can be made in a 10 in/25 cm sauté or frying pan with a tight-fitting lid.

For stovies with brown bits through them, continue cooking until they stick and brown lightly on the underside. Scrape this off and continue, mixing in the browned bits. This is known as 'Hash Browns' in America. It will only work with floury potatoes which go into a mush.

Before serving, sprinkle with a handful of finely chopped parsley, chives or spring onions. Serve with pickles or chutneys.

CHAPPIT TATTIES

Irish Champ: *Two stones or more of potatoes were peeled and boiled for the dinner. Then the man of the house was summoned when all was ready, and while he pounded this enormous potful of potatoes with a sturdy wooden beetle (potato masher) his wife added the potful of milk and nettles, or scallions, or chives or parsley, and he beetled till it was smooth as butter and not a lump anywhere. Everyone got a large bowlful, made a hole in the centre, and into this put a large lump of butter. Then the champ was eaten from the outside with a spoon or fork, dipping it into the melting butter in the centre. All was washed down with new milk or freshly churned buttermilk.*

Florence Irwin in *The Cookin' Woman* (1949).

A popular dish in the West of Scotland, largely due to Irish immigration to the industrial areas of Clydeside in the late 1800s and early 1900s, when it was handed on from one generation to the next.

1 kg/2lb 4oz floury potatoes – cooked, steamed dry, peeled and mashed
300 ml/½ pt hot milk
Pepper and salt
With either:
1 cup chopped or minced nettle tops or

½ cup chopped chives or
6 finely chopped spring onions or
2 large tablespoons chopped parsley or
1 cup fresh peas
Serve with:
250 g/8 oz butter

4-6 servings

Put the milk in a pan and bring to the boil. Reduce to a simmer and add the greens. Remove from the heat and add to the mashed potato. Beat till smooth and creamy.

Serve potatoes very hot in heated bowls with butter for making a pond in the middle 'Irish style' and with a glass of cold milk.

OATMEALED POTATOES

4-6 servings

This is best with new potatoes. Boil or steam **1 kg/2 lb 4 oz floury new potatoes** and while they are cooking toast **2 tablespoons coarse oatmeal** slowly in the oven. Drain the potatoes, toss in **1 tablespoon butter** and then coat with the toasted oatmeal. Sprinkle with **chopped parsley, chives or chervil** and serve.

DRIPPING POTATOES

Wash the potatoes and peel them very thin; boil them 10 minutes with a little salt, and then put them in a Yorkshire-pudding tin under the joint which is roasting before an open fire, to catch the gravy; when enough moistened, put them into the oven, still in the tin, turn the potatoes often, and baste them with a little dripping, till crisp and brown. Serve very hot, but not round the joint, or they will become sodden. Potatoes done in this way are mealy inside and crisp on the outside.

The Cookery Book of Lady Clark of Tillypronie, 1909.

These are the best roast potatoes, absorbing as they do all the dripping flavour from the meat. In the days when all roasts were cooked on a spit, cooking a starchy filler under the roasting joint was a well-developed art, to which Yorkshire pudding owes its existence.

TATTIE SCONES

These thin, triangular, unleavened scones have a dark-brown, mottled surface and should be so thin that they 'wiggle' when you hold one corner and give them a shake. They are traditionally eaten for high tea, spread with jam or butter and rolled up into a stick-of-rock shape. May also be fried with bacon for breakfast.

25 g/1 oz melted butter
Salt
250 g/9 oz mashed, floury maincrop potatoes
50 g/2 oz plain flour

Use a girdle or large frying pan.

To make

Add butter and salt to potatoes and stir in flour to make a firm but pliable consistency. Dust work-surface with flour and roll out thinly. Cut into a large round and divide into quarters or cut into small individual rounds with a plain-edged scone-cutter – prick with a fork.

Grease and heat girdle or frying pan till moderately hot. Bake for about 3 minutes on each side till lightly browned. Wrap in a towel. Eat rolled up with butter, jam or honey; or fried with bacon and eggs.

TATTIE SOUP

A hearty soup which makes a main meal dish. Potatoes combine well with all the onion family and also with kale, nettles, wild garlic leaves, chives, chervil or sorrel.

1 ham hough (knuckle)
OR 1-2 kg/2 lb 4 oz-4 lb 8oz piece of ham
2 L/3½ pts cold water
2 Bay leaves
1 kg/2 lb 4 oz floury potatoes (see p.248)
600 g/1 lb 5 oz leeks
2 tablespoons freshly chopped parsley or young kale or young
   nettles
250 ml/8fl oz milk (optional)
Salt and pepper

6 servings

To cook the ham

Put the ham into the cold water in a large pot and bring to the boil. Skim off any scum. Add bay leaf. Simmer gently for about an hour or until the meat is tender. Remove the meat, cover and leave to cool.

To make the soup

Wash and slice the potatoes thinly. Wash and chop the leeks finely, keeping the white and the green separate. Taste the ham stock for saltiness and adjust with more water if too salty. Add the potatoes and the white of the leek to the ham stock and bring to the boil. Simmer gently till the potatoes are cooked.

Chop the parsley, kale or nettles very finely. Remove the ham meat from the bone and chop into small pieces or chop up a few slices from the ham joint.

Add the green leek and the parsley/kale/nettles, chopped ham and the milk to the soup and heat through. Remove from the heat. Taste and season.

Serve

In deep, wide plates with crusty bread, oatcakes or bannocks and cheese.

Leeks

King of the onion family in the broth pot, leeks have a winter-growing tradition in Northern Europe and were a staple ingredient in winter broths. Now they are available all year, and picked young in summer they are so tender they can be sliced and tossed raw into a salad. But it's the thick stalk of the mature leek with its long green leaf (green flag) and short white root end (white blanch) that add distinction to broths, and especially to Cock-a-Leekie.

The original Scottish leek, raised for broth making, is a variety of the Common Long Winter Leek, which was first raised on the fertile soils of East Lothian. It has a longer, thicker stem and broader leaves and was described as the Musselburgh Leek by William Robinson in *The Vegetable Garden* (1885), when he said that the 'fine qualities of this vegetable are much better known to the Welsh, Scotch and French than to the English or Irish'.

The regions of Fife and Lothian, with their fertile soils, continue to be important leek-growing areas. Small to medium-sized leeks have the sweetest flavour. The hardy, winter-growing Musselburgh Leek is no longer grown commercially, though the seed is still available and it is sometimes to be found in farmers' markets.

Buying

Larger, older leeks have a stronger flavour and coarser texture than young thin ones, so are best used to flavour soups and stews. But for serving on their own as a vegetable or for salads, the young tender ones are best. Both winter and summer leeks should be lifted before they 'shoot', i.e. start forming the flower head, making a hard woody stalk in the centre which should be removed before use. English supermarkets in Scotland often sell leeks with a very long white blanch and practically no green flag, which is useless for a good pot of broth.

Preparing

Trim off root and any wilted green leaves. All of the green ought to be useable unless the leeks are mature, in which case the top inch or so may be too coarse and should be removed. If using the whole leek for soups, slit from the base to the tips to halve the stalk, and then make another slit at right angles which then opens up the leeks for easy washing and chopping. Leave to soak for a few minutes if they are very earthy to loosen the soil. For serving as a vegetable, slit through the green flag and rinse to remove grit. Cut in bite sized lengths.

STEAMED LEEKS
served hot or cold

8 medium-sized young leeks
For serving hot with poached eggs:
25 g/1 oz butter
Sea salt and ground pepper
4 poached eggs
2-3 tablespoons grated cheese
2 tablespoons chopped parsley
Or for serving as a salad with boiled eggs:
4 hardboiled eggs
Salt and ground pepper
2 tablespoons chopped parsley
Balsamic and Mustard Dressing (to store):
4 tablespoons balsamic vinegar
2 tablespoons Dijon mustard
250 ml/8 fl oz olive oil

4 servings

To steam

Remove any wilted outer leaves and trim the root end and the top if wilted. Slit open to just below the green stalk and wash well. Cut into bite-sized pieces. Place in a steamer over a pan of boiling water, cover with a lid and steam till tender, or put into a microwave bowl with a tablespoon of water. Cover with cling film. Pierce to let out steam and microwave on high (900w) for 2-3 minutes till soft.

To serve hot with poached eggs

Drain and put into a heated serving dish. Toss in butter. Season with salt and pepper. Sprinkle over parsley. Put poached eggs on top and cover with grated cheese. Put under a hot grill for a minute to melt the cheese and serve.

To make balsamic dressing

Put the balsamic vinegar and the mustard into a bottle or jar, screw on the lid and shake well. When they are well mixed, add all the olive oil and shake again until the mixture is emulsified. Taste and season (the mustard will hold the oil in an emulsion indefinitely, preventing separation).

To serve as a salad with balsamic dressing

Put leeks into serving dish and drizzle over some dressing. Turn the leeks in the dressing. Chop hard-boiled eggs finely and sprinkle on top. Finish with a tablespoon of finely chopped parsley. Serve with cold meats, fish or cheese and bread.

Carrots

Though carrots were first cultivated in the eastern Mediterranean, the Dutch are credited with developing the 'long orange' carrot, bringing it to Britain in the late 1600s as they fled religious persecution. They also grew pale yellow and purple varieties, but the orange has prevailed. Evidence of their arrival in Scotland by the early 1700s can be found in Scotland's earliest cookery books, while there is also a mention in the Clan MacDougall archive that carrot seeds, bought in Glasgow, were grown in Dunollie Castle garden in Argyll in the early 1700s.

At this time their main use was in rustic broths and stews, though their sweetness was also valued in more sophisticated light-airy soufflé puddings, flavoured with purees of cooked carrots. Their sweet, moist qualities also made them useful additions, grated raw, in Clootie Dumplings and American Carrot Cakes.

Buying

Young spring carrots are sold in bunches, usually with foliage attached. They should be about thumb-thickness. Maincrop varieties vary in thickness but should be tender with no woody core. It is worth checking for rotting carrots in poly bags which have been in this moist environment for too long. Supermarkets do not sell 'dirty' carrots. All their carrots are de-topped, washed and poly-bagged, which makes them more vulnerable to rot than a green-topped, dirty carrot which has never seen the inside of a poly bag. The best place to find a green-top dirty carrot – other than in your own garden – is in fruit and veg shops, farm shops and farmers' markets.

Unless carrots are organically grown, the Government's advice is to remove the tops and tails and peel off the skins, since higher than recommended levels of pesticides have been found in these parts of some commercially grown carrots.

CARROT AND BACON SOUP

An 'instant' soup, made using microwave and processor for a natural, fresh-tasting flavour. It is best made with young sweet carrots but would also work well with squash, sweet potato or parsnip.

350 g/12 oz onion, coarsely chopped
100 g/4 oz streaky bacon, coarsely chopped
3-4 tablespoons oil
500 g/1 lb 2 oz carrots, peeled and chopped
150 ml/5 fl oz water or stock

Salt and pepper
Milk

4-6 servings

Makes 1.1 L/2 pts

Put bacon, onion and oil into a bowl. Cover with cling film, pierce to release steam and microwave (900w) on high for 5-6 minutes. Remove and stir. Return for another 5-6 minutes or until the bacon is cooked and the onions are soft. Remove and add carrots and water. Cover again and microwave for 5 minutes. Remove and stir well. Return to the microwave and cook until the carrots are soft. Time will depend on the size of the carrots but keep checking every few minutes.

Put into the liquidiser and whizz till very smooth. Add milk, water or stock and adjust to required consistency. Reheat. Taste and season. Serve with bread or oatcakes and cheese.

GLAZED CARROTS

Because of their natural sweetness, carrots are ideal for this method of cooking vegetables. The slow cooking with butter and sugar gives them an attractive syrupy coating. They are a good partner for salty cured meats, especially ham and bacon.

500 g/1lb 2 oz carrots
1 tablespoon soft brown sugar
Salt
Cold water to just cover
25 g/1 oz butter
1 teaspoon lemon juice

4 servings

To make

Slice larger, older carrots into even-sized pieces and leave new carrots whole or cut in two. Put into the pan with sugar, salt and enough water to come halfway up the carrots. Simmer till the carrots are almost cooked – this will depend on age. Most of the liquid should have evaporated. Add butter and continue to cook, shaking the pan to prevent the carrots sticking. When very little liquid is left and they are all well glazed add a few drops of lemon juice and serve.

CARROT PUDDING

This late eighteenth-century soufflé type pudding is rich, light and buttery and partly sweetened with carrots. It is best baked in a ceramic dish and served immediately it is ready.

Boil as many good carrots as will be half a pound, cut them and pound them fine with half a pound of fine sugar; then beat ten eggs and three whites and mix them with the carrots; grate an orange in it, and just as you are going to put it in the oven put into it half a pound of clarified butter.

Mrs Fraser's *The Practice of Cookery* (1791).

HONEY AND CINNAMON CARROT CAKE

The American cake guru, Rose Levy Beranbaum (*The Cake Bible*, 1988) uses honey and cinnamon to add a warm, mellow spiciness to this cake which can also be served, as it was in the past, as a pudding. RLB makes her pudding in a savarin ring mould, but it works just as well in a round cake or loaf tin. It can be served with or without an icing. Her suggestion is a white chocolate and cream cheese 'frosting' – the generic name for all cake icings in the US. I've added the marmalade for extra flavour and sweetness.

Cake:
200 g/7 oz carrots, finely shredded
62 g/2 oz lemon juice (about 1 large lemon)
125 g/4½ oz sifted spelt flour

125g/4½ oz plain cake flour

½ teaspoon baking powder

1 level teaspoon bicarbonate of soda

1 teaspoon cinnamon

2 medium eggs (100 g/3½ oz beaten weight)

142 g/5 oz unsalted butter, softened (or oil)

250 g/8¾ oz runny honey

Icing 'Frosting':

125 g/4½ oz white chocolate

170 g/6 oz cream cheese

85 g/3 oz unsalted butter, softened

1 teaspoon cinnamon

1 tablespoon thick marmalade

Preheat the oven to 350F/180C/160Cfan/Gas 4.

Use a 23 cm/9 inch round cake tin or a 6-cup savarin ring mould, well buttered.

To make cake

Mix the carrots and lemon juice. Put all the dry ingredients into a bowl and beat with an electric beater for 30 seconds to blend. Make a well in the centre and add the carrot mixture, eggs, softened butter and honey and beat with a whisk or electric beater for 30 seconds till well mixed. Pour into tin and bake for about 45 to 50 minutes for the round cake and 30 to 40 minutes for the ring mould.

Icing 'frosting'

Melt the chocolate and butter in the microwave on half heat. Stir every 30 seconds. Or melt in a double boiler over boiling water. Leave to cool. Put the cream cheese in the food processor with the cinnamon and marmalade and whizz to blend. Add the white chocolate and butter. Whizz till smooth. Taste and adjust cinnamon and marmalade flavour if necessary. For cake, spread over top and sides. Decorate with a fork. To serve as a pudding, serve warm with crème fraiche or sour cream.

Cabbage and Related Vegetables: Turnips, Kale and Sprouting Broccoli

In the thousands of years since wild cabbage was first cultivated, it has produced a large number of *brassica* family relatives. In addition to turnips, kale and broccoli, there are cauliflower, Brussels sprouts and kohlrabi, not to mention many different forms of the Chinese cabbage and oilseed rape. The earliest records of cultivated cabbages date from around 600 BC, when kale is mentioned in early Greek literature.

Modern cabbages include many new and interesting varieties which have extended their potential in the diet, compared to the limited range of red and white cabbages available when they were developed first in Germany, before spreading to the rest of Europe in the early 1100s.

At present they are divided into eight main types: **Spring**, which have fresh loose leafy heads; **Summer**, which have either pointed or rounded hearts; **Autumn**, which are harvested in September; **Winter white**, which are large cabbages grown for storage as solid white heads; **Savoy**, which have crinkly, often bluish leaves; **Savoy hybrids**, which are crosses between Savoy and white cabbages – being denser than Savoys they will often stand in good condition in the ground until March; **January King** cultivators, hardy varieties which stand throughout the winter, and are particularly handsome cabbages with slightly crinkly and purplish leaves; and **Red**, which are harvested in October/November and can be stored through the winter.

Orcadians and Shetlanders share with Scandinavians an extensive use of cabbage in their diet in preference to other vegetables, and grow some very hardy varieties which are half cabbage, half kale.

These, eaten with fish, were at one time a staple item of diet, and cabbage was pickled in barrels for winter use as it still is in much of Eastern Europe and Germany. In Shetland the chopped cabbage was packed into wooden barrels with layers of animal fat, oatmeal, salt and spices, weighted down and used as required to add flavour to winter broths.

RUMBLEDETHUMPS

The curious name of this dish comes from the old Scots word 'rumbled', meaning mixed together, and 'thumped', meaning bashed. Eaten traditionally as a vegetarian dish, it can also be served as a vegetable with grilled bacon, sausages, black pudding or haggis.

750 g/1 lb 10 oz floury potatoes
50 g/2 oz butter
1 medium onion, finely chopped
500 g/1 lb 2 oz savoy, autumn or winter white cabbage, very finely chopped
75 g/3 oz grated Scottish cheddar
Chopped chives or spring onion

4 servings

Use a ceramic dish, 23 x 23 cm/9 x 9 in square, 6 cm/2½ in deep or pie dish 2 L/3½ pt capacity.

Boil potatoes in their skins, peel (only necessary if the skins are very thick) and mash. Melt the butter in a large pan and add the onion. Cook gently for 5 minutes without browning, add cabbage and a few tablespoons of boiling water. Cook over a high heat, stirring occasionally, till the cabbage is just cooked. Add potatoes and chives or spring onion and mix together. Taste and season. Put into serving dish. Cover with cheese and brown under the grill or in the oven. Serve as a main course or with grilled bacon, sausages, black pudding or haggis.

RED CABBAGE WITH APPLES

With its vibrant magenta colour and ability to absorb flavours in warming, slow-cooked dishes, red cabbage is the perfect partner for game and slow-cooked roasts such as lamb shanks and beef brisket. To prevent losing its beautiful colour during the cooking, it must have acid (lemon juice or vinegar) added. A small piece of good-flavoured fat bacon will add to the finished flavour.

2 oz/50 g lard/or 2 tablespoons oil
1 onion, chopped
450 g/1 lb red cabbage, finely chopped
4 tablespoons red wine vinegar or lemon juice
1 level teaspoon ground cloves
Bay leaf
Zest of 2 lemons
2 tablespoons soft brown sugar
Water
Piece of fat bacon
450 g/1 lb cooking apples, peeled and quartered

4-6 servings

To cook

Heat the lard or oil in a pan, and when hot add the onions. Fry until soft but not brown. Add the cabbage, vinegar (or lemon juice), cloves, bay leaf and lemon zest. Sprinkle the sugar on top and add water to almost cover. Push a piece of fat bacon into the centre. Cover and simmer gently for 3-4 hours. Add the apples near the end of the cooking and cook until they are just soft. Remove the bacon, slice and serve with the cabbage, or serve the cabbage with slow-roast meats or game.

Scottish Turnips (Neeps)

Our club [The Cleikum] put a little powdered gineger [sic] to their mashed turnips, which were studiously chosen of the yellow, sweet, juicy sort, for which Scotland is celebrated.
Meg Dods, *The Cook and Housewife's Manual*, 1826.

This yellow, sweet, juicy sort is *Brassica napus*, more commonly known in Scotland as a 'neep'. It is the sort which accompanies haggis and mixes so well with Orkney clapshot, and which is also known as a Swedish turnip, swede or rutabaga in the US. It came from Sweden to Scotland in the late 1700s, and is known in England as a swede.

The true turnip is the white-fleshed *Brassica rapa*, first used in the early 1700s by 'Turnip' Townsend to feed livestock through the winter, revolutionising agriculture by making it no longer necessary to kill most animals in the autumn because there was not enough winter food for them all.

Buying/Preparing

The Scottish neep is much hardier than the white-fleshed turnip and is at its best throughout winter when its flesh is less watery. Now available all year but best from August to April. Smaller sizes have a less thick woody outer layer, all of which must be removed before cooking. They also have a milder flavour.

BASHED NEEPS
Mashed Turnips (Swedes)

750 g/1lb 10 oz yellow turnip (swede)
Cold water to cover
Salt and ground pepper
25 g/1 oz butter
1 teaspoon finely grated ginger root or ground ginger to taste
Handful of chopped chives for garnish

4 servings

Remove all the hard, woody outer skin. Cut into thin slices. Put into a pan with water and boil till soft. Drain and dry off in the pan over a gentle heat for a few minutes, stirring to drive off excess moisture. Add salt, pepper, butter and ginger. Stir for another few minutes then mash thoroughly with a potato masher. Beat well till smooth. Taste and season. Serve with chives.

ORKNEY CLAPSHOT
with Burnt Onions

Traditionally eaten as a main course in Orkney when vegetables were your 'meat'. Neeps and tatties are cooked in the same pot then mashed together. This can be baked in the oven in a pie or gratin dish, thickly covered with grated cheddar cheese, or browned under the grill. George Mackay Brown, Orcadian writer and poet, liked an onion cooked in the pot with his neeps and tatties but at the Ubiquitous Chip restaurant in Glasgow's West End they serve it with a topping of caramelised 'burnt' onions. It is often served with haggis.

750 g/1 lb 10 oz each of neeps and floury potatoes (see p.248)
50 g/2 oz butter
Salt and ground pepper
To finish with cheese:
100 g/4 oz grated Orkney cheddar
To finish with burnt onions:
2 large Spanish onions (700 g/1 lb 9 oz) very thinly sliced
4 tablespoons oil
1 heaped tablespoon caster sugar

4-6 servings

Use a ceramic dish 23 x 23 cm/9 x 9 in square, 6 cm/2 ½ in deep or pie dish 2 L/3 ½ pt capacity, and a wok or frying pan to cook onions.

To make

Remove all the hard, woody outer skin of the neep. Cut into thin slices. Wash the potatoes. Bring a large pot of water to the boil and add the neeps first. Simmer for about 20 minutes then add the potatoes in their skins. They will take less time to cook and will disintegrate if boiled too long. Remove if cooked before the neeps. Drain off water when cooked and keep for vegetable stock.

To finish with cheese

Peel the potatoes. Return to the pan and add the butter. Mash potatoes and neeps together till smooth. To lighten and cream the mixture beat with a whisk or electric beater. Taste and season. Put into a pie or gratin dish, level top and cover with cheese. Bake in the oven till cheese is bubbling on top or finish under the grill.

To finish with 'burnt' onions

While the potatoes and neeps are cooking, heat the oil in a wok (or frying pan) and when hot add the sliced onions. Cook over a fairly high heat for 10 to 15 minutes, stirring frequently, till they are beginning to turn golden brown. Sprinkle over the sugar and stir continuously while the sugar caramelizes and begins to darken the onions. Remove when they are an even shade of mid to dark brown. Scatter on top of the clapshot and serve.

Kale

The old fashioned easy way of asking a friend to dinner was to ask him if he would take his kale with the family.
Dean Ramsay, *Reminiscences of Scottish Life and Character*, 1858.

Ramsay did not mean they would eat kale, just that it had become such an everyday item that the word had become generic for 'your dinner'. Its name comes from the Dutch 'Boerenkool', meaning 'peasants' cabbage'.

Kale applies to several varieties of non-heading brassicas. Most have a tall, thick stem, curled leaves and are very hardy. They are thought to have been the earliest type of cultivated cabbage and are closest to the wild forms. Kale's success in Scotland, and its claim to the title of Scotland's national vegetable, was largely due to its hardiness and, in particular, its improved flavour after a frost.

Green, curly-leaved varieties are the most common, but there are now many others in a variety of colours, both curly and flat-leaved. The very dark **Black Tuscan** (Cavolo Nero) is not as hardy as curly kale, but its young leaves can be used in salads and have a good flavour. **Red Russian, Redbor** and **Scarlet** can also be used young in salads.

Distinct Scottish varieties include the purple-veined, wrinkled-leaved **Shetland Kale**, which grows an open cabbage head at the top of its long stalk. Also **Pentland Brig**, which is broad-leaved and a good flavour, and **Sutherland Kale**, which is a very hardy ancient Highland variety. All kale is high-value food for its iron, and vitamin-rich antioxidant content.

Buying/Preparing

Supplies are now available throughout the year, though home gardeners value kale as a winter green which, depending on the variety, can be bitter when too young. Mature kale from a variety such as Pentland Brig is at its best from November through to May. The thicker, coarser leaves must be shaved with a sharp knife into very thin shreds – as they do in Portugal for their *Caldo Verde,* a green soup made with a similar textured coarse kale. Very woody stems in older kale should be removed. Less woody can be chopped and cooked for a bit longer than the leaves.

STIR-FRIED KALE

To retain as much food value as possible, chop very finely and stir-fry very quickly in a wok.

Lady Clark of Tillypronie (1903) says to 'add a dust of oat-

meal, or eat kale with a spoon and a piece of oatcake with it'.
She served hers with 'brown meat'.

250 g/9 oz long grain rice, cooked
2 tablespoons oil
2 onions, sliced
2-3 cloves crushed garlic
5 cm/2 in piece fresh root ginger, finely sliced
1 hot chilli, finely chopped
500 g/1 lb 2 oz kale tops, very finely shredded or ground finely
    in a food processor
250 g/9 oz cooked meat or fish
2-3 eggs, cooked in a frying pan into a flat omelette (optional)
1 head pak choy, very finely shredded
Soy sauce
Lemon or lime juice
Ground black pepper

4 servings

To prepare

Have all the vegetables ready to cook – onion, garlic, ginger,
chilli, kale (removing any very tough stalks from the kale). Chop
up the meat and fish into bite-sized pieces. Make the omelette
and cut into thin slices. Shred the pak choy finely.

To stir-fry

Heat the oil in a wok over a high heat. Add the onions and toss
until they soften and begin to colour. Add the garlic, ginger
and chilli. Stir through the onions and cook for a minute. Add
the kale and stir for a few minutes until it has wilted. Add the
cooked rice and mix through to mingle flavours. When hot, stir
through the meat, fish, sliced omelette and pak choy. Keep moving to heat through. Season with soy sauce, lemon or lime juice
and ground black pepper. Serve with chopsticks.

GREEN KALE SOUP WITH HAM

This is similar to Portuguese *Caldo Verde* (Green Soup), a peasant soup from the Douro Valley which uses a variety of kale
which grows to a height of about five feet and is fairly coarse-
textured. To tenderise it, the leaves are rolled up tightly and held
like a stick of rock while the top is shaved off in thin slivers with
a very sharp knife. Gathered into a pile on a chopping board,
it is then chopped so finely that it appears as just green flecks
in the soup. For the women of the Douro, it is not a soup to be
made in a hurry.

To make the stock:

500 g/1 lb 2 oz smoked or unsmoked ham*
500 g/1 lb 2 oz floury potatoes
1.8 L/3 pt water
1 medium onion, peeled or 2 cloves garlic, peeled
To make the soup:
250 g/9 oz kale
2 tablespoons oil
Salt and pepper

6–8 servings

For the stock

Put the ham in a large pot and add the water. Cover and bring
to the boil. Skim and simmer for about 30 minutes. Wash and
peel the potatoes and add with onion or garlic. Simmer till the
potatoes are soft and the meat cooked. Remove the meat. Leave
to cool.

To make the soup

Remove the coarse stalks from the kale, wash and chop very

*The use of the term Ham in Scotland loosely refers to any kind of
bacon and not merely the cured leg joint, and the cooked meat from
it, which is the usual English meaning of the word. In Scotland this is
usually called Cooked Ham or Gammon.

finely, as described above, with a sharp knife. Or put into the food-processor with the potatoes, onions/garlic and some stock and whizz. Return to the pot and bring to a simmer. Chop up the meat and add to the soup or serve separately. Taste and season. Serve with crusty bread.

Broccoli, Calabrese

This recent addition to Scotland's commercial vegetables has become so popular that growers are researching new varieties and growing methods. It is an Italian vegetable which was first known as Italian asparagus when it arrived in Northern Europe. Its name comes from the Italian '*brocco*' meaning 'shoot'. Calabrese is the region in Italy where it has been traditionally grown since the Middle Ages. There are two basic types: Calabrese, which is planted in the spring and harvested in the late summer when it produces small green cauliflower heads, and broccoli (green or sprouting), which is an outwintering annual, planted in early spring and ready the following spring. The sprouting varieties are purple or white.

BROCCOLI SALAD

The attractive colour and shape of the broccoli florets are the focal point of this green salad – a lively partner to any cooked meat, fish or boiled eggs.

500 g/1 lb 2 oz purple-sprouting, or young green, broccoli
1 gem lettuce
1 tub cress
3 tablespoons yoghurt or sour cream or a combination
2 teaspoons Dijon mustard
Juice of 1 lemon
2 tablespoons chopped chives
Salt and ground black pepper

Cooked meat, fish or boiled eggs

4 servings

To cook broccoli

Cut off the end of the broccoli stalks and discard if they look tough and woody (crunch a bit off the end if you are not sure). Break up florets into even-sized pieces. Steam for a few minutes till almost tender and still a bright colour. Drain and leave to cool.

To finish

Put the broccoli on a large oval ashet, platter or wooden board. Add the gem lettuce quarters. Cut the cress from its tub and scatter on top. Mix the yoghurt, mustard, lemon juice and chives together in a bowl. Place beside the salad. Serve with cooked meat, fish or boiled eggs.

Peas

Pea seeds have been found in deposits from Neolithic settlements in Jericho, while other early evidence of cultivation comes from the ruins of Troy, where a jar was found containing 440 lbs of peas.

They have been grown in southern Europe and the Near East for thousands of years, eaten either as fresh green peas when immature, or as dried peas for making into soup. Mangetout, sugar peas or snow peas do not have the stiff parchment-like walls on their pods, so are edible whole.

Peas were probably first cultivated in Turkey. At present there are several major groups of pea types: pod peas, which are for dried peas; pod peas for garden peas or petit pois; mangetout peas with flat pods; mangetout peas with swollen pods.

Peas must be picked and eaten young. A crop can come to ripeness in a matter of hours and must be picked and used quickly (or frozen) to preserve the sweet, fresh flavour.

GREEN PEA SOUP

500 g/1 lb 2 oz peas, fresh shelled or frozen
600 ml/1 pt water
100 g/4 oz streaky bacon
Bunch of fresh mint leaves
100 ml/3½ fl oz single cream
Salt and pepper

4 servings

To Make

Put the peas into the pot and add the water. Bring slowly to the boil and simmer for a minute. Remove from the heat. Grill the bacon rashers on both sides till cooked and chop roughly.

Whizz the peas, bacon, some mint leaves and water in a liquidiser till they are a fine puree. Return to the pot. Add the cream. Reheat gently. Taste and season. Serve with some chopped mint leaves.

MINTED PEAS
with greens

25 g/1 oz butter
25 g/1 oz plain flour
300 ml/½ pt ham stock and/or water
500 g/1 lb 2 oz fresh or frozen peas (defrosted)
200 g/7 oz lettuce, cos or gem or pak choy
Small bunch of fresh mint leaves, finely chopped
Squeeze of lemon or lime juice to taste
Salt and pepper

Making the peas

Put the butter into a pan and melt over a medium heat. Add the flour and stir to blend. Cook for a few minutes, then gradually add the stock, stirring all the time. When simmering and thickened, add the peas and cook for a few minutes till soft. Remove from the heat and stir in the greens and mint. Taste and season. Add lemon or lime juice. Adjust consistency with more stock if necessary. Serve with **Boiled** or **Baked Ham** (see p.237-8) or **Baked Pork Chops** (see p.239).

Mixed Vegetable Dishes

HOTCH POTCH
Spring Vegetable Soup

That's Hotch-Potch – and that's cocky-leeky – the twa best soups in natur. Broon soup's moss-water – and white soup's like scauded [scalded] milk wi' worms in't. But see, sirs, hoo the ladle stauns o' itsel in the potch . . .
The Ettrick Shepherd, James Hogg, *Noctes Ambrosianae*, 1822-1835.

The Shepherd's enthusiasm for Hotch Potch led him into another eulogy when he described it as 'an emblem o' the haill vegetable and animal creation.'

Its virtue lies in the freshness and variety of the young spring vegetables and the universal liking in Scotland for a soup which has as much in it as possible.

For the stock:
1 kg/2 lb 4 oz neck of mutton or lamb
3 L/5 ½ pt water
1 onion stuck with a few cloves
Bay leaf
Bundle of fresh herbs
Added vegetables:
50 g/2 oz fat from the stock

¼ medium turnip, peeled

2-3 young carrots, peeled

½ medium cauliflower, broken into small sprigs

125 g/4 oz fresh broad beans

125 g/4 oz fresh green peas

75 g/3 oz spring onions, finely chopped

½ lettuce, finely chopped

Chopped chives

Salt and pepper

8-10 servings

Making the stock

Put the mutton or lamb into cold water and bring to the boil, skim. Add onion stuck with cloves, bay leaf and bundle of fresh herbs. Simmer till the meat is tender. Strain, leave to cool, remove excess fat and take the meat off the bone. Chop it up finely.

To finish the soup

Melt the fat from the stock in the pan and add turnip and carrots (they can be grated by hand or in the food processor with

the grating disc) Add cauliflower and broad beans. Over a low heat toss the vegetables for about five minutes, cover and sweat for another five minutes, stirring occasionally, without colouring. Add the peas and the spring onions. Heat through. Add the strained stock, bring to a gentle simmer. The vegetables should be just tender. They will lose their fresh flavour if overcooked. Finally, just before serving, add meat, lettuce and chives. Taste and season. Serve.

LENTIL BROTH

This has an extra flavour kick, added at the end, of piquant tomatoes and vinegar, balanced with a spoonful or two of sweet treacle. It can be made thick or thin depending on taste. If thick it can be served with cooked rice, greens, spicy chutney and a spoonful of plain yogurt.

250 g/9 oz red split or yellow mung lentils
2 L/3½ pt water or stock (or use a ham bone)
50 g/2 oz butter
1 medium onion, finely chopped
2-3 stalks of celery or fennel, finely chopped
2 medium carrots, diced or grated
3-4 potatoes, sliced
¼ of a medium turnip, diced or grated
Finishing the soup:
1 tin chopped tomatoes
1-2 tablespoons apple cider vinegar
1-2 tablespoons treacle or molasses
Salt and ground black or cayenne pepper
Herbs to garnish, leaves of thyme, oregano or basil

6-8 servings

Use a large broth pot and a large sauté or frying-pan.

To cook lentils

Wash lentils till the water comes clear. Put in the water or stock (or use a ham bone) and simmer covered until the lentils have become a fine puree, which will take 1-2 hours. Beat with a whisk to make them smooth.

To prepare and cook vegetables.

Grate or slice the onion, celery or fennel, carrots, potato and turnip, using the appropriate blade of the food-processor, or chop by hand. Melt the butter in a large sauté or frying-pan and add the onion, celery or fennel, carrots, potato and turnip. Toss in the butter for a few minutes. Cover and sweat for about 5 minutes, stirring frequently to prevent sticking. Add to the lentil stock and simmer till all are just tender. Adjust consistency if necessary with stock or water.

Finishing

If using, add meat from the ham bone, finely chopped. Add chopped tomatoes, cider vinegar, treacle or molasses and black pepper. Blend into the broth. Taste and season. Adjust the balance of sweet and sour. Add thyme, oregano or basil. Serve either thin as a broth or thick as a soup-stew.

6: CHEESE

Many's the long night I have dreamed of cheese, toasted most-
ly, and woke up again and here I were. You might not happen
to have a piece of cheese about you now?
Robert Louis Stevenson, *Treasure Island*, 1882.

Poor Ben Gunn's first words to his rescuers, after being marooned
for three years on Treasure Island, are echoed by Patrick Rance,
cheese expert and author of *The Great British Cheese Book* (1982),
when he says, 'If you offered me a desert island with just one kind of
food, a farmhouse cheddar would be my unhesitating choice.'

Cheese is a rich area of gastronomy, where passions run high.
Its value in the past, however, was not just for its unique flavours
and textures but as a vital supply of portable, long-keeping protein.
Much transfer of cheese went on, particularly from the Highlands
to the Lowlands, in exchange for grain. Highlanders are said to have
survived, at certain times of the year and during bad harvests, solely
on cheese, fish and milk.

The Highland cheeses made by crofters were mostly of the soft
variety, made from skimmed milk and from ewes', cows' and goats'
milk. They were made into a light, soft cheese with a sharp citric
tang which was known as 'crowdie'. It was also known as 'hangman
cheese' or 'hangie', since the curds were tied in a cheesecloth and left
to hang as the whey drained out, usually from the branch of a tree
in the open air. To preserve crowdie it was mixed with butter and
packed into wooden barrels or stone crocks and kept cool in the barn
during winter. This was called 'Crowdie Butter', and remembered as
a special treat by the generation who ate it as children in the early
1900s.

'The great treat, though,' says Wallace Lockhart in *The Scot and*
His Oats, 1983, 'was to have crowdie mixed with fresh cream and

piled on an oatcake with fresh salted butter. Then you had a royal feast of flavours – acid, sweet and salt, and, better perhaps, a royal mixture of textures, soft, crisp and crunchy.'

While the crofter's crowdie was a relatively short-keeping cheese, other areas of the country became known for the quality of their longer-keeping cheeses. The special dairying areas of the country, where surplus cheese was bartered for other goods, included Ross-shire, Caithness, Orkney and the Borders. But it was in Ayrshire, Dumfries, Galloway and Kintyre, and on the islands of Arran, Bute and Islay, that cheesemaking became a larger-scale farm industry. These warm, wet lowlands, with their rich, heavy loam soils, were perfect for lush grass-growing, providing the best diet for dairy cattle to produce rich milk. This is home to the native dairying breed of Ayrshire cows, prized for the high quality of their milk.

It was in the late 1600s that new methods of making longer-keeping cheeses began to be developed in these areas. Much of the credit goes to a farmer's daughter from Ayrshire, Barbara Gilmour. She had fled to Ireland from religious persecution at the time of the Covenanters, but returned home in 1690, bringing with her a recipe for making cheese which revolutionised the old methods. It used full cream cows' milk, and the cheese was pressed till it was quite hard, to improve both the keeping quality and the flavour. While the old cheese was called 'common cheese', the new one was described as 'sweet-milk cheese'. Around a century later, in the 1790 *Statistical Account of Scotland*, it is described as Dunlop cheese, and was being made in five Ayrshire and two Lanarkshire parishes.

During the 1800s the Dunlop recipe was improved – with help from English cheddar-makers – and demand was increasing in the developing urban markets of Central Scotland. By the end of the century it had become Scotland's premier cheese. Though some large creameries were built to make it, it was also being made by single farmers in Ayrshire and the south-west in the 1930s. 'Each farm has a fully matured cheese open for cooking, and a softer one for eating,' says Patrick Rance, when staying in the area. 'At breakfast, porridge was followed on alternate days by bacon and eggs or toasted cheese on a scone made from home-ground flour, eaten in front of the fire.'

The subsequent demise of Dunlop was due partly to the general decline in farmhouse cheesemaking, during and after World War II, when milk was bought in bulk by the Milk Marketing Board (MMB) and taken in tankers to large creameries to make factory cheddar. But it was also under threat of extinction when the MMB decided that their creamery cheese should be called 'cheddar' rather than Dunlop. A leading rubber tyre company of the day (now extinct) was called Dunlop, and they thought the association of rubber with cheese was not a good idea.

Yet despite this, a few creameries persisted with the old Dunlop cheese. The revival of farmhouse cheeses in the 1980s and 90s, and in particular the success of Ann Dorward's Dunlop cheese made from unpasteurised milk in the old way, has saved it from extinction. In addition to its ancient pedigree, it is distinguished from the generic 'cheddar' by the taste and flavour in the milk from the local grass, and the cheesemakers' methods producing a mellower flavoured and softer, creamier textured cheese. Cheesemakers often describe it as a 'meatier' cheese than cheddar.

Methods of Cheese Production

'Pasteurisation eliminates 99 per cent of the worthwhile organisms, including the bacteria and esters vital to the character of cheese,' says Patrick Rance.

Post-World War II saw a decline in unpasteurised farmhouse cheese and an increase in block cheddar manufacture in creameries, now the dominant mass-market Scottish cheese. But the advantages of traditional farmhouse cheeses – clothbound, cylindrical and made from unpasteurised single-farm milk – are of flavour and texture, and they are now produced by a small group of artisan cheesemakers.

Those who make this cheese usually make it from one farmer's milk, which means they can ensure high levels of management and hygiene. Some farmhouse cheesemakers, though not all, are also farmers with their own milking animals. Making cheese from one farm's milk provides the cheese with a distinctive locality, and often special breed of cow, which is lost in the factory product when milk from numerous farms, covering a wide area, is mixed in 3,000-gallon tankers.

Cheesemaking methods today are highly scientific. Careful control of curd-making, by manipulating the recipe with lactic acid starters and bacterial cultures, give the cheese much of its character. And yet there will always be differences in the milk caused by the breed of the milking animal, the time of year and the soil and ecology of the region. Milk from cows feeding on fresh grass and wild clover will taste totally different to milk from those fed silage and turnips. When they eat the fresh, young spring grasses, their milk will taste different to milk from mature autumn grass. All of which makes for a subtle, but fascinating, variety in cheese.

Moulding, pressing, coating and storing cheese also affect its flavour and quality. Clothbound traditional cheese has the advantage of being able to breathe, mature and ripen to a fuller flavour. Vacuum-sealed, rindless blocks, however, must be kept at a lower temperature, to prevent the cheese from 'blowing' the wrap, with a consequent loss of flavour.

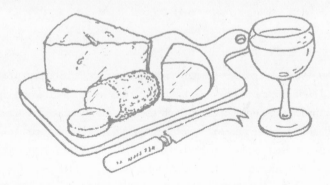

Uses/Buying and Storing Cheese

*Cheese is capital in the forenoons, or the afternoons either,
when you've had nae ither denner, especially wi' fresh butter
and bread; but nane but gluttonous epicures wad hae recourse
to it after they hae been stuffing themsels, as we hae noo been
doin for the last hour, wi three coorses, forby hotch-potch and
puddins.*

Christopher North, *Noctes Ambrosianae*, 1822-1825.

Less gluttonous modern epicures would disagree with these re-
marks. But then it's all a question of the size and content of the dinner. North, and his tavern cronies, are to be found on another night
ringing the bell for some toasted cheese. 'It's a gude while now sin'
dinner and I'm getting roun' again into hunger.'

Cheese is one of the best standby foods, available at a moment's
notice. Its endless variations of texture, flavour and aroma mean that
all palates can be satisfied. Buying from specialist shops usually allows a tasting before you buy, which means a better choice.

While there have been attempts to distinguish cheddar, and
other cheeses, according to strength, this is regarded by cheese experts as a poor way of judging a cheese. The strongest cheese is
not always the best. In cheese-speak, 'cleanness' is described as the
level of acidity balanced against other flavours. The acidity should
not be too high, but at the same time there should be enough there
to provide a tang. Badly matured cheese may have a dull, muddy
flavour or it might have sharpness at the first taste, but then no
follow-through.

Cheese should be served at room temperature (it is best stored
in waxed paper, in the vegetable compartment at the bottom of the
fridge). It needs about half an hour to an hour at room temperature
before serving, unwrapping just before eating and re-wrapping just
after. Oatcakes with crowdie are the classic combination, but scones
with toasted Dunlop (Rance's Ayrshire breakfast) are another good

partnership, also tangy farmhouse cheddar and Cox's pippins or Egremont russets. Crusty bread goes with all cheese. The French, who eat three times more cheese than the British, serve cheese immediately after the main course and before the dessert, usually with some of the main course's red full-bodied wine, when *le fromage* becomes a special course, a relaxing break for the cook, and a sign of unhurried eating.

Cheese Types

1. Fresh-Soft Cheeses (without rind or mould) and **Natural-Rind** (may have a light mould).

Made from milk which has been turned into floppy curds and whey by using rennet to form the curd. Alternatively a curd is formed naturally by the lactic acid in the milk as it sours, which is the traditional method for crowdie. Such cheeses are known as Lactic Cheeses and have a tangier, sharper flavour than rennet-started curds. The curds are separated from the whey by draining. For crowdie the cheese is hung up in a muslin bag. No pressing is involved. Or it may be put into a perforated mould and allowed to drain naturally. Revivalist cheesesmaker and pioneer of the crofter's crowdie, Susannah Stone, who began Highland Fine Cheeses in the 1950s, claimed that, 'The unusual thing about crowdie is that it is semi-cooked. The fresh milk is soured naturally beside the stove and then "scrambled" over the heat and hung up to drip in a muslin cloth. This ancient cheese is unique to the Highlands and Islands of Scotland, and as far as we know was made nowhere else in Europe – it has special qualities. Firstly, because of the natural curding (12 hours) it has a lovely citric flavour. Rennet was not traditionally used to speed the souring. We use no rennet on our large scale, lactic cultures, and stick rigidly to the old recipe and method which is believed to go back to Viking and possibly Pictish times.'

Another type of fresh cheese is Natural-Rind, a term which applies to young cheeses which have been left to drain longer and in a drier atmosphere than Fresh-Soft cheeses. They are put into moulds and may be simply turned regularly so the weight of the curd presses out the whey or they may be lightly pressed. This is a typical old-fashioned farmhouse cheese which might have been eaten very fresh, a couple of weeks old, or matured for a few months, when a natural rind developed.

Cheesemakers and Varieties

BRENDA LEDDY (Garden Cottage Farm, Stichill, Kelso): **STICHILL** is soft, fresh cheese from unpasteurised Jersey cows' milk, **KELSAE** is from the same type of milk and is similar to a Wensleydale, but has a stronger, richer flavour.

CAMBUS O' MAY (Ballater, Deeside): **CAMBUS O' MAY**, **LARIG GRUH** and **LOCHNAGAR**, natural-rind, white, crumbly young cheeses made with unpasteurised cow's milk from traditional farmhouse recipes, hand-pressed in truckles. Cheesemakers: Reid family.

CONNAGE HIGHLAND DAIRY (Ardeseer, Inverness): made from organic cow's milk, **CONNAGE CROWDIE** and **CROMAL**, crumbly, traditional farmhouse cheese. Cheesemakers: Clark family.

DEVENICK DAIRY (Banchory, Aberdeenshire): made from Jersey/Friesian cows' milk, **DEE'S CHEESE** (garlic or chilli flavour), soft cream cheese; **COWDIE**, their version of crowdie; **THE COOS ROOT**, a mild, soft farmhouse cheese. Cheesemakers: Groat family.

GALLOWAY FARMHOUSE CHEESE (Dumfries and Galloway): **CAIRNSMORE CHEESES** include a hard ewes milk cheese, available in various flavours, created from the organic milk from the farm's flock of Friesland sheep. The range also includes cheeses produced from organic cows' milk and goats' milk; they are natural-rind cheeses, also available clothbound. Cheesemaker: Alan Brown.

HIGHLAND FINE (Tain, Easter Ross): their varieties of **CROWDIE**, made from pasteurised cows' milk as lactic cheeses, include: **CABOC**, which is a double cream cheese with a buttery texture, rolled in toasted pinhead oatmeal; **BLACK CROWDIE**, a crowdie and cream-cheese mixture rolled in crushed peppercorns and toasted oatmeal, giving it a unique flavour. Cheesemaker: Rory Stone.

HILDA SEATER (Grimbister, Finstown, Orkney): **GRIMBISTER ORKNEY FARMHOUSE** is made throughout the summer months from unpasteurised cows' milk in various sizes and flavours.

HUMPHREY ERRINGTON (Walston Braehead, Carnwath, Lanarkshire): **MAISIE'S KEBBUCK** is an unpasteurised, unpressed, natural-rind cow's milk cheese about 3 months matured.

LOCH ARTHUR (Dumfries and Galloway): **CRANNOG** is a fresh, young soft cheese made from organically reared Ayrshire cows' unpasteurised milk. Cheesemaker: Barry Grahame.

ST ANDREWS FARMHOUSE CHEESE (Anstruther, Fife): **ANSTER** and **RED ANSTER** (flavoured with garlic and chives), made from unpasteurised cows' milk. Cheesemaker: Jane Stewart.

2. Soft-White Cheese (with white, penicillium candidum rind).

Made with full-cream milk, the floppy curd is put into perforated moulds and the whey drains out naturally, without pressing, in an atmosphere of high humidity so that the curd does not lose too much whey. The high moisture content, plus the high humidity, encourages the growth of the mould. Maturity is usually reached in about a month. The cheese is creamy and fairly mild in flavour – the texture buttery. There is a short period during which the cheeses are considered 'ripe', before they begin to start softening too much. This is a matter of taste; some like them quite runny. When they begin to smell too highly of ammonia, it is not wise to eat them.

Cheesemakers and Varieties

CONNAGE HIGHLAND DAIRY (Ardeseer, Inverness): made from organic cow's milk, **CLAVA BRIE** and **HIGHLAND HEART** (heart-shaped brie). Cheesemakers: Clark family.

DEVENICK DAIRY (Banchory, Aberdeenshire): made from Jersey/Friesian cows' milk, **MONARCH BRIE**. Cheesemakers: Groat family.

HIGHLAND FINE (Tain, Easter Ross): **MORANGIE BRIE** made from milk from Ayrshire and Friesian cows. Cheesemaker: Rory Stone.

LOCH ARTHUR (Dumfries and Galloway): **CRIFFEL**, a square, basket-shaped, washed-rind cheese with an outstanding texture and flavour (winner of many awards) made from organically reared Ayrshire cows' unpasteurised milk. Cheesemaker: Barry Grahame.

STANDHILL FARMHOUSE CHEESE (Hawick, Borders): **ROXBURGH ROONDIE**, soft white mould brie/camembert-type cheese made with Friesian cows' milk; **BORDERS BRIE**, one and a half kilo rounds; **FATLIPS CASTLE BLUE**, soft blue cheese made in the same size as the 'Roondie'. Cheesemakers: Jim and Annie Shanks, *standhillcheese@aol.com*.

3. Blue Cheeses

The rind varies from a fine bloom to thick rind. Often they are wrapped in foil. The blue mould, a strain of penicillium, is usually added to the cheeses at the beginning of the process. They are neither pressed nor cooked. The floppy curd is ladled into the moulds and left to set naturally. Turned frequently, it is the weight of the curd in the cheese which presses out the whey. Once they can stand on their own they are rubbed with salt and put in a controlled atmosphere (in the case of Roquefort in underground caves) for the blue mould to develop.

Cheesemakers and Varieties

DEVENICK DAIRY (Banchory, Aberdeenshire): made from Jersey/Friesian cows' milk, **BADENTOY BLUE**. Cheesemakers: Groat family.

HIGHLAND FINE (Tain, Easter Ross): **STRATHDON BLUE** is made from pasteurised cows' milk and is aged for 8-12 weeks; **BLUE MONDAY** is a wild blue-veined cheese made with cows' milk. Cheesemaker, Rory Stone.

HUMPHREY ERRINGTON (Ogscastle, Carnwath, Lanarkshire): **LANARK BLUE** is a revival – blue-veined ewes' milk cheese, unpasteurised, it is made from a Friesian-cross ewe in an area which was once noted for ewes' milk cheese. A Roquefort-style cheese. **DUNSYRE BLUE** is an unpasteurised, blue-veined cows' milk cheese made from a single herd of Ayrshire cows.

4. Hard Cheeses (thick-rind, often waxed, oiled or clothbound).

The curd must be cut more finely so more whey can be extracted. It may be warmed slightly to force out more whey, which is then drained off and the curd left to set. Next it is cut into blocks, and turned, until it reaches the correct acidity, when it is cut again (cheddaring) before salting and putting into moulds. The final hardness will depend on how much pressure is put on the cheese at this point.

Traditional, clothbound, matured hard cheese allows a rind with moulds to develop. In a cloth it can also breathe, so loses moisture as it matures. Hard cheeses, plastic wrapped or dipped in wax, will have less flavour and a softer texture. 'Mild' creamery cheddar is matured for about 4-5 months, while 'mature' is usually 9 months-1 year old, with some, 'extra mature', matured even longer for a stronger flavour.

Cheddar cheeses are given grades according to their quality and an ability to mature. Grades start with 'Choicest', which is a 'First Grade' cheese and is reckoned to have extra potential for improving for more than one year. 'First Grade' is cheese with a clean flavour, firm body and close texture, with bright colour, no gas holes, free from mould and of a regular shape, and which can be matured for up to a year. 'Graded' is when there is a slight fault, possibly weak 'body' or over-acid, when the cheese will not mature well and should be eaten within a few months. 'No grade' is unsuitable for counter sale and will be used for processing.

Farmhouse Cheesemakers and Varieties

CAITHNESS DAIRY (Lybster, Caithness): range of **CAITHNESS CHEESE**, natural and flavoured, made from own-farm pasteurised cows' milk. Cheesemakers: Sandy and Sandra Sutherland.

CONNAGE HIGHLAND DAIRY (Ardeseer, Inverness): **CONNAGE DUNLOP**, a crumbly, traditional farmhouse cheese made from organic cows' milk. Cheesemakers: Clark family.

DUNLOP DAIRY (Dunlop, Ayrshire): **DUNLOP** is made from unpasteurised cows' milk in both small clothbound truckles and in a large thirty-pound size similar to the original farmhouse Dunlop. May be matured for over a year. **BONNET** is a crumbly Wensleydale-style cheese made from goats' milk, and **SWINZIE** from ewes' milk is a cream-textured, nutty flavour. Cheesemaker: Ann Dorward.

SIGRIOB-RUADH FARM DAIRY (Tobermory, Isle of Mull): **ISLE OF MULL CHEDDAR** is a long-matured, clothbound truckle made from unpasteurised cows' milk. Cheesemakers: Christine and Jeff Read.

STANDHILL FARMHOUSE CHEESE (Hawick, Borders): **LILLIESLEAF** is a hard, crumbly Caerphilly-type cheese; **MINTO MELLOW** is somewhere between cheddar and a Gloucester cheese both made with Friesian cows' milk. Cheesemakers: Jim and Annie Shanks.

LOCH ARTHUR CHEESES (Dumfries and Galloway): **LOCH ARTHUR FARMHOUSE CHEDDAR** is a long-matured, clothbound truckle made from a single herd of organically reared Ayrshire cows' unpasteurised milk. Cheesemaker: Barry Grahame.

Creamery Cheddar and Dunlop – from Pasteurised Cows' Milk

Only one small creamery on the Isle of Arran, using milk from three farms at Kilmory, makes an **EXTRA MATURE DUNLOP** as well as an **EXTRA MATURE CHEDDAR**. A co-operative of 20 farmers on Orkney own and run the creamery in Kirkwall, which makes **ORKNEY MATURE** and **MEDIUM MATURE SCOT-TISH ISLAND CHEDDAR** from their own cows' milk.

There are large, high-tech creameries at Stranraer, where they make **MEDIUM MATURE GALLOWAY CHEDDAR** and **MACLELLAND SERIOUSLY STRONG** (14 months matured) **CHEDDAR**; at Campbeltown, where they make **MULL OF KIN-TYRE EXTRA MATURE CHEDDAR**; and at Lockerbie, where they make **LOCKERBIE CHEDDAR**.

For more information about sources of Scottish cheeses, see p.279.

TOASTED CHEESE

'Toasted mostly' – Ben Gunn's Dream.

Ben Gunn's dream cheese would have been sliced onto a plate and left in front of the fire to melt slowly. His toast would have been made separately, on a toasting fork, also in front of glowing embers. Then he would have mixed some favourite flavouring into the cheese: a dust of cayenne pepper, a slurp of ale, a knob of butter, a dab of mustard ... He might have soaked his toast in some wine or ale before pouring over the molten cheese to make the dish properly described as 'Toast and Cheese'.

The Welsh can lay claim to making this into a national dish. It appears that their description was entirely appropriate when they called it a 'rare bit', meaning something splendid ('Rabbit' is a shortening of the original word). The *OED*'s definition of Welsh Rarebit is: 'A dish consisting of cheese and a little butter melted and mixed together, to which are added ale, cayenne pepper, and salt, the whole being stirred until it is creamy, and then poured over buttered toast: also, simply, slices of toasted cheese laid on toast.'

CHEESE AND EGGS
with toast or cauliflower

This partnership of cheese and eggs appears in the *Household Book of Lady Grisell Baillie* (1692-1733) in a dish she calls 'Ramekins of Cheese'. In my grandmother's cramped tenement kitchen in Glasgow's East End in the mid-1900s she also made a dish she called 'cheese and eggs' which we had for high tea, usually poured over toast, occasionally over cooked cauliflower – but never 'in ramekins'.

It is a simple, fondue-type slow melting of cheese and gentle cooking of eggs, taking care to keep the texture smooth and creamy.

1 teaspoon cornflour
4 tablespoons milk
250 g/9 oz grated extra mature cheddar
2 large eggs, beaten
Salt and pepper
Mustard (optional)
4 slices of hot toast
Or cooked cauliflower
Or small crusty loaf cut into bite-sized chunks

2-4 servings

To make

Blend the cornflour with a little milk till smooth in a small, thick-based pan. This can also be made in a double boiler over boiling water, but will take longer. Add the remaining milk and the cheese. Heat very gently, stirring with a wooden spoon till the cheese melts. Remove from the heat and spoon some of the hot cheese mixture over the eggs. Beat together with a whisk or fork. Pour back into the pan and continue cooking. Stir over a low heat till the mixture becomes thick and smooth. Taste and season.

To serve

Pour over toast or cooked cauliflower and serve. Or put the pot in the centre of the table and serve with chunks of crusty bread for dipping.

Milk-Related Traditions

A dinner in the Western Isles differs very little from a dinner in England, except that in the place of tarts there are always set different preparations of milk.
Samuel Johnson, *Journey to the Western Isles of Scotland* (1775).

Besides the milk, buttermilk and whey, which were drunk in large quantities by all classes, there is also a rich tradition of distinctive dishes made of milk. Travellers to Scotland, such as the good doctor above, often commented on this fact. The food historian, F. Marian McNeill, researched these milk dishes in her book *The Scots Kitchen* (1929, revised ed. 2011).

These were traditions based on a self-sufficient system of rural life where households had their own cows and were able to milk the cow straight into a pail of buttermilk, meaning many of them are now obsolete. An exception is the fresh, soft, drained cheese which was known as Hattit Kit and very similar to the French *Coeur à la Creme,* made in a heart-shaped mould with holes in the base to drain the cheese.

HATTIT KIT

'Hattit kit, a dish of milk with a top-layer of cream. 1600.'
Dictionary of the Scots Language

PLAIN

Take equal parts whole milk and buttermilk and place them in a small keg in a warm spot. After two or three days a thick white paste or curd rises to the top [the hat]. Remove this and strain. If too thick, thin with whole milk and sweeten to taste. Best eaten as a dessert with oatcakes when preferred. Can be flavoured with whisky. This can be repeated several times by adding milk and buttermilk to the keg. Hence the name. A warm weather dish. Anon.

1.2 L/2 pts sweet whole milk
1.2 L/2 pts cultured buttermilk
Sugar or honey
Soft fruits

Bring sweet milk almost to the boil and add buttermilk. Stir over the heat until the curd separates. Heat gently, it must not boil. Pour into a colander lined with a piece of muslin and leave for 2-3 hours till the whey has drained off. While it is still quite soft, sweeten with sugar or honey. Put into a muslin-lined mould with holes in it (make holes in small plastic tubs with a red hot skewer). Leave to drain. When it has stopped dripping, turn out and serve with cream and fruit or oatcakes and butter.

RICH
for festive occasions

100 g/3½ oz unsalted butter
100 g/3½ oz caster or fine brown sugar

250 g/9 oz hattit kit or crowdie
1 egg yolk
50 g/2 oz raisins
1 tablespoon thick bitter marmalade
1 tablespoon blanched chopped almonds

Beat together the butter and the caster or fine brown sugar till creamy. Add the hattit kit or crowdie, egg yolk, raisins, marmalade. Mix together thoroughly and pour into a lined sieve or a mould with holes. Level the top and put a light weight on top. Leave overnight. Turn out and decorate with almonds. Serve as a spread for Plain Cookies, Hot Cross Buns, or a **Special Yeast Cake** (see p.346).

CHEESE CAKE
with chocolate and raspberries

A marbling of creamy cheese and dark chocolate is baked with a scattering of fresh raspberries or blueberries on top to make this colourful, multi-flavoured cheese cake.

For the chocolate mix:
250 g/9 oz unsalted butter, plus extra for greasing
175 g/6 oz dark chocolate
250 g/9 oz caster sugar
50 g/2 oz plain flour
50 g/2 oz self-raising flour
5 large eggs
2 teaspoons vanilla extract
For the cheese mix:
350 g/12 oz cream cheese
75 g/3 oz caster sugar
1 teaspoon vanilla extract
2 medium eggs
250 g/8 oz fresh raspberries or blueberries

8-10 servings

Preheat the oven to350F/180C/160Cfan/Gas 4.

Use a 20 cm/8 in round cake tin with removable base. Grease sides and line base with non-stick baking paper or line base and sides with a sheet of foil.

Heating the eggs

Put the eggs into a bowl and pour over hot water. Leave for 3-4 minutes. Pour off water and break eggs into a bowl and whisk.

To make the chocolate mixture

Melt the chocolate in a double boiler or in a bowl over a pan of hot water, stirring occasionally till it is just melted. Or melt slowly in the microwave (900W) on half-power for 60 seconds. Remove and stir. Melt for another 60 seconds on half-power, remove and stir. Continue removing and stirring till it is only just melted. Leave to cool till just lukewarm.

Put the sugar and softened butter into a mixing bowl and beat with an electric beater till creamy. Add a quarter of the eggs and beat till mixed in. Add another quarter and beat in. Then add half the flour and continue beating. Add the remaining eggs and the remaining flour and beat to make a thick creamy mixture. The warm eggs will prevent it curdling. Stir in the melted dark chocolate. Pour into prepared tin and level surface.

To make the cheese mixture

Put the cream cheese, sugar, vanilla extract and eggs into a bowl and beat till smooth and creamy with a whisk or electric beater. Pour over the chocolate mix in an even layer.

Use a large fork to marble the cheese mixture through the chocolate. Scatter the raspberries or blueberries on top and push them into the mixture. Bake for about 35–40 minutes. Leave to cool in the tin. Serve warm as a pudding or for tea.

7: Fruits & Puddings

She put into the carriage a basket of excellent gooseberries, and some of the finest apricots I ever saw or tasted, which have grown out of doors; the season has been unusually favourable and her husband was fond of cultivating his garden.

Robert Southey [at Inverness], *Journal of a Tour in Scotland in 1819.*

A colder, wetter climate than the rest of Britain, plus a lack of early gardening know-how, might appear to have put the Scots at a horticultural disadvantage, yet, as Southey noted, gardening expertise was not lacking and the climate was not always hostile. Some parts, certainly, were warmer than others and the terrain also varied considerably. But where the two combined favourably there was success. It was to these areas that Cistercian and Benedictine monks first came in the 1000s, settling in the fertile Borders, the valleys of Strathmore and the Morayshire coast, and bringing both improved horticultural varieties and growing expertise. The range of fruits and vegetables grown by them, and subsequently in the gardens of the aristocratic houses of the land, was impressive.

Ever enterprising, the Scots have also gathered wild fruits and berries: blaeberries, brambles, wild raspberries, rowans, sloes, rosehips and geans. Conserves, jams and jellies were made with these wild fruits and used in imaginative ways. They were regarded as flavourings, not just to spread on bread, but to use as sauces with puddings. They were even concocted into drinks, such as the warming drink which Thomas Pennant was given when he visited the Macleods of Arnisdale in 1769.

> I shall never forget the hospitality of the house: before I could utter a denial, three glasses of rum, cordialised with jelly of bilberries, were poured into me by the irresistible hand of good Madam MacLeod.

As one of the most eminent naturalists of the eighteenth century, his observations on fruits eaten on Jura are also revealing –

Sloes are the only fruits of the island. An acid for punch is made of the berries of the mountain ash [rowan]: and a kind of spirit is also distilled from them.

Commercial horticulture, to provide for growing markets in industrial towns, began in the 1700s. Everyone in Edinburgh at this time was familiar with the street cry for apples and pears: 'Fine rosey-cheekit Carse o' Gowries – the tap o' the tree'. But the Carse of Gowrie orchards were gradually abandoned around the 1960s and 70s as supermarkets began importing cheaper apples from warmer countries which produced higher yields. The economics of growing and picking the native crop were no longer viable and many orchards were dug up. Luckily, some were left.

Despite this setback, the horticultural industry has worked with the positive aspects of the Scottish climate and used to advantage the cooler climate and the longer hours of summer daylight to grow crops like berries and peas. They are slower to ripen, so develop a better flavour, while the cooler weather means fewer pests and diseases and less pesticide use. Scotland is a major producer of berries and peas.

For much of the 1900s, a high percentage of the commercial berry crop found its way into highly processed products which damaged some of the natural flavour as well as valuable nutrients. Much of the crop went to jam factories, such as Keillers of Dundee or canning factories like Baxters of Speyside, or it was blast-frozen or used to flavour sweet yoghurts. The push, which began in the late twentieth century to sell more of the berry crop fresh, rather than processed, has been successful and now fresh berries dominate the market.

Research into berry varieties which flourish best in the Scottish climate began in 1946, when the Scottish Raspberry Investigation was set up at University College Dundee, transferring to Mylnefield Farm in the Carse of Gowrie in 1951. This eventually became the Scottish Crop Research Institute (SCRI), where the focus has been on soft fruit, potatoes and barley. Over the years, it has supported the industry and been instrumental in its success: pioneering new breeding varieties of many Scottish horticultural crops with a view to increasing yields, producing disease-resistant plants which will fit the special needs of the consumer, while at the same time maintaining quality. In 2012 it was merged with the Macaulay Land Use Research Institute to become the James Hutton Institute (JHI).

Scottish Soft Fruits

Raspberries

It was a group of Scottish market gardeners in Angus in the early 1900s who decided to move out of traditional strawberry production and into raspberries. They formed a co-operative and in subsequent decades established the Scottish crop as the dominant British supply. On the fertile Tayside soils, once favoured by the farming monks of the Middle Ages, the raspberry matures slowly, producing a flavourful berry around the beginning of July. SCRI's raspberries were all named after Scottish valleys or glens. **Glen Clova** (1969) is one of the oldest, and was followed by **Glen Prosen**, **Glen Moy** and **Glencoe**, a purple raspberry (1989). The deep purple Tayberry is a cross between the European raspberry and the American Loganberry. **Glen Garry, Glen Lyon, Glen Magna, Glen Rosa** and **Autumn Bliss** (a late crop) are all varieties of the 1990s, as well as the excellent **Glen Ample**, which has become one of the most popular UK varieties – a high yielder, it is also a large fruit with an aromatic, sweet flavour. **Glen Doll** is one of the latest raspberries to be bred at the SCRI. With outstanding flavour, and large fruit size, it ripens slightly later than Glen Ample, thus extending the season.

With additional support from the Scottish Executive and the Horticultural Development Council, the Scottish Raspberry Breeding Consortium has been set up which includes growers, marketing organisations and propagators involved in the UK raspberry industry. Once the most promising varieties are identified in the breeding programme, they are propagated for small trials on commercial farms in a diversity of sites and cropping systems. Here, they are evaluated for 2 to 3 years and valuable feedback is given. There are several promising new selections currently under evaluation. In mid-July, at the peak of the raspberry season, a 'Fruit Walk' is held at the Invergowrie site when it is possible to see, and taste, new and developing varieties. The quest for the perfect raspberry – its colour, flavour, size, texture and growing qualities – is never-ending.

Strawberries

Though Tayside growers in the early 1900s moved out of strawberries and into raspberries, strawberry growing continued to flourish in the Clyde valley where it had started in the 1870s. Recently, however, it has become very successful on the arable farms of Tayside, Fife and the North-East, using polytunnel growing systems which protect the crop from damp and mildew. Compared with a strawberry, picked under-ripe in Spain in midwinter, Scottish strawberries ripen slowly in the long hours of summer daylight which develops the sugar content slowly, resulting in their superior taste.

First developed for Dutch glasshouse growing, **Elsanta** became the most popular eating variety in the 1990s and continues to be a supermarket favourite. It is a large, orange-red berry, with a deep pinkish-red flesh. When fully ripe it is neither too soft nor too firm: it's a berry to be squashed when eating, when it releases its finely balanced flavours. Elsanta has now, however, been overtaken by **Symphony**, which is widely grown in the UK, the Netherlands and Germany. It ripens slightly later then Elsanta and has a similarly high eating quality and flavour, as well as good resistance to disease, and an ability to tolerate more extreme soil conditions. Other large eating varieties, **Pegasus, Rhapsody, Sonata** and **Hapil,** are large, soft, juicy berries which are mostly grown on pick-your-owns. **Cambridge Favourite** and **Tamella** are the smaller-sized jam-making berries.

Blackcurrants and Redcurrants

Blackcurrants which were bred at SCRI were all named after Scottish mountains. **Ben Lomond** (1972) was one of the earliest, and since then **Ben Hope, Ben Avron, Ben Connan, Ben Sarek, Ben Tirran** and **Ben Alder** have become popular, with Ben Hope the most popular UK variety. The breeding programme is commercially funded by the blackcurrant drink industry and only 5% of the crop is eaten fresh, the rest is processed into juice.

Redcurrants have never had the same commercial juice-making potential as blackcurrants, but they do contain high amounts of pectin, which is useful as a setting agent in jams. They can be found in fruit farm shops, pick-your-own and farmers' markets. They are also popular with amateur growers.

Brambles (Blackberries)

Brambles were taken up by the SCRI, and a breeding programme producing thornless, flavourful berries which ripen earlier for commercial and amateur growing has produced varieties named after Scottish lochs. **Loch Ness** has become the number one variety in the world, while the later varieties **Loch Tay** and **Loch Maree** have also become popular with growers.

Blueberries

In the 1970s some farmers in Angus were persuaded by the SCRI to grow American high bush blueberries, but they didn't see much future in a crop that took five years to mature. It also ripened over too long a period, making hand-picking more laborious, and they dug out their bushes. What fortunes could have been made if they had been more adventurous. About 20 or so of these discarded bushes were planted in the peaty/acid soil of a garden in Wester Ross, where they continue to produce huge yields annually, without fail, whatever the weather, some 40 years on.

It is only in the last decade that some Scottish fruit farmers have made the blueberry investment as the value of the crop in the marketplace has rocketed. They are the same genus as the low-grown wild blaeberry, and therefore compatible with an acid soil. Varieties include **Bluecrop,** the most common variety which fruits well in Scotland, also **Chandler, Darrow, Duke, Hardyblue** and **Spartan.**

Gooseberries

Not regarded as an important commercial crop, they are one of the hardiest berries and very easy to grow in the Scottish climate. They are popular with amateur fruit growers. Some enterprising fruit farms, which also have farm shops and pick-your-own, grow a field of gooseberries for enthusiasts. The easiest to grow are the mildew-free **Hinnonmaki** (red and yellow), **Invicta, Lancashire Lad** (green), **Martlet** (red) and **Pax.**

Apples, Pears and Plums

Despite the abandonment of Scotland's commercial apple, pear and plum orchards in the twentieth century, like the seemingly eccentric old potato hoarders there have been old-fruit-tree hoarders too. There have also been organisations showing an interest in preserving the old, and developing new commercial orchards. The Perth and Kinross Countryside Trust, whose area includes the old orchard-fruit-growing area of the Carse of Gowrie, have done a survey of the area and found records of 50 orchards, of which 17 have not been dug up. Nine of them, they reckon, still have some commercial potential. Their research has also discovered a record of the quantities of fruit produced. One estate at Grange had 10,000 fruit trees, of which only one remains. Though allowed to go wild, it is a sign of these heritage trees' stamina that some in the nine surviving orchards, possibly around 200 years old, are still producing good-quality fruit of a decent size.

In Angus too there have been efforts to revive fruit orchards. The Angus Orchards Project began in 2009, with ten heritage fruit trees planted at Glamis Castle by local schoolchildren. Three years later, over three hundred fruit trees have been planted in Angus orchards, many attached to schools. The planting has been supervised by Fred Conacher, tree officer for Angus Council. Sourcing heritage fruit trees was solved for Conacher by John Butterworth, who has an organic fruit tree nursery in Ayrshire (Butterworths Organic Nurseries). An old-fruit-tree hoarder, he had been saving varieties from extinction for years and was able to supply, and advise, on which varieties grow best in different parts of Scotland.

Scottish varieties include: **Oslin (Arbroath Pippin)**, a sharply spiced eating apple, one of the oldest known Scottish varieties, it is thought to have been introduced by monks at Arbroath Abbey in the 1100s: **Seaton House**, a cooking apple thought to have been developed by a house gardener in the mid-1800s; **James Grieve**, a dessert apple with yellow fruit, speckled and striped with orange, savoury and juicy with a strong acidity; **Coul Blush**, which is Britain's most northerly apple, hailing from Coul in Wester Ross, it is gold with a faint flush and sweet-tasting, with a soft, cream flesh; **Bloody Ploughman**, cultivated in the Carse of Gowrie around 1880, is a deep, dark, blood-red eating apple with a pink-stained flesh, which was named after a ploughman who was caught stealing the apples and was shot by a gamekeeper; **Cambusnethan Pippin** is a popular scab-free dessert apple from either Clydesdale or Stirling which is tender and juicy with mild acidity; **Lass o' Gowrie**, a sweet, juicy cooker from Perthshire, favoured for keeping its shape; **Hood's Supreme**, a large handsome sweet cooker from Angus, and **White Melrose**, raised at Melrose Abbey before 1831, a large, ribbed, green fruit with a sweet, sub-acid flavour popular in Tweedside orchards in the nineteenth century.

Other apples with a Scottish heritage which are available from another old-fruit-tree hoarder, Andrew Lear in Bankfoot, Perth, include: EATERS: **East Lothian Pippin; Lord Rosebury; Early Julyan; Galloway Pippin; Port Allen Russet; Ellisons Orange; Hawthorden**. COOKERS: **Beauty of Murray; Clydeside; Cutler Grieve; Howgate Wonder; Lady of Wemyss; Scotch Bridget; Scots Dumpling; Stobo Castle; Tower of Glamis; Lemon Queen**.

Preserving Heritage Varieties

At many historic properties owned by the National Trust for Scotland, fruit orchards have been preserved, a number with very old varieties. Some of the fruit is for sale locally, but some is also made into apple juice. At Geilston Garden in Dunbartonshire and Priorwood Garden in Melrose, some unusual varieties are supplied to artisan juicemakers, Cuddybridge (see p.451), who hand-press the juice.

Pick-Your-Own Fruit, Farm Shops and Farmers' Market Stalls

A new demand in the marketplace for in-season, peak-condition, locally grown, fresh – rather than processed – soft fruits has encouraged the development of local farm shops, pick-your-own and farmers markets. These are the places to find the best-flavoured fruit which has been allowed to ripen to full maturity on the plant. They have become outlets for many commercial growers who have small areas of production and prefer to avoid supplying large multiple retailers.

The peak berry-picking season is the summer months, but new early and late varieties now extend the season from May into September. Perthshire and Tayside are the areas with the greatest concentration of fruit farms. Many PYOs provide a full-time telephone answering service throughout the season, when state of the crop information is given, the varieties available and the weather conditions for picking. There is space to park and picnic and sometimes there are teas and home baking as well as playground areas for children. Children are encouraged to pick. Most PYOs also sell ready-picked fruit, while some farms have shops selling soft fruit and other farm produce, which are worth seeking out.

Supermarket Soft Fruit Distribution and Demands

The central distribution system, operated by supermarkets, demands that soft fruit (and other fruit too) has a longer than natural shelf life so it will retain its good appearance during lengthy periods of transportation. The downside to this is that when the fruit is removed early from the plant, and kept chilled during transportation, the flavour and texture are compromised.

When the fruit is left to ripen naturally in the warmth of the sun it develops its full, natural, sweet flavour and soft texture in the long hours of daylight. Extending the season to the colder, less sunny months may increase production, but without warmth and sun the fruit will still lack quality.

There is also an environmental issue when supermarkets truck strawberries from Kent to their supermarkets in strawberry-growing areas of Tayside during peak summer months. Even less eco-friendly are those strawberries in December from even further afield.

Soft Fruit and Cream

It was quite a pantry; oatcakes, barley scones, flour scones, butter, honey, sweetmeats, cheese, and wine, and spiced whisky, all came out of the deep shelves of this agreeable recess, as did the great key of the dairy; this was often given to one of us to carry to old Mary the cook, with leave to see her skim and whip the fine rich cream, which Mrs Grant would afterwards pour on a whole pot of jam and give us for luncheon. This dish, under the name of 'bainne briste', or broken milk, is a great favourite wherever it has been introduced.

Elizabeth Grant of Rothiemurchus, *Memoirs of a Highland Lady 1797-1827.*

To 'pour on a whole pot of jam' suggests this was a runny type of conserve, rather than a spread-on-bread British jam. Other countries make much less fuss than the British about getting their fruit preserves to set solid for just this reason. A sauce in a jam-pot, with cream and soft fruit, is a fast-and-easy pudding idea with endless permutations. Here are a few others.

1. Fresh Soft Fruit and Cream. Combine fruit, either singly or in a combination with cream, whipped or pouring, as a garnish. Soured cream, crème fraîche, fromage frais and natural yoghurt can also be used in combinations.

2. Fresh Soft Fruit, Cream and Fruit Sauce. Fruit plus cream with the addition of the juice of the berry or another berry for a sauce or a syrup sauce.

3. Puréed Fresh Soft Fruit and Cream. Consistency and texture will depend on the type of fruit and thickness of the cream.

4. Iced Fresh Soft Fruit Purée and Cream. The answer for strawberries which are the only soft fruit which freezes badly whole.

5. Fresh Soft Fruit, Cream Cheese, Honey, Oatmeal and Whisky.
These two are combined in the classic Scottish dish of Cream-
crowdie (Cranachan).

1. Fresh Soft Fruit and Cream

FRESH SOFT FRUIT
on a platter with cream

*At the end of the meal a huge dish was put on the table, and on
it an abstract design of prepared fruit, very bold and Matisse-
like. We were each given a fork, to spear little pieces of this
and that as we sat back and talked. It seemed to me the best
possible way to end a meal with glory and without exhaustion
for the cook.*

Jane Grigson, *Observer Magazine*, December 1982.

This can make a stunning centrepiece for a cold table or a serve-
yourself ending to a simple family meal. Creating colour contrasts and textures is all part of the fun.

A **whole pineapple** can be cut in wedges without removing
its green leaves. Remove the hard centre core from each wedge,
then cut the flesh from the outside edge with a sharp knife and
cut into bite-sized pieces. All varieties of **melon** can also be cut
into boat-shaped wedges and then into bite-sized pieces like
the pineapple. **Peaches, apricots, nectarines, greengages** and
plums should all be stoned and cut into bite-sized pieces. **Oranges** and sweet **grapefruit** should be segmented, either with or
without the pith. **Tangerines** can be peeled and sliced into rings,
mangoes cut into hedgehogs, **fresh figs** cut with a cross and
pressed open, **papaya** cut in wedges with seeds removed, **passion fruit** and **kiwi** cut in half. **Strawberries, raspberries, redcurrants, blueberries, blackcurrants, brambles, grapes, cherries,**
and **gooseberries** need no special preparation.

Assembling the fruits

This should be done in two stages. First, put in place those which can be arranged in advance without any drying out or discolouring. Have some rough idea of how the finished platter is going to look and then prepare as much as possible ahead of time. It's not necessary to spend hours arranging patterns of fruit – like a good watercolour painting it should not be 'over-worked'.

Serving

Serve with icing sugar, dusted from a sieve, over sharp fruits like raspberries. Or with wedges of lime or lemon for squeezing over very sweet fruits like mangos, papayas and strawberries. Or scatter over some fresh mint leaves. Serve with a bowl of whipped cream, crème fraiche or sour cream.

2. Fresh Soft Fruit, Cream and Fruit Sauce

'GOURMET' STRAWBERRIES

The sauce is a simple purée of the fruit, sharpened with lemon.

500 g/1 lb 2 oz strawberries, washed and hulled
Juice of 1 lemon
Sugar to taste
Whipped cream

4 servings

To prepare

Take about a quarter of the strawberries and purée in the liquidiser or processor with lemon juice and sugar. Taste for sweetness. Put the strawberries in a bowl and sieve the purée on top. Chill for about half an hour before serving. Serve with cream.

Note: this also works with raspberries, or could be used with any other soft fruits in any kind of mix. i.e. serve strawberries with raspberry purée and vice versa. A good combination is a redcurrant purée with strawberries. Backcurrants and redcurrants are also good in raspberry purée.

HOW ESCOFFIER SERVED STRAWBERRIES
at the Carlton Hotel

Soak some large strawberries in orange juice and Curaçao. Put them into a silver or glass dish and cover them with Chantilly cream.

Auguste Escoffier, *Ma Cuisine*, 1934.

Known in classical cuisine as *Strawberries Romanoff*, there have been many versions inspired by Escoffier's original partnership of strawberries and oranges.

500 g/1 lb 2 oz strawberries
150 ml/5 fl oz freshly squeezed orange juice
5 tablespoons orange-flavoured liqueur
300 ml/10 fl oz double cream
Vanilla sugar to taste

4 servings

To prepare

Taste strawberries to check their sweetness and add sugar accordingly. Leave overnight.

Add freshly squeezed orange juice and the liqueur and soak for 1 hour.

Transfer to serving dish. Whip the double cream and sweeten with 2 tablespoons vanilla sugar. Cover fruit with the cream and serve.

BRANDIED FRUIT CUP

This combination of dried and fresh fruits allows plenty of scope for variation according to season. It is a cross between a 'compote' and a fruit salad, but will keep well in the fridge for a few days, so is worth making up in quantity.

150 g/5 oz dried apricots
350 g/12 oz mixed dried fruit, stoned
500 g/1 lb 2 oz fresh cherries
1 grapefruit, segmented
125 g/4 oz preserved kumquats
500 g/1 lb 2 oz figs in syrup
3 bananas, sliced
Strawberries, raspberries or any other soft fruits in season
Juice of 1 lemon
Sugar to taste
Cognac – a few tablespoons
Whipped cream

8-10 servings

To prepare the dried fruit

Place the dried apricots and mixed dried fruit in a saucepan with boiling water to cover. Leave to soak for several hours or overnight. Simmer till tender – cool and cut up into pieces.

Add the rest of the fruit and combine in a large bowl; add the lemon juice, sugar and cognac to taste. Leave overnight for flavours to develop and blend together.

Serve slightly chilled with a bowl of cream and **Almond Nutball Biscuits** (see p.373).

STRAWBERRIES AND RASPBERRIES
with Whipkull

Whipkull is a Shetland speciality which was originally eaten with thin, crisp, butter shortbread for Yule breakfast (see p.332). Eggs and sugar are beaten over heat till thick and creamy, then flavoured with rum.

Fruit marinade:
250 g/9 oz strawberries
250 g/9 oz raspberries
4 tablespoons freshly squeezed orange juice or kirsch
Sugar to taste
Sauce:
3 egg yolks
3 tablespoons sugar
1½ tablespoons kirsch
1 teaspoon lemon juice
1 teaspoon grated lemon rind
125 ml/4 fl oz whipped double cream

Serves 4

To marinade the fruit

Slice the strawberries and leave the raspberries whole. Put into a glass dish and sprinkle with orange juice or kirsch and sugar. Cover and leave in a cool place for a few hours.

To make the sauce

Beat the eggs and sugar together over hot water till they are thick and creamy, then beat in flavourings and finally fold in the cream. Pour over the marinated fruit and serve immediately. Serve with thin crisp shortbread (see p.332).

3. Fresh Fruit Purée and Cream

Fruit purée, mixed through whipped cream is a simple idea. Variety comes with different textures of puree, from very smooth to fairly rough. A liquidiser or food processor will provide the smoothest result while mashing with a fork will make a more varied texture.

WHIPPED FRUIT PUDDING

This is a good method for 'stretching' the fruit, if in short supply.

It is similar to a Russian *Kissel* (from Slavic meaning 'sour'), a popular dish which appears in many forms and varieties, originally made with sour fruits. It can be hot or cold, firm or liquid, and made using many kinds of soft fruits as well as cranberries and rhubarb which have to be cooked. The most popular in Russia are cherries, redcurrants and cranberries. Other parts of Eastern Europe also use strawberries, blueberries, raspberries, gooseberries or rhubarb. It can be served in a cup for drinking or in a bowl to be eaten with a spoon, and is usually topped with sweet cream. It is also used as a topping for pancakes or waffles. Maple syrup with strawberries gives a special fragrance.

450 ml/¾ pt fresh orange juice
25 g/1 oz potato flour, arrowroot or cornflour
Juice from ½ lemon
3 tablespoons maple syrup or 2 tablespoons honey
Pinch of ground cinnamon and grated nutmeg
250 g/9 oz raspberries and strawberries
150 ml/5 fl oz whipped cream or crème fraiche or a mix of the
    two

4 servings

To make the syrup

Blend the potato flour, arrowroot or cornflour with a little of the orange juice in a bowl. Heat the juice in a pan and pour some over the flour and juice in the bowl. Return to the pan and simmer to thicken, stirring all the time. Pour into a large bowl and whip with a beater. Leave to cool. Add lemon juice, maple syrup, cinnamon and nutmeg. Taste and adjust flavouring.

Finishing the dish

Reserve a few whole berries and mash up the rest. Fold in with the cream/crème fraiche. Chill. Serve with whole berries for garnish.

4. Fruit Purée with Cream – Iced

Ice-cream making in Scotland has been dominated by Italians and their descendants for over a century. The classic Italian ice-cream cone in Scotland comes with a topping of raspberry syrup. Of uncertain origins, this was originally known as a MacCallum. According to legend it was made by a Glasgow 'Tally' for Mr MacCallum, a supporter of Clyde Football Club, whose colours are red and white.

Ice-cream became a 'street food' for the ordinary people around the 1850s, though it had been eaten by the wealthy classes for much longer. According to Henry Mayhew, writing in *London Labour and the London Poor* (1850), the initial reception was not all favourable. People who tried it complained that it gave them the 'shivers', and he forecast an uncertain future for the trade.

A RICH ICE-CREAM
suitable for moulding

3 egg yolks

3 tablespoons icing sugar

2–3 teaspoons lemon juice

150 ml/5 fl oz whipping cream, whipped

250 g/9 oz strawberries or raspberries or any other fresh fruit
in season

This is the simplest method of making ice-cream at home. Described as a 'parfait', it has a high proportion of egg yolks and cream which will not form large crystals as they freeze, removing the need to churn the mixture as it freezes. It is best made in small quantities, since some of the delicate flavouring will be lost if kept frozen for longer than a month.

To prepare

Put the eggs and sugar in a bowl over a pan of simmering hot water and beat till thick and creamy. Purée fruit in the liquidiser or food processor. With fruits like strawberries and raspberries, sieve after liquidising to remove the pips. Add the lemon juice. Mix the egg and sugar with the purée, folding in lightly, and then fold in the cream. Taste for flavour and pour into a plastic container or mould and freeze.

Serving

Ice-cream should be allowed to soften slightly for about 30 minutes at room temperature, which will greatly improve the texture and also the flavour. If the mixture has been set in a special mould, put in a bowl of hot water to loosen for a few minutes before removing.

ETTRICKSHAWS HOME-MADE ICE-CREAM

Mix 500 g/1 lb 2 oz each of fruit pulp and sugar to every 600 ml/1 pint of whipped double cream. Add a 'generous measure of any complementary liqueur' and freeze. Serve with a homemade cinnamon biscuit.

From Peter Slaney, Ettrickshaws Country House Hotel in Selkirkshire.

FRUIT-FLAVOURED WATER ICE
(Sorbet)

Simple mixtures of fruit purée and sugar syrup give the kind of clean, penetrating flavours which were used in formal dinners of many courses, somewhere about the middle, to 'refresh the palate'. Queen Victoria is said to have favoured a rum sorbet for this purpose. More suited to the end of a meal in less formal eating occasions, a sorbet is one of the best ways of preserving soft fruit like strawberries which do not freeze well whole.

250 g/9 oz granulated sugar
300 ml/10 fl oz water

Juice of 1 lemon
Juice of 1 orange
500 g/1 lb 2 oz strawberries or any other soft fruit
1 egg white

To make syrup

Dissolve the sugar in the water, bring to the boil and simmer for about five minutes. Cool and add the orange and lemon juice.

To prepare fruit

Put the fruit into a food processor and whizz till smooth. Sieve to remove seeds.

To freeze

Mix the purée and syrup together and pour into a plastic container with a lid. The shallower it is, the quicker it will freeze. Put into the deep-freeze and remove every half-hour. Beat with a whisk or beater to prevent large crystals forming. When it is uniformly solid, but not too hard, beat the egg white in a bowl till fairly stiff. Add spoonfuls of the sorbet gradually to the white of egg, beating together till all is mixed in. This will give the sorbet more volume and a lighter texture. Refreeze. Do not keep too long in the freezer, since flavours begin to fade after a month or so.

5. Fresh Soft Fruit, Cream Cheese, Honey, Oatmeal and Whisky

Fresh fruit with a complementary cheese is one of the easiest ways of ending a meal. Soft fruits with a soft cheese are ideal.

CRANACHAN
(Cream-Crowdie)

A unique blend of Scottish flavours, enriched with cream and sharpened with tangy berry fruits in this versatile tradition. The best way to make and eat this is in the traditional way; mixing your own, to your own taste, as you sit round a table with family or friends. The ritual eating was originally a celebration of 'harvest home', when wild brambles and blaeberries would have been picked by children from the hedgerows and moors.

Set on the table the following:

A bowl of **cream** – freshly whipped double cream. This was traditional but it was often varied according to taste and availability, with some crowdie to make cream-crowdie (see p.279). (Sour cream, fromage frais or crème fraîche are modern variations.)

A bowl of **oatmeal** which has been toasted slowly and gently in the oven. This drives off excess moisture, concentrates and greatly improves the flavour. **Buttered Oats** (see p.17) is another option.

A bowl of fresh soft **fruits** – either a single fruit, or combination, but must be soft and fresh.

A jar of **heather honey** to sweeten.

A bottle of favourite **whisky** or **Scottish liqueur**.

Give each person a bowl and spoon (in old Scots households the bowls would have been wooden and the spoons hand-carved horn). The ingredients are then passed round the table and each person creates their own mixture, lubricating with a slurp of whisky or liqueur.

Other Scottish Cream Sweets

TRIFLE

*That most wonderful object of domestic art called trifle . . .
with its charming confusion of cream and cake and almonds
and jam and jelly and wine and cinnamon and froth.*
Oliver Wendell Holmes, *Elsie Venner*, 1861.

A trifle is the passing triviality, creating an element of fun at the end of the meal. It was not always an informal dish. At upper-class dining tables in the early 1800s the trifle was an elegant centrepiece to a formal dinner table. As Meg Dods (1826) instructs: 'Make the dish high and handsome . . . and garnish with a few sprigs of light flowers of fine colours . . . or a sprinkling of Harlequin comfits. This last we think vulgar, but it is in frequent use.'

TO MAKE A TRIFLE

Cake/Biscuit/Jam Layer:

250 g/9 oz sponge cake

125 g/4 oz almond biscuits

375 g/12 oz strawberry or raspberry jam

Sherry or Madeira to taste, for children use fresh orange juice

Custard Layer:

500 ml/18 fl oz milk

6 large eggs

1 tablespoon caster sugar

1 teaspoon cornflour

Vanilla extract

Cream Layer:

600 ml/1 pt whipping cream

1 tablespoon caster sugar

4-6 servings

Cake/biscuit/jam layer

Put cake in the bottom, crumble biscuits on top and soak everything with sherry or Madeira. Cover with a layer of jam. Leave for at least an hour.

Custard layer

Put the milk in a pan and heat till almost boiling. Beat the eggs, sugar and cornflour together in a bowl. Pour the hot milk over,

stirring well. Strain and return to the pan. Cook very gently, stirring all the time till it thickens. This can be done in a double boiler. Leave till almost cold; add a few drops of vanilla extract before pouring over the first layer.

Cream layer

When the custard is cold and set, beat up the cream with the sugar till it thickens and pour over custard. Chill and serve decorated with edible fresh flowers such as old fashioned scented roses, borage flowers, primroses, marigold petals or violets.

To crystallise flowers, pick them on a dry day, remove all stems and green. Wash and dry thoroughly. Paint each flower with lightly beaten egg white, then hold with tweezers and dip in caster sugar till thoroughly coated. Place on a baking sheet and dry off in a warm airy place. When dry place between sheets of greaseproof paper and store in an airtight tin.

CALEDONIAN CREAM

This is a version of Mrs Dalgairns's Caledonian Cream (1829) which she made with Seville orange marmalade, brandy and lemon juice to flavour '2 pints of cream'. A quick and easy mix with a good-flavoured result.

125 g/4 oz crème fraiche
1 tablespoon thick marmalade
2 tablespoons brandy (or rum)
2 teaspoons lemon juice
125 ml/4 fl oz double cream, whipped
Sugar to taste
4-6 tangerines

4 servings

To make

Put the crème fraiche, marmalade, brandy or rum, lemon juice and sugar into a food processor or liquidiser and whizz till smooth. Remove and mix through the cream. Peel the tangerines and slice thinly removing any stones.

To serve

Divide the sliced tangerines between four glasses. Sprinkle over a teaspoonful or two of brandy. Pile the cream mixture on top. Serve slightly chilled.

BISCUITS AND CREAM

Unbelievably simple to make – layers of biscuits and cream are stuck together in a log-shape then covered in cream. Left for a few hours, the cream softens the biscuits and the flavours mingle.

284 ml/9 fl oz carton whipping or double cream
1 packet of biscuits
Jam or chocolate spread
Bar of dark chocolate

To make

Whip the cream till it just thickens to a spreading consistency. Spread each biscuit, first with jam or chocolate spread and then cream. Sandwich one on top of another to make a tower shape.

When it is about six inches high lay on its side on the serving plate. Make another tower joining it to the one on the plate. Finish by spreading the cream on the top and sides. Leave to soften for at least 2-3 hours. The longer it is left the softer the biscuits will be.

Decorate with chocolate 'curls'. Draw a sharp knife over the surface of the chocolate, scraping off slivers which will curl. Scatter over the top of the log.

LEMON CREAM
soufflé

This was made by Scottish Hotel School students for the Queen's lunch, during a sail up Loch Lomond on *The Maid of the Loch* in 1970, after she had opened the Loch Sloy Power Station. Individual portions were made in wine glasses with greaseproof paper tied round the top to extend the soufflé above the rim. When set, the greaseproof paper was removed and the exposed sides were coated in finely chopped pistachio nuts. Tiny rosettes of cream were piped round the top edges. Lots of emergency back-ups were made for possible disasters in transit from Crookston to Loch Lomond.

2½ fine-leaf quick dissolving sheets gelatine (Costa brand)
2 large lemons, juice of
3 large eggs
125 g/4 oz caster sugar
175 ml/6 fl oz double cream
25 g/1 oz finely chopped pistachio nuts

Serves 4-6

To dissolve gelatine

Put the gelatine into cold water for a few minutes till it softens. Remove and put into a small bowl. Cover with half the lemon

juice. Heat the bowl in a pan of simmering water until the gelatine dissolves. Or put into the microwave (900w) and heat on 70%. It should dissolve in about 60 seconds. Do not overheat. Leave to cool.

Mixing the eggs, sugar and cream

Separate eggs and beat whites till fairly stiff. Do not overbeat. Put yolks and sugar in a bowl and place bowl in a pan of boiling water. Beat till thick and creamy and the whisk leaves a trail on the surface.

Beat the cream till fairly thick. Do not overbeat. Fold the lemon juice and gelatine into the sugar and egg mixture. Next fold in the cream, cutting and folding until thoroughly mixed.

Finally fold in the egg-white in two batches, again cutting and folding more carefully this time to preserve as much air as possible.

Finishing

When thoroughly folded in, pour into a glass dish, sprinkle over the chopped pistachios and serve with thin shortbread (see p.332).

SYLLABUB
A richly flavoured cream

An infusion of cream and alcohol which has an English heritage going back to Tudor times. In its original form the mixture was served slightly warm, the cream and flavourings separating into two layers.

50 g/2 oz caster sugar
1 lemon, grated zest and juice
1 cinnamon stick
4 tablespoons whisky or brandy
4 tablespoons dry sherry, or dry white wine
300 ml/10 fl oz double cream

4 servings

Use a heated jug or bowl.

To prepare

Put the lemon zest, juice, sugar and cinnamon in a pan, dissolve the sugar and simmer gently for a few minutes to concentrate flavours. Add the alcohol and heat through. Cover and leave to infuse for a few hours or overnight.

Whip the cream till thick but not too stiff. Reheat the infused flavourings and pour into a heated jug or bowl. Add the cream. Mix through. Serve warm, poured into warmed individual glasses, with crisp shortbread (see p.332).

Some Other Ways with Scottish Soft Fruits

SOFT FRUITS
with Scone Dumplings

This popular American pudding is known as a 'slump'. It is any mix of stewed fruits topped with squares of plain scone dough which absorbs the fruit flavours and juices as it cooks. Louisa May Alcott named her house Apple Slump after this dish.

It is particularly colourful with fruits like blackcurrants, blueberries, brambles (blackberries), redcurrants, plums, raspberries and strawberries which also have a lot of juice. These fruits can also be mixed with apples or rhubarb. Quick and easy to prepare in a frying or sauté pan, it is a 'good fun' pudding for children to make.

600 g/1 lb 5 oz soft fruits or a mix with apples or rhubarb
3-4 tablespoons sugar
Water
Scone mix:
150 g/5 oz plain flour
1½ teaspoons baking powder
50 g/2 oz butter
Milk to mix

4 servings

Use a 25-30 cm/10-12 in frying or sauté pan with a lid.

To prepare

Put the fruit and sugar into a large frying or sauté pan with a lid and add water to come about halfway up the fruit. Use less water with fruit such as raspberries and redcurrants which have a lot of juice. Cover with the lid and simmer very gently till the fruit is heated through and the juice just beginning to run. If using apples or rhubarb they should be cooked till soft. Taste for sweetness and add more sugar if necessary. The fruit mixture should be about three-quarters covered with juice. Add more water if necessary. Pour off excess if there is too much.

To make the scone mix

Put the flour and baking powder into a bowl, rub in the butter and add enough milk to make a stiff paste. Roll out the mixture about 1 cm/½ in thick and cut up into 2.5-5 cm/1-2 in squares.

Scatter over the top of the fruit, cover with a lid and simmer very gently for about 15 minutes to steam the scone. The scone will be well risen on top and soaked in fruit juices underneath. Serve hot with cream.

HAZELNUT MERINGUE CAKE
with fresh raspberries and cream

Two layers of chewy hazelnut meringue are sandwiched with a thick layer of whipped cream and an equally thick layer of raspberries. The top should be crisp, the centre soft, moist and slightly chewy – the flavour heavy with hazelnuts. It should be assembled a few hours before eating to allow the flavours to mingle.

This is a cook-ahead-and-stop-worrying cake, since the meringues will keep for several weeks if they are tightly, but carefully, wrapped in foil and kept in an airtight tin.

For the meringue:
225 g/8 oz hazelnuts
4 egg whites
225 g/8 oz caster sugar
For the filling:
300 ml/10 fl oz whipping cream, stiffly whipped
250 g/9 oz raspberries
Icing sugar for dusting on tops

4-6 servings

Line 2 x 20cm/8 in sandwich tins with non-stick baking paper or a sheet of foil.

Preheat the oven to 350F/180C/160Cfan/Gas 4.

To make meringue

Toast the hazelnuts in a cool oven for about 10 minutes, then cool. Grind them till fairly fine. Whisk the egg whites till well bulked up but not too stiff, and then add the sugar a tablespoon at a time, beating well. Finally fold in the ground hazelnuts and pour into the prepared tins. Spread out evenly. Bake for 20 minutes till the meringue is set but not dried out. Remove from the tins and leave to cool.

To assemble

Spread the cream thickly on one half, cover with raspberries and place the other half on top. Dust thickly with icing sugar and leave for an hour at least before serving.

LEMON TART

This is the forerunner of the Lemon Meringue Pie. Instead of separating the eggs and making a meringue topping, whole eggs are added to make a rich, sharp, creamy filling.

Rich Shortcrust Pastry:
100 g/3½ oz unsalted butter
50 g/2 oz icing sugar
1 egg yolk
150 g/5 oz plain flour
For the filling:
8 eggs (350 ml)
275 g/9½ oz caster sugar
250 ml/9 fl oz lemon juice (approx 4-5 lemons)
1 tablespoon grated lemon zest
150 ml/5 fl oz double cream
Icing sugar for dusting (optional)

8-12 servings

Use a 23 cm/9 in flan tin with removable base 3-4cm/1¼–1½ in deep.

Preheat the oven for pastry 350F/180C/160Cfan/Gas 4, reduce to 325F/160C/140Cfan/Gas 3 for lemon filling.

To make the pastry

Beat the butter and sugar in a mixer or with an electric beater till light and fluffy. Add egg and beat for a minute to mix in. Add the flour and mix on a slow speed until it forms a smooth paste. Do not overmix. Knead to a smooth pliable dough. Wrap in clingfilm and leave to rest in a cool place for an hour before use.

To bake the flan

Roll out pastry and line flan tin. Do not cut off overhang. Bake blind with foil/or greaseproof paper and beans or rice, for 20-30 minutes till cooked through, removing the foil/greaseproof paper for the last 15 minutes. Bake till a light golden brown. Leave to cool. Cut off overhang.

To make the filling

Put the eggs into a bowl and beat lightly together, then add sugar and lemon juice and beat till the sugar is dissolved. Pour a few spoonfuls of the egg and lemon mixture into the cream and mix till blended together. Transfer to the egg mixture and mix in. Add the lemon zest. If a lot of froth has gathered on the top from beating, cover and put into the fridge for a few hours, stirring occasionally till it subsides.

To bake

Put the pastry flan into the preheated oven and pour in the filling (this is easier to do in the oven). Bake for about 30 minutes or until the filling is set in the middle. Dust with sieved icing sugar when it comes out of the oven and caramelise briefly under a hot grill (optional). Eat warm or cold with whipped cream.

8: Sugar & Spice, Cakes & Baking, Scottish Sweeties & Preserves

Besides such homely sweets as gundy, glessie, cheugh jeans and black man, there were bottles of 'boilings' (Scotch Mixtures) that glittered like rubies, emeralds, topazes and all the jewels of the Orient, and tasted of all the fruits of the orchard and spices of the Indies.

F. Marian McNeill, *The Scots Kitchen*, 1929.

Sugar

With such temptations it is not surprising the Scots have a sweet tooth. Sweetie boiling, it seems, was a national pastime in the days before multimedia distractions when every household had its brass sugar-boiling pan. The heyday for sugar-boilers was around the end of the 1800s, when sugar became cheap enough for everyone to indulge. The sugar trade across the Atlantic had started as Britain acquired sugar-cane producing colonies in the New World. In 1765 the first sugar-refining factory was built in Greenock, and a century later it had become Scotland's major sugar-refining port. Around 400 ships a year transported sugar from Caribbean holdings for processing in fourteen sugar refineries, and as the volume of sugar imports increased, so the price fell.

Previously, honey had been the popular sweetener but was not used to boil sweeties. Only the upper classes had access to expensive sugar loaves made from Arabian sugar cane, processed to extract the syrup, and then poured into long conical moulds. When sugar was required, it was chipped off with pincers. While it was used to make elaborate sugar fantasies to decorate their dining tables, it had another more practical purpose in the instant rush of inner warmth it provided for those living in cold Northern countries.

The health benefits of sugar were based on medieval beliefs, similar to those in ancient Chinese medical culture, which taught that those in a physical state of cold (yin) required the heating (yang) power of a warming dose of medicinal sugar or other such 'heating' food. Apothecaries made humbugs, toffees, tablets, lozenges and liquorice to relieve the symptoms of coughs, colds and other ailments. Though it is no longer thought of as a medicine, Scots tablet originated as a small, flat disc or 'tablet' containing some natural health-giving substance, or some bitter potion, mixed with medicinal sugar.

Sugar Types

Granulated white sugar is refined from cane or beet and is 100 per cent pure sucrose. Caster, which is finer, and icing, finer still, are also 100 per cent pure sucrose.

Brown sugars may be made in two ways: either from highly processed white beet sugar with all its trace elements removed, and then mixed with a small proportion of cane molasses, or they can be made by halting the refining process, in which case they should be described as 'unrefined' on the label. These will most likely come from ex-colonial countries such as Mauritius, Barbados and Guyana, where entire communities depend on sugar for jobs in harvesting and refining. These sugars have a better, fudgier flavour and produce a more interesting end result. They also contain trace elements and vitamins that occur naturally in sugar cane, but are lost when refined to 100 per cent pure. They are now available in various grades from 'golden' (equivalent to white granulated but a golden colour) to 'soft brown', which is akin to caster sugar.

Muscovado has less molasses removed and Demerara is a larger crystal than granulated. Black treacle is a more refined form of the more bitter pure cane molasses.

Spices

The history of spices is a rich tapestry of Arab monopoly, Italian intrigue and dangerous journeying across the globe. The spice trade developed in the first century AD, but British enthusiasm first took off after Crusaders returned from the 'holy wars' (1100-1300) with supplies of spices, dates, figs, almonds, sherbets and sweetmeats. From then on, simple British tastes were transformed by spices. These added such interest and variety, becoming fully integrated into the food culture when Britain began trading with the spice countries of the East as the British Empire expanded.

While some spicy customs like sprinkling a layer of pepper over sweet custards have fallen by the wayside, others have survived. Sugar and spice innovations such as gingerbread, mincemeat, plum puddings and black bun can be traced back to the first recipe books and beyond. Except for gingerbread, which is eaten now at any time of the year, the others remain distinctly festive foods, reflecting their early restricted use on festivals and holidays. Ginger continues to be used, like sugar, as a 'heating' food in natural medicines.

Spice Sources

India is the leading spice exporter (mostly pepper, cardamom, chillies, ginger, turmeric and cumin) followed by Indonesia (pepper, nutmeg, mace, cassia, ginger, cardamom, vanilla), Madagascar (vanilla, cloves) and Malaysia (pepper, ginger). More than 80 per cent of spices are from developing countries, and production and export are an important element of their agricultural economy.

Differences in quality depend on the climate, the soil and how the growers have managed the crop. Though ginger is grown throughout the spice world, Jamaican ginger is widely regarded as the best. It is also the most expensive. Grown in small quantities, it is the extra special growing conditions, plus the rich soils, which have increased the level of essential oil in this ginger, giving

it a deep-yellow colour. Most Jamaican ginger is made into oil and none is now sold as ground ginger in the UK.

Other differences in quality depend on the methods of processing, distribution and storing. Ginger can lose its pungency if it has been treated to remove some of its oils before grinding. Cinnamon and cloves are the other spices most likely to have had some oil extracted. It is surprising the differences in pungency between brands. Top spice-buyers will laboratory-test spices before buying to check the oil content. They also prefer to buy whole, rather than ground.

Exposure to light, warmth and air will also deplete spice-pungency. Ultraviolet light dries out the oil and lightens the colour of the spice. Those spices sitting on shelves in clear glass jars for too long will eventually lose their potency. To test the quality of a spice, buyers judge first the aroma. Then, if it is ground, they will put a pinch in the palm of the hand and rub gently with the thumb to release the full aroma.

The best and cheapest way to buy spices is from small companies. They will usually buy in small quantities and the spices will be sold faster and will therefore be fresher. Buying from small mail-order companies can result in a saving of 30-50 per cent compared with the prices of the larger market leaders, who have higher overheads and large advertising budgets to finance.

Honey

Honey from a single type of blossom is the most expensive but has the best flavour. Highly blended honeys have nondescript flavours and some may contain amounts of ordinary sugar. These often taste sickly-sweet, whereas pure honey will have greater depth of flavour. Scottish heather honey comes from bees which have been taken to the heather-clad hills during the summer months, giving the honey its uniquely aromatic flavour and dark colour.

Honey does not deteriorate if stored for 1-2 years at around room temperature. It does not like the cold, however, and must be kept away from strong smells. Viscosity varies according to the amount of water in the honey. If it is too runny, its water content will be too high and it will not be a good buy. It will also be lacking flavour. Of the heather honeys, pure ling is the only one which sets like a jelly (thixotropic). Honey that has crystallised and set should be put in a bowl of warm water (not hotter than 50C) to melt. Honey has a high food value and contains traces of minerals, iron, calcium, magnesium, phosphorous, vitamins C, B, B2, B5, B6, nicotinic acid and other residues, including enzymes, gums and resins. Some of this will be destroyed if the honey is heated above 50C.

Scottish Baking

If every Frenchwoman is born with a wooden spoon in her hand, every Scotswoman is born with a rolling-pin under her arm. There may be a divergence of opinion as to her skill in cooking, but it is certain that she has developed a remarkable technique in baking – not only in bannocks, scones and oatcakes, but also in the finer manipulations of wheat – in cakes, pastry and shortbread.

F. Marian McNeill, *The Scots Kitchen*, 1929.

Shortbread

'Remember: six, four, two,' said the teacher: 'six ounces of flour, four of butter and two of sugar.' It was our first shortbread lesson. The method was also easy to remember. The lump of butter was put in the middle of a wooden pastry board and kneaded by hand into a pile of sugar beside it. Then small amounts of flour, from another heap, were kneaded into the sugary butter and it began to grow and change texture. Too much flour added at once, we soon discovered, did not work. It had to be added gradually until the texture changed into a smooth, pliable shortbread dough ready to roll out into shapes.

Feeling the 'life' of the dough is the best way to judge consistency. No recipe is a foolproof guide, especially when using flour and butter which both have varying degrees of moisture content. The delicate balance between the right and wrong consistency is crucial to making a good shortbread, and I'm glad we got our hands into things at an age when habits are formed.

Origin of Shortbread

'Short' has been used for at least five centuries to describe anything which is crisp and easily crumbled. In medieval times they made 'shortpaste' for Lent. Later the word was prefixed to both cake and bread, but by the early 1800s Scots were commonly referring to short 'bread' rather than short 'cake', though it would have been more logical to have kept continuity with the oat 'cake' and the pan 'cake'. However, by deviating from the rest of Britain and America, one of Scotland's most defining food items was created. No common biscuit, according to the professional baking industry, it is classed as an item of 'flour confectionery'. This is a status which the Scottish Association of Master Bakers fought to preserve when EU bureaucrats thought it should be taxed as a biscuit.

Flour

A soft, white flour with a low gluten content is best. If a strong flour is used, the dough will be tough and the baked shortbread a hard texture. A soft fine wholemeal may be used in a mixture with white but it will have a stronger flavour and the essential buttery taste may be lost. Replacing some flour with oats (see Tiree Shortbread p.334) does not affect the butter taste. Replacing 25 g/1 oz of flour with rice flour or semolina will give a crunchier texture, while replacing the same amount with cornflour will make a more 'melting' texture.

Butter

This is the main flavouring and shortening agent which gives distinction to shortbread – the finished flavour will be rated by the quality of the butter. It should have a low moisture content.

Sugar

Caster sugar gives the best result, though some icing sugar may be used for a finer result. The butter flavour tends to get lost if brown sugars are used.

SHORTBREAD
to knead by hand or mix in a food-processor

170 g/6 oz plain flour
113 g/4 oz butter, at room temperature
57 g/2 oz caster sugar
Caster sugar for dusting

Preheat the oven to 335F/170C/150Cfan/Gas 3 for thin and 320F/160C/140Cfan/Gas 2½ for thick.

Prepare a greased or lined baking tray.

Kneading the dough by hand

Put the sugar and butter on the board and knead together. Sift the flour into a corner and start working in gradually till the dough is still soft and pliable and not too firm. Add more flour if you think it can take it without the dough breaking up. If it is too soft the shortbread will spread. Too stiff a dough will be too difficult to roll out and shape. Wrap the dough in clingfilm and leave in the fridge for an hour; it can be left longer – overnight if necessary. This allows the sugar to dissolve into the moisture in the dough, making a smoother texture.*

Shaping the dough

Remove from fridge and allow to soften at room temperature. Roll out into a round or cut into fingers or fancy shapes. The thickness is a matter of taste. Thicker should be baked at a lower temperature and will take longer to bake. The above quantity may be pressed into a tin 18 x 28 cm/7 x 11 in and then cut into fingers. (Makes about 18-20 biscuits.)

Wooden decorative shortbread mould

Flour the mould well. Knock out excess flour and press in the dough. Level off with a rolling-pin. Then invert the mould, holding one hand underneath to catch the shortbread. Knock it on the edge of the work surface several times at different places till it comes out of the mould. If it sticks, start again, re-flouring the mould. Once moulds have been used a lot they become seasoned and the shortbread will come out easier.

Sugar-edged small shortbread rounds

Roll into a sausage shape and then roll in either granulated or demerara sugar. Leave for an hour to harden in the fridge before slicing into round biscuits.

Baking

Before baking, shortbread of all shapes or sizes should be

---

*To mix in a food-processor: Put the sugar, butter and all the flour, except for one tablespoonful, into the food-processor and whizz to mix the butter through the other ingredients. Turn out onto a work surface and knead till it comes together into a soft pliable dough. Knead in the remaining flour if necessary.

pricked all over with a fork (docked) to let the steam escape evenly and avoid it distorting the shape.

It should be baked slowly to develop the rich butter taste and have an even light-golden colour throughout. If the temperature is too low it will have an undesirable greyish colour inside, while if it is too high it will have a 'bone' in the centre. If not using a convection fan oven, place in the middle of the bottom shelf in the oven: thick shortbread can take up to an hour; very thin can be baked in 25-30 minutes. About five minutes before it is ready, it can be removed from the oven and scored with a sharp knife to make it easier to break into pieces when cold. It should also be dusted lightly with caster sugar, which will stick to the hot surface better if done at this stage.

TIREE SHORTBREAD
with oats

The recipe for these very thin, crisp, round shortbread biscuits came from Tiree, made by an unknown baker and handed on from one to another in the way all the best recipes are.

113 g/4oz caster sugar
225 g/8 oz butter, softened
175 g/6 oz plain flour
175 g/6 oz porridge oats
Caster sugar for dredging

Preheat the oven to 325F/160C/140Cfan/Gas 3.

Makes about 36-38.

To Make

Cream the butter and sugar with an electric beater. Add the flour and oats and mix with a wooden spoon. Turn the mixture onto a floured work surface and knead together. Roll out thinly to about 5 mm/¼ in thick. Cut with a 6 cm/2½ in fluted cutter.

Bake for 25-30 minutes. Dredge with caster sugar while still hot.

RICH SHORTBREAD

Shapes

Oval and oblong shapes are described in early recipes with some variations. Mrs MacIver (1773) shaped hers into an oval, then made a decorative plaiting at the ends. Some other ovals are cut in two 'the narrow way, so as to have two cakes somewhat the shape of a Saxon arch' – Meg Dods (1826). Others divide it into squares or oblongs, but all seem to agree that the thickness should be one inch (2.5 cm).

Rich Shortbread for festive occasions and as a present

This is a one-inch thick round of shortbread with ground or chopped almonds and caraway seeds added to the mixture. It is decorated on top with crystallised lemon and orange peel and sometimes caraway comfits. Because of its thickness, recipes advise putting a band of paper round the outside, as well as sitting it on several layers of paper while baking, so that it does not brown too quickly round the edges and on the base. This special shortbread was baked for New Year celebrations, and in some areas was known as a Pitcaithly Bannock. At least as early as the 1820s it was sent as a present from Scotland, as Meg Dods advises her readers to make a rich Scotch Shortbread with almonds 'for sending as a holiday present to England'.

PITCAITHLY BANNOCK

This thick, golden round of festive shortbread, in its original form, was flavoured with almonds, caraway and crystallised orange and lemon peel, which decorates the top. It can be simplified using only almonds, some flaked almonds in the mixture and whole blanched almonds pressed on top, Dundee cake-style.

Double quantity basic mix (See p.332)
Add:
57 g/2 oz toasted flaked almonds
1 tablespoon caraway seeds
Decorate with:
25 g/1 oz candied orange or lemon peel
Or:
57 g/2 oz blanched whole almonds

To bake

Make up a double quantity of the basic mix and add the toasted almonds and caraway seeds. Decorate the top with the orange/lemon peel or blanched almonds or a mixture of both. Shape into a 2.5 cm/1 in thick round or rectangle. Decorate the edges by pinching with thumb and forefinger. Protect the edge with a strip of greaseproof paper and bake as for the basic mix.

Scones
'Fine Bread'

We lay upon the bare top of a rock like scones upon a girdle.
Robert Louis Stevenson, *Kidnapped*, 1886.

Scones have a Scottish pedigree which goes back at least to the late 1700s, when Robert Burns, rightly, described them as 'souple [soft] scones, the wale [choicest] of food'. How they got their name is uncertain. The *Scottish National Dictionary* suggests that the word may be a shortened version of the Dutch 'schoonbrot', meaning fine bread. There is no confusion, however, about their pronunciation, at least in Scotland, where they are universally known as a 'skawn', as in gone. English pronunciation varies, since in some regions it is the same as the Scots, while in others it is 'skown', to rhyme with own.

When to eat

They should not be limited to afternoon teatime with butter or cream and jam. Unsweetened, they can be eaten as an impromptu substitute for bread at any time of the day, as Patrick Rance discovered when he got a slice of Dunlop cheese toasted with a scone for his breakfast while staying with an Ayrshire cheesemaker in the mid-twentieth century.

The secret of a good scone

The dough should be light and soft. Too wet will be doughy inside, too dry will be hard. The mixing should be done quickly and lightly. There should be the minimum of handling and they should be baked quickly in a hot oven until they are just risen and dried out. The outside should be very crisp: the inside light and soft.

Ingredients

Scots unsweetened scones, baked as 'fine bread', are made with buttermilk and bicarbonate of soda and are known as soda scones. There is a subtle difference in the result which is softer, lighter, moister and with a sharper flavour than scones made with fresh milk and baking powder. If buttermilk is not available then fresh milk may be soured by adding lemon juice to make it curdle.

Mixing and shaping

'Deftly mixed' is probably as good a description as any of the technique, which depends on light, quick handling for a perfect result. The flour should be well sifted and all the milk poured into a well in the centre. Stir with a fork, gradually bringing in the flour; if the mixture is too dry and 'ragged' looking, the scones will not be light. The mixing should be done with as little 'working' as possible and it should be a soft, elastic consistency, but not too wet and sticky. It should be handled as little as possible. It may be kneaded for a few seconds, then rolled out with a rolling pin or pressed out by hand into a large round shape (a bannock) for the girdle about 1 cm/½ in thick, and for the oven 2.5–4 cm/1–1½ in. Then it is cut into 6 or 8 triangular scones. They may be separated or touching; if the latter they will take longer to cook but can be broken after baking.

Baking

All scones may be baked either on a girdle in the traditional way or in the oven. There will be differences in shape and texture. Those baked on the girdle will have smooth, flat top and bottom surfaces, while the oven ones will be rough on top. Oven ones are more likely to be drier, while girdle scones will be moister.

The girdle-baking technique allows more control over the baking, since they can be watched as they cook. The girdle should not be too hot to begin with, or the scones will brown too quickly. Cook slowly, till risen, and till there is a white skin on top. This usually takes about five or six minutes. The heat should have penetrated to the top, and the centre should be well set before turning. Increase the heat if necessary till brown underneath, then turn and brown on the other side. Open up a little at the edge to check they are quite dry. Wrap in a towel to keep them soft. It is more difficult to judge when they are in the oven but they will take a shorter time than you imagine. Overcooked or undercooked, they lose their softness and lightness.

Types of Scones

SODA SCONES
'Fine bread'

Using bicarbonate of soda and buttermilk (or soured milk) will make the softest scones. To make the lightest scones with the best rise, use a low gluten flour such as a fine plain flour for cakes and pastry or a '00' Grade premium plain white flour (used for making pasta). To make a less 'fine' scone, use some or all wholemeal. Irish soda bread is traditionally made with a high percentage of coarse wholemeal.

250 g/9 oz plain cake or pastry flour, or '00' grade premium plain flour, or wholemeal flour
2 level teaspoon bicarbonate of soda
30 g/1 oz butter, softened
30 g/1 oz vegetable fat for pastry
240 ml/16 fl oz buttermilk (or fresh milk soured with 1 tablespoon lemon juice to make up this amount)
Pinch of salt

Makes 4/8 scones or 1 round divided into 4/6.

Preheat the oven to 450F/230C/210Cfan/Gas 8.

To make

Sift the flour and soda together into a bowl. Add the fats and blend into the flour either by rubbing in with tips of fingers or, briefly (10 seconds), in the food-processor.

Make a well in the centre and add nearly all the milk. Using a fork, start by bringing in the edges gradually until it forms a softish sticky dough. The consistency should be neither too soft nor too stiff. Add more milk if too stiff.

To shape and bake

Flour work surface and turn out mixture. Handle lightly. Knead for about 10 seconds to make the dough smooth. Press out to 1.5-2 cm/½-¾ in thick with fingers, or a rolling pin, and shape either into a large round and cut into quarters, or cut into individual scones with a well-floured scone cutter. Do not twist when cutting. Handle lightly and as little as possible.

Place on a floured baking tray, dust with flour and bake for

10-15 minutes till risen and lightly browned. Cool on a rack in a tea-towel to keep soft.

Variations

SWEET MILK SCONES

Instead of buttermilk use **sweet milk** and either **plain flour** with **2 level teaspoons baking powder** or **fine self-raising flour** for cakes. Add **2 tablespoons caster sugar** with the dry ingredients.

FRUIT SCONES

Add **75 g/3 oz dried fruit** and **1 tablespoon golden syrup** or **caster sugar** to the basic soda scone.

TREACLE, HONEY or SYRUP SCONES

Add **1-2 tablespoons treacle** or **runny honey,** or **golden syrup** to the milk and mix in before adding to the basic mix.

CHEESE SCONES

Add **150 g/5 oz grated extra mature Scottish cheddar cheese** and a **large pinch of cayenne pepper** to the sifted flour. Season well with salt. Brush tops with **egg** and grate some more cheese on top.

Cheese and Onion Scones (see below).

SOUR CREAM SCONES
with raspberry jam

Sift **113 g/4 oz self-raising cake flour** and **113 g/4 oz fine plain flour** together with **1 teaspoon bicarbonate of soda.** Add **1 egg, 2 tablespoons oil** and **200 ml/7 fl oz soured cream.** Mix with a fork to a light dough and divide into six. Flour well and bake at

450F/230C/210Cfan/Gas 8 for 20 minutes. Serve warm with **raspberry jam** and **whipped cream**.

APPLE OR RHUBARB SCONES

Add to the basic mix **1 egg**; an extra **50 g/2 oz butter; 3 tablespoons sugar** and **500 g/1lb 2 oz peeled, cored and roughly chopped cooking apple** or **chopped rhubarb**. Spread in a greased baking tin 28 x 18 cm/11 x 7 in. Sprinkle a thick layer of **granulated sugar** on top and bake at 450F/230C/Gas 8 for 30-40 minutes or until the fruit is soft. Can be served as a pudding with cream.

ONION SCONES

Melt **2 tablespoons bacon fat** in a pan, add **1 small onion**, finely chopped and cook till soft but not browned. Leave to cool. Add to the dough. Fry some slices of onion and put on top. Brush with **egg**. For **Cheese and Onion Scones** add the onion mix to the cheese scones and put both onion slices and cheese on top.

SODA SCONE
'fine bread' baked in a pot

In Ireland this was the original method of baking soda bread. The dough was put into a special iron pot with a lid which was buried in the burning peats to make a 'pot oven'. A heavy-based enamel, or other similar pot, which will go in the oven, will do just as well. This method creates steam inside the pot which prevents a crust forming too quickly, thus allowing full 'oven spring' when the dough swells to its maximum size before the top sets. The soda-scone mix made in this way is much lighter and better risen. The Chinese make steamed bread with this method. See also **Buttermilk Bread** with oats and barley, p.26.

SCOTTISH PANCAKES AND CRUMPETS

The word 'cake' was originally applied to a small regularly shaped item which was eaten as bread and known as a 'kaak of bread' (see origins of oatcake, p.6). The sweet cake came later. The Scottish 'pan-cake' is a throw-back to the original meaning, as is the Yorkshire 'tea-cake'. In the North of England, and in some parts of Scotland too, this pancake is also called a 'drop' scone because the mixture is dropped onto the girdle.

In the late 1600s the crumpet – another type of cake – arrived. This got its name 'crompid cake' from the fact that it curled up or bent into a curve when baked. The verb to 'crump' or 'crimp' means to curl. The original crumpet was baked very thinly and cooked on a girdle, which is why it curled. English crumpets are now quite different affairs, but the Scottish crumpet remains true to the original meaning and is thin and usually curled into a stick-of-rock shape when eaten.

The same mixture can be used for both pancakes and crumpets; the difference is in the consistency, with crumpets mixed to a much thinner consistency.

125 g/4½ oz plain flour, beremeal or fine oatmeal
125 g/4½ oz self raising cake flour
1 teaspoon bicarbonate of soda
1 tablespoon golden syrup or honey or sugar
2 tablespoons oil
1 large or 2 medium eggs
To mix with:
Buttermilk or fresh milk soured with the juice of a lemon
For thick pancakes: 250-275 ml/9-10 fl oz
For thin crumpets: 440 ml/15 fl oz

Preheat the girdle till moderately hot and grease lightly with oil. A large non-stick frying pan may also be used or a plug-in electric teriyaki hot plate.

Mixing the ingredients

Sift the dry ingredients into a bowl. Whisk the honey or syrup, oil and eggs together with a fork or whisk. Make a well in the centre of the flour and add with most of the milk. With a wooden spoon, gradually bring in the dry ingredients. When everything is mixed in, beat with a whisk till smooth. The mixture should drop easily from a spoon. Adjust with more milk to make a thinner pancake. For crumpets add enough milk to make the mixture very runny.

Size

Drop spoonfuls onto the heated, greased girdle. Size and shape as desired. Scotch bakers' crumpets are usually about 14 cm/6 in, and their pancakes about half this size. For an American pancake stack, served with maple syrup and grilled bacon, the thick pancakes are about the size of a Scotch bakers' crumpet.

Firing

For pancakes, turn when the heat has penetrated to the top surface and it is beginning to bubble. They should be lightly and evenly brown underneath, and should only take 1-2 minutes on each side.

For crumpets, turn when the whole surface is covered with burst bubbles and it has almost dried out. This will make a 'lacy' crumpet, which is almost see-through when held up to the light.

Wrap in a tea towel on a cooling rack immediately they are cooked. Pancakes or crumpets may be served warm with butter and jam for tea, and with grilled bacon and honey, maple or golden syrup for breakfast. Crumpets can be sprinkled with lemon juice and caster sugar and rolled up to eat like a stick of rock.

Scottish Cookies

I want a plain ham-and-egg tea . . . and some cookies and cakes.
R.M. Williamson in *Scotland, Readings etc.*, edited T.W.
Paterson, 1929.

A cookie is a plain, round, yeasted, sweet bun. It is very light in texture with a dark-golden, shiny top. Split open and filled with whipped cream with a dusting of icing sugar on top, it is known as a Cream Cookie: with an iced top only it is known as an Iced Cookie. These three types are the most commonly available in high street bakers' shops in Scotland. Spice and fruit may also be added, with the appropriate description.

The name was probably adopted from the Dutch 'koekje' which is actually the diminutive of 'koek' – cake. A Scottish cream cookie is almost the same as a Devon Split, but an American cookie is a British 'biscuit'. A 'cookie shine' is an old Scottish name for an English 'bun fight'.

PLAIN COOKIES

500 g/1 lb 2oz strong plain flour
1 teaspoon salt
75 g/3 oz sugar
75 g/3 oz butter, softened
1 teaspoon (½ pkt) quick-action yeast
2 medium eggs, beaten
125 ml/4 fl oz milk
125 ml/4 fl oz warm water
For glazing:
1 egg yolk beaten with 1 teaspoon water

Makes 14–16

Preheat the oven to 425F/220C/200Cfan/Gas 7. Prepare 2 large greased baking trays.

To mix the dough

This can be done by hand, mixing all the ingredients to make a soft sticky dough, or it can be mixed quickly in a mixer with a dough hook. Put the flour, salt, sugar, butter, yeast, eggs, milk and most of the water into the bowl. Using the dough hook, start the mixer on a slow speed and mix, adding more water if necessary to make a very soft, sticky dough. Beat on a higher speed for a minute until everything is thoroughly mixed. Cover the bowl with a cloth and leave for 10 minutes or longer. This allows the flour to absorb the moisture.

Knead by fold-stretch-and-rest

Oil the work surface and your hands, and turn out the dough. Scrape the bowl clean and oil it lightly. Press out the dough into a round shape. Fold in two, bringing the top edge down to the bottom edge making a half circle. Push down lightly with the 'heel' of your hand and push and stretch the dough away from you to about 5-10 cm/2-4 in. Turn the dough a quarter, clockwise, and repeat fold-push-and-stretch. After three or four times the stretchy gluten in the flour will develop and it will become more difficult to push and stretch. When this happens, stop and leave dough to relax for at least 10 minutes, or longer. Repeat push-and-stretch twice more, and the dough will become smooth, silky and elastic. Put back into the bowl.

Rising the dough

Cover with a cloth and leave to rise in a warm place until it has risen by 50%.

Shaping the cookies

Divide into 14-16 pieces. Shape into rolls. Place on baking tray leaving space for rising. Cover with lightly oiled clingfilm and put in a warm place till they have risen again by 50%.

Baking

Brush the tops with egg and bake for about 25-30 minutes, when the crust and base should be firm and browned.

CREAM COOKIES

Split when cold and fill with whipped cream. Dust on top with icing sugar.

ICED COOKIES

Make up a fairly stiff water icing, leave plain or colour, and coat the top of the cookie.

CURRANT COOKIES

Add **125 g/4 oz currants** to the dough.

A SPECIAL YEAST CAKE
using the Cookie dough

This rich yeast cake, with its dark golden sticky top, is a good New Year alternative to Black Bun. It was the speciality of Neil Rieley, a retired Glasgow grocer, who baked for a hobby in a remote Highland glen fifty miles from the nearest bakers, firing his weekly bread supply in a wood-burning stove. His deep-freeze stood in the porch at the back door, and as you left a frozen, malty-crusted loaf would be put in a bag as a leaving present.

Dough as for Cookies (see p.344)
Sticky top:
25 g/1 oz butter
25 g/1 oz brown sugar
1 tablespoon golden syrup
3 tablespoons currants

Preheat the oven to 425F/220C/200Cfan/Gas 7.

Grease base and sides of a 20-25 cm/8-10 in round tin or similarly sized rectangular bread tin with non-removable base.

To make the sticky top

Melt butter, sugar and syrup together and bring to the boil. Remove from the heat and pour into the base of the tin. Sprinkle over half the currants.

Shaping the dough

Shape the dough into about 20 to 30 small balls. Arrange the balls in the tin in loose layers, sprinkling the rest of the currants between the layers. Cover with oiled clingfilm and leave to rise in a warm place by 50%. Bake for 20 minutes, then turn down to 400F/200C/180Cfan/Gas 6 for 40 minutes or until the crust is firm and browned. Turn upside down onto a plate when still warm from the oven. Scrape off any bits which have stuck to the bottom of the tin and put on top of the cake. Serve with rich Hatted Kit (see p.293).

MR JIMMY'S SPICED COOKIES

An aromatic spiced bun which ex-high street master baker, Jimmy Burgess, made in 'the pastry' at One Devonshire Gardens in Glasgow, where he became a legend for his fine bread, rolls and pastries.

For the starter sponge:
350 ml/12 fl oz tepid water
25 g/1 oz fresh yeast
1 tablespoon sugar
25 g/1 oz dried milk powder
75 g/3 oz strong white flour
For the spice mix:
3 nutmegs
3 teaspoons allspice berries

1 cinnamon stick
1 teaspoon whole cloves
1 teaspoon ground ginger
For the cookies:
25 g/1 oz spice mix
650 g/1lb 7 oz strong white flour
75 g/3 oz solid vegetable fat
50 g/2 oz sugar
250 g/8 oz dried mixed fruit
For brushing the top:
1 egg beaten with 1 teaspoon water

Preheat the oven to 400F/200C/180Cfan/Gas 6.

To make the starter

Mix everything together and leave in a warm place until the top is frothing and bubbling.

To make the spice mix

Blend the spices (except nutmeg which should be grated) in a coffee grinder. Grind till fine. They will not be quite as fine as the commercial variety, but this does not matter for baking. Store in an airtight jar, label with the date and keep in a cool place out of direct light and use within a month or two.

To mix the dough

This can be done by hand, mixing all the ingredients together to make a soft sticky dough, or it can be mixed quickly in a mixer with a dough hook. Put the spice mix, flour, fat, sugar, dried fruit and starter sponge into the bowl. Using the dough hook, start the mixer on a slow speed and mix, adding more water if necessary to make a very soft, sticky dough. Beat on a higher speed for a minute until everything is thoroughly mixed. Cover the bowl with a cloth and leave for 10 minutes or longer. This allows the flour to absorb the moisture.

Knead by fold-stretch-and-rest

Oil the work surface and your hands, and turn out the dough. Scrape the bowl clean and oil it lightly. Press out the dough into a round shape. Fold in two, bringing the top edge down to the bottom edge to make a half circle. Push down lightly with the 'heel' of your hand and push and stretch the dough away from you to about 5-10 cm/2-4 in. Turn the dough a quarter, clockwise, and repeat this fold-push-and-stretch. After three or four times the stretchy gluten in the flour will develop and the dough will become more difficult to push and stretch. When this happens, stop and leave dough to relax for at least 10 minutes, or longer. Repeat push-and-stretch twice more and the dough will change texture to smooth, silky and elastic. Put back into the bowl.

Rising the dough

Cover with a cloth and leave to rise in a warm place until it has risen by 50%.

Shaping into buns

Divide up the dough and shape into round buns. Put on a greased tray. Make a pastry cross for hot cross buns. Cover with lightly greased clingfilm and leave to prove till risen by 50%. Brush with egg and bake for 20-30 minutes. Serve warm.

WHITE FLOURY BAPS

He grew, the great Macguldroch grew,
On butter'd baps and ale.
R. Couper, *Poems*, 1804.

Lady Clark of Tillypronie (1909) says that '"Baps" are mixed very slack – water, flour, salt, yeast. (Neither butter, eggs, nor milk.) They are well dusted with flour and eaten fresh as soon as baked.'

The etymology of the word is unknown but it seems that they were always breakfast rolls made from a very plain bread dough, and the shapes and sizes varied greatly from one part of the country to another, possibly even from one household to another. 'Are ye for your burial baps round or square?' says Mrs Lion in *Reminiscences of Scottish Life and Character* by Dean Ramsay (1870).

Whatever size or shape, they are distinguished by their fresh, soft, white, floury qualities. The most common shape today is round, and they may be called morning rolls or baps. The thick floury coating which Lady Clark advises prevents an early crust forming and allows them to rise well. She belonged to Aberdeenshire where a floury bap was popular. Other variations include the Glasgow Roll which has a hard, crisp, well-fired exterior and an open texture inside like an Italian ciabatta. A dusting of semolina on top adds to the crisp exterior. There are also special well-fired 'burnt' Glasgow Rolls.

500 g/1 lb 2 oz strong white flour
50 g/2 oz lard, softened
1 level teaspoon salt
1 teaspoon (½ pkt) quick-action yeast
1 teaspoon sugar
**300 ml/10 fl oz mix of half water and half milk, heated and
  cooled**

Makes 9

Preheat the oven to 425F/220C/200Cfan/Gas 7.

Use 2 greased baking trays.

To mix the dough

This can be done by hand, mixing all the ingredients together to make a soft sticky dough, or it can be mixed quickly in a mixer with a dough hook. Put the flour, lard, salt, yeast, sugar and most of the liquid into the bowl. Using the dough hook, start the mixer on a slow speed and mix, adding more water if necessary to make a very soft, sticky dough. Beat on a higher speed for a minute until everything is thoroughly mixed. Cover the bowl with a cloth and leave for 10 minutes or longer. This allows the flour to absorb the moisture.

Knead by fold-stretch-and-rest

Oil the work surface and your hands, and turn out the dough. Scrape the bowl clean and oil it lightly. Press out the dough into a round shape. Fold in two, bringing the top edge down to the bottom edge to make a half circle. Push down lightly with the 'heel' of your hand and push and stretch the dough away from you to about 5-10 cm/2-4 in. Turn the dough a quarter, clockwise, and repeat this fold-push-and-stretch. After three or four times the stretchy gluten in the flour will develop and the dough will become more difficult to push and stretch. When this happens, stop and leave dough to relax for at least 10 minutes, or longer. Repeat push-and-stretch twice more and the dough will change texture to smooth, silky and elastic. Put back into the bowl.

Rising the dough

Cover with a cloth and leave to rise in a warm place until it has risen by 50%.

Shaping

Divide dough into 9. Shape into round or oval baps. Dust tops with flour. Place on baking tray leaving space for rising. Cover with cling-film and put in a warm place till they have risen again by 50%. They may be pressed lightly in the centre with your forefinger to make an indent in the middle.

Baking

Bake for about 20-25 minutes, when the base should be firm and browned. Leave until cold before removing from tray.

Gingerbread

An had I but one penny in the whole world,
Thou shouldst have it to buy gingerbread.
William Shakespeare, *Love's Labour's Lost.*

Gingerbread began its life as a hugely popular 'fun' biscuit sold at annual fairs. The gingerbread booth was a colourful affair with gingerbread 'crowns, kings and queens, cocks, etc., dazzlingly resplendent with pseudo gold leaf' and brightly decorated with coloured satin ribbons.

Unlike today's soft gingerbread, recipes in the early 1400s were for a hard biscuit, dried out rather than baked. To make it, honey was mixed with grated bread into a stiff paste, which was flavoured with spices and coloured red and yellow. It was rolled out and shaped into amusing figures, letters and numbers which were used to teach children to read and count.

Robbie Salmond was an eccentric itinerant gingerbread seller, according to J.H. Jamieson in his article on 'Street Traders and Their Cries' in the *Book of the Old Edinburgh Club* (1909). At the Hallow Fair in Edinburgh he was to be found 'encouraging' his customers by occasionally tossing samples of his gingerbread into the crowd and shouting – 'Bullock's blood and sawdust – Feed the ravens, Feed the ravens.'

Another Edinburgh gingerbread biscuit appears in Robert Chambers' *Traditions of Edinburgh* (1868) when he refers to the shop and 'tavern' run by Mrs Flockhart in the Potterrow. Her nickname was 'Lucky Fykie' and, in a fifteen-feet-square room, she had a shop selling a variety of miscellaneous items; a living area; a tiny closet (side room); and adjoining this a small room described as a 'hotel'. 'Each forenoon this place was . . . put into the neatest order; at the same time three bottles, severally containing brandy, rum, and whisky, were placed on a bunker-seat in the window of the "hotel", flanked by a few glasses and a salver of gingerbread biscuits. About noon anyone watching the place from an opposite window would have observed an elderly gentleman entering the humble shop, where he saluted the lady with a "Hoo d'ye do, mem?" and then passed into the side space to indulge himself with a glass from one or other of the bottles. After him came another, who went through the same ceremonial; after him another again; and so on. Strange to say, these were men of importance in society – some of them lawyers in good employment, some bankers, and so forth ... On special occasions Lucky could furnish forth a soss – that is, stew – which the votary might partake of upon a clean napkin in the closet, a place which only admitted of one chair being placed in it.'

GINGERBREAD MEN, WOMEN
and other shapes

This makes a firm biscuit when baked, which can also be used for making Christmas tree decorations.

125 g/4½ oz butter
100 g/3 ½ oz soft brown sugar
3 tablespoons golden syrup
1 teaspoon ground ginger
1 teaspoon ground cinnamon
1 large egg
320 g/11½ oz self-raising flour
1 tablespoon currants or chocolate chips

Grease two large baking trays.

Preheat the oven to 350F/180C/160Cfan/Gas 4.

Making and shaping

Put a large pan over a low heat and add the butter, cut up into small pieces. When melted, add the sugar, syrup, ginger, cinnamon and egg. Remove from the heat and beat with a wooden spoon till smooth. Add the flour and mix to a pliable but stiff paste. Knead for a minute till smooth. Cover and rest for 30 minutes in the fridge.

Dust the work surface, and a rolling pin, with flour and roll out the dough to about 3 mm/one eighth of an inch thick. Cut into shapes using gingerbread man/woman cutters. Or make shapes, drawing first on thick paper or cardboard, cutting out and placing on top of the dough, then cutting round them. Use currants/chocolate chips or other commercial cake decorations, pressing into the dough before baking.

Baking and decorating the dough

Bake for about 15-20 minutes till lightly browned. Leave to cool on the tray. They can also be decorated using ready-made fondant. To make different colours, use cake decoration colourings and work into the fondant. Roll out thinly and cut into shapes. Stick on with some icing sugar mixed with a little water to a thick paste. Decorate with commercial cake decorations.

DARK GINGERBREAD

This remarkable gingerbread is dense with spices and treacle and may sink slightly in the middle – not a sign of failure. For a less dense result add a little more flour. Replace some or all the butter with oil to make a more moist crumb which will keep better.

175 g/6 oz butter or oil
175 g/6 oz soft brown sugar
175 g/6 oz treacle
2 eggs
1 tablespoon ground ginger
1 tablespoon ground cinnamon
1 teaspoon allspice
175 g/6 oz plain flour (195 g/6¾ oz for lighter result)
1 teaspoon bicarbonate of soda

250 ml/8 fl oz buttermilk or fresh milk soured with the juice of a lemon
Optional:
125 g/4 oz raisins
50 g stem/2 oz ginger, chopped
25 g/1 oz flaked almonds

Use a 23 cm/9 in round or 28 x 18 x 4.5 cm/11 x 7 x 1¾ in deep tin. Grease sides, line base with non-stick baking paper or press a large sheet of foil across base and up the sides.

Preheat the oven to 350F/180C/160Cfan/Gas 4.

Mixing in a pan

Put the butter/oil, sugar and treacle into a large saucepan which will hold the finished mixture. Warm slightly to melt the butter. Remove from the heat and beat in the eggs. Add the spices and beat in. Sift in the flour and soda and beat in. Mix in raisins or ginger if using. Add the milk and mix to make a fairly runny consistency. Pour into the tin. Sprinkle almonds on top if using.

To bake

Bake for about 45–50 minutes till springy on top when pressed lightly.

May be served hot as a pudding with **Sticky Toffee Sauce**. Keeps well.

STICKY TOFFEE SAUCE

This is a versatile – as well as a long-keeping – sauce for using hot with ices in a sundae or on warm gingerbread served as a pudding. It can also be used hot on Scotch pancakes and crumpets (p.342), cold as a toffee icing on cakes and hot with a **Clootie Dumpling** (see p.27).

85 g/3 oz butter
150 ml/5 fl oz double cream

150 g/5 oz muscovado brown sugar

To make

Place the butter, cream and sugar in a pan and stir till the sugar is dissolved, then boil for 3 minutes, stirring when necessary to prevent sticking. Serve hot or leave to cool, cover and store. It will keep in the fridge for at least a month.

'BLACK' BUN
with a yeast dough

This 'Rich Bun' or a 'Scotch Christmas Bun' or just 'Scotch Bun', shaped like a round cob loaf, was first made by commercial bakers who were only allowed to use spices and dried fruits for festive occasions. They took a lump of their bread dough and worked in the fruit and spices to flavour it. Selkirk Bannocks have their origins in this custom. But the festive Scotch Bun was a much richer and spicier affair, so much so that it was held together with a thin casing of plain bread dough. This was later converted to pastry, and the spice and fruit mixture made even more dense, when it was more appropriately renamed a 'Black Bun' sometime in the mid to late 1800s. This is a version of the original method using a yeast dough, and is more dark and speckled than 'black'.

For the dough: use **Plain Cookie** recipe, see p.344.

Fruit and Spice Mix:

200 g/7 oz raisins

200 g/7 oz currants

125 g/4 oz flaked almonds

2 tablespoons dark muscovado sugar

½ teaspoon ground cloves

25 g/1 oz freshly ground cinnamon

15 g/½ oz ground ginger

2-3 tablespoons rum or brandy

1 egg yolk plus 1 teaspoon water for glaze

Preheat the oven to 350F/180C/160Cfan/Gas 4.

Grease a 20 cm/8 in round cake tin.

Make the plain cookie dough

Once mixed, oil another bowl lightly and put in the dough. Cover with a damp cloth or lightly oiled clingfilm and put in a warm place to rise by 50%. Divide into two pieces, a third and two-thirds.

To make the bun

Mix all the fruit, sugar and spice ingredients together and moisten with rum or brandy. Roll out the two-thirds piece of dough and place the fruit/spice mix on top. Fold over and knead till the fruit and spices are mixed evenly through the dough. This can be done in the mixer with the dough hook.

When well mixed in, roll out the smaller piece to a large round a few inches larger than the bun. Place the bun in the centre and bring up the sides to meet in the centre at the top. Bring all the edges together and mould evenly round the bun.

Turn over on the join and put into the cake tin. Leave to prove in a warm place till it has risen by about a third. Prick all over with a long skewer right through to the bottom of the bun, brush with glaze and bake for about 1 hour. To test for readiness, remove from the tin; the crust and base should be firm and browned. Cool and wrap in clingfilm or foil to store.

SELKIRK BANNOCK

This rich yeasted bannock is shaped like a round cob loaf and is generously filled with sultanas. It is sold in bakers' shops in the Borders in small and large sizes. When Queen Victoria visited Sir Walter Scott's granddaughter at Abbotsford she is said to have refused all else with her tea but a slice of The Bannock.

900 g/2 lb strong plain flour
125 g/4½ oz butter, softened
125 g/4½ oz lard or vegetable fat, softened
225 g/8 oz sugar
1 x 7 g packet quick-action yeast
½ teaspoon salt
450 ml/15 fl oz milk, warmed
450 g/1 lb sultanas
1 egg yolk plus 1 teaspoon water for glazing

Preheat the oven to 425F/220C/200Cfan/Gas 7: bake for 15-20 minutes. Reduce to 375F/190C/170Cfan/Gas 5: bake for 20-30 minutes.

Use a large greased baking tray or two small baking trays.

To mix the dough

This can be done by hand, mixing all the ingredients together to make a soft sticky dough, or it can be mixed quickly in a mixer with a dough hook. Put the flour, butter, lard, yeast, salt and most of the milk into the bowl. Using the dough hook, start the mixer on a slow speed and mix, adding more milk if necessary to make a very soft, sticky dough. Beat on a higher speed for a minute until everything is thoroughly mixed. Cover the bowl with a cloth and leave for 10 minutes or longer. This allows the flour to absorb the moisture.

Knead by fold-stretch-and-rest

Oil the work surface and your hands. Turn out the dough. Scrape the bowl clean and oil it lightly. Press out the dough into a round shape. Fold in two, bringing the top edge down to the bottom edge to make a half circle. Push down lightly with the 'heel' of your hand and push and stretch the dough away from you to about 5-10 cm/2-4 in. Turn the dough a quarter, clockwise, and repeat this fold-push-and-stretch. After three or four times the stretchy gluten in the flour will develop and the dough will become more difficult to push and stretch. When this happens, stop and leave dough to relax for at least 10 minutes, or longer. Repeat push-and-stretch twice more and the dough will change texture to smooth, silky and elastic. At the beginning of the third push-and-stretch, work in the sultanas. Put back into the bowl.

Rising the dough

Cover with a cloth and leave to rise in a warm place until it has risen by 50%.

Shaping and Baking

Shape into four small or two large buns. Place on a greased baking tray, cover with some lightly oiled cling film, and leave in a warm place till they have doubled in size. Brush with the egg glaze and put in a hot oven for 15-20 minutes then reduce the heat to 390F/200C/180Cfan/Gas 6 and bake for another 20-25 minutes till the crust and base are firm and browned. Larger buns will take 30-40 minutes at the reduced temperature. Cool thoroughly on a rack.

SELKIRK BANNOCK TOASTS
with rum

6 slices of week-old Selkirk Bannock, or any other plain or rich bread
3 eggs, beaten
250 ml/8 fl oz milk
25 g/1 oz sugar
125 ml/4 fl oz rum
50 g/2 oz butter
2 tablespoons oil
1 tablespoon granulated or caster sugar, mixed with 1 teaspoon cinnamon

To make 6 toasts

Beat the eggs, milk, sugar and rum. Soak the bread on both sides. Heat the oil and butter in a large frying pan till hot. Fry the bread on both sides till brown and crisp. Sprinkle with cinnamon sugar and serve.

ECCLEFECHAN BUTTER TART

This rich buttery tart is a speciality of the Scottish Borders, available in bakers throughout the year but often preferred at Christmas instead of mince pies. It has a 'secret' ingredient (vinegar) which is undetectable when it is baked, but is essential since it acts as a balance to the butter. An A-list celebrity chef unwisely missed it out in his version of this popular tart.

Quick Shortcrust Pastry (or Rich Shortcrust see p.324):
175 g/6 oz plain flour
50 g/2 oz lard
50 g/2 oz butter
50 ml/2 fl oz boiling water
For the filling:
125 g/4½ oz butter, softened
175 g/6 oz soft brown sugar
2 large eggs
1 tablespoon wine or balsamic vinegar
250 g/9 oz mixed dried fruits
125 g/4½ oz chopped walnuts
To serve:
250 ml/8 fl oz whipped cream
100 g/3½ oz whole walnuts, toasted

Preheat the oven to 350F/180C/160Cfan/Gas 4.

Prepare a 23 cm/9 in flan tin, 3 cm/1¼ in deep.

To make the pastry

Cut the lard and butter into a bowl and pour over the boiling water. Beat with a wire whisk till the fats are melted and the mixture is creamy. It does not matter if it separates. Sift in the flour. Mix together. Knead till smooth. Wrap in clingfilm and put in the fridge for at least an hour till it hardens.

To bake the flan

Roll out pastry and line flan tin. Do not cut off overhang. Bake blind with foil/or greaseproof paper and beans or rice, for 20-30 minutes till cooked through, removing the foil/greaseproof paper for the last 15 minutes. Bake till a light golden. Leave to cool. Trim off overhang.

To make the filling

Beat the sugar and butter till light and creamy. Beat in the eggs gradually. Mix in the vinegar, dried fruits and walnuts. Stir to mix and pour into the pastry flan. Level top and bake for 30-40 minutes. Serve with whipped cream and toasted walnuts.

MINCEMEAT 'STREUSEL'

This is not only a fast alternative mince-pie recipe but also includes an ingenious 'topping' which fuses with the mincemeat as it bakes. It's a speciality of Glyn Meredith, one of the Torridon Tea Ladies in Wester Ross, who supply the Community Hall with baking for all events.

Quick Shortcrust Pastry, see previous recipe
or **325 g/12 oz ready-made shortcrust**
Filling:
2 x 411 g/1 lb jars mincemeat *

*Variations: some spoonfuls of mincemeat can be replaced with vintage marmalade. Mincemeat can be flavoured with rum or brandy.

361

Topping:

75 g/3 oz white self-raising flour

40 g/1½ oz semolina

40 g/1½ oz caster sugar

75 g/3 oz butter

Makes 16

Preheat the oven to 400F/200C/180Cfan/Gas 6.

Grease a Swiss Roll tin approx 30-33 x 23 x 2 cm deep/12-13 x 9 x ¾ in deep.

To make the pastry

Cut the lard and butter into a bowl and pour over the boiling water. Beat with a wire whisk till the fats are melted and the mixture is creamy. It does not matter if it separates. Sift in the flour. Mix together. Knead till smooth, wrap in clingfilm and put in the fridge for at least an hour till it hardens.

To make the topping

Put the flour, semolina, and caster sugar into a mixing bowl. Melt the butter, allow to cool slightly, pour onto the dry ingredients and mix together to form a dough. Wrap tightly in clingfilm. Chill for 30 minutes in the freezer till hard, which makes it easier to grate.

To line tin, fill and bake

Roll out the pastry to fit the tin. Line the tin. Spread the mincemeat evenly over the pastry base. Grate the topping over the mincemeat with a coarse grater. Spread evenly. Bake for 30 minutes until golden brown on top. Cut into 16 slices. Serve warm with cream or brandy butter.

Quick and Easy Cakes

These are a late-twentieth-century development, which are made, not by the time-consuming method of creaming butter and sugar, but by beating everything together in seconds. This breakthrough for home-bakers has been made possible by the availability of special cake flours. These were previously only available to professional bakers in the UK, though they have been available for home-bakers in America for decades. A pioneer of this radically different cake-making method is the American cake guru, Rose Levy Beranbaum (*The Cake Bible*, 1988) who identified this difference between UK and US flours when her publisher asked her to write a UK edition of the book. When she arrived in the UK to do some recipe-testing for this edition, she was dismayed to discover that UK flours would not work with her recipes. But they do now.

They are variously described as 'ideal for cakes and scones', 'light', 'supreme sponge', and 'extra fine'. What they all achieve is a higher rise and finer texture than standard plain or self-raising flour. The main reason for their success is a very high starch content, which is required to emulsify the butter and eggs and make a tender crumb. They are low in gluten, which toughens a cake. They have also been well sifted and aerated, so that they sieve and mix in more easily than standard flours. Another reason for their easy mixing and smooth finished texture is that they have been selected from the highest grade of flour particles which are finer and more even than other flours. They may also have been heat-treated to modify the gluten content.

Self-raising (SR) or **plain**? Always self-raising for quick-and-easy cakes, but if the flour is near, or past, its best-buy date its raising qualities may be less efficient, and a teaspoon of baking powder should be added to every 250 g/9 oz just in case. Professional bakers like to control the baking powder content and always use this with plain flour.

SUCCESSFUL CAKE BAKING

Balance

This depends on getting the correct balance of strengthening and tenderising ingredients.

Flour and eggs contain the proteins which strengthen the structure of the cake. Sugar, butter and liquids weaken it, though they are essential to soften and tenderise the finished texture. If the proportion of flour and eggs is too high, the cake texture will be too dry and heavy. If it is too low, the cake will not hold its shape and may sink in the oven or as it cools. To prevent failure, it is necessary to weigh ingredients accurately, which is best done with digital scales.

Temperature – warming butter and eggs

Butter and eggs, if they are too cold, can separate when cakes are mixed, which will spoil the finished texture. To prevent this they should both be around the same temperature i.e. lukewarm. Butter can be warmed slightly, till just soft without melting, in the microwave. The eggs in their shells can be warmed in a bowl of hot water for a few minutes.

SPONGE CAKE
cup cakes and tray bakes
Basic Easy-Cream Method

Sponge:

4 large eggs (250ml)

250 g/9 oz self-raising extra-fine cake flour

250 g/9 oz caster sugar

250 g/9 oz butter, softened

1-2 teaspoonfuls vanilla extract

1-2 tablespoons milk

Flavoured 'Buttercream' icing:*

175 g/6 oz unsalted butter at room temperature

*not true buttercream, which is made with egg whites.

250 g/9 oz icing sugar

Flavouring options:

1 teaspoon vanilla extract

4 tablespoons milk *or*

4 tablespoons liqueur, rum, brandy, whisky *or*

4 tablespoons orange or lemon juice *or*

50 g/2 oz cocoa powder

4 tablespoons boiling water

Preheat the oven to 350F/180C/160Cfan/Gas 4.

Use 2 x 20 cm/8 in round cake tins *or*

1 x 23-25 cm/9-10 in round cake tin *or*

1 x 25 x 18 cm/12 x 7 in rectangular traybake tin (16-18 squares) *or*

16-18 cup cake tins.

Grease sides, line base with non-stick baking paper or press a large sheet of foil across base and up the sides of tins.

To make

Warm the eggs: put into a bowl of hot but not boiling water. Leave for 2 minutes. Take out eggs and break into a measuring jug. Whisk till thoroughly mixed. Put the self-raising flour, baking powder and sugar into the bowl and beat with electric beater for 30 seconds. Make a well in the centre. Add most of the eggs, butter and vanilla and beat for 60 seconds when the mixture should change to a lighter colour and become thick and creamy. Add the remainder of the eggs and beat for another 30 seconds. The mixture should be a soft dropping consistency. Add some milk if it's too stiff. Put into prepared tins. Level the tops.

To bake

Bake for 30-40 minutes if two cakes, or 50-60 minutes if one large cake. Cup cakes take 20-30 minutes. Test with a skewer which should come out clean. Remove from the tin and cool on a rack.

To finish sponge sandwich with jam and cream or *'Buttercream' icing*

Spread jam on underside of one sponge. Beat 250 ml/9 fl oz double cream till stiff and spread on top. Place underside of other sponge on top of jam and cream and dust top with icing sugar. Or make butter icing and spread in the middle and on top. Decorate with a fork to make a rough surface. Finish with special cake decorations.

To make 'Buttercream' icing

Put butter into the bowl and beat with electric beater till soft and fluffy. Add flavourings and beat till mixed into the butter. Sift half the sugar on top. Beat to mix in. Add remainder of the sugar and beat till light and smooth. Add colourings.

Variations

CHOCOLATE CAKE: Follow the basic recipe ingredients but use only **200g self-raising flour** and make up the remainder with **50 g/2 oz cocoa powder**. Follow the basic method. For icing use **Buttercream Icing** recipe using cocoa powder.

LEMON DRIZZLE CAKE: Grate the **zest of one lemon** into the basic sponge recipe. Bake in 23-25 cm/9-10 in round cake tin or a 28 x 18 cm/11 x 7 in rectangular tin. Mix the **juice of a large lemon** with **4 tablespoons of granulated sugar**. Spread over the top of the cake when it comes out of the oven and while it is still in the tin. Leave to cool in the tin.

'A CAKE WITH APPLES IN IT'

This was made in the autumn to use up excess fruit: clearly a very popular cake, it was mentioned frequently in Grisell

Baillie's *Household Book* (1692-1733). Perhaps they also used other fruits in season. Pears and plums would work equally well. For another version made with a scone mix, see Apple Scone (p.341). The apples in this cake are the decoration on top, fanning out as it bakes.

Easy-Cream Sponge Cake mix:
200 g/7 oz SR cake flour
175 g/6 oz caster sugar
175 g/6 oz butter, softened
3 large eggs, warmed (see Basic Easy-Cream Method p.364)
1 tablespoon milk
4-5 eating apples
2 tablespoons melted butter for brushing
1 tablespoon caster sugar mixed with 1 heaped teaspoon
  ground cinnamon

Preheat the oven to 350F/180C/160Cfan/Gas 4.

Use a 23-25 cm/9-10 in cake tin. Grease sides, line base with non-stick baking paper or press a large sheet of foil across base and up the sides.

Making the sponge and finishing

Follow the **Basic Easy-Cream Method** (see p.364). Beat flour with sugar for 30 seconds. Add butter and three-quarters of the eggs/milk. Beat for 60 seconds. Add remaining liquid and beat for another 60 seconds. Pour into the tin, level the top.

Preparing the apples

Peel and cut in half. Scoop out the core, then turn onto cut side and make about 4-5 incisions, almost, but not quite, through the apple, cutting from north to south pole rather than round the equator.

   Lay apples on top of sponge. Do not press in. Brush liberally with the melted butter and coat the whole surface with cinnamon sugar. Bake for ¾-1 hour. Serve warm as a pudding, then use later as a cake.

It will keep for a few days.

MINCEMEAT SANDWICH CAKE

A sandwich cake of contrasting textures – velvety sponge base, mincemeat middle and crunchy oat top – its charm lies, not just in its flavours and textures, but also in the fact that it needs no fancy adornment save a dust of icing sugar, and is a useful last-minute alternative to a traditional Christmas cake.

Easy-Cream Sponge Cake mix from 'A Cake with Apples in It' (see p.367)
Mincemeat layer:
411 g/ 1 lb jar mincemeat
Crunchy oat top:
75 g/3 oz soft brown sugar
125 g/4½ oz buttered oats (see p.33) or use a 'crunchy' oat cereal
3 teaspoons freshly ground cinnamon
50 g/2 oz fine plain flour
50 g/2 oz butter, chopped roughly
Icing sugar for dusting

Preheat the oven to 350F/180C/160Cfan/Gas 4.

Use a 23 cm/9 in cake tin with removable base.

Grease sides, line base with non-stick baking paper or press a large sheet of foil across the base and up the sides.

To make

Make the sponge cake mix and put into the tin. Level the top and put spoonfuls of mincemeat on top, spread evenly. Put all the ingredients for the crunchy oat topping into the food processor and whizz until it forms fairly fine crumbs. Sprinkle on top of the mincemeat. Bake for 1 hour or until a skewer comes out clean.

Remove the sides of the cake tin, dust top with icing sugar, and serve hot or cold with whipped cream.

MAPLE SYRUP CAKE

A simple but perfect combination of aromatic maple syrup and velvety butter sponge. Reminiscent of an old-fashioned steamed pudding, it is turned out upside-down to serve and needs no other adornment save the syrupy topping. It can also be made with golden syrup, but this will give a sweeter flavour with none of the maple aroma. It can be eaten – as in America – for breakfast with crisp, fried bacon.

250 ml/8 fl oz maple syrup
125 g/4½ g SR cake flour
125 g/4 ½ g caster sugar
125g/4 ½ oz butter, softened
2 medium eggs, warmed (see Basic Easy-Cream Method
    p.364)
2 tablespoons milk

Preheat the oven to 350F/180C/160Cfan/Gas 4.

Prepare an 18 cm/7 in round soufflé or earthenware ovenproof dish, well greased.

To bake

Put the maple syrup into a pan and heat through but do not boil. Keep warm. Make Easy-Cream Sponge (see p.367). Beat flour and sugar for 30 seconds. Then add butter and three-quarters of the eggs. Beat for 60 seconds. Finally beat in the remaining liquid, beat for 60 seconds.

Pour hot maple syrup into the dish. Cover evenly with spoonfuls of the cake mixture. Bake for 45-50 minutes or until a skewer inserted in the centre comes out clean. Remove from the oven and invert onto a serving dish. If some of the syrup has stuck to the base, scrape off, or microwave for 30 seconds, and pour over cake. Serve warm.

CHOCOLATE
Sour Cream Cake

A good-keeping moist, tender cake which is quickly mixed in a food processor with boiling water, which releases the maximum chocolate flavour in cocoa powder. A very easy cake for children to make and decorate. Can also be served as a pudding.

40 g/1½ oz cocoa powder
200 g/7 oz self raising extra-fine cake flour
½ teaspoon bicarbonate of soda
200 g/7 oz soft brown or caster sugar
85 g/3 oz butter, softened
2 large eggs
60 ml/4 tablespoons sour cream or double cream soured with
   1 teaspoon lemon juice
1 teaspoon vanilla extract
2 tablespoons boiling water
Icing sugar for dusting on top to serve with crème fraiche *or*
Chocolate or vanilla butter icing (see p.262) and
Dark chocolate for chocolate curls to decorate

Preheat the oven to 325F/160C/140Cfan/Gas 3.

Use a food-processor.

Grease sides and line base with non-stick baking paper or press a large sheet of foil across the base and up the sides of 1 x 1.2 L/2 pt loaf tin; or 8-10 paper cup cakes; or a 19 cm/7½ in round cake tin.

To mix in a food processor

Put the cocoa powder, flour, bicarbonate of soda and sugar into the food processor. Put on the lid and whizz to bring all the ingredients together, about 20-30 seconds. Remove the lid. Add butter, eggs, sour cream and vanilla. Whizz for another 15-20 minutes. Remove the lid and check that everything is thoroughly mixed in and there are no lumps. Scrape down sides and whizz for another 10-15 seconds. Pour in all the boiling water. Whizz for another 20-30 seconds. Remove the lid. The mixture should be a glossy, smooth, creamy consistency with no lumps or bubbles.

To bake in 1 large loaf tin or a round cake tin

Pour into prepared tin and bake for 50-60 minutes or until a skewer comes out clean. Cool in the tin for 10 minutes then turn out onto a rack. Dust loaves lightly with icing sugar and serve warm with crème fraiche for pudding. Or leave till cold and decorate the top with chocolate buttercream icing and chocolate curls. To make curls, scrape a very sharp knife across the flat side of the bar of chocolate.

To bake in cup cakes

Pour mixture into paper cup cakes and bake for 20-30 minutes till risen and cooked through. Decorate as for cakes above.

DUNDEE CAKE

Whole almonds cover the surface of this cake before it is baked, roasting gently to a golden brown during the baking, giving the cake its attractive finish. The flavourings are sultanas and candied orange peel. This is the cake that was first made in Keillers' marmalade and confectionery factory in the late 1800s when production lines turned from marmalades and jams to festive midwinter baking.

Using the Seville orange peel from the marmalade process, and employing all their high-quality principles of production, they made this outstanding cake which eventually took on the name of the town. While its fame spread, commercial bakers else-where changed and altered the Keillers' original. Currants, raisins, cherries and lemon peel were added, and flaked almonds, instead of whole, were put on top. Though the Keiller family lost control of the company, their unique cake lives on, thanks to a Dundo-nian baker who worked for Keillers, and recalled the original's special features when he returned from World War I in 1918.

280 g/10 oz plain flour for cakes/pastry
250 g/9 oz caster sugar
250 g/9 oz butter, softened
5 eggs (259 g/9 oz) medium, warmed
2 tablespoons sweet sherry (optional)
450 g/1 lb sultanas
50 g/2 oz thick peel marmalade, pureed
Grated zest of orange and lemon
85 g/3 oz whole blanched almonds for the top

Preheat the oven to 350F/180C/160Cfan/Gas 4.

Use an 18-20 cm/7-8 in round cake tin, lined with non-stick baking paper, or press a large sheet of foil across the base and up the sides.

To make mixture

To warm the eggs, put them, still in their shells, into a bowl of hot water and leave for about 2 minutes till they are lukewarm. Beat flour and sugar with an electric beater for 30 seconds. Then add butter and three-quarters of the eggs. Beat for 60 seconds till creamy. Beat in remaining eggs and sherry, if using, for 60 seconds. Finally fold in the sultanas, pureed marmalade and or-ange zest. It should be a soft, dropping consistency.

To bake

Turn into a lined tin. Level the top and cover with whole al-monds. To protect the cake, make a strip of thick brown paper which will come above the height of the cake and wrap round the sides of the tin. Secure with string or tape. Bake till lightly browned on top and until a skewer inserted into the centre of the cake comes out cleanly, about 1¾ -2½ hours depending on depth of cake. If browning too much on top, cover with a sheet of foil. Cool, wrap in foil and store.

Biscuits to eat with puddings or serve with tea

The drop biscuits and almond biscuits that so often appeared
heaped high between dishes of jelly, cream and syllabub on
the dinner table, at dessert, might also be offered at tea.
Marion Lochhead, *The Scots Household in the Eighteenth*
Century, 1948.

ALMOND NUTBALLS

These plump little almond-flavoured nutballs are rolled in icing sugar and are more of a confection than a biscuit. Children love them.

75 g/3 oz toasted flaked almonds
175 g/6 oz plain flour
57 g/2 oz caster sugar
100 g/3½ oz unsalted butter
1 teaspoon vanilla extract
Icing sugar for dusting

Use 2 greased baking trays, 28 x 18 cm/11 x 7 in.

Preheat the oven to 325F/170C/150Cfan/Gas 3.

To make

Put the toasted almonds into the food-processor and whizz for about 10 seconds. They should not be too fine. Remove. Put the flour, sugar and butter – cut up into small pieces – into the food-processor and whizz for a minute. Add the almonds and the vanilla extract. Turn the mixture onto a work surface and bring it together, kneading to make a firm but pliable dough. Divide into 12-15 small balls about the size of a walnut. Place on a greased baking tray. They should not spread.

To bake

Bake for 20-30 minutes till the base is lightly golden brown. When they are still slightly warm, sift some icing sugar into a bowl and roll them till thoroughly coated.

OAT AND WALNUT BISCUITS

Very easy-to-make 'spreading' oaty biscuits which are both nutty and slightly chewy with a buttery flavour.

125 g/4½ oz butter
2 tablespoons golden syrup
1 level teaspoon bicarbonate of soda
1½ tablespoons water
75 g/3 oz plain flour
50 g/2 oz coconut
125 g/4½ oz rolled oats
175 g/6 oz caster sugar
50 g/2 oz chopped walnuts

Lightly oil two large baking trays or cover with non-stick baking paper.

Preheat the oven to 350F/180C/160Cfan/Gas 4.

To make

Put the butter in a large pan and add the syrup, melt together. Leave to cool. Mix the bicarbonate of soda with the water and add to the cooled butter mixture. Put the flour, coconut, rolled oats, sugar and walnuts into the pan. Mix all together into a stiffish paste. It should not be runny. Shape into walnut-sized balls. Put on the baking tray, leaving plenty of room for spreading. Bake for 30-40 minutes until lightly browned. Cool in the tin. Remove and store in an airtight tin.

Other Baking Specialities

Aberdeen Rowie or Butteries: A hand-crafted roll (rowie), it is a roundish, high-fat, crisp, misshapen roll about half an inch thick. In and around Aberdeen they tend to be very crisp and salty. Elsewhere they often become more 'bready' than crisp. They are thought to have been made originally for fishermen as a long-keeping roll. They are an East Coast product seldom seen on the West Coast.

Abernethy Biscuit: Pale-golden, shortbread-type biscuit, pricked on top, which contains less butter and sugar. Its name comes, not from the town of Abernethy, but from a Scots surgeon, John Abernethy (1764-1831) who suggested the recipe to his local baker.

Border Tart: Variants are Eyemouth Tart and Ecclefechan Butter Tart. A shortcrust pastry flan is filled with a mixture of dried fruit, sugar, melted butter and egg. When baked it is usually coated with white water icing.

Cumnock Tart: A regional and sweet variation of the Scotch pie which is made with apples or rhubarb. It was originally made by an Ayrshire baker, Mr Stoddart, around 1920, and is now made by Bradfords of Glasgow. The recipe came to Bradfords via the founder, who was apprenticed to Mr Stoddart. It is a hand-crafted, oval, double-crust individual tart with a sugary browned surface and lightly burnt edges, and they make about 800 a week.

Glasgow Roll: A morning roll with a hard outer surface with a light and very open, well-aerated texture inside. Sometimes described as a 'chewy' roll. Specially designed as a roll for hot fillings with its hard crust and airy centre, the traditional filling used was bacon and egg. It is made with a high-gluten flour and is entirely handcrafted. The largest bakery in Glasgow makes 300,000 a night.

Kirriemuir Gingerbread: This was first made by Walter Burnett in Kirriemuir, who sold his recipe to a large plant baker in East Kilbride near Glasgow in the 1940s. It was made in this bakery until 1977, when the recipe was sold again to Bell's of Shotts, who continue to make it. It is a light-textured, dumpling-type gingerbread which is sweetly malted and lightly spiced.

Parkin: Also known as 'perkin'. The recipes vary according to the baker, but they range from thick, biscuity cakes to thin, hard biscuits. They are a light ginger-brown, with a sweet ginger flavour, and most have some oatmeal added.

Softie: This is the description for a round bun on the East Coast, the name used to distinguish it from a hard, crisp 'rowie'. It contains double the amount of sugar in a plain bap.

Square Loaf: A loaf specially designed for making 'pieces', sandwiches which fit into a square lunch box. It is also known as a 'plain' loaf (distinguished from a 'pan' loaf which used to be considered a posher version since it was made in a tin, and became used as a description for those who had aspirations above their station). It is also known as 'batch bread': a system of baking bread when the loaves are tightly packed on a tray and rise upwards rather than outwards, which gives them their tall shape. It is the half slice which is square.

Water Biscuit: A thick circular biscuit which is made in Orkney, they are irregular cream to pale golden, blistered in places with gold-brown bubbles and dotted with small holes. They have a rich, nutty flavour and are very crisp with a flaky texture. Developed from the ship's biscuit, they were originally used as bread substitutes in remote areas.

Sweeties

The ecstasy of acquiring a 'Sugar Hert', a handful of 'Curly Murlies' or a bottle of 'Treacle Ale' and a slab of 'Gingerbread' is impossible to describe.

G.M. Martin, *Dundee Worthies*, 1934.

Sugar Hearts were, as you might imagine, fondant shapes, but the Curly Murlies were a more specialised Angus delicacy. They are described by Martin as 'mixed sweets of various shapes and sizes of the texture of pandrops although the Curly Murlie proper had a rather gnarled exterior. They were formed on a seed or other foundation such as a carvie [caraway], clove or almond. The nucleus of the Curly Murlie proper was probably aniseed. It was about the size of a large pea. These sweets were popular on feeding-market days when Jock was expected to give Jenny her "market" in the form of a pockie of market sweeties or Curly Murlies.' (Murl means a crumb or fragment and pockie a paper bag.)

BASIC SUGAR BOILING PROCESS

450 g/1 lb granulated sugar
300 ml/½ pt ml water
Pinch of cream of tartar to prevent granulation

This can be done easily without professional equipment such as a sugar thermometer, since the practical test of putting a few drops of the boiling sugar into a cup of cold water will tell you exactly what stage the sugar is at. If the result is a little past the desired stage, remove the pan from the heat, add a little warm water to lower the temperature and continue.

Dissolve the sugar over a low heat in the liquid, stirring with a wooden spoon until no particles of sugar are left. To test, examine the back of the spoon for any sugar crystals. Brush the sides of the pan with water to remove any crystals.

When all is dissolved, bring gradually to the boil and simmer gently till required stage is reached.

Stages in Sugar Boiling

Smooth/Transparent Icing for crystallising purposes and fondant. The mixture begins to look syrupy. To test, dip finger in water and then very quickly into the syrup, the thumb will slide smoothly over the fingers, but the sugar will cling.

Soft ball (115-120C/235-245F) for soft caramel, candy, fudge and tablet. To test, drop a little syrup into cold water and leave for a few moments. Pick up between the finger and thumb, when it should roll into a small soft ball.

Firm or hard ball (121-130C/245-265F) for caramels, marshmallows, nougat, Edinburgh Rock and soft toffee. Test as above when the syrup should roll into a hard ball.

Small crack (135-140C/280-290F) for toffees and rock. Test as above, when the thread of syrup should break lightly.

Hard crack (150-154C/300-310F) for hard toffees, boiled sweeties and drops, pulled sugar and rock. Test as above, when the thread of syrup should break sharply.

Caramel (165C/335F upwards). When the syrup begins to discolour, turning a darker brown colour, caramel stage is reached. If it is allowed to become too dark, the taste will be bitter.

TABLET

'Taiblet for the bairns,' writes Lady Grisell Baillie in her shopping list (*circa* 1692-1733).

Slightly harder than fudge, but not chewy like toffee, tablet has a slight 'bite' to it. In its plain form it has a special flavour to it which comes from boiling sugar and milk together. Its early versions were medicinal, carrying plant remedies and sometimes bitter medicines (see p.379), though now it has many other flavourings added. The earliest Scots recipe, in Mrs McLintock (*circa* 1736), is flavoured with oranges, which at that time were taken as a 'strengthening' medicine.

800 g/1 lb 12 oz caster sugar
175 g/6 oz unsalted butter
200 ml/7 fl oz milk
1 tin condensed milk

Use a large 3 L/5-6 pt thick-based stainless steel pot.

Line an 18 x 22 cm/7 x 11 in baking tray with kitchen foil. Cover with a layer of clingfilm and place in the freezer for a few hours.

To make

Put the sugar, butter and milk into the pot and heat gently, without boiling, stirring with a wooden spoon to melt the butter and dissolve the sugar. Check the back of the wooden spoon to make sure there are no sugar crystals. Add the condensed milk and stir in. Bring up to a slow simmer. Stir continuously. This rich mixture can stick and burn very quickly. When it begins to turn golden brown, test a few drops in a cup of cold water. It should reach soft-ball stage (or use a sugar thermometer, see basic sugar-boiling process p.377). Remove from the heat, place the pan on a cool surface.

Beating, setting and marking

Beat with a wooden spoon as it cools, when it will change in texture from smooth and silky to thicker and grainy. This can take several minutes or longer. Check the back of the spoon for signs of texture change. The mixture will begin to thicken as it grains. It should be poured at this point before it becomes too thick, when it will turn into fudge rather than tablet. Add flavourings at this point. Pour into tin, level top and leave to cool.

When cold, cover with a layer of clingfilm and put in freezer for 1½ hours. Remove from freezer, remove clingfilm, turn out of the tin onto a work surface. Take off foil and clingfilm. Leave for 30 minutes. Score the underside with the heel of a chopping knife about 3 mm/1/8 in deep to divide into two halves. Break along the cut. Continue scoring and breaking into preferred sizes. Store, tightly wrapped in clingfilm in an airtight tin.

Flavourings and colourings

Orange – Add **fresh orange juice** instead of milk.

Vanilla and Walnut – mix in **2-3 drops of vanilla essence** and **50 g/2 oz finely chopped walnuts** when the sugar is removed from the heat.

Cinnamon – Add **1 teaspoon cinnamon oil** before pouring.

Ginger – Add **50 g/2 oz chopped preserved ginger** before pouring.

Peppermint – Add **2-3 drops of peppermint oil** before pouring.

Fruit and Nut – Add **50 g/2 oz finely chopped nuts** and **50 g/2 oz dried fruit** before pouring.

'TOFFY FOR COUGHS'

From *The Cookery Book of Lady Clark of Tillypronie*, 1909

125 g/4 oz butter
125 g/4 oz black treacle
450 g/1 lb granulated sugar
1 teaspoon ground ginger
1 teaspoon grated lemon zest

To make

Melt the butter and treacle together in a pan, stir and add the sugar. Continue till the sugar dissolves. Increase the heat gradually until it simmers. Keep stirring. Test by putting a few drops in a cup of cold water when it should form a firm ball. (Or use a sugar thermometer, see basic sugar boiling, p.377.) Remove from the heat and add the lemon and ginger. Pour out very thinly into a buttered baking tin. Crack into pieces when cold. Store in an airtight tin.

Traditional Scottish Sweeties Past and Present

Almond Cake: a rich, buttery, toffee mixture, poured into a tin which has a thick layer of flaked almonds on the base. A version of this is made in Orkney.

Barley Sugar: usually made into a twisted stick of hard rock, flavoured with barley water and liquorice.

Berwick Cockles: peppermint flavoured boilings, white with pink strips and shaped like the cockle shells which used to be fished up near Tweedmouth harbour. Sold in tins.

Bon-Bons: strips of candied lemon or orange peel which are dipped into barley sugar.

Black Man: treacle toffee. Also known as **Treacle Gundy**.

Black Striped Balls: black and white striped balls of hard toffee with a strong peppermint flavour.

Butterscotch: a hard boiling with a buttery flavour. Made as a quality sweetie by Keillers in Dundee, shaped into a rectangular shape and wrapped in silver foil with a dent in the middle where it broke into two pieces. Packaged in cigarette-sized packets.

Cheugh Jeans: chewy (cheugh) toffee which was made in different flavours – clove, cinnamon, peppermint, ginger or chocolate.

Coltart's Candy: pronounced Coolter, and made famous by the song which the sweetie man sang as he travelled round the country selling his wares. The candy was aniseed-flavoured, but the recipe and the custom were lost when Coltart died, greatly lamented, in 1890.

Claggum or **Clack**: made with treacle and water, boiled till the soft-ball stage and then pulled into long sticks of rock.

Curly Andra: a white coral-like sweet with a coriander seed in the centre. The name comes from the Scots corruption of coriander which is 'curryander'.

Curly Murlies (see p. 377) also known as **Curly Doddies**.

Edinburgh Rock: not the customary solid stick with letters down the centre, but a light, pastel-coloured, sugary confection, delicately flavoured. It was discovered by accident when Alexander Fergusson, popularly known as Sweetie Sandy, came across a piece of confectionery which he had overlooked and left lying for several months. He became one of Edinburgh's most successful confectioners in the nineteenth century and the rock is now exported all over the world.

Glessie: 'But the glessy! Who that ever tasted it can forget the stick of sheeny, golden rock, which stretched while you were eating it to gossamer threads of silver glistening like cobwebs in the sun.' *Scots Magazine*, 1925.

Gundy: toffee, also an aniseed or cinnamon-flavoured hard boiling.

Hawick Balls: cinnamon-flavoured hard toffee with a subtle hint of mint.

Helensburgh Toffee: more of a fudge than a toffee, it has a rich, creamy flavour which comes from the use of condensed milk.

Horehound Boilings: well-loved by Dundonian jute workers who sucked them to relieve their dry throats from the jute dust in the factories. Still a popular sore-throat boiling.

Jeddart Snails: dark-brown toffees, mildly peppermint-flavoured. The name and shape were given to them by a French prisoner-of-war from Napoleon's army, who made them for a Jedburgh baker.

Lettered Rock: long sticks of hard rock with a strong peppermint flavour, bright pink on the outside, white in the middle with red letters down the middle spelling the name of the appropriate town.

Mealie Candy: a hard boiling flavoured with treacle and ginger and with oatmeal added.

Moffat Toffee: a hard toffee, amber and gold striped, with a sherbet-like tangy centre. It is now made commercially by a local Moffat family who have been making toffee for generations. One of its early names was Moffat Whirlies. The Moffat Toffee Shop in the town is Mecca for sweetie lovers.

Oddfellows: soft lozenges which are made in delicate colours and aromatic flavours such as cinnamon, clove and rose geranium. Made originally by Wishaw confectioners..

Pan Drops: mint imperials, or **Granny Sookers**. The sweetie grannies slipped to young children in church to get them through the minister's sermon.

Soor Plooms: originated in the Borders where they were made to celebrate an incident in local history when a band of English marauders were surprised and overcome while eating unripe plums. They are round, bright-green balls with an acid, astringent tang.

Starrie Rock: available from the Star Rock shop in the Roods in Kirriemuir, Angus. It was made originally by a stone mason who was blinded in 1833. Sticks are short and thin, slightly chewy and with a delectable buttery flavour. (They also make excellent horehound boilings here.)

Sugar-ally-water: liquorice water. Hard block liquorice was chipped into small pieces and mixed with water in a lemonade bottle. It was then shaken every day until it dissolved. It could take up to a week as it improved in flavour.

Sugar-bools: small round sugar plums like marbles.

Sugar-hearts: pink, heart-shaped fondants.

PRESERVES

For fifteen shillings a quarter Mrs McIver taught cookery, preserving and pickling. In her earlier . . . days she sold preserved cherries and raspberries, and also 'plumb-cake'.
Alexander Law, *Education in Edinburgh in the Eighteenth Century*, 1965.

Marmalade

To his delight Henry VIII was given a 'box of Marmalade' as a present in 1524. It was a box of preserved quinces, however, which so pleased the greedy Henry, and not marmalade as we know it today. The first mention of this confection is in port records at the end of the 1400s. The name, it seems, came from Spain and Portugal, where quinces were known as 'Marmelos'. In English this became 'marmalade' and was used to describe any kind of thick preserved fruit. Marmalades of cherries, plums and apricots were common. The first English recipes appear in the 1600s, among them one using oranges by Sir Kenelm Digby (*The Cook's Oracle*, 1602-1665) after his travels in Italy and Spain.

The Scottish contribution to marmalade's history began in a small way in a family grocer's shop in Dundee, run by Janet Keiller, whose husband kept a sharp eye on the cargos from around the world coming into the nearby Dundee docks. One day he picked up a shipment of bitter Spanish Seville oranges and Janet began her experiments with marmalade.

She had an idea that – instead of making it into a solid paste in the old way – she would make a jelly-type marmalade with 'chips' (chopped up orange peel) set in it. This greatly increased the volume produced as well as the profit. It also had an excellent flavour and was much a better 'spread' on toast or bread than the old version.

In 1797 the Keillers built their first marmalade factory in Dundee, and throughout most of the nineteenth century they continued to perfect the process. They visited the Seville orange growers in Spain to ensure they got the very best quality Seville oranges. As in all their other products, their aim was to make the best marmalade.

In the late 1800s, the Keiller family lost control of the company, and though the name and the marmalade survived into the next century, it was eventually a victim of takeover and asset-stripping by a multinational confectionery company. The Albert Museum in Dundee has a rich archive of Keiller memorabilia, and the history of the family has been researched and written by W.M. Mathew in *Keiller's of Dundee: The Rise of the Marmalade Dynasty* (Abertay History Society 1998).

CHIP MARMALADE

This is a traditional chip marmalade, of the Keiller brand, which can be varied according to taste by the amount of more bitter pith added. The pips are the main source of pectin (gelling material) in oranges and should be put in a bag and boiled with the rest of the oranges and sugar.

900 g/2 lb Seville oranges
900 g/2 lb jam preserving sugar
2 lemons

Preparing the fruit

Wash the oranges well and put in the preserving pan. Pour over boiling water to cover. Cover with a heavy plate to keep the fruit submerged. Simmer until the fruit softens. Keep topping up with boiling water so the fruit is always covered. It will take between one and two hours.

When cool, cut in half, remove the pulp with a spoon and put into a bowl. Cut up the skins into thick or thin chips. Put the pulp through a sieve and press through some or all. More will make a thicker marmalade with more of a tang. Extract the pips and put into a muslin bag and tie up.

Finishing the marmalade

Put the chips and pulp into the water the fruit was boiled in. Measure and add **450 g/1 lb preserving sugar** for every 600 ml/1 pt. Put into the pan with the zest and juice of the lemons. Bring to the boil and simmer till set.

Testing for a set

Test by putting a teaspoonful on a chilled saucer and placing in the deep-freeze compartment for a few minutes to chill and give a quick result. The surface should set and crinkle when pushed with the finger. Do not boil the marmalade too vigorously while the test is being made, otherwise the setting point may be missed.

Finishing

Remove from the heat, skim with a slotted spoon, and leave

for ten minutes to cool before potting – this prevents the chips sinking. Pour into clean hot jars. Seal and cover. Or leave a space at the top of the jar and add one or two tablespoonfuls of spirits or liqueurs (whisky, rum, brandy, Glayva or Drambuie). This both flavours and seals the marmalade, preventing mould developing on top.

FORTINGALL MARMALADE

During the time I was the lessee of the Fortingall Hotel, about thirty-four years, we always made our own Orange Marmalade, rising at the end to a quarter of a ton every spring.

William 'Hep' Heptinstall, *Gourmet Recipes from a Highland Hotel*, 1967.

This is a less time-consuming recipe than the previous one, since a processor is used to cut the skins and pulp. It is also a sweeter marmalade.

1.8 kg/4 lb Seville oranges
Juice of 4 lemons
5 L/9 pts water
1.8 kg/9 lb preserving sugar

The day before

Halve the oranges and squeeze out the juice. Soak the pips in 600 ml/1 pt water. Shred the orange skins on the slicing disc of the food processor and soak them in the remainder of the water.

Making the marmalade

Put the shredded peel with the water on to boil, and when soft (1-2 hours) add the sugar, orange and lemon juice and the water in which the pips have been soaking. Boil to 218F/105C; test for a set. Pot, seal and cover.

RASPBERRY OR TAYBERRY JAM

The full, fresh raspberry tang is preserved in this non-cooked jam which is thickened with liquid pectin, then deep-frozen. It can be stored in the refrigerator for several weeks. If the fruit is very ripe it may not set well, but then it becomes a runny 'conserve' for pouring over ice creams, hot pancakes etc (see p.342).

450 g/1 lb fruit
490 g/1 lb 4 oz caster sugar
2 tablespoons lemon juice
125 ml/4 fl oz liquid pectin

To make

Put the fruit into a bowl with the sugar and lemon juice and stir. Leave overnight, when the sugar will have dissolved. Add the pectin and mix in well. Ladle into small plastic containers. Leave to set. Cover with lids and put into the freezing compartment if you want to store for some time. Otherwise it can be kept in the refrigerator for a month or two, but will not keep for more than about two weeks at room temperature.

STRAWBERRY JAM

Strawberries lack both pectin and acid, so both have to be added to make the jam set. To keep the berries whole, it is better to use small fruit rather than large.

1.3 kg/3 lb strawberries
1.3 kg/3 lb preserving sugar
250 ml/8 fl oz liquid pectin
2 tablespoons lemon juice

Makes 2.2 kg/5 lb

To make

Put the fruit and lemon juice into a preserving pan and add the sugar. Heat gently till all the sugar is dissolved. Add the pectin and bring to the boil. Boil rapidly till the setting point is reached (see marmalade recipe p.386 for how to test). Remove from the heat. Skim with a slotted spoon and leave to settle for ten minutes. Stir before pouring into hot jars, seal and cover.

ROWAN JELLY

With its sharp, astringent tang, this is perfect with game roasts as well as lamb and mutton. For a more intense rowan flavour use fewer cooking apples. Crab apples can be used but will provide a lot of pectin, so should be mixed with other apples or the jelly will be too solid.

1 kg/2 lb 4 oz slightly under-ripe rowan berries
1 kg/2 lb 4 oz unpeeled cooking apples, coarsely chopped
Preserving sugar

To make

Remove stalks from the rowan berries. Put into pan with the apples and just enough water to cover and bring to the boil. Simmer the fruit till soft and put into a preserving bag or muslin to drip overnight. Measure the juice and add **450 g/1 lb of sugar** to every **600 ml/1 pt liquid**. Put into the pan and bring to the boil, simmer till set (see marmalade recipe p.386 for how to test for a set). Pot, seal and cover.

HERB JELLY

This apple-based jelly can be flavoured with fresh herbs such as mint or tarragon. Some whole cinnamon sticks can also be added for extra flavour. Crab apples can be used but will provide a lot of pectin, so should be mixed with other apples or the jelly will be too solid.

1.3 kg/3 lb cooking, crab or eating apples, coarsely chopped
4 oz/125 g fresh herbs or 3-4 whole cinnamon sticks
Water
Sugar

To make

Place the coarsely chopped apples in a pan. Cover with water and cook till soft and pulpy. Pour into a jelly bag and drip overnight without squeezing.

Measure juice and weigh out **450 g/1 lb sugar** to each **600 ml/1 pt juice**. Stir over a low heat till the sugar is dissolved. Add the fresh herbs tied in a muslin bag, and/or 3-4 whole cinnamon sticks. Bring to the boil and simmer till set (see marmalade recipe, p.386, for how to test for a set). Remove from the heat and allow to stand for about 5 minutes. Add one or two whole herb leaves to each of the pots once they have cooled, or a 1-in piece of cinnamon. Pot, cover and seal.

SPICED DAMSONS

This remarkable preserve has a mulled wine flavour and deep crimson colour, which enlivens both cold meats and hot roasts, particularly game.

600 ml/1 pt full-bodied red wine
900 g/2 lb ripe damsons
2 x 10 cm/4 in sticks cinnamon
150 g/5 oz sugar

To make

Dissolve the sugar in the wine, add the cinnamon and bring to the boil for 1 minute. Add the damsons and simmer until they are just soft. Pack the damsons into jars. Chop the cinnamon into small pieces and put into the jars. Pour over the syrup. Seal with a lid.

APPLE CHUTNEY

The taste and aroma of this chutney depends on a subtle blending of spices, cinnamon, cloves and ginger with the sharp-sweet tang of cooking apples. Orange juice, honey and cider vinegar, yet more sweet-sour notes.

675 g/1½ lb cooking apples, coarsely chopped
1 tablespoon fresh ginger root, grated
125 ml/4 fl oz orange juice
1 teaspoon ground cinnamon
½ teaspoon ground cloves
250 ml/8 fl oz honey – to taste
250 ml/8 fl oz cider vinegar
Salt

Bring to the boil and simmer uncovered, stirring occasionally, for about 45-50 minutes. Cool a little, pot, cover and store.

RAISIN CHUTNEY

Plump raisins, cooked slowly in tomatoes, blended with cinnamon and cloves, make this characterful chutney which combines well with cold meats and game, as well as mature hard cheeses and pickled onions.

50 g/2 oz butter
450 g/1 lb large raisins
2 tins chopped tomatoes

300 ml/½ pt water
4 whole cloves
2 sticks cinnamon
Salt and ground black pepper to taste
150 g/5 oz brown sugar
5 tablespoons cider or wine vinegar

To make

Melt the butter in a large wide pan and add the raisins. Sauté the raisins for a few minutes, then add the tomatoes, water, cloves, cinnamon, salt and pepper. Cook uncovered for about 1 hour, stirring occasionally, till very thick.

Add the brown sugar and cider or wine vinegar.

Mix through, simmer for a few minutes. Taste for flavour. Remove cinnamon, pot, cover and seal.

STORE MUSTARD

A Scandinavian recipe which makes a rich, glossy and slightly sweet mustard, which they serve with dill-cured salmon.

1 x 113 g/4 oz tin Colman's mustard
Same volume of caster sugar and double cream
½ teaspoon 00 pasta or potato flour
2 eggs, beaten
1 tablespoon balsamic vinegar

To make

Empty the contents of the mustard tin into a pan. Then fill up the tin with sugar and empty into the pan. Add flour and mix together. Fill the tin with cream and add to the pan with the eggs. Beat with a whisk till smooth and cook gently over a low heat, stirring all the time till it thickens. This can be done in a double boiler. When cold, stir in the vinegar and pour into pots. Cover and seal.

PICKLE VINEGAR

The outstanding flavour of this vinegar is dependent on the many spices and flavourings – plus a long roasting in the summer sun.

4 L/7 pts white wine vinegar
150 g/5 oz black mustard seeds
50 g/2 oz fresh ginger root
75 g/3 oz whole allspice
15 g/½ oz cloves
50 g/2 oz black peppercorns
15 g/½ oz celery seeds
675 g/1½ lb brown sugar
40 g/1¾ oz grated horseradish
1 head garlic
1½ sliced lemons

To make

Combine all the ingredients in a large glass jar and leave on a sunny window ledge all summer, or at least four months. Strain and pour over parboiled or raw fruits and vegetables or use in salad dressings.

9: CULINARY INTERCHANGE

> *... For there is much, not only in the actual cookery but also in the Domestic Economy of our ingenious neighbours, worthy of profound attention. In the hope that the foreign graces transplanted into this volume may considerably enhance its value to the practical cook, and in the belief that a culinary system superior to either the French or the English, may be drawn from the combined excellencies of both countries.*
>
> Meg Dods, *Cook and Housewife's Manual*, 1826.

Since the Auld Alliance with France in medieval times there has been a lively interest in adapting, refining and developing the 'excellencies' of food from other countries. Long established food traditions, such as broths and baking, were improved in the early days by culinary interchange between the Scots and the French. Over the years, people from diverse cultures – Scandinavians, Irish, Italians, Indians, Chinese, Americans, English, Jews and many others – have brought new customs which have mostly enriched the native food culture.

When the Jewish Hofman family, fleeing the Russian pogroms in the early 1900s, moved to Lerwick, they became the first Jewish-Shetlanders. The cultural divide could not have been greater. But their Jewish tradition of home-cooking and hospitality was based on years of living in ghettos, where there were always good things to eat at home despite the misery outside. They carried this with them wherever they went, and in Shetland formed strong relationships through an exchange of food cultures, which is recalled by Ethel Hofman (third generation Jewish-Shetlander) in her book *Mackerel at Midnight* (2006).

Similar exchanges have occurred as Italians, Indians, Pakistanis, Bangladeshis and Chinese settled in the twentieth century, each finding a way to cook in their own style, and in the process to create an appetite for some features of their food culture among native Scots. Many others have followed from many countries. Their long-term influence has yet to be discovered. Will curried haggis become more popular than the native version? I don't know. But there is certainly no lack of enthusiasm for culinary interchange among those Asian-Scots who have made Scotland their home, as they devise their own tartan, dress up in kilts and, of course, eat curried haggis on Burns Night.

The Auld Alliance with France

One of the most important influences on the Scots kitchen came from France. This began around the end of the 1200s, when England, after subduing Wales and much of Ireland, turned its expansionist plans towards Scotland and France, prompting the Scottish and French kings to sign a pact against the English in 1295. Known as the Auld Alliance, it lasted for over three centuries, during which time the two countries became close both politically and culturally. There was much royal intermarriage. A district of Edinburgh became known as Little France. French craftsmen built many Scottish palaces and churches. And though the alliance ended without acrimony with the Scottish Reformation in 1560, the friendship and cultural interchange between Scotland and France has continued.

Early evidence of French influences can be seen in a series of leatherbound household books written between 1671 and 1707 by John Foulis of Ravelston, a typical Lowland laird farming a modest estate of rolling fields on the north east shoulder of Corstorphine Hill just outside Edinburgh, which was still surrounded by a medieval wall with a city guard. Sitting at his desk each day to write his expenses, he adds other information, revealing a lively, generous, fun-loving, uninhibited *bon viveur* who visits Leith to buy large quantities of French wine and brandy.

French claret has been described as the 'lifeblood of the Auld Alliance' and was drunk by all classes. When shipments arrived at Leith, a hogshead was put on a cart and trundled up into the town, where a large jug was filled for sixpence. French wine drinking became a badge of Scots identity during many centuries, while many entrepreneurial Scots involved in the wine trade flourished. Families in the trade became legends. Even today, the port of Leith retains its position as a wine importer, with many of the old buildings still standing which would have been familiar to John Foulis on his many trips there for supplies of French wine and brandy.

In the Foulis kitchen there is another sign of French influence when his cook, Marie, concocts a 'strong broth' in her large black cauldron hanging over the open fire. It's an intensely flavoured potful of meat, vegetables and herbs which is not the finished broth but a stockpot replica of the French 'pot au feu'. The meat is removed. Then the well-flavoured liquid is used to add character to a large repertoire of other dishes including soups and broths.

For Scots cooks, it's an important lesson which will affect the development of their food culture in the years which follow. Classic Scotch Broth, Cock-a-leekie, Cullen Skink, Hotch Potch and others have yet to be invented. But when they are, the guiding principle to their success is the foundation of an aromatic 'strong broth' or 'pot au feu'. Evidence of this are the 'strong broth' recipes which appear in all the early cookery books and manuscripts of the time, such as those of Martha Brown in Ayr (1710), Lady Castlehill at Cambusnethan (1712) and Mrs McLintock in Glasgow (1736). The full influence of nearly three centuries of liaison with the French on Scotland's early food culture has never properly been unravelled, but it is likely to have changed the course of other Scottish food traditions, besides traditional broths.

French 'haute cuisine'

The infiltration of French 'haute cuisine', which happened when

French chefs were employed in upper class and royal kitchens in the early 1800s, was a less positive culinary interchange. Fleeing France after the Revolution in 1789, they were welcomed in Britain. Queen Victoria staffed her kitchens with French chefs. Before long they were writing cookery books based on a French system of 'haute cuisine'. In Scotland, the Duke of Buccleuch's kitchen was managed, in the latter part of the eighteenth century, by Joseph Florence, a French chef.

When the railways opened up the country to travel in the second half of the 1800s, and hotels became essential at every station, it was this French system of kitchen organisation which prevailed and a menu written in French replaced the old British 'bill of fare'. But a wholesale importation of another country's cooking style, to the point that British menus are written in a foreign language, is not an interchange.

Till well into the second half of the twentieth century, French 'haute cuisine' and French-written menus prevailed in all quality hotels throughout Britain. The least positive effect of this largely extravagant style of cooking, which depended on rich saucing and expensive foreign ingredients – truffles, foie gras, caviar etc – was a lack of pride in native dishes, local foods, distinctive varieties of fruits and vegetables and artisan skills. The backlash was slow to take off, but now it has gathered momentum. This is Scotland (and Britain), not France.

East Coast Fishwife's Norse Heritage

While the medieval Scots-French alliance developed out of friendship, the relationship between the Scots and the Vikings began with invasion, pillage and destruction. The outermost groups of Scottish islands – Shetland, Orkney and the Hebrides – were ruled by Norway from the mid-800s. Although the pagan invaders from the north came to conquer, they eventually settled peaceably and even embraced the Christian church. Recent evidence of their burial grounds proves that they brought women with them on their raids, with the intention of settling.

The strength of the Vikings was their skill as seamen and their ability to harvest the seas. They introduced more advanced boat-building skills and fishing techniques to the less adventurous Scots. The Viking women also brought highly developed skills of fish preservation to the areas around the Scottish coast where they settled. Early Scots already knew how to dry fish with salt and smoke them in the rising smoke from the open hearth fire, but the Vikings had more advanced developments of this too.

Perched on a cliff-top on the east coast of Scotland, just north of Arbroath in the village of Auchmithie, some families – bearing Viking names such as Spink – settled and built houses. Fish was plentiful as they continued their adventurous harvesting of the seas. Gathering bait was women's and children's work. Women and men together baited the line. The men fished while the women packed their wicker creels with fresh fish and headed off to sell it in the neighbouring countryside.

This fishwife – descendent of Vikings – was an intriguing character in her distinctive outfit: a white mutch (bonnet) tied under her chin, starched and ironed frills framing her brown, weatherbeaten face; stout knee-high leather boots; black woollen stockings; a navy skirt with an apron; a blouse and a woolly cardigan; and on cold days a thick woollen shawl.

Her method of preserving the surplus fish produced a hot-smoked, cooked fish quite unlike the hard salted variety which was the norm. It was a whole, deheaded fish, lightly salted, a dark coppery colour on the outside with light, creamy, cooked flesh inside. It was known as an Auchmithie lucken (closed) to distinguish it from the more common open-salted fish. As the railways began to make accessible a wider marketplace, its fame spread and demand grew.

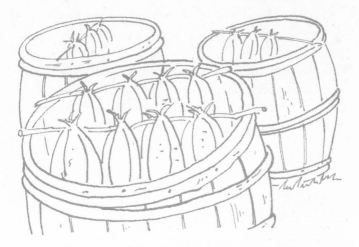

By the closing years of the 1800s, Auchmithie fisher families were relocating to nearby Arbroath, a larger port where the opportunities to expand were better. Gradually, more families transferred to the area at the Fit o' the Toon, replacing their old half barrels with a square brick pit in their back gardens but continuing to call it 'the barrel'. So the old Auchmithie lucken became an Arbroath smokie. (An Arbroath native is commonly known as a 'smokie'.)

Descendents of the Vikings have continued to make the cure, but not just in the Fit o' the Toon. A new angle on its promotion has been developed by Iain Spink, who has become a popular feature at farmers' markets and food fairs setting up the old wooden barrel and lighting a fire in it to smoke the fish in the old way. He is easy to find – just follow the wafting smokie aroma. And there is nothing to beat a smokie 'hot off the barrel'.

The Arbroath smokie has now received the distinction of a preservation order in the form of a PGI (Protected Geographical Indication) from the EU. Its character remains, protected and preserved by law from unscrupulous opportunists in the food industry. Preserved, too, as an ancient symbol of culinary interchange between the Vikings and their adopted homeland.

Italian Peasants Add Mediterranean Colour to the National Diet

While the French came in friendship, and the Vikings to make war, the Italians came in abject poverty but bringing with them all the flavours of the warm Mediterranean to cold Scotland. The first wave set out on the long walk to Scotland around the 1860s when they left their mountain villages, which could no longer support them and their families.

The story of poverty-stricken peasant families finding a new home in Scotland is one of colossal struggle, enormous sacrifice and great love of their native food culture. In their remote mountain villages they were self-sufficient: farming sheep to make pecorino and ricotta cheese with ewes' milk; keeping a pig to use up scraps and the by-products of the cheesemaking; growing grain to make polenta; olives to press for olive oil; grapes to make into wine; and tomatoes, garlic, rosemary, thyme and oregano to flavour everything. There was no running water, no electricity, no telephone, no post office and no shops.

Father was usually the first to leave this peasant lifestyle when there was no longer enough food to feed the family. A boat trip across the channel was the only transport he could afford. The rest of the journey was done on foot, hitching lifts when he could, and he arrived in Scotland knowing no English and barely able to write his name. But he had come to join others who had already made the trip. And he found friendship among them – and among the Scots too, once he had mastered the language. Besides, there was a ready market for the ice cream which he sold from a barrow in summertime as he moved about, and in wintertime there was the new invention of potatoes cut into thick fingers which he fried in a deep pan of oil and sold in pokes from a stall in the market. With hard work he could make enough to save some money.

Soon, he would go back for his family, piling the family belongings onto a barrow and wheeling it back to Scotland. Then he set up on his own. Business flourished. There was always a new town or village ready to welcome his cooling cones of ice cream in summer and warming pokes of fried chips in winter.

Around the turn of the century, some Italians became ice-cream café owners. Others bought new deep-frying equipment and set up as fish and chip shops since, by this time, fish had joined up with chips to make a complete meal. Wonderfully fresh fish was being landed by the fishing boats every morning. Potatoes were in plentiful supply from local farmers, and soon no Scottish town was without its Italian 'chippie'. The other important culinary interchange was when some Italian families in city centres saw the opportunity of importing the essential ingredients of their peasant culture which they missed so much, and needed so badly, to continue making their fresh, simple Italian dishes, and the Italian grocer hit the high street. Pasta, olive oil, pecorino cheese, tins of tomatoes and garlic became more readily available to the Italian Scots, and soon native Scots were hooked on these flavourful Mediterranean ingredients.

Transformed in his lifetime from poor Italian peasant into prosperous Italian/Scots businessman, some of the Italian immigrant's family went on to become owners of luxurious ice-cream parlours with mirrored walls, discreet partitions and leather seats. However, not all went smoothly for the ambitious Italian families who were now capturing the prosperous middle-class market in industrial cities such as Glasgow. Some native Scottish traders resented this invasion of their territory. There was religious prejudice too. Xenophobic Presbyterian sects, such as the United Free Church, held a conference in 1907 on 'Ice Cream Hells', claiming they were a moral threat to the people.

But others supported the Italian enterprise. Influential in changing attitudes was A. J. Cronin, one of the most popular novelists of the day, who took his middle-class heroine, Mary, into an Italian ice cream café and did much to improve their image:

He [the hero Denis] took her arm firmly and led her a few doors down the street, then, before she realised it and could think even to resist, he had drawn her inside the cream-coloured doors of Bertorelli's café. She paled with apprehension, feeling that she had finally passed the limits of respectability . . . looking reproachfully into Denis' smiling face, in a shocked tone she gasped,

'Oh Denis, how could you?'

Yet as she looked round the clean, empty shop, with its rows of marble-topped tables, its small scintillating mirrors and brightly papered walls, while she allowed herself to be guided to one of the plush stalls that appeared exactly like her pew in church, she felt curiously surprised, as if she had expected to find a sordid den suited appropriately to the debauched revels that must . . . inevitably be associated with a place like this.

By the 1930s, the so-called 'Ice-cream Hells' had morphed into sophisticated art deco cafés with low wicker chairs and delectable sundaes arriving in tall glasses with glitter sticks and swirls of cream on top. No problems of class prejudice here for Cronin's Mary, or for any child of the first half of the twentieth century living within walking distance of an Italian café when, in these days before fridges, they would be sent with the largest jug in the house to have it filled up with scoops of vanilla ice by their neighbourhood 'Tally'. While the rest of Europe regarded Italian *gelati* as a luxury, for Scots of this generation it was as common as mince and tatties.

Thus diverse cultures mix and mingle to everyone's benefit. But in addition to the specific foods and dishes brought by the Italian peasants and their descendants, they also brought their love of the simple pleasures of seasonal foods, the importance of home cooking and the bonding value of eating together in friendship. Scots also have a history of an impoverished peasantry and know the value of these traditions, thus making a strong culinary bond between the two countries which survives into the fifth generation, to the advantage of both.

Recipes from Diverse Food Cultures

ITALIAN

O RAGU DI MAMA

Italian poet, Eduardo de Fillipo (1900-1984), wrote a poem with this title to celebrate the cooking women of Italy. A ragu, he maintained, should never be described as just a 'meat and tomato stew'. It is a culinary system which provides many meals for many people, usually throughout the weekend. Friday is the shopping and cooking day. Saturday and Sunday there is meat – pork, meatballs and sausages – for eating with vegetables, while the constant supply of tomato sauce for pasta and pizzas means that mama can put her feet up.

50 g/2 oz dried mushrooms
4 tablespoons oil
250 g/9 oz streaky bacon, finely chopped
4-5 large onions, finely chopped
2-3 stalks celery, chopped
4 carrots, sliced thinly
2 tablespoons tomato puree
6 tins chopped tomatoes
1 tablespoon brown sugar
1 tablespoon wine vinegar
1 large head of garlic, crushed
Herbs: parsley, bay leaf, thyme, fennel, oregano, wild garlic
    (a good handful of stalks, leaves, flowers, depending on
    season) wound together with strong thread

1-2 kg/2¼ – 4½ lb fresh pork, preferably on the bone
Water to cover
Salt
Ground black pepper or cayenne pepper to taste
For the meatballs (optional):
500 g/1 lb 2 oz minced beef
1 egg
125 g/4 oz breadcrumbs
1 onion, finely chopped
2 tablespoons grated parmesan
2 tablespoons oil
250 g/9 oz sausages
handful of fresh basil

To make

Pour some boiling water over the dried mushrooms to reconstitute and leave for 30 minutes. Remove and chop finely. Reserve cooking liquor. Put one tablespoon of oil in a very large pot over a medium heat and when hot add the bacon. Cook till crisp. Add the remainder of the oil and when hot add the onions. Cook till soft and transparent. Add celery and carrot and cook for about five minutes, stirring frequently over a low heat. Add the tomato puree, stir and cook for another few minutes before adding the mushrooms and their liquid, tinned tomatoes, sugar, vinegar, salt, garlic, the bundle of herbs and pork. Add water to just cover the pork.

Bring up to a gentle simmer, cover and simmer very gently till the meat is tender, stirring occasionally. The time will depend on the cut, a shoulder joint taking longer than a tenderer cut of leg.

Remove the meat and serve separately or cut up and return to the ragu. Taste and season the ragu, adding ground pepper and/or cayenne for more heat. Adjust sweet/sour balance by adding more sugar or vinegar.

To make the meatballs

Mix the mince, eggs, breadcrumbs, onion, parmesan, salt and pepper in a bowl to a stiff consistency. Roll into small balls the size of an egg. Heat the oil in a frying pan and add the meatballs and/or sausages. Fry on all sides until lightly browned. Add to the ragu. Season, add basil and serve with pasta or polenta.

Vegetarian ragu

Omit the meat and add extra celery, carrots and mushrooms, plus 2 tins of cooked haricot or other beans.

FRENCH

Faites simple, mais faites parfait.
(Make it simple, but make it perfect)
Auguste Escoffier (1846-1935)

GRATIN DAUPHINOIS
Potatoes baked in cream

Cooks in the Dauphine area, on the Alpine border of France, devised this perfect partnership of cream and potatoes, golden on top and softly melting layers of creamy potatoes underneath. It can be made with a waxy or floury potato.

750 g/1lb 10 oz waxy or floury potato (see p.248)
1-2 cloves garlic, crushed (optional)
Salt
¼ grated nutmeg
300 ml/10 fl oz milk
300 ml/10 fl oz single or double cream

4 servings

Preheat oven to 350F/180C/160Cfan/Gas 4.

Use a medium-sized, sturdy roasting tin approximately 1.75 L/3 pt capacity.

Preparing the dish

Wash and slice potatoes wafer-thin. Or use the food-processor slicing disc and whizz. Put the sliced potatoes and crushed garlic into the roasting tin – it should be about two-thirds full. Season with salt and nutmeg. Pour in milk and cream. Place tin on a medium heat and heat gently till the milk/cream just begins to simmer. Cook for a few minutes. Keep the potatoes moving so they don't stick and burn.

Baking

Put into oven and bake for about 45 minutes or until the potatoes are soft and have absorbed all the milk and the cream has formed a golden crust on top. Serve.

TARTE TATIN

This simple, but ingenious, solution to soggy pastry in the base of a fruit tart is to cook the pastry on top of the fruit then reverse it. The method was devised by restaurateur Mademoiselle Tatin, who gave her name to the tart. According to Monet, the French painter who often lunched at Mlle Tatin's restaurant, she used firm-textured Egremont Russet apples, a variety he had planted in his own garden to make his favourite tart.

40 g/1½ oz unsalted butter
85 g/3 oz caster sugar
3 large firm-fleshed eating apples, Egremont russet or Cox's Pippins
250 g/9 oz puff pastry

20-23 cm/8-9 in shallow metal frying or sauté pan with a thick base, or Tatin tin which can be put on the stove and in the oven.

Preheat oven to 400F/200C/180Cfan/Gas 6.

To prepare the apples and pastry

Peel, quarter and core apples a few hours before cooking. Leave uncovered to dry out. They will turn brown but will be browned anyway in the cooking. Roll out the pastry to a round 20-23 cm/8-9 in. Prick all over with the point of a sharp knife and chill for a few hours in the fridge.

To caramelise the apples

Slice the butter thinly and put in the base of the tart tin. Sprinkle over sugar. Press apples, core side up, on top, arranging them in circles. Place pan over a medium to low heat. When the butter begins to melt shake the pan gently so the butter and sugar dissolve and mix together. Cook the apples in the sugar and butter slowly till they are just slightly softened. It may take 10-15 minutes. Turn down the heat if the sugar is caramelising too quickly. When the apples are beginning to soften and the sugar is a rich brown caramel colour, remove from the heat.

To bake pastry and serve

Place the pastry on top and press round the edges with a fork. Bake for 20-30 minutes till the pastry is risen and browned. Turn upside down onto a round dish. If some of the caramel remains in the pan, heat the pan over a low heat and when it is melted, scrape out over the apples. Serve warm with some thick whipped cream or clotted cream.

ENGLISH

Today our Scots porridge and barley broth and scones and or-
ange marmalade are as popular south of the Tweed as are ham
and eggs, bath buns, and Yorkshire pudding in the north. But
native dishes have a habit of deteriorating on alien soil, and
despite their similarity to a casual observer, the cuisines of the
two countries remain, in many respects, curiously distinctive.
F. Marian McNeill, *The Scots Kitchen* (1929, revised 2011)

ENGLISH RIB ROAST AND YORKSHIRE PUDDING

In the oven's fierce heat, a Yorkshire pudding is expanding and
rising like a large flower opening its petals in the summer sun,
soon to be served with roast gravy. Next is the roast; the carving knife, sharpened to a keen edge, moves easily through the
crisp brown skin to where the centre of the roast rib is lean,
pink and juicy. Glistening brown potatoes and parsnips have
been roasted with it. There is more gravy plus a sauceboat of
'hot' and creamy horseradish sauce. It's a culinary masterpiece
which goes back to the earliest days of cooking. But, crucially,
to the time when a spit-roast was first cooked in front of the
fire.

Cooks, naturally keen to catch the drips from the roasting meat which had previously dripped into the fire, put a pan
underneath. And as the meat dripped its juices, 'dripping pans'
were created with a hollow in the centre, so the cook could put
in her ladle and pick up a spoonful of the 'dripping' every so
often to baste the meat. The first recorded mention of a north
of England 'dripping pudding' to be poured into the dripping
pan towards the end of the roasting time appears in 1737. The
pudding was made with a flour and milk batter, and cooked a
few inches below any kind of roasting meat. It appears ten years

later as a 'Yorkshire' pudding in a cookbook written by Hanna Glasse, who herself came from the north of England.

There are three types of rib roast of beef. The **Sirloin** is the middle section of the back. Moving towards the head, the next up is the **Wing Rib**, also known as an **English Rib Roast**. On the bone it looks like a giant cutlet and is easy to carve. Further up, nearer the head, are the **Fore Ribs**, which have arguably the best flavour with more lubricating fat, but they also have a thick 'lip' of meat and fat on the outer edge, which tends to be slightly tougher than the rest of the meat and will take longer to cook.

Boned and rolled may be easier to carve, but meat gains flavour from the bone; the bone also supports and protects the meat during the cooking and prevents it drying out and shrinking – it does not increase the cooking time. The English eat more meat on the bone than the Scots.

Allow about 250 g/9 oz per person on the bone, 175-225 g/6-8 oz off the bone.

2.5 kg/5 lb 8 oz joint
25 g/1 oz butter, melted
1 tablespoon flour
1 teaspoon ground black pepper
1 teaspoon powdered mustard
Sea salt
1-2 glasses robust red wine
stock or water for adjusting consistency of gravy
salt and ground pepper
Yorkshire Pudding:
Makes 6-8 large, 12 small
113 g/4 oz plain flour
pinch of salt
1 egg
300 ml/½ pt milk

8–10 servings with leftovers

Preheat the oven to 450F/230C/210Cfan/Gas 8.

Use a large roasting tin and a Yorkshire pudding tin; instant-read internal thermometer.

Preparing the meat

Brush the top surface and ends of the meat with melted butter. Lightly brown 1 tablespoon flour in a pan and mix with 1 teaspoon freshly ground black pepper and 1 teaspoon powdered mustard. Rub this into the buttered surface. Leave at room temperature for a few hours or overnight to absorb flavours before cooking.

Roasting

Place the meat bone-side down in a roasting tin. Sprinkle some sea salt over the fat surface. Roast for 10 minutes at the highest heat, then reduce the temperature to 400F/200C/180Cfan/Gas 6 and roast till the internal temperature reaches 54C for rare or 57C for medium rare on an instant-read thermometer. Allow a roasting time of 15 minutes per 450 g/1 lb for underdone pink meat. Remove, place on a warmed ashet or serving platter, cover with two layers of foil and leave the meat to rest for 20 minutes in a warm place, when the meat will go on cooking, increasing its internal temperature by 2C.

Making the pudding

Make up the batter in advance – at least an hour before cooking.

Sift the flour into a bowl. Add the salt and make a well in the centre. Break in the egg and add the milk. Beat to a smooth consistency. Pour 1 tablespoon of dripping or lard into each pudding tin and put into a very hot oven 450F/230C/210Cfan/Gas 8. Leave for five minutes till the fat is really hot, remove and then add the batter. Bake till the puddings are puffed and golden – 10–15 minutes for small ones.

While puddings are baking, make the gravy

Drain off some of the fat from the pan, add some robust red wine and scrape up all the residues from the pan. Simmer for a few minutes to reduce and concentrate the flavours. Now add some stock/water and continue reducing, stirring all the time. Some juices will, by now, have dripped out of the meat and should be added to the gravy. When it has a good consistency, taste and season.

Serving

In Yorkshire and other parts of the north of England the pudding is served first with gravy. The meat and vegetables follow with more gravy.

Serve with mustard (see p.392) or horseradish sauce.

To make horseradish sauce: hold the head well back to avoid irritating the eyes and grate a small piece of fresh horseradish root into the juice of half a lemon to prevent browning. Or put in a food-processor with the lemon juice and whizz. Mix with crème fraiche to the required 'hotness'.

SUSSEX POND PUDDING

This classic English steamed pudding is an inspired fusion of mellow pastry, rich buttery sauce and sharp tangy secret lemon hiding in the middle. The drama when it is opened is the buttery, lemon-scented sauce, which spills out to make the 'pond'.

For the pastry:
350 g/12 oz self-raising flour
1 level teaspoon baking powder
¼ teaspoon salt
175 g/6 oz beef suet, finely chopped
Cold water
2 L/3½ pt greased pudding basin

Filling:
200 g/7 oz butter
200 g/7 oz demerara sugar
1 large or 2 small unwaxed lemons, washed

To make

Mix all the ingredients for the pastry with water to make soft, elastic dough. Dust the work surface with flour, knead the dough lightly and roll out to a large circle which will fit into the pudding basin. Cut out a wedge about ⅓ of the circle. Lift the remaining pastry into the bowl. Press cut edges together and press evenly to fit the bowl.

Put a layer of half the butter and sugar in the base. Roll the lemon back and forward on the work surface, pressing down well to release its juices, then prick all over with a fork. Lay the lemon on top and cover with remaining butter and sugar.

Roll out the remaining pastry into a round lid for the top. Wet the top edges of the pastry in the bowl and press the pastry lid on top, sealing well. Cover with the pudding bowl lid or two layers of greaseproof paper tied on with string. Place in a pot of boiling water which comes half-way up the bowl, cover and simmer gently to steam for 3 hours.

To Serve

Turn out onto deep serving dish: an ashet is ideal but make sure there is enough room on the plate for the 'pond'. Cut up the lemon and serve a piece with each serving.

IRISH

IRISH STEW

The dish originated in the Irish cabin. In it utensils were scarce – a frying pan, a griddle, a kettle and a potato pot sometimes constituting the entire cooking apparatus. When a pig or sheep was killed at the 'big house' the griskin, spare-ribs, or scrag-end of the neck of mutton were shared with the peasants. Having limited vessels and more limited experience, the potatoes were peeled when meat was used, otherwise they were boiled in their 'jackets'; and meat, potatoes and onions were put in the pot, covered with water and all boiled to-gether. So Irish Stew was made, and without much change has remained as a popular dish to this day.

Florence Irwin, *The Cookin' Woman*, 1949.

2 tablespoons dripping or lard
500 g/1 lb 2 oz onions, sliced
1.3 kg/3 lb neck or ribs of lamb, mutton or pork
1.3 kg/3 lb potatoes, peeled
Salt and pepper
Few sprigs of thyme
2 tablespoons chopped parsley

4 servings

To make

Heat the dripping or lard over a medium heat in a large heavy-based pan. Add the onions and cook gently till soft and lightly browned. Add the meat and continue browning. Finally, add the potatoes. Cover with water and bring to the boil briefly, skim. Slice about a third of the potatoes very thinly; these will disintegrate and thicken the stew. Leave the rest in large pieces. Add the thinly sliced potatoes, salt, pepper and thyme to the meat and stir well. Cover and simmer gently till the meat is almost tender. Add the larger potatoes and continue cooking till they are soft. Taste and season. Finish with chopped parsley.

Often served in Ireland with **Pickled Red Cabbage**: Shred a large red cabbage finely, spread out on a large tray and lightly cover with salt. Leave for 2-3 days, turning daily. Drain the cabbage and pack into jars, then cover with spiced vinegar (see p.393). Put a cayenne pod and a few peppercorns into the jars, cover and seal. Ready for use in a fortnight.

Variation

Use a leftover joint, removing all meat from the bones. Cover the bones with water and simmer for about 2 hours to make a stock. Strain. Prepare the potatoes and onions as above and add to the stock, cook till tender then add the cooked meat thinly sliced and heat through.

Amongst half a dozen families in the entry there was a broth exchange. Each family made a few extra quarts and exchanged them. Each can was emptied, washed, refilled and returned.

'Did ye ever think, Jamie, how like folks are to th' broth they make?'

'No,' he said, 'but there's no raisin why people should sting jist because they've got nothin' but nettles in their broth!'

The potatoes were emptied out of their pot on the bare table, my father encircling it with his arms to prevent them from rolling off. A little pile of salt was placed beside each person, and each had a big bowl full of broth. The different kinds had lost their identity in the common pot.

Alexander Irvine, *My Lady of the Chimney Corner*, 1966.

COLCANNON

You can make this into a main meal dish by adding crowdie (cottage cheese) and some sour cream. It's an Irish version of Scots Rumbledethumps (see p.264).

2 medium onions, finely chopped
50 g/2 oz butter
2 tablespoons oil
450 g/1 lb 2 oz shredded cabbage
1.3 kg/3 lb floury potatoes (see p.248)
Half a small turnip (swede)
150 g/5 oz cottage cheese or crowdie
150 ml/5 fl oz sour cream or crème fraiche
salt and ground pepper
50-100 g/2-4 oz cheddar, grated

6–8 servings

Use a gratin or pie dish, 1.75 ml/3 pt size.

Sautéing the onions and cabbage

Heat the butter and oil together in a large pan and add the onions. Cook till soft and yellow. Add the cabbage and sauté till just tender.

Preparing the other vegetables

Cook and mash the potatoes and turnip. Season, and while still warm add crowdie and sour cream.

Finishing the dish

Mix together the two lots of vegetables. Add ½ teaspoon ground caraway and 2 tablespoons cider vinegar (optional). Taste and season. Spread in a gratin or pie dish and cover with grated cheddar cheese. Brown under the grill or finish in the oven. (400F/200C/180Cfan/Gas 6).

SCANDINAVIAN

The Scandinavians are widely known as brilliant design-ers, and much of what they have designed, crafted and sent out into the world for the past three decades has been for the beautification of the table – porcelain, silverware, crystal, linen. It is not so widely known that they are excellent cooks as well. It should stand to reason, however, that a people who could care so much about the way a table looks would also care vitally about food, and the Scandinavians do.

Dale Brown, *The Cooking of Scandinavia*, 1969.

SALT HERRING WITH LEEKS

This Finnish combination has a strong personality of contrasting flavours. It should be eaten with plainly boiled or baked potatoes.

8 salt herring, boned and skinned
3 medium leeks, white and pale green only, cleaned and finely sliced
2 hard-boiled eggs
50 g/2 oz unsalted butter, melted and very hot
4 large baked potatoes

4 servings

To assemble

Arrange the herring in a row up the centre of an ashet. Put the hard-boiled eggs on one side and the leeks on the other. Pour the very hot melted butter over everything and serve immediately with baked or boiled potatoes.

MARINATED FRIED HERRING

This method is in two parts: first the frying, then the marinating. In theory it is the same idea as sousing, but frying the fish first gives it a firmer texture and fuller flavour.

8 herring fillets
Seasoned flour
50 g/2 oz butter

300 ml/½ pt cider vinegar
300 ml/½ pt water
6 tablespoons granulated sugar
1 bay leaf
6 peppercorns
1 medium onion, finely sliced

To cook

Coat 8 herring fillets in seasoned flour. Fry in butter till golden brown on both sides. Leave to cool. Bring the cider vinegar and water, with the sugar, bay leaf, peppercorns and onion, to the boil and then cool.

When both are cold, pour marinade over the fish and leave overnight before using. Serve cold with brown bread and butter. The dish will keep in a cool place for about a week.

PAKISTANI/INDIAN

Chana-jora-garam!*
Brother, I have come from a long, long distance
To bring you this unimaginably tasty
Chana-jora-garam.
I use the most excellent and secret masala –
You can know, because all kinds of famous people
Eat my chana-jora-garam.
Indian street seller's song

PAKORA
with hot tomato chutney dip

These deep-fried vegetables are street food in India, sold at street corners or in bazaars to nibble during the day. Every pakora-maker has their own version of vegetables and spices. The only

*A spicy savoury snack.

constant factors are besan (gram flour made from ground chick peas) as the binding ingredient, and deep-frying in oil. They are often translated on British restaurant menus as 'indescribables'.

225 g/8 oz besan/gram flour (ground chick peas)
125 g/4½ oz each onions, potatoes, cabbage
1 teaspoon salt
1 teaspoon chilli powder – or to taste
1 tablespoon tomato paste

To cook

Put the gram flour into a large bowl. Halve the onions and slice lengthways into paper-thin slices. Peel and slice the potatoes and cabbage into very thin slices. Or cut vegetables in a food-processor on the slicing disk. Add all the ingredients to the flour as they are prepared and mix with the salt, chilli powder and tomato paste to make a stiffish mixture. Fry in spoonfuls in deep fat. Drain and serve hot or warm.

Serve with Tomato Chutney

Pound together in pestle and mortar: **2 green chillies, chopped; 1 onion sliced; 2 cloves garlic, peeled; 2 tomatoes, chopped; few leaves of mint;** and mix with a **tablespoon of mango chutney**. Or put into food-processor and whizz. Taste and season with salt.

MRS ANWAR'S CHICKEN

The subtleties of cooking chicken in yoghurt were revealed to me by Mrs Anwar when we made this dish together. The delicate spicing and the gradual evaporation of the yoghurt during cooking leaves the chicken moist inside but with a crisp, nicely flavoured skin. The crucial point is at the end of the cooking when the outer skin is crisping. Too long in the oven will dry out the meat, too short a time and the skin will still be too soggy.

1.3 kg/3 lb chicken, jointed
Curry powder:
50 g/2 oz coriander seeds
50 g/2 oz cumin seeds
4-6 small dried chillies
50 g/2 oz turmeric
5 cardamom pods
15 g/½ oz cinnamon
7 g/¼ oz each of cloves; nutmeg; mace
50 g/2 oz fenugreek
Flavouring:
250 ml/8 fl oz natural yoghurt
2 green chillies, finely chopped
2½ cm/1 in piece of ginger root, peeled and grated
1 grated onion
Salt
50 g/2 oz ghee or butter, melted
Chapati:
225 g/8 oz wholemeal flour
2½ tablespoons ghee or melted butter
Water

4-6 servings

Use a large roasting tin or 2.5L/3½ pt ceramic dish.

Curry Powder

Grind the curry spices in blender till powdered.

Marinating in yoghurt

Put the flavouring ingredients, 2 tablespoons curry powder and the yoghurt into the roasting tin or dish. Stir to mix. Add the chicken and turn it in the mixture. Leave overnight, turning the chicken once or twice.

Roasting the chicken

Preheat the oven to 375F/190C/170Cfan/Gas 5.

Turn chicken skin side up and drizzle melted ghee or butter over. Roast in the oven for about an hour or until the skin is brown and crisp and nearly all the yoghurt has evaporated.

Serve with chapati

Put wholemeal flour into a bowl and add melted ghee or butter. Mix through the flour. Make a well in the centre and add 3 tablespoons lukewarm water. Knead into the dough. Continue adding water a tablespoon at a time till the dough comes together into a firm compact ball. Knead the dough till it becomes smooth and elastic. Leave to rest for 30 minutes. Shape into small balls about the size of a small egg and roll out to a 13 cm/5 in round. Cook on a heated, but ungreased girdle or large frying pan till lightly brown on both sides. Serve warm.

CHINESE

One can compare Chinese cooking with Chinese painting and calligraphy, where the aim is to achieve a very high degree of delicacy and refinement within a traditional and sometimes stylized framework, but at the same time never lose sight of the need for character, quality and meaning which should be the foundation of every artistic expression.

Kenneth Lo, *The Chinese Cookery Encyclopedia*, 1974.

CHINESE CRISPY ROASTED BELLY PORK

'Ideally, the pork should be in one piece, like the pork you see hanging in the windows of some Cantonese restaurants,' says Deh-Ta Hsiung. *'But if you prefer, the meat can be cut into large strips for cooking.'*
The Chinese Kitchen: A Book of Essential Ingredients (1999).

Finely ground five-spice powder (*wuxiang fen*), it seems, was originally based on the ying-yang balance of flavours found in the five basic flavours in Chinese cooking – sweet, sour, bitter, hot and salty. Sometimes described as the Chinese *bouquet garni*, it is a variable mix which may include more than five spices. The basic five are: star anise, cassia bark, fennel seeds, Sichuan pep-percorn and cloves. Other additions, depending on the brand, are coriander seeds, dried orange peel, ginger and cardamom.

1.5kg/3lb 6oz belly of pork with rind on
1 tablespoon salt
1½ tablespoons five-spice powder
Lettuce leaves for serving
For the dips:
3-4 tablespoons light soy sauce
1 tablespoon chilli sauce

Preheat the oven to 475F/240C/220Cfan/Gas 9.

Use a metal rack and roasting tin.

To prepare the meat

Pat the skin dry with kitchen paper and score with a Stanley knife. Make sure that it is free from hairs. Mix the salt and five-spice together and rub all over both sides with the salt and five-spice powder, then leave to stand for at least one hour or overnight in the fridge.

To roast

Place the pork, skin side up, on a rack over a roasting tin of hot water and roast at the high heat for 20-25 minutes. Reduce the heat to 400F/200C/180Cfan/Gas 6 and cook for another 45-50 minutes or until the skin has turned to crackling.

To serve

Chop the meat into small, bite-size pieces, place them on a bed

of lettuce leaves and serve hot or cold with the dips. Any leftovers can be used in other dishes.

JEWISH

*The real crystallisation of Jewish cuisine took place in the
sixteenth century, when the Jews were confined to ghettos by
edict. It may seem surprising that interest in food should blossom in a ghetto, especially one devoted to religious worship:
but people focused on their home lives as an antidote to the
misery and degradation outside. Hospitality became a means
of survival and the celebration of religious festivals . . . made
it possible to remain indifferent to the world outside the gates.
Banquets were held on top of the bakehouse which was the
hub of bustling activity where housewives exchanged hints,
stuffed necks and cabbage leaves, rolled meat balls and dumplings, fried potato pancakes and grated horseradish while they
waited for their goose and chicken drippings to melt down
and their pickled beef to boil.*
Claudia Roden, *The Good Food Guide*, 1985.

CHALLAH

A handsome plaited white loaf, glazed and decorated with poppy seeds, which rises in the middle and tapers at the ends. It
is traditionally plaited with four strips making an interesting
weave, though it is just as attractive in a simpler three-plait.

550 g/1¼ lb strong white flour
2 tablespoons sugar
1 teaspoon salt
1 teaspoon (½ pkt) quick-acting yeast
50 g/2 oz butter, softened
300 ml/½ pt warm water

3 eggs + 1 white

Glaze – 1 yolk from egg-white above with 1 teaspoon water

½ teaspoon poppy seeds

Preheat the oven to 425F/220C/200Cfan/Gas 7.

Prepare 2 large greased baking trays.

To mix the dough

This can be done by hand, mixing all the ingredients together to make a soft sticky dough, or it can be mixed quickly in a mixer with a dough hook. Put the flour, sugar, salt, yeast, butter, eggs and most of the water into the bowl. Using the dough hook, start the mixer on a slow speed and mix, adding more water if necessary to make a very soft, sticky dough. Beat on a higher speed for a minute until everything is thoroughly mixed. Cover the bowl with a cloth and leave for 10 minutes or longer. This allows the flour to absorb the moisture.

Knead by fold-stretch-and-rest

Oil the work surface and your hands, and turn out the dough. Scrape the bowl clean and oil it lightly. Press out the dough into a round shape. Fold in two, bringing the top edge down to the bottom edge to make a half circle. Push down lightly with the 'heel' of your hand and push and stretch the dough away from you to about 5-10 cm/2-4 in. Turn the dough a quarter, clockwise, and repeat this fold-push-and-stretch. After three or four times the stretchy gluten in the flour will develop and the dough will become more difficult to push and stretch. When this happens, stop and leave the dough to relax for at least 10 minutes, or longer. Repeat push-and-stretch twice more, and the dough will change texture to smooth, silky and elastic. Put back into the bowl.

Rising the dough

Cover with a cloth and leave to rise in a warm place until it has risen by 50%.

Shaping bread and baking

Divide into three or four equal pieces. Roll out each piece into a rope about 30 cm/12 in long, thicker in the centre and tapering at the ends. To make a four-plait loaf place the four pieces in the form of a cross, joining the four tapered ends together at the centre of the cross. Lift the ends of the two opposite ropes and twist them over the other pair to reverse their positions but still preserve the cross shape. Then lift and reverse the other pair. Repeat, lifting and reversing one pair at a time to weave the four ropes into a compact plait, rising in the middle. Tuck loose ends under the loaf, cover with lightly greased clingfilm and leave in a warm place to rise for 30 minutes. When risen, brush with glaze, sprinkle with poppy seeds and bake for about 30-40 minutes till golden brown and crusty.

AMERICAN

Today American cookery is at a crossroads somewhere between technology and tradition.
James Beard, *American Cookery*, 1980.

SOUTHERN CRISP FRIED CHICKEN
with Corn Fritters

The colour should be an even golden-brown, the crust crisp but tender and the meat moist and well flavoured.

1.3 kg/3 lb chicken thighs

For coating:

4 tablespoons wholemeal flour

1 teaspoon salt

½ teaspoon ground pepper

1 teaspoon ground cinnamon (optional)

For frying:

100 ml/3½ fl oz vegetable oil

Or 100 g/3½ oz lard or dripping

For the sauce:

4 tablespoons chicken or other suitable stock

150 ml/¼ pt single cream

Salt and pepper

½ teaspoon fresh thyme leaves

1 tablespoon lemon juice

4-6 servings

To cook

Heat the oil or lard in a 25-30 cm/10-12 in frying or sauté pan. Put the flour for coating, salt, pepper and cinnamon into a polythene bag, mix well and then add the chicken pieces two or three at a time and toss in the bag till they are well coated. Shake off excess flour. Heat the fat till moderately hot – it should come about half way up the chicken. Maintain heat at a moderate temperature, allowing the skin to brown slowly; the frying process may take around 30-40 minutes. Pile on serving dish and keep warm.

Corn Fritters

150 g/5 oz sweetcorn kernels

1 egg

125 g/4 oz self-raising flour

Salt and pepper

150 ml/¼ pt milk

To make

Put the sweetcorn into a bowl, add the egg and beat together. Add the flour and mix in. Add milk to make a dropping consistency, adding more milk if necessary. Drain off most of the fat from frying pan and reserve. Reheat pan and when hot drop spoonfuls of the mixture into the pan. Cook on both sides till golden brown.

Gravy

Use the leftover flour from coating, about 2 tablespoons. Put about two tablespoons of saved cooking fat from the frying into the pan and add flour. Stir for a few minutes, then add the chicken stock and cream. Simmer gently to reduce to the correct consistency. Add thyme and lemon juice. Taste for seasoning and serve with the chicken and fritters.

BROWNIES

Best served slightly warm, which releases their moist, dense, chocolatey character. All they need is a dusting of icing sugar and crème fraiche or whipped thick cream, though in America they are usually coated with a rich chocolate icing, often with nuts on top or mixed through.

350 g/12 oz butter, softened
300 g/10½ oz soft brown or caster sugar
4 large eggs
113 g/4 oz plain, super-refined cake flour
85 g/3 oz cocoa powder
2 teaspoons vanilla extract
Icing sugar for dusting

Preheat the oven to 350F/180C/160Cfan/Gas 4.

Use an 18 x 28 cm/7 x 11 in tin with 4 cm/1½ in sides. Grease sides, line base with non-stick baking paper or press a large sheet of foil across the base and up the sides.

To make

Warm eggs: put them, still in their shells, into a bowl of hot water and leave for about 2 minutes till they are lukewarm. Break into a bowl and beat together. Cream the butter and sugar together with an electric mixer till light and creamy. Add the vanilla and beat in the eggs gradually. Sift in the flour and cocoa powder. Mix in well but do not beat. It should be a fairly thick consistency. Spread evenly in the tin.

To bake

Bake for about 45 minutes or until risen and firm on top. Test with a skewer, which should come out clean. Remove from the oven. Leave to cool for about five minutes, then cool on a rack.

Dust with icing sugar and serve slightly warm with crème fraiche or whipped thick cream.

STRAWBERRY SHORTCAKE

Often served as a summertime birthday cake. A shortcake is the American word for a British scone.

Berry mix:
700 g/1 lb 9 oz ripe strawberries
2-3 tablespoons caster sugar
Lemon juice
Shortcake (scone) mix:
250 g/9 oz self-raising cake flour
30 g/1 oz butter, softened
30 g/1 oz vegetable fat
50 g/2 oz caster sugar
240 ml/16 fl oz milk
For serving:
600 ml/20 fl oz whipping cream

Preheat the oven to 450F/230C/210Cfan/Gas 8.

To prepare strawberries

Sprinkle the caster sugar and lemon juice over the strawberries and marinate for a couple of hours.

To make the shortcake

Sift the flour into a bowl. Add the sugar and fats. Blend into the flour either by rubbing in with tips of fingers or, briefly (10-20 seconds), in the food-processor. Make a well in the centre and add nearly all the milk. Using a fork, start by bringing in the edges gradually until it forms a softish sticky dough. The consistency should be neither too soft nor too stiff. Add more milk if too stiff.

To shape and bake

Flour work surface and turn out mixture. Handle lightly. Knead for about 10 seconds to make the dough smooth. Roll or press out to about 2 cm/¾ in thick with a rolling pin or your fingers, and shape into a large round. Place on a floured baking tray, dust with flour and bake for 10-15 minutes till risen and lightly browned. Cool on a rack in a tea towel to keep soft.

To assemble

Split shortcake in half. Whip cream till stiff. Spread the shortcake base with about a third of the cream and cover with half the strawberries. Spread over another third of the cream and put on the lid. Cover the top with the final third of the cream and decorate with remaining strawberries. Dust the top heavily with icing sugar. The strawberries may fall down the sides and onto the plate. Serve immediately.

Early Scottish Cookery Writers

Mrs McLintock

Mrs McLintock's Receipts for Cookery, Glasgow 1736

Thought to be the first collection of Scottish recipes, it is a rare little book (only two copies are known to exist, both in Glasgow University Library) and Mrs McLintock has clearly been influenced by the need for preservation of food, since more than half the book is taken up with recipes for pickling, potting, preserving and making wines. This perhaps explains why there are few Scottish national dishes. No Haggis, Barley Broth or Black Bun, though there is a recipe for Shortbread. She has one or two excellent soups, a Lobster Soup which is finished with oysters and mussels and a basic soup recipe which starts with, 'great whole onions stuck with cloves, a bunch of sweet herbs,' and lots of beef and veal bones. It is finished with toasted bread floating in the soup and a cooked marrow bone in the centre of the plate.

Mrs Johnston

Mrs Johnston's Receipts for all sort of pastry, cream, puddings, etc., Edinburgh 1740

A small collection of recipes for plain basic fare thought to be either copied from Mrs McLintock or written by her under another name. Of the 117 pages in the book the first 92 are the same as in Mrs McLintock's 1736 edition.

Elizabeth Cleland

The Practice of Cookery, pastry, pickling, preserving, containing…a full list of supper dishes…directions for choosing provisions: with two plates, showing the method of placing dishes upon a table etc., Edinburgh 1759

Mrs Cleland also had a cookery school in Edinburgh and her book has the feeling of an elementary manual of instruction—there is much emphasis on methods of preservation. A whole chapter is dedicated 'To pot and make hams', but Scottish national dishes are also well represented.

Susanna MacIver
Cookery and Pastry, Edinburgh 1773

She began by selling cakes, jams, chutneys and pickles from her shop, but later opened a cookery school where she taught a sophisticated range of dishes to the well-to-do of Edinburgh. In 1773 her pupils encouraged her to publish her recipes. The collection is well mixed with French influence. Unlike many contemporary English books which are at pains to denounce the French as spoiling good English fare, possibly because of the long Scottish association with the French, she, like most Scots, seems to have had a more relaxed attitude to their incursions.

She includes a fair representation of Scottish dishes, like Scotch Haggis, Parton Pies, Rich Bun, Shortbread, Diet Loaf, Chip Marmalade, To Make Tablets and To Make Barley Sugar. It seems, though, that she was not a broth-lover, since no recipe appears for the universal Scotch Broth, which was considered so much of a national institution both at home and abroad that it is included in *The London Art of Cookery* by John Farley (1785).

Mrs Fraser
The Practice of Cookery and Pastry, Edinburgh 1791

She helped to run Mrs McIver's cookery school, took over after her death and then published her own recipes. This is a more sophisticated and comprehensive collection than Mrs McIver's. Her aim was to 'reconcile simplicity with elegance, and variety with economy'. She has organised the book in a more logical structure, dividing it up into three parts—I cookery; II Pastry; and III Confectionery, which includes all the preservation methods. Plain simple fare predominates, with all the basic Scottish dishes, and little French or foreign influence besides the odd 'ragoo' and 'fricassy'. Curiously she also, like Mrs McIver, has no recipe for Scotch Broth among her nineteen soup recipes of which only three could be termed traditionally Scottish. In place of Cock-a-Leekie she has a poor version of Leek Soup with prunes but no chicken.

Mistress Margaret (Meg) Dods of the Cleikum Inn, St Ronan's
The Cook and Housewife's Manual, Edinburgh 1826

Meg Dods was a fictitious character whom Sir Walter Scott created in his novel *St Ronan's Well*, but is said to have been modelled on Miss Marian Ritchie, the landlady of his local inn, the Cross Keys in Peebles. Meg was a capricious and eccentric old landlady with a detestable bad humour. Potential guests were turned away if she disliked the 'cut of their jib', and the ones who stayed had to be prepared for her blunt couthy ways. Her saving grace, and the reason why gourmets flocked to her inn, was that she was a superb cook.

The real author of the cookery book was Mrs Isobel Christian Johnston, wife of an Edinburgh publisher. The connection with Scott and his novel is not made clear in the introductory 'The St Ronan's Culinary Club'. Mrs Johnston is the first Scottish cookery writer of the century to make an accurate assessment of the changes taking place, cutting her cloth accordingly, while at the same time carrying out the task with expert professionalism. Public horizons were widening far beyond the basics of Plain Roast and Boiled, although these were still important. Curiosity and the desire to learn were cultivating the made dishes of beef, mutton, veal and venison, etc. In the second chapter the whole system of French Cuisine is thoroughly explored, while the next deals with national dishes— Scottish, Irish, Welsh, German, Spanish and Oriental. She is one of the first cookery writers to isolate these subjects, recognising the public interest in them. Both before and after her, the tendency was to create a hotch-potch of foreign and national dishes with no clear distinction.

She was careful also not to adopt these dishes purely for their novelty, but claims that she has set out to embody 'all in Foreign culinary science that is considered really useful'. She was a very practical lady.

Mrs Dalgairns
The Practice of Cookery, Edinburgh 1829

First published only three years after Meg Dods, and competing with her for popularity, this is a large cookery book with 1,434 recipes. It seems, however, that the public did not take to Mrs Dalgairns with the same enthusiasm they felt for Meg Dods, but her book is just as large and comprehensive. Despite this, there is a feeling of muddle about the structure of the book. There are all the basic Scottish national dishes, but French, English, Irish and other foreign dishes occur randomly throughout the book. Apart from the lack of form she has a vague style of writing, so that when you read the recipes you are constantly frustrated by lack of quantities and instruction. None of these criticisms apply to Meg Dods, which explains why her book was reprinted frequently throughout the century and Mrs Dalgairns' was not.

Lady Clark of Tillypronie
The Cookery Book of Lady Clark of Tillypronie, arranged and edited by Catherine F. Frere, London 1909

Lady Clark was an obsessional collector of recipes. When she died her husband asked Catherine Frere to edit her manuscript collection. She took on the task of sorting out 'the gatherings of many years' which consisted of sixteen books of various sizes, containing nearly three thousand pages of manuscript, some of the page written on every available margin, plus recipes written on loose sheets pinned in; or on backs of envelopes; or on backs of paid bills; or any available piece of paper.

The collection begins in 1841 when emigrés from the French Revolution stayed with Lady Clark's family. Her culinary curiosity was aroused by them and consolidated when she travelled with her family to Italy and France. When she married in 1851, her husband was in the Diplomatic Service and they lived in both Paris and Turin. Her collection has a strong hidden implication that if you give fifty different chefs the same recipe they will all produce a different dish. She spent so much time gathering recipes from so many different people that there are many variations of the same recipe, reflecting always the personality of the individual. It makes interesting reading; especially since her roots were in the North East of Scotland, and it was to this part that she returned frequently, absorbing also the culinary traditions of her home.

F. Marian McNeill

The Scots Kitchen, Its Traditions and Lore, Blackie 1929 (new edition Birlinn, 2010)

Because she thought that our old national dishes were in danger of sinking into oblivion through modern standardisation of food, F. Marion McNeill set about preserving everything hallowed by age.

She ranged the country from north to south and from palaces to island sheilings in her search for the authentic food of the people. Being by profession a historian, she also sketched the development of Scottish food throughout the centuries, and set about showing how 'the pageant of Scottish History is shadowed in the kitchen.' She highlights the distinctive traditions and customs, not out of 'antiquarian zeal', but from a 'healthy national sentiment', and our debt to her is infinite.

William Heptinstall

Gourmet Recipes From a Highland Hotel, Faber and Faber 1967

In the 1920s when railway hotels were the only outposts of serious gastronomy in Scotland, an enterprising Yorkshire-born chef, with a formidable international reputation, bought Fortingall Hotel— eight miles from the nearest railway station and on a quiet back road in Perthshire.

During the thirty-five years of Heptinstall's reign at Fortingall he not only created an outstanding hotel off the beaten track, but stimulated, encouraged and trained many young chefs who continue to keep his cooking philosophy alive in hotels and restaurants in Scotland and further afield. He was particularly well known for his Cold Table, only offered once a week, preceding Sunday lunch. On an average Sunday, forty dishes could appear on the table, half of which probably had to be prepared before breakfast. He felt that the start to a meal was vitally important—'Just as a good or bad start may win or lose the race,' he said, 'so may hors-d'oeuvres make or mar a meal. Unless they are dainty, little, and tasty, they will dull the keen edge of your appetite.'

In *Gourmet Recipes* he exploits the natural produce of Scotland with originality and flair, but mindful always of the practicalities— his infectious enthusiasm shines through.

HOUSEHOLD BOOKS, JOURNALS, LETTERS, DIARIES

Lady Grisell Baillie

The Household Book of Lady Grisell Baillie 1692-1733, edited by Robert Scott-Moncrieff, 1911

Besides much information on household expenditure, Lady Grisell also kept a special book in which she recorded 'Bills of Fair'. Not all of the hundred and seventy in the book are meals in her own family home, but she recalls meals with friends and in other countries. The list of dishes give an indication of the types of foods which were popular at this level of society. She has carefully preserved the exact layout of the dishes on the table, so that the book shows clearly the type of eating in the days when they arranged everything on the table at once.

Edward Burt

Letters from a Gentleman in the North of Scotland, 5th ed., 1822

Edward Burt was an English engineer who served with General Wade building roads in the Highlands from 1724-28. His letters are unique, since he was travelling in the area before the very roads he was helping to build brought 'travellers' to the Highlands. His record of the manners and conditions of the people is vivid and detailed, interspersed with much humour—a good read ('I was invited to sup at a Tavern. The cook was too filthy on Object to be described: only another English Gentleman whispered me and said, he believed, if the fellow was to be thrown against the Wall, he would stick to it'). He lived for some time in or near Inverness and made a number of journeys along the Great Glen and into some of the adjacent country.

Ochtertyre House Booke of Accomps 1737-1739, edited by James Colville, Edinburgh 1907

While Grisell Baillie's bills of fare give an indication of the dinner

435

party fare of sophisticated Edinburgh society, then the Ochtertyre House Book gives the picture of the standard of daily living in an average baronial establishment just before the 'Forty Five. It is a detailed catalogue of daily meals, purchases and home-grown or home-produced food. You can follow the rhythm of the seasons in the foods they ate and see the way they utilised all the odds and ends in a most economical way when beasts were killed.

Thomas Pennant

Tour in Scotland, 1771 [Describes a journey made in 1769]

According to Pennant his book was such a success that Scotland was, as a result, '*inondée* with Southern visitors'. He was one of the most eminent naturalists of the eighteenth century, and as a traveller showed a lively curiosity about people and customs as well as the natural things of the country. His comments on the things he saw growing, and which the people were eating, are an important record of the Scots diet. His 1769 *Tour in Scotland* went into five editions between 1771 and 1790. He made another tour round the West Coast and the Islands in 1772, but this was less popular with the public since these areas were much less accessible.

Christopher North (Professor John Wilson)

Noctes Ambrosianae 1822-1835

Ambrosian nights in an Edinburgh tavern were brought to life by Wilson, a professor of philosophy, in a series of imaginary colloquies which entertained the readers of *Blackwood's Magazine* for more than a decade. They were so popular that Blackwood's allowed other writers besides Wilson to write the dialogues when, for one reason or another, he couldn't contribute. But none of them could match his style, and the published collection in four volumes is confined only to Wilson's work.

His principal characters, Christopher North (Wilson himself), Timothy Tickler (Robert Sym) and James Hogg, The Ettrick

Shepherd, only bear the slightest resemblance to the original people. They formed the prototypes, and Wilson's imagination expanded and developed them. Besides talking a great deal, they also ate.

Most of the vivid and detailed descriptions of what and how they would have eaten in early nineteenth century Edinburgh ring true. There is just the occasional doubt that Wilson's imagination has elaborated over much. His description of the 'Deluge of Haggis', likening it to a flood when the haggis was first burst open, while highly entertaining, goes well beyond the bounds of reality by the time he is finished.

His comments, though, on attitudes to food indicate current taste and style, and occasional pieces on subjects like how they ought to eat these new things called 'pineapples' are both revealing and amusing:

Shep. And what ca' ye thae, like great big fir cones wi' outlandish-looking palm-tree leaves arching frae them wi' an elegance o' their ain…What ca' ye them?

North. Pineapples.

Shep. I've aften heard tell o' them—but never clapped een on them afore. And these are pines! Oh! but the scant is sweet, sweet—and wild as sweet…I'll join you noo in a pair o' pines.

[NORTH gives the SHEPHERD a pine-apple]

Hoo are they eaten?

Tickler. With pepper, mustard, and vinegar, like oysters, James.

Shepherd. I'm thinking you maun be leein.

Tickler. Some people prefer catsup.

Shepherd. Haud your blethers. Catchup's gran kitchen [relish] for a' kinds o' flesh, fish and fule, but for frutes the rule is 'sugar or naething',—and if this pine keep the taste o' promise to the palat, made by the scent he sends through the nose, nae extrawneous

sweetness will he need, self sufficient in his ain sappiness, rich
as the colour o' pinks, in which it is sae savourily enshrined.—I
never pree'd ony taste half sae delicious as that in a' ma born
days! Ribstanes, pippins, jargonels, peaches, nectrins, currans and
strawberries, grapes and grozets, a' in ane!'

Samuel Johnson and James Boswell

Johnson's Journey to the Western Islands of Scotland, 1775
Boswell's Journal of a Tour to the Hebrides with Samuel Johnson, 1785

The 64-year-old English lexicographer and the 33-year-old Scot
spent four months together on a tour which took them round a large
part of Scotland and into many different types of Scottish homes.
They went from Edinburgh northwards to Aberdeen, then along
the Morayshire coast to Inverness. This was the easy part. In Inverness they bade 'farewell to the luxury of travelling' and continued on
horseback across to Glenelg, over to Skye, down to Coll, across to
Mull and back to the mainland at Oban. From there they travelled
south to Glasgow and then into Ayrshire before going back to Edinburgh.

Boswell's journal is more detailed and, according to literary experts, also a better travel book than Johnson's. Johnson seems to allow his prejudices about the Scots and their customs to influence his
opinions, and his likes and dislikes, while interesting and relevant,
perhaps don't always reflect the true nature of things. He was, after
all, a brilliant critic and he naturally came, not like the Wordsworths
in 1803, to see and feel, but to pass his own judgment. He was a
colourful character, highly amusing, witty and notoriously rude, in
which he was occasionally matched by his Scottish hosts. When
he was eating Hotch Potch at his Edinburgh landlady's she is reputed to have asked him, 'And how do you like the Hotch Potch, sir.'
'Good enough for hogs,' replied Johnson. 'Shall I help you to a little
more of it, then?' retorted the landlady.

Besides all kinds of opinions on all kinds of topics, the two men both noted how the people lived. They described the conditions, the traditions and the diet of the people and have provided a revealing and valuable account of life in different parts of Scotland and at different levels of society in the late eighteenth century.

BUYING GUIDE

General and Regional Information

ABERDEENSHIRE GRAMPIAN FOOD FORUM *www.grampianfoodforum.co.uk*

AYRSHIRE FOOD NETWORK *www.ayrshirefoodnetwork.co.uk*

BLACKFACE SHEEP BREEDERS *www.scottish-blackface.co.uk*

CASTLE DOUGLAS FOOD TOWN INITIATIVE *www.cd-foodtown.org*

CLYDE VALLEY FARMS DIRECT *www.clydevalleyfarmsdirect.co.uk*

COMMUNITY FOOD AND HEALTH *www.communityfoodandhealth.org.uk*

CROFTING CONNECTIONS *www.croftingconnections.com*

EAST LOTHIAN *www.foodanddrinkineastlothian.co.uk*

FARM SHOP *www.farmshop.uk.com*

FEDERATION OF CITY FARMS AND COMMUNITY GARDENS *www.farmgarden.org.uk*

FIFE FOOD NETWORK *www.fifefarmersmarket.co.uk*

FOOD FROM ARGYLL *www.argyllandtheisles.com/food_from_argyll.html*

FORTH VALLEY FOOD LINKS *www.forthvalleyfoodlinks.org.uk*

HOPE GARDEN TRUST, HOSPITALFIELD HOUSE, ARBROATH *www.hopegardentrust.org.uk*

LEWIS AND HARRIS HORTICULTURAL PRODUCERS *www.stornowayfarmersmarket.co.uk*

LOCHABER CRAFT AND FOOD PRODUCERS ASSOCIATION *www.lcfpa.co.uk*

MULL AND IONA COMMUNITY PARTNERSHIP FOOD FESTIVAL *www.mict.co.uk*

MUTTON RENAISSANCE *www.muttonrenaissance.org.uk*

NEWBURGH ORCHARD GROUP *www.newburghorchards.org.uk*

NORTH HIGHLAND INITIATIVE *www.mey-selections.com*

ORKNEY QUALITY FOOD AND DRINK *www.oqfd.co.uk*

PERTH FARMERS' MARKET *www.perthfarmersmarket.co.uk*

PERTHSHIRE PRODUCE GUIDE *www.perthshire-produce.co.uk*

ROYAL DEESIDE LARDER *www.discoverroyaldeeside.com*

SAVOUR THE FLAVOURS (Dumfries and Galloway) *www.savourtheflavours.co.uk*

SCOTTISH CROFTING FEDERATION *www.crofting.org*

SCOTTISH BORDERS FOOD NETWORK *www.bordersfoodnetwork.co.uk*

SCOTCH BUTCHERS CLUB (Ouality Meat Scotland) *www.qmscotland.co.uk*

SCOTTISH FOOD FORTNIGHT *www.scottishfoodfortnight.co.uk*

SCOTTISH FOOD GUIDE
www.scottishfoodguide.com
SCOTTISH ORGANIC PRO-
DUCERS ASSOCIATION
www.sopa.org.uk
SOUTHERN UPLAND PART-
NERSHIP *www.sup.org.uk*
SEAFOOD SCOTLAND *www.
seafoodscotland.org*
SHETLAND ISLANDS *www.
foodshetland.com*
SHETLAND SEAFOOD *www.
fishuk.net/seafoodshetland*
SKYE AND LOCHALSH *www.
tastelocal.co.uk*
SLOW FOOD UK *www.slowfood.
org.uk* PERTH *www.cittaslow.
org.uk*
TASTE OF ARRAN *www.taste-
of-arran.com*
TASTE OF GRAMPIAN FOOD
FESTIVAL *www.tasteofgram-
pian.co.uk*

Useful Organisations

ATLANTIC SALMON TRUST,
Perth: *www.atlanticsalmontrust.
org*, 01738 472032
MARINE CONSERVATION
SOCIETY UK, Ross-on-Wye:
www.mcsuk.org, 01989 566017
MARINE STEWARDSHIP
COUNCIL (Worldwide),
London: *www.msc.org*, 020
72468900
RIVERS AND FISHERIES
TRUSTS (Scotland), Dollar:
www.rafts.org.uk, 0131 272 2800
SCOTLAND FOOD AND
DRINK: *www.scotland-
foodanddrink.org*, 0131 335 0940

SCOTTISH ASSOCIATION
OF FARMERS' MARKETS:
www.scottishfarmersmarkets.co.uk
SCOTTISH SALMON PRO-
DUCERS' ORGANISATION,
Perth: *www.scottishsalmon.co.uk*,
01738 587000
SCOTTISH FEDERATION OF
SEA ANGLERS, Kelso: *www.
fishsea.co.uk*, 01592 657520
SEAFISH UK, Edinburgh: *www.
seafish.org*, 0131 558 3331
SEAFOOD SCOTLAND, Edin-
burgh: *www.seafoodscotland.org*,
01315579344
SHELLFISH ASSOCIATION
UK, London: *www.shellfish.org.
uk*, 020 72838305
QUALITY MEAT SCOTLAND
www.qmscotland.co.uk, 0131
4724040

Meat, Game, Farm Shops and Delis

AA beef = Aberdeen Angus

ABERDEEN ANGUS DIRECT
(Farm Shop) Banchory: *www.
aberdeenangusdirect.com* 01339
882 882
ABERFOYLE BUTCHERS by
Glasgow: *www.aberfoylebutcher.
co.uk* 01877 382473
ALLAN, JAMES (Butcher)
Hyndland, Glasgow: *www.craft-
butchers.co.uk* 0141 334 8973
ANDERSON'S (Butcher) North
Berwick 01620 892964
ANGUS ORGANICS (lamb and
AA beef) Airlie Estate, Kirrie-
muir 01307 860355

ARDALANISH FARM (organic beef and mutton) Bunessan, Isle of Mull 01681 700265

ARDARDAN ESTATE (farm shop) Cardross: *www.ardardan.co.uk* 01389 849188

ARDROSS FARM SHOP (beef) Elie, Fife: *www.ardrossfarm.co.uk* 01333 3314005

BALLENCRIEFF RARE PEDIGREE PIGS East Lothian: *www.ballencrieffrppigs.co.uk* 01875 870551

BALGOVE LARDER (farm shop/butcher) St Andrews: www.balgove.com, 01334 898145

BEECRAIGS COUNTRY PARK (venison) West Lothian: *www.beecraigs.com* 01506 844516

BEL'S BUTCHERS, High Street, Edzell, Angus 01356 648409

BLAIRMAINS FARM SHOP Manor Loan, Blairlogie: *www.blairmainsfarmshop.co.uk* 01259 762266

BOGHALL (butcher/game) Bathgate: *www.boghallbutchers.com* 01506 630178

BOWER G. (butcher) Stockbridge, Edinburgh: *www.georgebowerbutchers.co.uk* 0131 332 3469

BRASH, J. (butcher) Corstorphine, Edinburgh: *www.johnbrashbutcher.co.uk* 0131 337 3730

BRIG FARM SHOP (beef/game) Bridge of Earn, Perthshire: *www.brigfarmshop.co.uk* 01738 813571

BROWN & TURRIF (butcher) Aberdeenshire: *www.brownthebutcher.co.uk* 01888 563379

BUCCLEUCH HERITAGE BRANDS Dumfries and Galloway: *www.buccleuchfoods.com* 01556 503399

BUTCHERY, THE Goods Station Road, Lockerbie Dumfriesshire 01576 203329

BRYMER, BRUCE (butcher/game) Brechin, Angus 01356 624645

CAIRNTON FARM SHOP (AA beef) Banchory : *www.cairntonaberdeenangus.co.uk* 013398 83536_

CAITHNESS FREE RANGE EGGS Castletown: *www.caithnessfreerangeeggs.co.uk* 01847 821417

CAMPBELL (butcher) Port Ellen, Islay: *www.meatislay.co.uk* 01496 300480

CARMICHAEL ESTATE FARM SHOP Biggar, Lanarkshire: *www.carmichael.co.uk* 01899 308 336

CHISHOLMS OF AYR (local produce): *www.chisholmsofayrdeli.com* 01292 269555

CORNER ON THE SQUARE (deli) Beauly, Inverness: *www.corneronthesquare.co.uk* 01463 783000

COTTONRAKE (artisan bakery) Hyndland, Glasgow: *www.cottonrake.com* 07910 282040

CRAIGADAM ESTATE (lamb/game) Castle Douglas: *www.craigadam.com* 01556 650233

CROMBIE'S (butcher) Broughton St, Edinburgh *www.sausages.co.uk* 0131 557 0111

DALDUFF FARM SHOP

Crosshill, Ayrshire: *www.dalduff.co.uk* 01655 740271

DEE LARDER (deli) Banchory, Aberdeenshire: *www.deelarder.com* 01330 820388

DELI ECOSSE Ancaster Square, Callander: *www.deliecosse.co.uk* 01877 331220

DELIZIQUE (deli) Partick, Glasgow: *www.delizique.co.uk* 0141 3392000

DONALD RUSSELL DIRECT (meat) Inverurie: *www.donaldrusselldirect.com* 01467 629666

DOUNBY (butcher/farm shop/local prodcue) Dounby, Orkney: 01856 771777

DUNCAN C. (butcher) Ayr Street, Troon: *www.charlesduncanbutchers.co.uk* 01292 312755

EWART J. (butcher/AA beef) Moniefieth/Carnoustie: *www.ewartsbutchers.co.uk*, 01382 532029

FAIR AND SQUARE GAME (estate game) Auchessan Estate, by Crianlarich 01567 820975

FARM FRESH (deli/fresh:fish/meat/fruit/veg/cheese) Aberfeldy, Perthshire 01887 820327

FINDLAY'S PORTOBELLO (butcher) East Lothian:*www.findlaysthebutchers.co.uk* 0131 6692783

FLETCHERS (farmed venison) Auchtermuchty, Fife: *www.fletcherscotland.co.uk* 01337 828369

FOREMAN R.G. (butcher) Eyemouth and Coldstream : *www.borderbutcher.co.uk* 01890 883881

FRASER, DUNCAN (butcher/game and fish) Queensgate, Inverness 01463 232744

GALBRAITH, DONALD (butcher) Blackwaterfoot, Arran, Argyll 01770 860354

GARDEN HOUSE (farm shop/local produce) Milngavie, Glasgow 0141 9550011

GARLETON PRIME BEEF (farm shop/beef/lamb) East Garleton, East Lothian 01620 880212

GARTMORN FARM (poultry/eggs) Alloa: *www.gartmornfarm.co.uk* 01259 750549

GLOBE BUTCHERS, Lerwick, Shetland: *www.globebutchers.co.uk* 01595 682819

GLOGARBURN (farm shop) Tibbermore: *www.glogarburnfarmshop.co.uk* 01738 840864

GOSFORD BOTHY (farm shop) Aberlady: *www.gosfordfarmshop.co.uk* 01875 871234

GRIERSON, HUGH (organic AA beef/lamb/eggs) Tibbermore: *www.hughgrierson.co.uk* 01738 730201

GRIEVE, LINDSAY (butcher) Hawick: *www.lindsaygrievehaggis.co.uk* 01450 372109

HANSON'S KITCHEN (deli/local produce) Comrie: *www.hansenskitchen.com* 01764 670253

HATTONCROOK (farm shop/beef) Whiterashes: *www.mcgregoraberdeenangus.com* 01651 882271

HERDS THE BUTCHER Rosemont Place, Aberdeen 01224 638293

HIGHLAND GAME Baird Avenue, Dundee, Angus *www.highlandgame.com* 01382 827088

HIGHLAND GEESE Corranmor Farm, Ardfern, Argyll: *www.highlandgeese.co.uk* 01852 500609

HIGHLAND WILD BOAR (farm-reared boar) Millcraig Mill, Alness, Ross-shire 01349 883776

HILTON WILD BOAR (farm-reared boar) Peerth: *www.hilton-wildboar.co.uk* 01337 842867

HONEST FOOD CO LTD (farm butcher/beef/lamb) Hawick, Berwickshire 01450 372 072

HOUSE OF BRUAR (food hall) Blair Atholl: *www.houseofbruar.com* 01796 483236

INGRAM'S HOMECURE (bacon/sausages, farm shop) Newburgh, Ellon Aberdeenshire 01358 789548

ISLAND BAKERY AND DELI TOBERMORY, Isle of Mull: *www.islandbakery.co.uk* 01688 302225

ISLAY FINE FOOD (farm smoker) Bruichladdich, Islay: *www.islayfinefood.com* 01496 850350 .

JACK, ALEX (butcher) Stranraer, Ayrshire *www.alexjackbutchers.co.uk* 01776 702780

JAMESFIELD ORGANIC CENTRE (farm shop) Abernethy: *www.seedsofhealth.co.uk* 01738 850 498

JENNERS (food hall) Princes Street, Edinburgh: *www.jenners.com* 0131 260 2242

JOLLY, WILLIAM (fishmonger/smoker) Kirkwall, Orkney: *www.jollyfish.co.uk* 01856 873317

KATHELLAN FINE FOODS (farm foods) Kelty, Fife: *www.kathellan.co.uk* 0871 2262218

KINTALINE PLANT AND POULTRY CENTRE (eggs) Oban: *www.kintaline.co.uk* 01631 720223

KITCHEN GARDEN, THE (deli) Oban, Argyll *www.kitchengardenoban.co.uk* 01631 566332

LOCHABER FARM SHOP (café) Torlundy: *www.lochaberfarmshop.com* 01397 708686

LOCHEND FARM SHOP, Scotlandwell, Kinross: *www.lochendfarmshop.co.uk* 01592 840745

MACBETH'S (butcher) Forres, Morayshire *www.macbeths.com* 01309 672254

MACDONALD (butcher/AA beef) Pitlochry: *www.macdonald-bros.co.uk* 01796 472047

MACDONALD, W J (butcher/black pudding) Stornoway: *www.wjmacdonald.com* 01851 702077

MACLEOD, C (butcher/black pudding) Stornoway: *www.charlesmacleod.co.uk* 01851 702445

MACSWEEN (haggis) Edinburgh: *www.macsween.co.uk* 0131 440 2555

MCCALLUMS (butcher/deli/AA beef) Auchterarder, Perthshire *www.bestbeef.co.uk* 01764 662128

MCKIRDY BROTHERS (butcher) Port Seton, East Lothian 01875 811726

MILLERS, THE (deli) Midmar, Inverurie: *www.millersmidmar.info* 01330 833463

MILTON HAUGH FARM SHOP (food hall) Carmylie, Angus: *www.miltonhaugh.com* 01241 860579

MITCHELL J R (deli/butcher) Kelso, Berwickshire 01573 224 109

MORGAN MCVEIGH'S (deli/café) Colpy, Nr Inverurie: *www.morganmcveighs.com* 01464 841399

MULL BUTCHERS Tobermory, Isle of Mull 01688 302021

NEWTON DEE STORE (deli/bakery) Bieldside, Aberdeen 01224 868609

NITHSDALE COUNTRY LARDER, Sanquhar: *www.nithsdalecountrylarder.co.uk* 01659 67212

OLD KNOCKELLY SMOKE-HOUSE (farm shop) Penpont, Thornhill, Dumfriesshire 01848 600298

ORMSARY FARM (beef/lamb/game) Lochgilphead: *www.ormsary.com/farms.asp* 01880 770700

PARDOVAN (farm shop/own veg/game) Philpstoun, Linlithgow: 01506 834470

PEAT, COLIN (butcher/game) Haddington, East Lothian 01620 823192

PEEL FARM SHOP, Lintrathen, Kirriemuir: *www.peelfam.com* 01575 560718

PEELHAM FARM PRODUCE (meat/game) Foulden, Berwickshire: *www.peelham.co.uk* 01890 781328

PENTLAND HILLS PRODUCE (farm co-op) Hillend: *www.pentland-hills-produce.co.uk* 0131 445 3383

PHOENIX COMMUNITY STORES (deli) Findhorn Bay: *www.findhorn.com* 01309 690110

PILLARS OF HERCULES (organic farm shop) Falkland: *www.pillars.co.uk* 01337 857749

PIRIE, JAMES (butcher, own-cured pork) Newtyle, Perthshire 01828 650301

PROVENDER BROWN (deli) Perth: *www.provenderbrown.co.uk* 01738 587300

PUDDLEDUB PORK AND FIFESHIRE BACON Auchtertool, Fife: *www.puddledub.co.uk* 01592 780246

RAMSAY (Ayrshire bacon/butcher) Carluke, Lanarkshire: *www.ramsayofcarluke.co.uk* 01555 772277

RANNOCH SMOKERY (cured meats) Kinloch Rannoch: *www.rannochsmokery.co.uk* 0870 1501559

RAVENSTONE DELI (local foods) Whithorn/Wigtown: *www.ravenstonedeli.com* 01988 500329

REIVER COUNTRY FARM FOODS Eyemouth, Berwickshire: *www.reiver-foods.co.uk* 01890 761355

ROBERTSON'S (deli) Broughty

Ferry/Dundee: *www.robertsonof-broughtyferry.co.uk* 01382 739277

ROBERTSONS OF PIT-LOCHRY (butcher) Perthshire 01796 472011

ROBERTSONS THE LARDER at Tomich Farm Shop, Beauly, Inverness 01463 782181

ROTHIEMURCHUS FARM SHOP (beef/game) Aviemore: *www.rothiemurchus.net* 01479 812345

SAULMORE FARM SHOP (own beef/lamb) Connel, Oban: 01631 710247

SCOTTISH DELI, THE (local produce) Pitlochry/Dunkeld: *www.scottish-deli.co.uk* 01796 473322

SETON EAST FARM SHOP (fruit/veg/poultry/eggs) Near Longniddry, East Lothian 01875 815946

SHERIDAN (butcher/game) Ballater, Aberdeenshire: *www.hmsheridan.co.uk* 013397 55218

SPEY LARDER, THE (deli) Aberlour, Morayshire *www.speylarder.com* 01340 871243

STORE, THE (farm shop) Foveran, Ellon: *www.foveranstore.com* 01358 788083

TASTE FRESH (deli) Dundee: *www.tastefresh.co.uk* 01382 224300

TEVIOT GAME SMOKERY (& deli) Kelso: *www.teviotgamefaresmokery.co.uk* 01835 850 235

TOMBUIE SMOKEHOUSE (game) Aberfeldy, Perthshire: *www.tombuie.com* 01887 820127

URADALE FARM (Shetland lamb/mutton) Scaloway: *www.uradale.com* 01595 880689

VALVONA AND CROLLA (deli) Edinburgh: *www.valvona-crolla.com* 0131 556 6066

WARK FARM (native breeds/beef/lamb/pork) Cushnie, Alford: *www.warkfarm.co.uk* 01975 581149

WHITMUIR (organic farm produce) West Linton: *www.whitmuirtheorganicplace.co.uk* 01968 661908

WINSTON CHURCHILL VENISON, Dunoon: *www.winstonchurchillvenison.com* 01369 705319

WOODLAND FARM SHOP, Girvan, Ayrshire: *www.woodlandfarm.co.uk* 01465 710700

WOODSIDE FARM SHOP Drumoak, Aberdeenshire 01224 732081

YORKES OF DUNDEE (butcher) Strathmartine Road: *www.yorkesofdundee.co.uk*: 01382 825901

Fish, Shellfish and Seaweed

ARBROATH FISHERIES (fishmonger): *www.arbroath-smokie.co.uk*, 01241 872331

ARMSTRONG (fishmonger/smoker): *www.armstrongsofstockbridge.com*, 0131 315 2033

BELHAVEN SMOKEHOUSE, Dunbar: *www.belhavensmokehouse.com*, 01368 863224

BEVERAGE, ALAN (fishmonger) Glasgow: *www.alanbeveridge.com*, 0141 6201809

BLYDOIT FISHMONGER'S,

Scalloway: *admin@blydoitfish.shetland.co.uk*, 01595 880011

BURNS COUNTRY SMOKE-HOUSE, Minishant: *www.burnsmoke.com*, 01292 442773

CAITHNESS SMOKEHOUSE, Barrock: *www.caithness-smoke-house.com*, 01847 635007

CLARK BROTHERS (fishmonger), Musselburgh: *info@downiefish.co.uk*, 0131 665 6181

COCKLES (deli/fish shop), Lochgilphead: *www.cocklesfinefoods.com*, 01546 606292

DEE FISH (fishmonger), Castle Douglas: *www.deefish.co.uk*, 01557 870466

DUNKELD SMOKED SALMON: *www.dunkeldsmokedsalmon.com*, 01350 727639

EAST PIER SMOKEHOUSE, St Monans: *www.eastpier.co.uk*, 01333 405030

EDDIE'S (fishmonger), Edinburgh: *www.eddies-seafood-market.com*, 0131 229 4207

FENCEBAY FISHERIES (farm shop), Fairlie: *www.fencebay.co.uk*, 01475 568918

FISH IN CRIEFF (fishmonger), Perthshire: 01764 654509

FISH PEOPLE, The (fishmonger), Glasgow: 0141 429 1609

FISH PLAICE, THE (fishmonger), Glasgow: 0141 552 2337

GALLOWAY (smoker/fish) Newton Stewart: *www.galloway-smokehouse.co.uk*, 01671 820354

GIHA HALIBUT (fish farmer): *www.gighahalibut.co.uk*, 01700 821226

GOURMET'S CHOICE (smoked salmon), Portsoy: *www.gourmetschoice.net*, 01261 842884

GRANITE CITY (fishmonger), Aberdeen: *info@granitecityfish.com*, 01224 587065

HAND-MADE FISH (fish/smoker), Lerwick: *www.hand-madefish.co.uk*, 01950 422214

HEBRIDES HARVEST (organic/farm salmon) Benbecula: *www.hebridesharvest.com* 01870 602081

HEBRIDEAN SMOKEHOUSE (peat/smoked salmon): *www.hebrideansmokehouse.com*, 01876 580209

INVERAWE SMOKEHOUSES: *www.smokedsalmon.co.uk*, 08448 475490

ISLE OF EWE SMOKE-HOUSE, Altbea: *www.smoked-lyewe.com*, 01445 731304

ISLE OF SKYE SEAFOOD, Broadford: *www.skye-seafood.co.uk*, 08007 813687

JOLLYS (fishmonger/smoker/deli), Orkney: *www.jollyfish.co.uk*, 01856 872417

JUST SEAWEED, Isle of Bute: *www.justseaweed.com*, 01700 505823

KERACHER (fishmonger) St Andrews: *www.georgecampbellandsons.co.uk*, 01738 638454

KISHORN SEAFOOD BAR/SHOP, Wester Ross: *www.kishornseafoodbar.co.uk*, 01520 733 240

KYLE OF TONGUE OYSTERS, Lairg: *kotoysters@live.co.uk*, 01847 601 271

LOBSTER STORE, The (lobster and crab), Crail Harbour, Fife: 01333 450476

LOCH DUART (farmed salmon), Scourie: *www.lochduart.com*, 01674 66 01 61

LOCH FYNE OYSTERS (fish shop/smoker), Cairndow: *www.lochfyne.com*, 01499 600264

LOCHLEVEN SHELLFISH, Onich: *www.lochlevenseafoodcafe.co.uk*, 01855 821048

MacCALLUM OF TROON (Glasgow fishmonger/Oyster Bar Troon): 0141 204 4456

MACMILLAN (fresh and smoked Fish), Campbeltown: 01586 553580

McNAB'S KIPPERS (fish smokers), Lerwick: *mcnabkippers@aol.com*, 01595 693 893

MHOR FISH (fishmonger), Callander: *www.mhor.net*, 01877 330213

MILNE, J. H. (traditional fish smoker/finnans), Peterhead: 01779 490024

MURRAY, H. S. (fishmonger), Inverkeithing: 01383 412684

OBAN SEAFOOD HUT 'The Shack', Oban Pier (John Ogden): 01631 566000

ORKNEY FISHERMEN'S SOCIETY (crab), Stromness: *www.orkneycrab.co.uk*, 01856 850375

ORKNEY HERRING (sweet-pickled), Stromness: *www.orkneyherring.com*, 01856 850514

RACE, ANDY (fish shop/smokery), Mallaig: *www.andyrace.co.uk*, 01687 462626

SALAR SMOKEHOUSE, South Uist: *www.salar.co.uk*, 01870 610324

SOMETHING FISHY (fishmonger/smokery), Edinburgh: 0131 556 7614

SPINK, ALEX (Arbroath Smokies) Arbroath: *www.arbroathsmokiesonline.co.uk*, 01241 879056

SPINK D. (fishmonger/smokies) High St, Arbroath, Angus 01241 875732

SPINK, G&A (fish bar/shop), St Andrews: *www.tailendfishbar.co.uk*, 01334 474070

SPINK, Iain R. (smokies at events): *www.arbroathsmokies.co.uk*, 01241 860303

SPINK, M&M (fish/smokies) Marketgate, Arbroath: *www.arbroathsmokies.co.uk*, 01241 875287

STEPHENS (fishmonger), Montrose: 01674 672276, and Brechin: 01356 622037

UGIE SALMON (fish smoker), Peterhead: *www.ugie-salmon.co.uk*, 01779 476209

USAN SALMON (wild salmon), Montrose: *www.usansalmon.com*, 01674 676989

WATT, D. (fishmonger/cheeses), Railway Pier, Oban: 01631 562358

Dairy, Fruit, Vegetables, Bakery, Confectionery, Preserves

(For full range of Scottish cheeses see Chapter 6, p.284-90)

BS = Box Scheme

PYO = Pick-Your-Own

ALDERSTON, T. DAIRIES (cheese) Haddington: *alderstondairies@btconnect.com* 07767 276736

ALLANHILL FARM SHOP (fruit farm PYO) St Andrews, Fife: *www.allanhill.co.uk* 01334 477999

ANDERSON, GEORGE (fruit/veg) Musselburgh 0131 665 9595

ARGO'S BAKERY, Stromness, Orkney: *www.argosbakery.co.uk* 01856 850245

ARRAN CHOCOLATE FACTORY AND SHOP, Shore Rd, Brodick, Arran 01770 302873

ARRAN DAIRIES (milk/cream/ice cream) Brodick: *www.taste-of-arran.co.uk 01770 302374*

ARYSHIRE FARMHOUSE ICE CREAM, Mauchline: *www.ayrshireicecream.co.uk* 01290 552083

BARONY MILLS (water-mill/beremeal/oatmeal) Birsay, Orkney: *www.birsay.org.uk* 01856 771276

BELLFIELD ORGANICS (BS) Abernethy: *www.belfieldorganics.com* 01738 850589

BELHAVEN (fruit/veg farm/ices) Dunbar: *www.belhavenfruitfarm.co.uk* 01368 860573

BELLS BAKER Hawthorn Bakery, Torbothie Rd, Shotts: *www.bellsbakers.co.uk* 01501 820222

BLACK ISLE BERRIES (farm shop) Tore, Muir of Ord: *www.blackisleberries.co.uk* 01463 811276

BLACKETYSIDE FARM SHOP (fruit/veg PYO) Leven: *www.blacketysidefarmshop.co.uk* 01333 423034

BLAIRGOWRIE (farm shop/BS) Reform St.: *www.blairgowriefarmshop.co.uk* 01250 876528

BRIARNEUK NURSERY (tomatoes/soft fruit) Braidwood, Carluke: 01555 860229

BRIDGEFOOT ORGANICS (BS) Newmachar: *www.bridgefootorganics.co.uk* 01651 862041

BRIN HERB NURSERY (herbs/deli/café) Flicihity: *www.brinherbnursery.co.uk* 01808 521288

CAIRNIE FRUIT FARM (shop/PYO) Cupar, Fife: *www.cairniefruitfarm.co.uk* 01334 655610

CAITHNESS CHEESE Moorings, Occumster, by Lybster, Caithness 01593 721309

CALEDONIAN WILD FOODS (fungi/wild foods) Whiteinch, Glasgow 0141 9502412

CAMBUS O'MAY CHEESE, Craigmyle, Torphins: *www.cambusomay.com* 01339 889327

CARSEGOWAN ICE CREAM Newton Stewart: *www.carsegowan-icecream.co.uk* 01988 402259

CASTLETON (farm shop) Laurencekirk: *www.castletonfarmshop.co.uk* 01561 321155

CHARLETON (fruit farm/café) Montrose: *www.charleton-fruit-farm.co.uk* 01674 830226

CHEESERY, THE (cheese shop) Exchange St. Dundee: *www.thecheesery.co.uk* 01382 202160

CLARKS FOODS (artisan cheese) Bruntsfield, Ed.: *www.clarksfoods.co.uk* 0131 8560500

CLERKLAND FARM CHEESE

Stewarton, Ayrshire *www.dun-lopdairy.co.uk* 01560 482494

CLYDE ORGANICS (milk/ cream) Carnwath: *www.clydeorganics.co.uk* 01555 840271

CONNAGE HIGHLAND DAIRY (cheese/farm shop) Ardesier: *www.connage.co.uk* 01667 462000

CRAIGIE'S (farm shop/butcher) South Queensferry: *www.craigies.co.uk* 0131 319 1048

CRAIGMYLE CHEESE COMPANY Torphins, Kincardineshire: *www.craigmylecheese.co.uk* 013398 89340

CRANNACH (artisan baker) Cambus o May, Ballater: *www.crannach.com* 01339 755126

CREAM O' GALLOWAY (ice cream/café) Gatehouse: *www.creamogalloway.co.uk* 01557 814040 ORISP

CRUNCHY CARROT (fruit & veg shop, BS) Dunbar: *wwwcrunchycarrot.co.uk* 01368 860000

CUDDYBRIDGE APPLE JUICE, Innerleithen: *www.cuddybridgeapplejuice.com* 07522 424596

D AND D DAIRIES (milk/ cheese) Crieff, Perthshire: *www.danddairies.co.uk* 01764 652031

DALCHONZIE (farm shop) Comrie, Perthshire: *www.dalchonzie.co.uk* 01764 670416

DAMHEAD ORGANICS (farm shop) Edinburgh: *www.damhead.co.uk* 0131 6602128

DEVENICK DAIRY (cheese/ butter/farm shop) Banchory: *www.devenickdairy.co.uk* 01224 782476

DIFFERENT BREID (artisan bread) Garscube Rd, Glasgow: *www.differentbreid.co.uk* 07890 244965

DRUMMUIR FARM ICE CREAM Collin, Dumfries: *www.drummuirfarm.co.uk* 01387 750599

DRUMULLAN ORGANICS (fruit & veg/BS) by Girvan: *www.drumullan.co.uk* 01465 713080

EARTHY FOODS (local produce deli) Edinburgh: *www.earthy.co.uk* 0131 6672967

EAST COAST ORGANICS (fruit/veg BS) Pencaitland: *www.eastcoastorganics.co.uk* 01875 340227

ENGINE SHED (bakery/café/ Rudolf Steiner) Edinburgh: *www.engineshed.org.uk* 0131 6620040

FALKO (artisan bakery) Bruntsfield Edinburgh/Gullane: *www.falko.co.uk* 0131 6560763

FENTON BARNS (farm shop) North Berwick: *www.fentonbarnsfarmshop.com* 01620 850294

FINDHORN BAKERY (artisan bread) Near Elgin: *www.findhornbakery.co.uk* 07965 504296

FISHER & DONALDSON (bakers) St Andrews/Cupar: *www.fisheranddonaldson.com* 01334 472201

GALLOWAY FARMHOUSE CHEESE Sorbie: *www.gallowayfarmhousecheese.co.uk* 01988 850224

GALLOWAY FUDGE COMPANY Twynholm: *www.gallowayfudge.com* 01577 860608

GALLOWAY LODGE PRESERVES, Gatehouse: *www.gallowaylodgepreserves.co.uk* 01557 814357

GETDELI.CO.UK (mushrooms) Aviemore: www.getdeli.co.uk 01479 810583

GILL J.L. (specialist grocer/cheese/local foods) Crieff, Perthshire 01764 6530111

GOLSPIE MILL (water mill/beremeal/peasemeal) Dunrobin: *www.golspiemill.co.uk* 01408 633278

GOWRIE GROWERS (fruit/veg) Longforgan *www.gowriegrowers.co.uk* 01382 360620

GRAHAMS (milk/cream/butter) Bridge of Allan:*www.grahamsfamilydairy.com* 01786 833206

GRASSROOTS (deli/veg/fruit) Glasgow: *www.grassrootsorganic.com* 0141 353 3287

GREEN CITY WHOLEFOODS (workers co-op) Glasgow: *www.greencity.co.uk* 0141 5547633

GRIMBISTER FARM CHEESE Kirkwall, Orkney 01856 761318

GROW WILD (organic BS) Edinburgh: *www.growwild.co.uk* 0131 443 7661

HAMLYNS OF SCOTLAND (oatmeal/porridge oats) Banff: *www.hamlynsoats.co.uk* 01261 843330

HEATHER HILLS Bridge of Cally, Blairgowrie: *www.heatherhills.com* 01250 886252

HERBIE (deli/bread/cheese) Stockbridge, Edinburgh 0131 332 9888

HEBRIDEAN TOFFEE, Barra: *www.hebrideantoffeecompamy.com* 01871 810898

HENDERSON'S (bread/wholefoods) Edinburgh: *www.hendersonsofedinburgh.co.uk* 0131 226 6694

HIGHLAND FINE CHEESES, Blarliath Farm, Tain: *www.hfcheeses.com* 01862 892034

HOGARTH, JOHN (miller/oats/barley) Kelso, Roxburghshire *www.johnhogarth.co.uk* 01573 224224

HUNTLY HERBS (also potatoes organic) Huntly, Aberdeenshire *www.huntlyherbs.co.uk* 01466 720247

HYDROPONICUM GARDEN (fruit/veg) Achiltibuie: *www.the-hydroponicum.com* 01854 622202

INVERLOCH CHEESE Campbelltown: *www.inverlochcheese.com* 01586 552692

IRVINGS HOMESTYLE BAKERY, Castle Douglas: *www.irvingsbakery.co.uk* 01556 504162

ISABELLA'S (homemade) PRESERVES Edzell: *www.isabellaspreserves.co.uk* 01356 648500

ISLAND BAKERY, Tobermory, Mull: *www.islandbakery.co.uk* 01688 302223

ISLAND CHEESE COMPANY Brodick, Arran: *www.island-cheese.co.uk* 01770 302788

ISLE OF COLONSAY WILDFLOWER HONEY Poll Gorm: *www.colonsay.org.uk/honey* 01951 200365

ISLE OF MULL CHEESE, Tobermory: *www.isleofmullcheese.co.uk* 01688 302235

ISLE OF SKYE FUDGE COMPANY: *www.skyefudge.co.uk* 01470 521293

JACKIE LUNN (baker/Selkirk Bannock) Galashiels: *www.jackielunn.com* 01896 753877

JANNETTA (ice cream/confectionery) St Andrews: *www.jannettas.co.uk* 01334 473285

KNOWES FARM SHOP (fruit/veg/herb garden) East Linton: www.knowes.com 01620 860010

LAPRIG FRUIT AND VEG Hardacres, Greenlaw, Duns: *laprigveg@yahoo.co.uk* 01890 840215

LENSHAW ORGANICS (BS) Rothienorman, Inverurie: *jborganic@hotmail.com* 01464 871243

LIME TREE LARDER (chocolate/ice cream) Kilbirnie:*www.limetreelarder.co.uk* 01505 685258

LOCH ARTHUR CREAMERY (organic/farm shop/café) Dumfries: *www.locharthur.org.uk* 01387 760296

LOCH FYNE ORGANIC (fruit/veg) South Bairdon, Argyll: *www.lochfyne.com* 01499 600138

LUCAS OF MUSSELBURGH (ice cream): *www.lucasicecream.co.uk* 01316652237

LUVIANS ICE CREAM PARLOUR, St Andrews 01334 477128

MACKAYS (marmalade/preserves) Carnoustie: *www.mackays.com* 01241 853109

MACLAREN (bakers/Forfar bridies) Forfar/Kirriemuir: www.thebridieshop.co.uk 01307 463315

MACLEOD ORGANICS (BS fruit/veg) Ardesier, Inverness: *www.macleodorganics.com* 01667 462533

MELLIS, IAN Glasgow, Edinburgh, St Andrews: *www.mellischeese.com* 0141 3398998

MEWES G. (artisan cheese) Byres Rd, Glasgow: *www.georgemewescheese.co.uk* 0141 3345900

MHOR BREAD (bakery/café) Main Street, Callander: *www.mhorbread.net* 01877 339618

MITCHELLS (deli/cheese/dairy) Inverurie, Aberdeenshire: *www.mitchells-scotland.com* 01467 621389

MOFFAT TOFFEE SHOP (confectionery) Moffat: *www.moffattoffeeshop.com* 01683 220032

MOLLINSBURN ORGANICS (BS) Glasgow: *www.mollinsburnorganics.com* 07847 181063

MONIACK CASTLE HIGHLAND WINERIES Inverness: *www.moniackcastle.co.uk* 01463 831283

MORTONS (crispy Glasgow rolls) Glasgow: *www.mortonsrolls.com* 0141 9443111

MUDDY BOOTS (farm shop/soft fruits) Cupar, Fife: *www.muddybootsfife.com* 01337 830255

NATURAL VEG COMPANY (BS) Torbeck, Inverness: www.natvegco.com 01463 250440

NORTH STREET DAIRY (milk/cream/butter) Forfar:

www.northstreetdairy.co.uk
01307 463796

OATMEAL OF ALFORD (water mill) Laurencekirk: *www.oatmealofalford.com* 01561 377356

ORCHARD (fruit/veg) High St, Biggar 01899 221449

ORKNEY CHEESE COMPANY (cheddar) Kirkwall, Orkney: www.*orkneycheese.com* 01856 872542

ORKNEY CREAMERY (ice cream) St Ola, Orkney: *www.orkneyicecream.com* 01856 872542

OXENFOORD ORGANICS (fruit/veg BS) Pathhead: *www.oxenfoordorganics.com* 01875 320359

PATTULLO, SANDY (asparagus and sea kale) Eassie, Perthshire 01307 840303

PETRIE FINE FOODS (veggie/ vegan foods) Fenwick: *www.ayrshirefarmersmarket.co.uk* 01560 00184

PHANTASSIE (organic BS) East Linton: *www.phantassie.co.uk* 01620 860285

PITTORMIE FRUIT FARM (PYO) Dairsie, Fife: *www.pittormiefruitfarm.co.uk* 01334 870233

REAL FOODS EDINBURGH Tollcross, Broughton Street: *www.realfoods.co.uk* 0131 228 1201

REALLY GARLICKY CO. (garlic/oils) Nairn: *www.thereallygarlicky.co.uk* 01667 452193

REID, IAN (farm shop/restaurant) Newbigging Farm, Tealing, Angus: 01382 380255

ROOSTER POTATOES Albert Bartlett, Airdrie: www.*albertbartlett.com* 01236 762831

ROOTS AND FRUITS (fruit/ veg) Glasgow: *www.rootsandfruits.co.uk* 0141 334 3530

ROWAN GLEN DAIRY (yogurt/ butter/cheese) Newton Stewart: *www.rowan-glen.com* 01671 403633

SCARLETTS (heather/blossom honey) Longleys. Meigle: *www.scarlettshoney.co.uk* 01828 640821

SCOTGRO (BS) Aldearn, Nairn: www.scotgro.com 07719 343097

SCOTHERBS Kingswell, Longforgan, Dundee: *www.scotherbs.co.uk* 01382 360642

SCOTTISH PRESERVES Blairgowrie Perthshire: *www.scottishpreserves.co.uk* 01250 872038

SKYE BERRIES (organic soft fruits) Edinbane, Skye: 01470 582462

SKYE FRUIT and FUNGI (strawberries/mushrooms): *www.misty.croft@btinternet.com* 01471 855310

SOLITOTE NURSERY (soft fruit/veg) Duntulm, Skye 01470 552242

STAIR ORGANICS (BS) Tarbolton, Mauchline: *www.organicgrowing.com* 01292 541389

ST ANDREWS FARMHOUSE CHEESE, Anstruther: *www.standrewscheese.co.uk* 01333 312580

STANDHILL CHEESERY, Minto, Hawick: *www.standhillcheesery.co.uk* 01835 870225

STEAMIE BAKEHOUSE (artisan bread) Dunfermline: *www.steamiebakehouse.com* 07965 504296

STEWART TOWER DAIRY (ice cream) Stanley, Perth: *www.stewart-tower.co.uk* 01738 710044

STITCHILL JERSEYS (cheeses/butter) Garden Cottage Farm, Stichell, Kelso 01573 470263

STOCKAN & GARDENS (oatcakes) Stromness :*www.stockan-and-gardens.co.uk* 01856 850873

STRAWBERRY SHOP (soft fruits) Lethendy, Blairgowrie Rd, Perth 01738 5511135

STRUAN APIARIES (local honeys/preserves) Burnside Lane, Conan Bridge, Ross-shire 01349 861427

SUMMER HARVEST OILS (Rape seed oil) Madderty: *www.summerharvestoils.co.uk* 01786 474770

TATTIE SHAWS (fruit & veg) 35 Elm Row, Edinburgh: 0131 5576720

THISSELCOCKRIG (farm veg/chutneys) Whitsome, Duns, Berwickshire 01890 870370

TILQUHILLIE (steamed) PUDDINGS, Banchory: *www.tilquhilliefinefoods.com* 01330 822037

TUNNOCKS (snowballs/teacakes/caramel wafers) Uddingston: *www.tunnock.co.uk* 01698 813551

TWEED VALLEY ORGANICS (poultry/BS) Greenlaw: *www.tweedvalleyorganics.co.uk* 01361 810503

ULLAPOOL BAKERY Morefield Estate: *www.ullapoolbakery.co.uk* 01854 613034

VANILLA SKYE (chocolates) Portree: *www.vanillaskye.co.uk* 01478 611295

VITAL VEG (BS) Aboyne, Aberdeenshire: *www.vitalveg.co.uk* 01330 833823

WEST CRAIGIE (farm shop) South Queensferry, *www.the-jamkitchen.com* 0131 3191048

WEST HIGHLAND DAIRY (cheese) Stromeferry: *www.westhighlanddairy.co.uk* 01599 577203

YOUR LOCAL FARM (fruit & veg/BS) Slamannan, Falkirk: *www.yourlocalfarm.co.uk* 01324 851750

YOUR PIECE BAKING (oatcakes etc) Monimail: *www.yourpiecebakingcompany.com* 01738 622851

Select Bibliography

Cookery Books

Beard, James *Delights and Prejudices*, 1964
  James Beard's American Cookery, Little, Brown and Company, 1972
British Deer Society (Scotland) *Venison Recipes*
Boyd, Lizzie (Ed.) *British Cookery*, Croom Helm, 1976
Brown, Catherine *Scottish Regional Recipes*, Molendinar, 1981/Penguin 1983
Clayton, Bernard *The Complete Book of Breads*, Simon and Schuster, 1973
Clifton, Claire *Edible Flowers*, Bodley Head, 1983
Craig, Elizabeth *The Scottish Cookery Book*, Deutsch, 1956
David, Elizabeth *English Bread and Yeast Cookery*, Allen Lane, 1977
Davidson, Alan *North Atlantic Seafood*, Macmillan, 1979
Dods, Meg *The Cook and Housewife's Manual*, 1826
Drysdale, Julia *The Game Cookery Book*, Collins, 1975
Escoffier, August *Ma Cuisine*, first edition Flammarion, 1934, Paul Hamlyn, 1965
Fitzgibbon, Theodora *A Taste of Scotland*, Dent, 1970
Fletcher, Nichola *Venison, The Monarch of the Table*, Nichola Fletcher, 1983
Fulton, Willie *The Hebridean Kitchen*, Buidheann foillseachaidhnan Eilean an Iar, 1978
The Glasgow Cookery Book: Queens College Glasgow, John Smith, Revised Edition, 1962
Grigson, Jane *Good Things*, M. Joseph, 1971
  Fish Cookery, Penguin, 1975
  Jane Grigson's Vegetable Book, M. Joseph, 1978
  Jane Grigson's Fruit Book, M. Joseph, 1982
Harben, Philip *Cooking*, Penguin, 1960
Heptinstall, William *Gourmet Recipes from a Highland Hotel*, Faber, 1967
Katzen, Mollie *The Mosewood Cookbook*, Ten Speed Press, California, 1977
  The Enchanted Broccoli Forest, Ten Speed Press, California, 1982

457

King, A. and Dunnet, F. *The Home Book of Scottish Cookery*, Faber, 1967

Mabey, Richard *Food For Free. A guide to the edible wild plants of Britain*, Collins, 1972

Mabey, David and Rose *The Penguin Book of Jams, Pickles and Chutneys*, Penguin 1975

Menhinick, Gladys *Grampian Cookbook*, Aberdeen University Press, 1984.

Murray, Janet *Wartime Cookery Book*, Fraser, 1944
  Janet Murray's Cookery Book, London, 1950
  Traditional Recipes from Scotland, BBC, 1964
  With a Fine Feeling for Food, Impulse, 1972.

Nelson, Janet M. (Ed.) *A Mull Companion*, Mull 1977

Nice, Jill *Home-Made Preserves*, Collins, 1982

Olney, Richard *Simple French Food*, Penguin, 1983

Phillips, Roger *Wild Food*, Pan, 1983

Reid, Nancy (Ed.) *Highland Housewives' Cook Book*, Highland Printers, 1971

Scottish Women's Rural Institutes Traditional Scottish Recipes Cookery Book 6th Edition, 1946

Simmons, Jenni *A Shetland Cook Book*, Thuleprint, 1978

Stout, Margaret B. *The Shetland Cookery Book*, Manson, 1968 (first published in 1925 as *Cookery for Northern Wives*)

Taste of Scotland Ltd. and Catherine Brown *Chef's Manual*, 4th edition, 1985

Troisgros, Jean and Pierre *The Nouvelle Cuisine*, edited and adapted by Caroline Conran, Macmillan, 1980

Whyte, Hamish *Lady Castehill's Receipt Book, A Selection of Eighteenth Century Scottish Fare*, Molendinar, 1976

Wolfe, Eileen *Recipes from the Orkney Islands*, Gordon Wright, 1978

General

Anderson, W. *The Poor of Edinburgh and Their Homes*, Menzies, 1867

Brown, P. Hume (Ed.) *Early Travellers in Scotland*, Edinburgh, 1891

Burt, Edward *Letters from the North of Scotland* 5th ed., London, 1822

Campbell, John *An Exact and Authentic Account of the Greatest White-Herring Fishery in Scotland, carried on yearly in the Island of Zetland*, Edinburgh, 1750

Chambers, Robert *Walks in Edinburgh*, Edinburgh, 1825
  Traditions of Edinburgh, 2nd ed. Edinburgh, 1868
  Domestic Annals of Scotland, Edinburgh, 1859

Chapman, R.W. (Ed.) *Johnson's Journey to the Western Islands of Scotland and Boswell's Journal of a Tour to the Hebrides with Samuel Johnson*, Oxford University Press, 1961

Cheke, Val *The Story of Cheese Making in Britain*, Routledge, 1959

Colville, James (Ed.) *The Ochtertyre House Booke—1737-1739*, Scottish History Society, Edinburgh, 1907

Cutting, Charles L. *Fish Saving*, (Leonard Hill, 1955)

Edmonston, Elizabeth *Sketches and Tales of Shetland*, Edinburgh, 1856

Faujas de Saint-Fond, B. *Travels in England, Scotland and the Hebrides etc.*, London, 1799

Fenton, Alexander *Scottish Country Life*, John Donald, 1976.

Foulis, Sir John *Foulis of Ravelston's Account Book, 1671-1707*, Scottish History Society, 194

Fyfe, J.G. *Scottish Diaries and Memoirs*, Volume I (1550-1746), Volume II (1746-1843), Maclean, 1928

Grant, Elizabeth *Memoirs of a Highland Lady*, London, 1898

Hodgson, W.C. *The Herring and its Fishery*, Routledge, 1957

Jamieson, John *Etymological Dictionary of the Scottish Language*, new ed. 1879-82

Jamieson, J.H. *The Edinburgh Street Traders and their Cries*, in *Book of the Old Edinburgh Club*, Volume II, Constable, 1909

Kitchen, A.H. *The Scotsman's Food*, Livingston, 1949

Lochhead, Marion *The Scots Household in the Eighteenth Century*, Moray Press, 1948

Lockhart, G.W. *The Scot and His Oats*, Luath Press, 1983

MacCarthy, Daphne (Ed.) *Prodfact 1985, a Comprehensive Guide to British Agricultural and Horticultural Produce*, British Farm Produce Council, 1985

MacClure, Victor *Scotland's Inner Man*, Routledge, 1935
  Good Appetite, My Companion, Odhams Press, 1955

Martin, Martin *A Description of the Western Islands of Scotland, etc.*, 1703, Stirling, 1934

Mitchison, Rosalind *Life of Scotland*, Batsford, 1978

Newton, Lily *A Handbook of British Seaweeds*, British Museum, Natural History, 1931

Seaweed Utilisation Sampson and Low, 1951

Page, E.B. and Kingsford P.W. *The Master Chefs*, Arnold, 1971

Plant, Marjorie *The Domestic Life of Scotland in the Eighteenth Century*, Edinburgh University Press, 1952

Pococke, Richard *Tours in Scotland, 1747, 1750, 1760*, Scottish History Society, 1887

Ramsay, Dean *Reminiscences of Scottish Life and Character*, first published 1857, Robert Grant, 1947

Robertson, Una A. *Let's Dine at Hopetoun*, published in aid of the Hopetoun House Preservation Trust, 1981

Salaman, Redcliffe N. *The History and Social Influence of the Potato*, Cambridge University Press, 1970

Samuel, A.M. *The Herring: Its Effect on the History of Britain*, Murray, 1918

Sibbald, Sir Robert *What the Poor might eat; Provision for the Poor in time of Dearth and Scarcity*, Edinburgh, 1707

Sinclair, Sir John (Ed.) *The Statistical Account of Scotland*, Edinburgh, 1791-99

General View of the Agriculture of the Northern Counties and Islands of Scotland, Edinburgh, 1795

Southey, Robert *Journal of a Tour in Scotland in 1819*, The Mercat Press, 1972

Steven, Maisie *The Good Scots Diet*, Aberdeen University Press, 1985

Stuart, Marie W. *Old Edinburgh Taverns*, Hale, 1952

Sutherland, Douglas *The Salmon Book*, Collins, 1982

Tannahill, Reay *Food in History*, Stein and Day, 1973

Thornton, R. and Sieczka J.B. *Potato Atlas*, International Potato Centre, Lima, 1978

Torry Research Station *Fish Handling and Processing*

Victoria, Queen *Leaves From a Journal of Our Life in the Highlands, 1846-1861*, 1867

Wilson, C. Anne *Food and Drink in Britain*, Constable, 1973

Youngson, A.J. *Beyond the Highland Line, Three Journals of Travel in Eighteenth Century Scotland*, Collins, 1974

INDEX